THE RITES OF MEN:
MANHOOD, POLITICS, AND THE CULTURE OF SPORT

Varda Burstyn

Sport gathers more spectators on a global basis than any other activity today, yet it is widely regarded as being outside the dominant political and social systems. Varda Burstyn challenges this view, showing not only that sport generates an elitist, masculinist account of power and social order, but that it is central to the constitution of political power in contemporary life.

Burstyn begins by describing the emergence of sport as a masculinist secular religion by the close of the nineteenth century. Today, she argues, masculine dominance continues to be constructed and promoted by the multibillion-dollar nexus that has harnessed sport as the consummate sales agent. She goes on to show that the super-aggressive ideal of manhood, as practised, modelled, and animated through the culture of sport, has profound social and political consequences.

Combining some of the best insights of feminist theory with the perspectives of history, political science, economics, psychology, sociology, and cultural criticism, this book brings a new dimension to sport as a subject for serious scholarship.

VARDA BURSTYN is a political writer, cultural critic, and public policy consultant.

VARDA BURSTYN

The Rites of Men: Manhood, Politics, and the Culture of Sport

UNIVERSITY OF TORONTO PRESS
Toronto Buffalo London

© University of Toronto Press Incorporated 1999
Toronto Buffalo London
Printed in Canada

ISBN 0-8020-2844-6 (cloth)
ISBN 0-8020-7725-0 (paper)

∞

Printed on acid-free paper

Canadian Cataloguing in Publication Data

Burstyn, Varda
    The rites of men : manhood, politics, and the culture of sport

    Includes bibliographical references and index.
    ISBN 0-8020-2844-6 (bound)   ISBN 0-8020-7725-0 (pbk.)

    I. Sports – Social aspects.   2. Masculinity (Psychology).   I. Title.

    GV706.5B87 1999   306.4'83   C98-932677-2

This book has been published with the help of a grant from the Humanities and Social Sciences Federation of Canada, using funds provided by the Social Sciences and Humanities Research Council of Canada.

University of Toronto Press acknowledges the support to its publishing program of the Canada Council for the Arts and the Ontario Arts Council.

For my parents

Contents

Foreword

They are our heroes. They are eulogized as modern-day warriors. Whether in Olympic or professional team sports, they have a worldwide audience, command enormous respect, and, often, enormous salaries. They smile, they scowl, and they sell products. Virtually every boy wants to grow up to be just like them. They are our athletes. Their world may be the arena, the court, the track, and the playing field, but their performances fuel vast institutions where media and industry come together in a powerful and profitable embrace with local, national, and international politics. This world is, in Varda Burstyn's phrase, the sport nexus.

In this extraordinary book, Burstyn argues compellingly that sport has become the great masculine secular religion of our era. And as such, it plays a profound and usually invisible role in our interpersonal, work, and political lives.

We have both followed Varda Burstyn's work with ever-increasing interest. Over the past three decades, she has written broadly on sport, gender, politics, and cultural matters, as well as on issues of sexuality, the politics of human reproduction, and health policy. It is a range of interests that begins to suggest the tremendous sweep of social and intellectual terrain covered in this breathtaking book.

In a rich narrative that strides through the nineteenth and twentieth centuries, *The Rites of Men* tells the story of how the secular religion of sport came to be, and how athletes came to occupy their current social status as its demigods. Burstyn is without peer in the way she integrates issues of gender, family, and fatherhood with the economic and political dimensions of sport culture itself and society at large. Through such connections, she poses challenging questions to athletes, officials, educators, parents, and politicians alike.

As much as *The Rites of Men* is a critique of our dominant forms of masculinity and the institutionalized world of sport, one of the great strengths of this
book is that Burstyn writes with tremendous compassion about men, and with
enormous empathy for athletes themselves. After all, she says, much of institutionalized sport represents the brutalization of boys and men in the service of
the corporate and political interests at the heart of the sport nexus.

Woven through the book is an outstanding account of the links between
sport, manhood, and gender systems, in which she draws on a rich legacy of
studies of sport and gender, as well as on her own experience as a writer,
policy adviser, and former therapist. Embedded in this is a deep understanding
of the place of sexuality and homoeroticism present in men's sport in spite of
everyone's denials.

For those interested in how sport, economics, and gender interact, the book
addresses the corporate embrace of sport that has created an ever-more-as-
tounding manipulation of the male media audience. A multi-billion-dollar sports–
media nexus uses masculinist ideals to sell products (both sport itself and other
commodities) and, in turn, plays a strong role in constructing those ideals
anew. However, the problem isn't simply one of ideals, as we see when Burstyn
turns to the now-commercialized – and always politicized – Olympics, where
we witness with horror the biotechnologization of the human body, and to the
rampant anorexia in women athletes.

Perhaps the most disturbing questions arise when she traces the ways that
sport re-creates and amplifies strong emotional links between manhood, violence, war, and socioeconomic inequality. Sport becomes an anchor to neoliberal
economics and neoconservative politics through its strong beliefs in inequality
and the ideal that heroic masculinity is based on inequality. Central to this
world, says Burstyn, is an institutional emphasis on increasingly large, violent
male athletes. The commercial elevation of the masculine warrior to hero is a
central feature of the development of sport culture. By creating this hero in
sport culture, Burstyn argues, sport has been central, in our era, to the celebration of force, violence, and coercion as ideals of manhood. In this way sport
has acted as a political reservoir of anti-democratic and elitist values that
coexist with, and have often overwhelmed, egalitarian, cooperative, and democratic values. If this is true – and her argument is cogent – all of us, not just
those working in sport, should take sport seriously.

Burstyn's sweeping analysis does not end until she identifies some of the
possible mechanisms of change: change in sport culture, and in the gender
arrangements and masculine ideals that promote sport and, in turn, are promoted through sport. Hers is not a saccharine optimism. Rather, she makes an

impassioned and intelligent plea to radically alter the culture of sport and its place in society. Varda Burstyn's *The Rites of Men* is an important and exciting contribution to that goal.

Michael Kaufman, Toronto
Michael Messner, Los Angeles
March 1999

Acknowledgments

As my family, friends, and colleagues know too well, this book has been more than a decade in the making, much longer than I had initially anticipated when I first conceived its thesis in 1985. Between that year and 1990, when I began the first draft, I had some important opportunities to research and present my ideas in a number of different ways that aided enormously with the book. In this regard I warmly thank Max Allen, Jill Eisen, Bernie Lucht, and Alison Moss at CBC Radio's *Ideas*; John Fraser and Diana Symonds at *Saturday Night*; and June Callwood, who graced me with her support when I sought funding for the book.

I also would like to thank several colleagues in sports and gender studies whose practical support and intellectual encouragement were critical at many steps along the way. Bruce Kidd, Michael Kaufman, Geoffrey Smith, and Karen Dubinsky provided invaluable comments on the manuscript, and precious moral support. David Strand, a physical fitness innovator, read and provided feedback on the first draft. Jean-Marie Brohm generously shared ideas and materials with me in 1992. As well, my thanks are extended to Roberta Hamilton, Pamela Walker, and Selma Leydersdorff, all scholars of gender and politics, for their special insights and their encouragement at different stages of the project.

I have two older intellectual debts I also want to acknowledge here. I want to thank Gad Horowitz for many years of illuminating discussions about gender and politics, and for his work in psychoanalytic and political theory. I also wish to thank Robin Wood, who reminded me in the late 1970s that culture was just as important as economics where politics is concerned, and encouraged me to set down my ideas about its politicization.

As well, I wish to thank my parents and brothers, and my aunt, uncle, and cousins, for the myriad forms their support to me has taken over this time. I will be eternally grateful to Ian and Sylvia McLeod, who provided a refuge in rural France, far from the daily swirl of events, where I drafted this work. Andrea Knight provided immense help in research, editing, referencing, and indexing. To Wally Seccombe and David Fujiwara, many thanks for the conversations about sport and politics over many years. To Lynne King, Jackie Larkin, Deirdre Gallagher, Judith Weisman, Lin Grist, and Carol Kushner, thank you for your unwavering encouragement, insights, and friendship.

My thanks go to Virgil Duff at the University of Toronto Press for his support and belief in this book, and his gracious tolerance of the vicissitudes of my life and ability to produce. I am also grateful to Jim Leahy for his rigorous editing and perseverance through a long, difficult task. I want to acknowledge my heartfelt appreciation for the financial support of the Social Sciences and Humanities Research Council, the Canada Council, and the Ontario Arts Council, as well as the people of Canada who support a public sector in culture. Without public support, this book would never have been written. I hope these Councils will be happy to see the fruition of a long-overdue project.

I am also very much indebted to the many athletes, sports scholars, and educators – many of whose words and ideas are included in this work – who took the time to talk with me about their experiences of and ideas about sport and culture over the years. As an outsider to their world, I feel honoured by the time they have spent with me, and by the insights they have given me.

Finally, I want to express my loving gratitude to David Fenton, for his affection, his unfailing good humour, his wit, knowledge, patience, and constant support, which, in the end, made it all possible.

Varda Burstyn

THE RITES OF MEN:
MANHOOD, POLITICS, AND THE CULTURE OF SPORT

Introduction

The rituals of sport engage more people in a shared experience than any other institution or cultural activity today. World Cup soccer gathers upwards of a billion electronic spectators on a global basis. According to generally accepted estimates, between two billion and three billion people – close to half of the humans on this planet – followed the 1996 Atlanta Olympic Games on television or radio.[1] According to the *Toronto Star*, Edson Arantes do Nascimento, the Brazilian soccer superstar better known as 'Pele,' was 'the most recognizable face in the world in 1994.'[2] *Sports Illustrated* insisted in the same year that this distinction belonged to former heavyweight champion Muhammad Ali.[3] When the U.S. space probe landed on Mars in July 1997 and began sending back photographs of the planet's surface, a NASA spokesman compared the moment to 'winning the Superbowl, the World Cup, and the World Series three days in a row.'[4] This was the only metaphor he could find, he explained, that was sufficiently marvellous to convey the wonder of *Sojourner*'s discoveries.

These examples attest to the place that sport occupies in our psyches and our mythologies, to the global power of its language and culture, and to the extraordinary interest and allegiance it claims. There have certainly been moments of public alienation from commercial sport in the 1980s and 1990s in North America: witness the Pete Rose gambling incident, Ben Johnson's steroid scandal, Mike Tyson's rape conviction, and the baseball strike and hockey lockout of 1994 and 1995. Yet the appeal and the reach of the sport nexus – that web of associated and interlocking organizations that includes sports, media, industry, government, public education, and recreation – continues to grow each year. Born in the nineteenth century, sport as we know it adapted brilliantly to the twentieth, and shows every sign of flourishing in the twenty-first, even as many other nonindustrial forms of culture struggle to survive.

This book explores the close and abiding relationship between masculinism and capitalism – practised, modelled, and animated through the culture of sport. It explores how masculine dominance is constructed, embodied, and promoted in the associations, economies, and culture of the modern sport nexus. And it is about how masculinism, through sport, encourages and promotes other ideologies and other forms of inequality – notably economic, racial, and biotic hierarchies. It seeks to show how sport, interacting with other forms of culture, generates the ideology of what I call *hypermasculinity*, that is, an exaggerated ideal of manhood linked mythically and practically to the role of the warrior. This book seeks in a number of ways to link the hypermasculine culture of sport to antisocial tendencies in society: to militarist impulses and institutions and to the rise of neoliberal economics and neoconservative politics in North America.

When I began working on this book more than ten years ago, I did not believe that masculinism – the political ideology of our male-superior gender order – was all that sport is or can be about. Nor did I complete the project with such a view. Sport has been, at times, the site of many experiences of bonding and solidarity, pleasure, achievement, and healthful activity for people of both sexes and all ages, classes, and racial, ethnic, and linguistic groups. Many of its physical activities and game forms have promoted personal well-being, community coalescence, and social equality. Large numbers of people pursue physical activity in such ways today, outside the framework of competitive sport, even as they utilize skills and gestures they may have learned within it. Recreational sport often delivers just these positive experiences.

Yet for all these realities – to which I will return at appropriate moments in the pages that follow – it remains true that the culture of big-time sport generates, reworks, and affirms an elitist, masculinist account of power and social order, an account of its own entitlement to power. Because of my own preoccupation with egalitarian politics – too often downplayed or omitted from our understanding of sport culture – this is the account I have set out to elucidate. By necessity, this has meant a prolonged focus on some of the most troubling and antisocial dimensions of sport culture. These dimensions coexist in dynamic and contradictory tension with the more positive experiences of sport, both institutionally and in the lives of individual athletes and those involved in sport culture.

I am not an athlete, and I did not decide to write about sport because of formative athletic experiences. When I was young I was physically active, first in a rural environment and then in a suburban one. But aside from the usual obligatory participation in sport at school and summer camp, I had little to do with it or with school jock culture. The focus of my extracurricular activities lay elsewhere. In my twenties I became active in several social movements: the civil rights movement, the antiwar movement, the women's movement, the environmental movement, and left-wing politics. It was through these political movements that I met and became acquainted with a number of thoughtful athletes. They gave me insight into and knowledge about a fascinating world I might otherwise never have known.

Thanks to the friendship of these athletes I developed an abiding interest in sport as a sociopolitical institution, and early on I came to think of this institution as a 'school for masculinity.' But this interest remained more of a hobby than a systematic preoccupation. One reason for this is that throughout the 1970s and early 1980s, the focus of analysis within the women's movement and feminist scholarship rested on women themselves, and on understanding the myriad facets of the construction of femininity as a special and subordinate reality. In the late 1970s and early 1980s, I too explored this construction, with respect to film and visual art on the one hand, and to government and state-linked politics on the other. By the mid-1980s, however, like many other observers, I felt a profound dissatisfaction with the unifocal emphasis on women and femininity, particularly in the context of the 'pornography wars' that were then agitating society and dividing the women's movement. It seemed to me that we needed an understanding of the construction of men and masculinity equally sophisticated as the one we had developed of women and femininity. This was critical if we were to understand the whole ecology of gender, and the problems in heterosocial relations that so many feminist struggles were high-lighting.

One day in the summer of 1984 I was on my way to participate in a debate about pornography and censorship. I was thinking about this need for a discussion of masculinity when my eye was arrested by a newsstand display featuring *Playboy* and *Sports Illustrated* placed side by side. I went closer to look. On the cover of *SI* was NFL superstar Walter Payton, caught by the camera just after breaking Jim Brown's rushing record. Far from an image of joy or even brutal triumph, however, I was surprised and rather moved to see a look of considerable pain on his face – whether physical or existential pain, or both, it was hard to say. When, later on the podium, my pro-censorship opponent held up for scorn a centrefold from *Hustler*, I held up the picture of Walter Payton. 'If we want to talk about violence against women,' I said, 'let's start talking about violence among men.'

I decided then that sport and its broader culture would serve well as a case study for learning about the idealization of manhood and the construction of masculinity, and in 1985 I began to investigate sport more closely. I have only become more convinced of the role of sport and sport culture in generating masculinity. I have also become increasingly persuaded of the importance of gender – and hence of sport as a profoundly gendered institution – to the deep structures of ideology that affect political culture as a whole, generally in regressive and antisocial ways.

An implicit and partial political critique is not completely absent from sport journalism. In North America and Europe a small number of sports journalists write about the socioeconomic dimensions of sport with intelligence, concern, and style.[5] If these writers share a collective weakness, however, it is their failure to take the full measure of the implications of their own critiques. As well, these journalists are a minority. Most sports fans do not rely on the written word, much less the lengthy written word, for their relationship to and understanding of sport. It is primarily the television and radio sports 'journalists' who frame sport for large numbers of people. From the radio call-in programs to the commentary of former pro athletes, to the celebrity pieces in *People, Time,* and *Vanity Fair,* most of this journalism is geared, more or less shamelessly, to promoting big-time sport, not reporting on it.

In fact, as a result of processes I trace in detail in chapters 4 and 5, much of contemporary sport journalism is rapidly melting into publicity and advertising. For example, the CBS television network's coverage of the Masters golf tournament in Augusta, Georgia, in April 1997, led off with a one-hour special feature on Tiger Woods, who emerged from the event a new athletic superstar. Rather than being an objective portrait, this prepackaged special was actually purchased by CBS from International Management Group (IMG), a powerful sports agency that earns about $400 million a year. 'In short,' as Doug Saunders wrote in the *Globe and Mail* sports pages, 'the hour long special was essentially a commercial, paid for by the network, and presented as a straightforward TV documentary.'[6]

As well, not even the best journalists (save for Alison Gordon, former *Toronto Star* sports columnist) seriously address the gendered dimensions of sport, except peripherally and episodically. This omission is not a minor one; the implications of gender cannot simply be tacked onto a larger account as an afterthought. By not grappling with these dimensions, sports journalists also avoid some of the most profoundly political of sport's functions and influences, and some of its most destructive.

Over the years I have been writing about sport, I have become increasingly disturbed by its profound and far-reaching commercial appropriation, and by the effects of this on gender relations and on political life. In this sense, sport is a perfect example of neoliberal economics and neoconservative culture – a commercialized, gendered cultural enterprise, subsidized by the state, that encroaches on and finally occupies and defines public space. As sport and commerce fuse more closely, and expand more widely, it is more important than ever to consider what kind of physical culture sport provides for society and what kind of physical culture we really want to have.

These issues are the subjects of ongoing discussion within a substantial body of scholarship dealing with sport that has emerged as a distinct field ('sports studies') since the 1970s. Helen Lenskyj has compiled an annotated bibliography of research on women, sport, and physical activity that includes thousands of titles.[7] As well, having chronicled the historical exclusion of women from the social privileges conferred by sport, feminist scholars have extended their analyses to address the social-integrationist implications of women's commercial recruitment by sport – and sport equipment.[8] Much of the early scholarship produced by men in the field of sports studies centred around issues of sport and class, race, and national formation. In the last ten years, however, an impressive cohort of scholars has addressed the central issues in the construction of masculinity through sport and the political valence of masculinist sport culture.[9]

Because of my personal history and specialization, I approach sport culture from perspectives that are somewhat different from the athletocentric paradigms of sport studies. I approach sport in four primary ways. As a political scientist, I am concerned with how sport affects politics and how government and the state are involved in sport culture. As a student of the family, gender, and sexuality, I am concerned with the influence of sport within a conflicted gender order and with the broader political valence of gendered culture. As a cultural critic, I am concerned with the gendered distortion of communication, in this instance in physical culture, that results from the commercialization of that culture. And as a health reformer, I am concerned with the associations between poor population health and public support for high-performance sport. I hope, from these perspectives, to make a contribution to the larger discussion of gender, sport and politics.

Most people use words such as 'games,' 'fun,' or 'entertainment' to describe sport, and consider sports to be apolitical. As a society we give little thought to the ideological valences of sport and its culture. Its triumphs and virtues we describe as essential and normative; its failures and flaws we dismiss as secondary or anomalous. Furthermore, most of us think of sport as an activity of choice or preference, as something voluntarily done or left aside, as a realm of innocence and frivolity, as intense and healthy physical release for those who play it, and as a form of 'harmless entertainment' for those who do not. We think of sport as leisurely, benign. In effect, without giving it much thought, athletes and couch potatoes alike trivialize the importance of sport.

Implied in this popular assessment is the belief that sport is a mere byproduct of more important phenomena in economic, governmental, and family forms, and completely dependent on them. But from the point of view of the actual constitution of civil society and political power – that is, of how we organize ourselves as a society stratified along lines of gender, colour, ethnicity, class, sexuality, and physical ability – the institutions of sport, as the guardians of masculinist ritual, are among the most important regenerating sources of individualist, competitive, and coercive values and behaviours today. I see these as antisocial qualities, particularly when they dominate, rather than form smaller components of, a culture.

Sport's political impact is linked both to the symbolic operations that masculinist ideals effect in the public world and to the practical associations men make with each other in and through sport organizations. While many girls and women are athletic, women are not organized in and through sport such that it serves as an economic, cultural, and associational backbone for their gender interests. These are functions sport plays with respect to men as a gender, indeed as a gender class. In the words of sport sociologist Brian Pronger, 'The athletic world of power, speed and pain is an expression of the masculine ideals of our culture.'[10]

Chapter 1 provides a conceptual introduction to the themes, approaches, and terms of my study. In it, I spell out the parameters of my subject matter; explain why it is useful to regard sport much as one would an established religion; discuss a number of ideas concerning ideologies, the gender order, the body, ritual, and society; and, in the last sections, spell out some of my perspectives on two of the most important issues involved in the study of sport: sex and aggression.

Chapters 2 and 3 sketch gender relations and divisions of labour, family forms and sexuality, industrialization, militarization, and imperialism in the evolution of sport culture from the early nineteenth to the early twentieth centuries. Even though the games from which individual sports evolved long predated the nineteenth century, sport as a phenomenon emerged as a new masculine industrial culture during this time. The founding features of sport as an institution, and the key contributions it made to the culture of masculinity and gender are important in understanding its present evolution and its social and political impact.

Chapters 4 through 9 address sport culture, masculinity, and politics in the twentieth century. The relationship between sport and the media (the 'sport–

media complex') is at the economic and mythic centre of the sport nexus. For this reason, Chapter 4 discusses the economic and masculinist evolution of the sport–media complex in relation to changing gender relations. In Chapter 5, I trace how modifications in the nature of play, spectacle, and audience relationships have favoured the hypermasculine sport hero, and how changing body aesthetics influenced by sport are implicated in gender relations and conflicts. In chapters 6, 7, and 8, I tackle, respectively, the relationship of sport culture and masculinity to organized violence and war (especially in relation to the wars in Vietnam and the Persian Gulf); to working-class dislocation, racism, and the emergence of open homosexuality; and to the masculinist technomodification of the athletic body. Finally, Chapter 9 outlines some strategic issues for change.

In these latter chapters, I present my main themes sequentially. But because changes in sport–media relationships, larger economic dynamics, foreign policy, gender and race relations, and popular culture unfold simultaneously and interactively, not one at a time, each chapter should be approached as addressing one level or dimension in dynamic relation to the others.

Though I am Canadian, the emphasis in this text is on Great Britain and the United States. These two societies gave birth to the major global sport forms dominant today. Caught historically and geoculturally between England and the United States, Canada has experienced similar dynamics in the growth and evolution of its own sports industry. The distinctive aspects of Canada's sports history, captured in Bruce Kidd's study *The Struggle for Canadian Sport,* were significant for Canadians, and provide much food for thought for would-be sport reformers. But, as Kidd's work, including his previous book, *The Death of Hockey*, showed, these distinct qualities did not change the course of the evolution of 'Canada's national sport,' either in Canada or on a continental or global basis.[11] Nor were they able to stop the corporatization and Americanization of other sports. In fact, with respect to the core men's sports I focus on in this study, the border between Canada and the United States has virtually disappeared, forming a coherent North American system, dominated and determined by U.S. developments. It is thus important for Canadians to know about American sport. In addition, American readers may find the thoughts of an observer who is both inside and outside American culture of some use.

Although Chapter 1 clarifies the vocabulary I use in relation to sport, ideology, religion, organized violence, and sexuality, I would like to explain here the terms used to discuss the relations and institutions of gender. To designate the broad social arrangements of male-superior gender hierarchy common to many different cultures and modes of production, I employ the term *masculine domi-*

nance rather than the more common *patriarchy*.[12] For the specific contemporary form of masculine dominance that characterizes late industrial society, I prefer the term *masculinism*, since the power of men and the ideology of hypermasculinity are no longer extensions of the power of an omnipotent family father. Across the vast array of human cultures, we have seen many different forms of masculine dominance with meaningful differences in the extent and mechanisms of gender inequality. Generally people employ the terms 'patriarchy' and 'patriarchal' to refer to all these social arrangements and values, and I have no quarrel with this general usage. But technically speaking, patriarchy – the power of the family father – is only one form of masculine dominance characteristic of many agrarian and early capitalist family forms. And since I am concerned in this text with changing family forms and the place and power of the family in industrial societies, I want to be as precise as possible by opting for the more specific terms.

The adjective derived from masculinism is *masculinist*, a word that connotes a stance both about and supportive of men's gender dominance. It is not simply pro- or about men (masculine). Nor is it a description of the 'essential' and timeless biological characteristics of being male; rather, it is about masculine gender power. I use the term *hypermasculinity* to describe the ideal man in the masculinist conception. As well, for reasons I have written about elsewhere, I think that the term 'class' is appropriately applied to the respective members of gender groups under most conditions of masculine dominance.[13] Social classes are usually thought of as including both sexes, and of being based on economic and political disparities – for example, the working class, the owning class, the managing class, and so on. The meaningful core of this terminology revolves around relations between the classes characterized by appropriation, conflict, oppression, and domination.[14] These kinds of characteristics are also found in the relations between sexes in many societies of masculine dominance. By these definitions, in such societies, men and women are also members of distinct gender classes as well as economic ones.

Because I am interested in gendered patterns of signification in the culture of sport, of necessity I make generalizations about its symbolic/ideological nature and impact. For example, I draw a number of correlations between American football and the notion of manifest destiny, corporate business practice, racism, and war. These correlations are valid, I believe, at the ideological and symbolic level. By drawing these patterns, however, I am not saying that all football players share these values and orientations. The same may be said with respect to racism and sexism. Both are institutionalized in professional sport in a variety of ways, some of which I explore. In order to make the case for the systemic presence of those prejudices, there is no need to ascribe to individual athletes the systemic prejudices of their larger subculture or to deny that some individuals can and do transcend those prejudices.

Whether I suggest that physical culture can heighten the validity of a set of positive values (physical pleasure, solidarity, skill development, creativity), or negative ones (mindless consumerism, violence, jingoism, homophobia), I am not suggesting that sport has a uniform impact on everyone or that everyone interprets or accepts its values in the same way. The meaning of any given communication – whether a film, a book, or a sporting event – takes place at the point where the consciousness of the viewer meets the message(s) of the transmission. There is no single consciousness or mentality in our society that either represents or interprets for all of us. Individuals are not simply passive receivers. To greater or lesser extents, we attempt actively to make sense of what we see for ourselves, sifting what we get through the filter of our own experience.

So when I make generalizations about the categories of 'men' or 'masculinity,' I am not suggesting that all men, everywhere, experience identical anxieties and desires, have identical values, have an identical experience of sport and behave in identical ways. On the contrary. We are living through a period of major change and transition in the norms that govern relations between the sexes, and there is perhaps a greater diversity of responses and ambivalence to expectations and ideals of manhood than ever before. Men and women interpret the culture of sport in many different ways. Some cherish the experiences it offers, others find them offensive, and many are ambivalent about sport and its ideals, more or less articulately. My generalizations about the ideals and ideology of sport should not therefore be read as descriptions of individuals, so much as the mentality or point of view they encounter when they are engaged by athletic culture.

While this book is certainly about capitalism and its imperatives and methods writ large – for sport is nothing if not a capitalist success story – it is first and foremost an extended consideration of the engendering process of boys and men. I use the term 'engender' to refer to the process whereby boys and men are socialized into masculinity in a gender order.[15] As such, this work is a study of the economic, physical, and mythical disparities of the gender order and how these become constituted in the political order. While I have devoted a good deal of attention to many different aspects of sport and its socializing functions, my larger goal has been to make a contribution to our understanding of the gendered political economy of sport, one that organizes our understanding of it the better to change it.

In this aim, I have wanted to lend support to the widespread questions and growing objections of many parents and physical educators who are working to improve the conditions for active physicality in childhood, in adolescence, and throughout our lives. The many critiques of sport they advance and their innovative and much-loved initiatives in communities across this continent – these rarely make the news. Yet they represent an important part of the future of a pro-social physical culture. This book is my contribution to validating those important questions – partial or comprehensive – being raised in many communities today about the way we organize our physical play and socialize our children. It is written in the hope that by discarding the more violent and dominating elements in sport and by more vigorously reclaiming and remaking pleasure within our physical culture, we can more easily remake other aspects of ourselves and our society.

1

Societies, Bodies, and Ideologies:
Terms and Approaches

Kids calling to each other on a baseball diamond in summer. A cheering crowd in a football stadium amid the glories of the northeastern autumn. The sounds of a puck being slapped back and forth across a frozen pond on a sparkling, frosty winter day. The swift moves, shouts, and patter of inner-city basketball courts on a spring evening. All these sights, sounds, and sensations are woven into the fabric of North American culture, and mark both the closing of the work (or school) day and the passing of the seasons. Those who play these games reap the pleasure of physical exertion and skill, sociability, prestige, and, in the case of those who succeed professionally, money. All these benefits, vicarious or direct, are the subject of much celebration and promotion. Early in life, physical education teachers and camp counsellors laud the benefits of sport, while televised sports announcers and the sport press never tire of singing the praises of sport and its stars.

Nevertheless, I will argue in this book that as the seemingly simple rules, rituals, and ideals of sport, and the culture that has grown around them, draw on the sensual glory and unrivalled symbolic power of the body, they also deliver a series of 'anti-benefits' to society, they exact a series of tolls from us, and they do us some considerable damage. It is my contention that the culture of sport celebrates many attitudes and behaviours toward nature and our fellow humans that are socially destructive and that these consequences cancel out much of the positive experience sport can deliver. Indeed, throughout much of the world of professional sport and the broad culture it has spawned, these antisocial attitudes and behaviours decidedly outweigh the prosocial ones.

The bulk of this book approaches relationships between the culture of sport, ideals of masculinity (manhood), and politics within a semi-historical narrative that travels through the nineteenth and twentieth centuries. I have brought a number of premises to this narrative and its main themes, and I employ a number of terms as I go along. By way of providing a more theoretical back-drop to this narrative, in this first chapter I want to address my approach to central preoccupations in the chapters that follow and make some terminological explanations. I begin by defining what I mean by the terms 'sport' and 'sport culture,' and other related concepts, in this study.

Defining the Parameters of Sport in This Study

The term 'sport' has multiple meanings. Some scholars such as William J. Baker, a distinguished sport historian, employ the word in an ecumenical, transhistorical sense, to describe any socially organized physical game or contest.[1] In this usage, medieval jousting and the contemporary Olympic games are, equally, 'sports.' The existence of a physical contest is taken as the defining criterion for sport. There is considerable merit to this perspective. The basic repertoires of bodily gestures (running, jumping, throwing, swimming) do appear transhistorically and cross-culturally. In this sense they can be said to span, rather than change with, larger economic and social periods. From my perspective, the nature of men's physical culture as competitive and violent across so many different types of societies is perhaps the single most important of its cross-cultural features. On the other hand, very important elements of physical culture do change along with major changes in economic organization and class structure. Therefore, the physical cultures of societies differ from each other in important ways as well. Ritualized physical activity can be delivered through many different kinds of physical practices including many rigorous yet 'non-sport' disciplines. Dance in its many varieties is a popular and elite field of physical culture, as are yoga, tai chi, and recreational hiking. All these activities involve muscle, skill, individual and group practice, and even ritual, but in ways different from those of modern sport.

The persistence of similar activities in the physical cultures of different groups and peoples within and across societies has been regarded as evidence of the naturalism and universalism of 'sport.'[2] I read it as evidence of a universal propensity to use the body in games – an important propensity, for people in all societies will gravitate to sanctioned opportunities for physical release and ritual sociality. But there is no escaping the fact that the way each society performs, observes, and contextualizes its physical cultures differs dramatically from period to period. In distinguishing sport per se from other kinds of physical cultures, I think these differences are also crucial. A simple example of how one generic gesture can have two very different social organizations and social meanings can be seen by comparing a favourite game of the Mbuti pygmies of the Ituri rain forest in Zaire – one of the most egalitarian human societies we know of and one of the happiest – with our game of tug of war.[3] The Mbuti game differs radically from ours in that its goal is to reach the *equalization* of two large, multigenerational 'teams' that begin as gender-distinct but end as gender-mixed. Our tug of war has as its goal the vanquishing of one team by the other. The Mbuti physical ritual seeks to create and ritually affirm the intermixing of teams (social groups) rather than their separation. It includes the dynamic of *polarization* (two sides), and therefore has drama, but not the dynamic of *competition*, for there is no winner or loser in the sense that we employ those terms. In the modern sport version, the basic physical dominance of one team over another – zero-sum competition – is at the very centre of the ritual.

More complex examples can be found by comparing the folk games of precapitalist Europe with the Native American games the Europeans encountered in the New World.[4] Europeans played many different kinds of ball games in the fifteenth, sixteenth, and seventeenth centuries. There were scores of different versions of foot and ball games, proto–field hockey, and the precursors of cricket, tennis, and golf. When they arrived in North America, European colonialists were astounded to find that the Aboriginal peoples played games remarkably similar to their own. There were many Native versions of bat and ball games, including lacrosse, and forms of football that rivalled in refinement those of the Europeans. But the religious contexts and ritual objects of the Native American games were different. For the Europeans, games were part of a secular holiday culture. Among the male youths of the ruling classes of the Aztec and Inca civilizations, on the other hand, the playing of these sports, associated with elements of human sacrifice, was part of their sacred and often deadly religious rituals for appeasing their gods.[5] Particularly in Central and South America, the meaning and social function of these games struck a resounding note of difference from the European physical culture. The culture that surrounds physical performances is as important as the physical acts performed.

As the ideological importance of sport depends more on its specific and distinct cultural forms than the actions it shares with other forms of physical culture, I will use the term 'sport' to refer to a limited field of physical activity quite distinct from the larger physical culture around it. Sport in this work refers to a physical culture that possesses, in the words of sport sociologist Allen Guttmann, 'a distinctive set of systematically interrelated formal–structural characteristics'; these qualities, taken together, differentiate 'sport' as such from other forms and traditions of physical culture. Five of these characteristics help us identify sport as the representative physical culture of modernity:

- *specialization* ('have evolved from less differentiated games, and ... have a gamut of specialized roles and playing positions');
- *rationalization* ('rules ... are constantly scrutinized and undergo frequent revision ... athletes train scientifically ... and strive for the most efficient employment of their skills');
- *quantification* ('the "stats" have become an apparently indispensable part of the game);
- *obsession with records* ('the unsurpassed quantified achievement ... [the] "record" ... is a constant challenge to all who strive to surpass it, and thereby to achieve a modern version of immortality.')
- *bureaucratization:* ('modern sports are typically governed ... by national and transnational bureaucracies' e.g., the United States Olympic Committee, or the Fédération Internationale de Football).[6]

These characteristics are indeed unique to sport as the dominant form taken by 'industrial play.' (These terms also describe the processes that took place in economy, society, and culture during the nineteenth century.) Hence swimming in a lake at the cottage for fun is not sport; competing in a swimming meet is sport. Performing a ballet, even though it may entail equivalent or superior physical discipline and skill, is not sport; competing in a figure skating competition, where the most athletic movements of dance are ranked and quantified, is sport.

Guttmann's two remaining criteria for the delineation of sport, examined as abstract characteristics and as historical processes, are more problematic. The first of these is secularism. As Guttmann writes, 'Modern sports are not related – as pre-modern sports often were – to some transcendent realm of the numinous or sacred.'[7] Certainly, sport's lack of reliance on traditional religions has enabled it to reach across pre-existing divisions and appeal to many different kinds of men and communities. But this formulation of secularity ignores something central in the numinosity of sport itself. It misses the way in which sport has become a locus of worship in its own right, and become in this sense a religion of its own.[8] I discuss the reasons to regard sport as a religion in the next section of this chapter. Equally problematic for the definition of sport is the characteristic of 'equality' that Guttmann ascribes to it. 'Modern sports require, at least in theory, that no one be excluded from participation on the basis of ascriptive traits (such as race or ethnicity) and that the rules of the game be the same for all participants.'[9] In theory this commitment to equality is true. But in practice, accepting it at face value trivializes the real inequalities on which the world of sport has historically been constructed: inclusion or exclusion from playing the game itself was historically granted on the basis of gender, class, and race. And the win–lose structure at the very core of the record-obsessed sport ritual ensures that ranking, not cooperation, is the dominant value. These inequalities and celebrations of inequality have been inherent in the practical and historical – if not theoretical and rhetorical – constitution of the major modern sports. As they have been challenged, they have provided some of the most exciting sport dramas of all time.

Today, in North America, many of the racial and class barriers typical of sport late in the last century have been overcome. Nevertheless, there are still systemic expressions of racism within sport, and class tensions are regularly played out through it (see Chapter 7). As well, women have made significant inroads into sport. By the end of the nineteenth century, sport was an established part of education for upper-class girls, and activities and sports such as cycling, tennis, and golf have been popular among middle-class women throughout the twentieth century. Over these same years, a remarkable cadre of women Olympic and team sport athletes has emerged. Yet, as I discuss at length in chapters 4 and 5, the lion's share of society's attention and resources continues to flow toward men's athletics; and the dominant cultural pressures through the culture of sport continue to forge a template of gender that is masculinist and antiegalitarian.

What I call in this book 'the sport nexus' is a highly lucrative, multibranched transnational economy of enormous scope and influence. The sport nexus is composed of distinct sectors of economic and political interests, associated together in various clusters of overlapping and interlocking organizations, strategies, and personnel. Sociologist Sut Jhally coined the term 'the sport–media complex' to refer to the new entity that came into being as sport and commercial media forged deep links over the course of the twentieth century.[10] This complex is at the centre of the nexus, which additionally includes other significant complexes, such as the sport–industry, sport–medicine, and sport–state complexes. Direct subsidies of national Olympic teams, huge indirect public subsidies for the infrastructure of commercial sport, and the inclusion of sport in public educational and recreational systems are all ways in which the public underwrites sport and the taxpayer becomes a partner in the sport nexus. These complexes and the sport nexus as a whole include both high-performance and professional sport, and overlap into many networks in popular leisure and recreation. At once an elite power apparatus and a form of lateral community organization, the sport nexus is also pyramidal in configuration: the layers at the top organize and commercially exploit the activities of those at the bottom. The term 'sport nexus,' then, refers to an entity consisting of sport in its associations with the mass media, corporate sponsors, governments, medicine, and biotechnology.

The sports that claim first place in North American society – football, hockey, baseball, basketball, Olympic athletics, and boxing – are the ones that primarily sustain the sport nexus. For the most part they are male-dominated and are constructed to display the most masculine qualities of the human body. When I use the umbrella term 'sport' in this book, then, I am referring to this particular cluster of core sports within the larger sport nexus, and not to the whole field of sports, much less of physical culture. I am interested in the way these sports, through the culture they generate and affect, become imprinted and elaborated in the collective imagination. I am interested in how these sports generate their meanings, and in how these meanings, detached from the athletic encounter, take the values of these sports into other arenas of life. I am equally interested in how – notably through the pressures of corporate capitalization, gender order change, the growth of the Black and gay movements, and the proliferation of biotechnology – the broader culture in its turn acts on sport.

The culture of sport is in fact made up of many different subcultures and many different dimensions and sites, unified by specific rituals and codes common to all. By the term 'sport culture,' then, I am referring to all those dimensions and sites in which sport has been a palpable point of reference or influence, including, but extending far beyond, its own dedicated networks. I include in this category fan culture and its traditions of rioting and violence; cultural genres and ritual practices that celebrate the athleticized, hypermasculine hero – from sport journalism to men's action blockbusters; sport-associated apparel and equipment industries and the commercial discourse of sport and the athleticized body; and the place of sport in the social life of youth and adults in our school and recreational systems.

Sport as Secular Sacrament

People who are indifferent to the magic of sport are often at a loss to explain the draw it has on its fans and practitioners. To such people it is not clear why the physical enactment of struggle by 'champions,' captured in the technical abstraction of records, resonates so powerfully, so emotionally with its fans. Yet clearly, these struggles provoke an intense and meaningful set of associations for their initiates: memories, fantasies, and identifications. Moreover, there is little understanding of why men in particular seem to need such apparently tribal genealogies that provide paternal, heroic, and protodivine ancestors.[11]

Yet these dimensions of feeling and identification approximate the experience of religion more than any other form of human cultural practice. This has long been acknowledged by commentators close to sport. Baron Pierre de Coubertin, founder of the modern Olympic Games, 'insisted repeatedly on the religious character of the Games,' according to Olympic historian John MacAloon. De Coubertin wrote in 1929 that 'the central idea' of the Olympic revival was that 'modern athletics is a religion, a cult, an impassioned soaring.'[12] Today, thoughtful journalists remark on the same qualities. Réjean Tremblay, for example, a senior sports writer in Montreal (where post–Stanley Cup parties have sometimes turned into destructive riots) observed in the middle of the 1994 Stanley Cup playoffs that 'many years ago people here were Catholics. Now they are Canadiens' fans. This is something unnatural. It goes much too far.'[13] Kirk Makin of the *Globe and Mail* reported sport psychologist Saul Miller's 'revelation' one day at a Denver Broncos football game 'while 75,000 fans roared and the team romped under its 40 foot Bronco mascot.' Miller was on the field and 'looked up at this huge horse up there, painted orange. I swear it looked like the great god Ba'al or something. It was their tribe, and they chanted and sang.'[14]

Such 'religious' fervour captures collectivities much larger than cities. Brazil's football culture is a form of national religion in itself. For example, in 1994, Isabel Vincent reported from Rio de Janeiro that 'a much-needed economic plan to combat inflation – running at more than 40 per cent a month – will be put on hold, and the presidential election campaign, which was in full swing until a few days ago, will be suspended as Brazilians turn their attention to a much more urgent issue: Just how will the national soccer team do in the *Copa*, the World Cup?'[15]

In June 1997, after the Detroit Red Wings won the Stanley Cup, an estimated one million people turned up for the city's celebration. The players were paraded to the ceremony in thirty identical red Ford Mustang convertibles. After a star player was critically injured in an automobile accident, prayer vigils spontaneously appeared on the street outside his hospital. Red ribbons were hung on trees and street signs. Red flags and bumper stickers appeared on city streets. In the United States, ESPN (the cable sports network) has advertised football with the following offer: 'Join our congregation this Sunday for an inspirational experience.' The words accompanied a photo of a player kneeling with bowed head in front of a huge stadium audience. U.S. coffin manufacturers even produce 'caskets in the colours of Alabama, Auburn and Georgia, as well as Tennessee' for that final touchdown.[16]

More than any church, sport and its associations have become the great cultural unifiers of the nineteenth and twentieth centuries, first in Anglo–North American culture, then throughout Europe and the rest of the world. Sport's success lay in the development of a physical and mathematical language of meanings and loyalties, based on the gendered body, that superseded divisions of culture and religion. This language presented in clear physical and symbolic terms a great gendered master narrative of the imperial age.[17] The athletic champion came to represent individuals, working groups, and communities; the quantified athletic record communicated his strength to other communities. As the French theoretician of sport Jean-Marie Brohm expresses it: 'Sport has powerfully contributed to a *cosmopolitan consciousness*; – a consciousness of a sporting humanity, in which the referential criteria are the records and the champion. In a sporting world the record and champions constitute a kind of *symbol of universality*.'[18]

I want from the beginning of this study to assert what I see as the effectivity, indeed the agency, of symbols and myths – particularly as they are mobilized by specific economic interests – as a guiding principle in understanding the place and power of the dominant sport forms in our society. The embodied athlete has become, on a social scale, the living mythic symbol-bearer, and the idea of the athlete–hero is fundamental to the nature and success of sport. The sport nexus, with its vast bureaucracies and enterprises, depends on him and the symbolic and mythological services he performs through the ceremonies and rituals of sport. These combine competition, physical skill, strength, and display.[19] This ritual practice generates and sustains a *mythology* – a set of story-beliefs about society and the cosmos – that is ideologically laden. The rituals and mythologies of sport are the account sport gives of the world, and the base on which its vast contemporary economies rise.[20]

Rituals are repetitive, sequenced actions that form the basis of ceremonies. In *Gender Advertisements*, Erving Goffman writes that

the function of ceremony reaches in two directions: ... the affirmation of basic social arrangements and the presentation of ultimate doctrines about man and the world. Typically, these celebrations are performed either by persons acting to one another or acting in concert before a congregation ... in brief, the individual is given an opportunity to face directly a representation ... of what he is supposed to hold dear, a presentation of the supposed ordering of his existence.[21]

Rituals encode and transmit information about basic, ideal social arrangements. They are, as anthropologist Lucia Nixon has pointed out, 'an essential part of human culture.' Nixon offers the following definition of rituals:

When people in a particular group engage in ritual behaviour, they transmit information to themselves and to each other about their current state of being ... The information that people communicate in rituals is often a symbolic duplication and restatement of beliefs and social relationships within the group. Rituals are powerful, then, because they legitimate and validate the way people in a given society interact – whether those people realize it or not.[22]

As a ceremonial ritual that actively involves unconscious as well as conscious participation, sport is a social text of information with the power of communication. While its more popular forms can communicate many different messages, its elite and professional forms communicate the dominant world view or 'mentality' of its age.

As a widespread ceremonial ritual of the industrial age, sport is remarkable for its ability to express two apparently contradictory sets of qualities: on the one hand, modernity, abstraction, efficiency, science, concept, and mind; on the other, the past, archaism, worship, emotionality, sex, and the body. Speaking of the growth of the Olympic movement and of spectacle as a performative genre, John MacAloon comments that 'the forging of a new genre of cultural performance out of diffuse cultural themes and anxieties is nothing else than an attempt to gain control over them.'[23] Reconciled in sport, these qualities are transmitted by it as the 'ultimate doctrine' about 'man and the world' both to its participants and to those around them. In the electronic age, sport does this in phenomenally powerful and far-reaching ways. Thus sport may include only a small part of society as active participants – largely, but not exclusively young males – yet still affect the whole.

The information of sport – the 'ultimate doctrine' about the world contained in its ceremonies and rituals – is the particular mythology it perpetuates and celebrates. Mythologies are collections of myths organized along a recognizable set of central themes. They condense a number of explanatory ideas and exemplary ideals. In the existing culture of sport these are structured around ritual physical actions of territorial appropriation and physical strength. As organizing principles within human culture, myths and mythologies shape the perception of reality by those who believe in them. Some schools of thought conceive of myths primarily as ideological delusions that carry and support the views of historically and culturally specific dominant social groups: in effect, value-laden lies or fabrications. Those who believe them are thought to suffer from 'false consciousness.' Other approaches – Carl Jung and Joseph Campbell, for example, as well as promoters of the male mythopoetic movement – claim that myths encode and communicate transhistorical and universal truths and need to be attended to for this reason. As Joseph Campbell writes:

The symbols of mythology are not manufactured; they cannot be ordered, invented, or permanently suppressed. They are spontaneous productions of the psyche, and each bears within it, undamaged, the germ power of its source ... It has always been the prime function of mythology and rite to supply the symbols that carry the human spirit forward, in counteraction to those other constant human fantasies that tend to tie it back. In fact it may well be that the very high incidence of neuroticism among ourselves follows from the decline among us of such effective spiritual aid.[24]

In my own view, myths are complex sets of ideas that combine both these dimensions. All cultures must face and give answers to similar – that is, transhistorical – questions: What is the origin and meaning of life and death? What roles should the sexes play? How can humans control the apparently uncontrollable course of existence? As a result, mythologies have similar elements from one culture to another. On the other hand, human cultures give very different answers to these questions, reflected in their differing mythologies. Mythologies combine elements of the continuity of such interrogation and the diversity of possible answers. They derive their power in no small measure from their special ability to address the contradictions between the two.

For the purposes of this particular study of sport and its broad relationships to specifically political ideology in the industrial epoch, the approach to myth taken by sport sociologist Jim McKay in his discussion of sport and the gender order is perhaps most useful.[25] McKay does not accept that contemporary myths purely embody fundamental, transhistorical truths; nor does he see myths as 'total delusions or absolute falsehoods.' Instead, 'myths are partial truths that emphasize specific versions of reality and conceal or overlook others. In all cultures myths are crucial in defining what is natural, normal and legitimate. They are inextricably involved in relations of power, because they ensure that some accounts of reality count more than others.'[26] It is in this sense – a partial account that emphasizes and privileges one version of reality over another – that myths and mythologies are ideological and political. If one account of reality – one mythology – predominates over all other existing but minoritarian accounts, it is the dominant ideology.

The core men's sports condition and inform the constitution of the gendered social order and its dominant ideology. The rites of men condition the rights of men, and hence the culture of sport influences broader political consciousness and capabilities. The rites of sport create value-bearing mythologies around particular kinds of heroic figures: large strong, often violent, record-setting champions. The sport culture related to these rites shares with them a supralinguistic but clearly coded symbolic system that embodies a template of values – 'manly' values – as social values. These values can often cut across differences in social station and conscious political ideology. Capitalists and communists, whites and Blacks, men and women of every nation, all enjoy sport and the heroic narratives with which it is bound up. The ways in which the elemental physical content of sport has been gendered are central to its appeal. The actions that the dominant sport forms practise and celebrate are 'higher, faster, stronger,' in the succinct words of the Olympic motto. This is at once an industrial and a masculinist motto, for it condenses within its ideal bodies and activities the technomorphism of industrial capitalism (the ideal of the machine) and the biomorphism of maleness (the muscular superiority of males). It is, in this sense, a hypermasculinist slogan. (The consequences it has had for the athletic body are explored at length in chapters 5, 6 and 8.)[27]

The linkage of the modern ideal of the machine to the archaic ideal of the physically powerful male took place in the late nineteenth century. This fusion produced a sort of 'maleness squared.' In his 1978 study of gender and capitalism, political scientist Gad Horowitz coined the term 'surplus masculinity' (an equivalent term to hypermasculinity) to define the hegemonic masculine and capitalist ideal of manhood. He noted that our gender arrangements, based on a template of compulsory heterosexuality, produce this surplus masculinity as a result of the denigration of femininity they require. A key product of this surplus masculinity, in Horowitz's view, is the 'surplus aggressivity' of men as a gender, and of a social order that values domination more generally. Horowitz defined 'surplus aggressivity' as more than the necessary aggressivity required to maintain relations of personal and social viability. In a gender arrangement of compulsory heterosexuality such as the one that has prevailed in capitalist societies, surplus aggressivity is produced through the creation of a feminine-phobic, overcompensating masculinity that tends to domination and violence.[28]

Many of the specific forms and actions of sport, and the idealizations of sport culture, are characterized by hypermasculinity and surplus aggressivity. They exhibit an excess of the qualities associated with 'the most extreme potentialities of the male body' (to borrow Michael Messner's eloquent phrase) and the competitive and violently instrumental masculine 'role,' and a relative deficiency of those associated with the possibilities of the female body and the cooperative, supporting feminine 'role.'[29] In this sense, sport is a religion of domination and aggression constructed around a male godhead. At the political level, it tends to gender political consciousness and thus the frame of political evaluation for ideas of collectivity and stratification and the role of the state. As I trace in my discussion of sport and the neoconservative state in chapters 6 and 9, health, education, and welfare are seen as 'feminine' and 'soft' apparatus of government, wasteful and of dubious value in this hypermasculine ideological frame. Police, prisons, and the military, on the other hand, perceived as masculine, 'hard' apparatus, are valued as disciplined and essential.[30]

The religious dimensions of sport and sport culture involve the interaction between two distinct yet interrelated levels of experience.[31] The first is the *personal-existential* experience of athletes – the way people who participate in sport feel about their own activities and the contexts in which they live them. The second is the *symbolic-ideological* experience – the dimension in which sport has shared meaning for broader numbers of people beyond its actual practitioners. This is the level at which sport is most influentially ideological for nonparticipants and participants alike. In many important ways these levels are clearly different. For the athlete, *achievement* (or 'failure') in the agonistic competitive act is the primary experience. The pleasure or pain of the audience, on the other hand, is based entirely on their *identification* with the athletes for, in, and through whom they feel vicarious pleasure or disappointment. Nevertheless, both athletes and participants respond to, in Roone Arledge's words, 'the joy of victory, the agony of defeat.' In this respect, the athlete's and the audience's experiences overlap and interpenetrate in the mythological dimension, creating a shared realm of belief and feeling in which the athlete and the spectator are united in many of their hopes, fears, and interpretations of the outcome of any event or contest. In this overlapping space, the meanings of sport are kept alive and regenerated by the complicit relationship of athletes and spectators, each playing their respective roles and reaping their respective rewards.

When moments of primal physical intensity are socially shared through the performance of physical ritual, the athlete's intrinsic pleasure of bodily performance and his sacrificial pain, if pain has been involved, are crowned and embellished by a sense of belonging. The crowd feels a similar pleasure and pain and, if victory is achieved, a feeling of representation and affirmation. At that moment, athletes and spectators are transcendentally united in the celebration of their champions – symbolic figures who represent the strength, well-being, and fate of their communities. Listen to how Stanley Chikosa, a Zambian living in Canada at the time, explained the effect of the tragic airplane crash that destroyed that country's national soccer team in 1993.

The country was in a state of total grief. People were weeping openly in the streets ... Flags were at half mast. A week of national mourning had been declared. Zambia is a country without a lot of heroes and in one blow we had lost many of our national heroes ... It will take years for Zambia to recover from something like this. It's more than the realization that Zambia's chances for qualifying for next year's World Cup are now gone. Soccer is the most popular game in Zambia, and the game is part of our national psyche.[32]

These feelings about soccer are shared by fans in the developed as well as developing world. They could equally be found in Italy, Germany, and Russia, as well as in England, where the game was first codified. In Canada, hockey plays the most important role in identifying the national population with a set of player-heroes who represent the country and are demigods of the 'national psyche.' In the fall of 1996, the Canadian national team lost the World Cup in hockey. Signs of depression, loss, and anger were evident across Canadian communities. When the team captured the Cup in 1997, there was jubilation.

The identification supporters have with their team – or, for that matter, with an individual athlete – can be very intense among boys and adult men. 'It's not a club, it's mine,' is how one supporter expressed it. 'It's one of the most important things in my life.'[33] Rick Parry, chief executive officer of England's Premier Football League, expressed the identification of supporters with sports teams this way: 'You can change your job, you can change your wife, but you can't change your football team ... You can move from one end of the country to another, but you never, ever lose your allegiance to your first team. That's what English soccer is all about. It's about fierce loyalty, about dedication.'[34] And – unspoken but so absolute as to be taken for granted – it is about those qualities in the masculine mode. For, even as this book is written, the ties that have bound athletes to their communities – whether in working-class England or postcolonial Africa – are being unravelled by commercialization and free trade in athletic labour. And as the ties of locality, ethnicity, and nation come more and more undone, the ties of gender, of masculinity, become increasingly important.

Sport locates its practitioners – including its active supporters – in a male-defined and male-populated universe that is dynamic, like the constantly changing circumstances created by capitalist industrial growth. But, at the same time, it provides a constant – perhaps the one constant – in an ever-changing world where the requirements of manhood and masculinity are so hard to fulfil. In England, when teams lose, their supporters often follow them out of the stadium singing 'You'll Never Walk Alone.' In this sense, too, sport is like the church used to be – an alternative family, a support system as well as a system of meaning. When this dearly held illusion of a stable patriarchal genealogy is disrupted, economic and emotional repercussions can follow. During the major league players' strikes and lockouts in baseball and hockey in 1994 and 1995, when owners and players abandoned their fans in order to haggle greedily among themselves, reactions among loyalists ranged from disgust to rage at the violation of the sacred trust the athletes supposedly shared with them.[35] Attendance dropped at major league games and increased at minor league events. And there is evidence to support the view that baseball has never fully recovered. In fact, in industrial society, sport has overtaken many of the previous functions of an established patriarchal church and organized religion: the moral instruction of children, the ritual differentiation of men and women, the worship by both of a common divinity forged in the masculine mode, and the national and international experience of collective bonding around that divinity. Our domed stadiums are cathedrals of men's culture. Like the Catholic Church at the height of its influence, organized sport is both an international masculinist network of community-based associations and an extended, elite power apparatus of enormous influence.

One compelling explication of the religious nature and functions of sport comes from French sport sociologist Jean-Marie Brohm in his two major works *Sport: A Prison of Measured Time* and *The Political Sociology of Sport.*[36] Brohm is a Freudian Marxist who sees in sport the contemporary 'opiate of the people' – a term Karl Marx used to describe organized religion. Sport acts as an opiate, in Brohm's view, in a number of ways. It mounts spectacles of physical mortification that model authoritarianism. It provides an integrative mechanism for the physical maintenance of the labour force. It teaches hierarchical social relations. And it displaces and shapes erotic energy in sadomasochistic ways. While Brohm's treatment of sport does not take masculinism sufficiently into account – much work of cultural theory inspired by traditional psychoanalysis and Marxism deserves the same criticism – his key ideas have great merit and are powerfully presented. Another explanation of the sport-as-religion thesis comes from Donald Mrozek in his more historical *Sport and American Mentality 1880–1920.* Where some scholars emphasize the ability of sport to deliver very personal and concrete identity anchors (such as those of neighbourhood, community, and class), Mrozek emphasizes the protoreligious functions that American sport played in the coherence of a gendered *national* culture and consciousness in the late nineteenth and early twentieth centuries. Like Brohm, Mrozek addresses sport in wider terms of cosmological placement and the ability of sport to represent and animate more abstract ideologies. He focuses particularly on what he calls sport's ability to provide a number of 'strategies of regeneration' – mythologies and social practices – that energized American society in the years covered by his study. Mrozek sees such strategies as binding together all human societies.[37] He also details, as we shall see further in chapters 2 and 3, how sport was able to answer the new needs for such strategies required by the evolution of American society in the era of industrial expansion and national formation. Essential to this role was sport's ability to renew and strengthen ideals and institutions of masculinity and masculinism, as modernization shifted and destroyed old modalities of gender.

Employing the sacred code of records and the mythology of hypermasculine champions, sport and sport culture convey masculinism itself and the rightness of it. The largest 'community' – a self-organizing collectivity with group identity, group agency, group differentiation, and group interests and rights – that sport constructs is the community of men and the dominant position of that community within mixed society. Insofar as sport is our way of preparing young males to act as physical enforcers of a vigorously defended economic and gender order grounded in inequality and domination, it is not fun and games. Instead, it should be understood as an established (state-supported) religion with a protomilitary ritual practice that serves to undemocratically demarcate the ownership of physical coercion, a territory that is still almost exclusively men's, and that spreads the values of domination within the larger social sphere.

The Masculinism of Sport

Is this masculine quality of sport a problem? If sport can provide for the psychological needs of identity and belonging so effectively while all other anchors of identity fall away in capitalism's continuously changing universe, why criticize it? If it answers profound gender-differentiated social needs and provides a massive child-care network for boys, is this wrong?

The problem – if the myriad difficulties of modern sport can be connected in one phrase – is that sport also divides people in ways that are often destructive and antisocial. Sport divides people against themselves. It separates children from children, men from women, men from men, and community from community. Sport models and exacerbates social conflict and encourages antisocial and antidemocratic values. And it does this most centrally through its inflection of gender, particularly its offering of ideal types and behaviours for men. Gendered institutions, values, and behaviours shape 'small p' political culture – the politics of interpersonal and social life – in ways that directly affect 'large p' political culture – the politics of government and the state – much more than has yet been taken into account in theories of political formation and social change.

To explain why sport tends to be as or more reactionary than progressive, most critical socialist scholars attribute its negative qualities directly to those of the capitalist mode of production. Thus the subordination of cooperation to competition and domination occurs because capitalism is not a humane socioeconomic system. If the fundamental relationships sport validates are competition and ranking; if the fundamental good is that of high performance (productivity); if the fundamental actions are those of overpowering and dominating, it is because these qualities are inherent in the capitalist system.

However, something extremely important has been left out of their account: sport's relationship to men organized as a gender-class. Sport mounts as spectacle a symbolic representation of the *masculinist system* and its fundamental principles. Indeed, masculinism must be understood as the primary ideological core of sport and its culture. Where sport is concerned, masculinism and gender-class are not 'add-on' categories to capitalism, economic class, or race. Rather, masculinism – the gender dominance of men – is organized and achieved by sport. The masculinist ideological reflexes sport nurtures in its narrative of masculine heroics energize and inform other political identifications such as locality, ethnicity, and nationality. Thus, we speak of a 'virile patriotism' – a political position driven by a masculine, gendered impulse – or a 'wimpy foreign policy.' The political position is framed in gendered and masculinist terms, often through sport tropes, in the rhetoric of politics and war. Sport is in this sense a unified men's culture – constituted by men for each other – as much as it is a variegated class and race culture in which its participants live out traditional divisions and competitions.

In addition to an economic order (the system by which a society organizes its production – e.g., slave, feudal, capitalist), every society has a gender order. This term refers to the way a group socially organizes and gives cultural meaning to the biological existence of two sexes and the inbuilt, bodily drive for sexual pleasure. The gender order is a product of the social choices and customs of groups of physical beings who possess a number of biological legacies and a consequent series of potentials. Looking only to the known past, we cannot hope to find an accurate record of what those potentials are. On the other hand, we cannot, by virtue of present cultural diversity, assume infinite malleability in the behaviours and options open to us, since some would violate our basic biological makeup and needs (for air, water, food, shelter, rest, love, and a sense of belonging).[38]

The rituals of physical culture are important in this gender order because practically and symbolically they empower and disempower certain members of society by casting lines of physical activity and passivity, inclusivity and exclusivity, entitlement and marginalization, skill and ignorance. The relationship between who is permitted to enact physical rituals of prowess, what these rituals celebrate, who is mythically constructed as a cultural hero, and who actually has societal power, is very strong cross-culturally. For example, in classical Athens, and for many centuries thereafter in the Hellenic world, the prevailing gender template was highly polarized, ranking women below men economically, politically, and physically. As a gender, women did not have independent property, or political and reproductive rights. Girls of the upper classes were permitted to participate in extensive sex-segregated athletics.[39] But as adults, women did not extensively engage in these activities. Secluded in the dark, often unpleasant private house, and confined to work associated with the household and children, the very location of women's lives contrasted with the bright, decorated *palestra* and *agora*, where men's politics and athletics unfolded.[40]

Both symbolically and practically, Greek athletics were rehearsals for military action; in a phrase, they were *war games*. Foot and chariot races, javelin throws, wrestling, running, and hoplite races – all these events ritualized the skills that ruling men needed to play a commanding role in the city–state armies whose campaigns were an essential part of the economy of the times. The ancient Olympic Games, conducted at four-year intervals from 776 BC to 394 AD, were the premier site in a network of city and intercity festivals and games for the display of this masculine military prowess. They were held during institutionalized truces agreed on by all participating city-states. And their associated functions – lavish feasts, parties, and religious rituals – enabled negotiated interactions between normally hostile parties, providing essential occasions for consolidating gains or losses on the battlefield, developing trade arrangements, shifting political alliances, and other important matters.[41] That adult women were excluded from participation and even spectatorship at the Olympics during most of their tenure, and that this exclusion was enforced on pain of death, also ensured that women were excluded from key economic, military, and religious networks and events that were decisive in these societies. Thus inclusion or exclusion in the most important forms of physical culture – forms close in many respects to our own sport – mirrored literal empowerment or disempowerment along gender lines, rigidly polarized and ranked in ancient Greek society.

In keeping with its sexual division of labour and accompanying belief systems, a culture generates a template of gender that exemplifies its gender order, the expression of its dominant ideology of gender.[42] In practice, this template exists in the real structure of family systems and the relative status of women and men in society. Discursively it is reflected in the structure of language and conventions of culture, understood and internalized by people of all sexes, whether in compliance with or transgression of its norms. In our own case, 'the "faded mythology" preserved within Indo-European languages and categorical structures' write Sandra Curry Jansen and Don Sabo,

is organized around what Harding called the 'totemism of gender.' This totemic organizes words, thoughts, images, objects, people and experiences into polarities that encourage binary perceptions and categorizations of difference such as male/female, human/nature, subject/object. Moreover, this process of binary coupling is weighted by hierarchical assumptions that implicitly attach primary importance to the first term in the system: the male, human, subject.[43]

These bipolar ascriptions are alive today in the sense that they are still being reproduced in interpersonal, social, and political life, in our myths, beliefs, and ideologies, from our traditional conceptions of politics and the state to the genres and conventions of Hollywood, to the culture of sport.

A product of previous gender divisions of labour and their corresponding ideologies, and reworked through the belief systems of our century, this polarized template does not function well for us today. With the unravelling of the male-provider family-wage system and its separate-spheres gender order, the template's ongoing prescriptions for masculine aggression and female acquiescence are at odds with the roles most adults of both sexes are required to play in family and economic life. This explains why the template no longer feels natural to large numbers of people and why it is under constant challenge. As some of the challenges posed by the great social movements of the postwar period suggest, there are a number of alternative ways to arrange a gender order – ways that could work with the actual requirements of men and women in a gender-inclusive, if not yet equal or integrated, labour market, and that could allow for the development of all – not simply 'gender-appropriate' – abilities in both men and women.

I define 'ideology' as a set of associated values, beliefs, and feelings that correspond to the world-view and interests of a social group. Just like class ideologies, ideologies of gender are not monolithic, even where they are powerful. Cultural theorist Raymond Williams suggests that many ideologies coexist in complex societies, and can be roughly categorized as *dominant, residual,* or *emergent.* The 'dominant' ideological stream is usually majoritarian, though it may only recently have become so or it may be past its social prime, already fracturing into residual and emergent fragments. The ability of a dominant ideology to 'incorporate' or co-opt opposing ideologies before they fully differentiate into distinct, alternative ideological forces is crucial to preventing the crystallization of dissident social forces and to maintaining stable class relations. The dominant ideology, if successful, is the here-and-now ideology. 'Residual' ideologies represent the tenacious ideas of superseded social and economic relations. 'Emergent' ideologies, by contrast, express new social and economic relations and the possibilities and ideas these create.[44]

Different kinds of sport represent different crystallizations of ideologies. The Arctic Games of Inuit and other First Nations held annually in northern

Canada are living examples of residual ideology embodied in the physical culture of hunting-and-fishing societies based on group solidarity and gender complementarity.[45] North American football, by contrast, expresses the complex hierarchical relations and interactions of mature masculinist capitalism with its extended complexities in social and gender divisions of labour, and is an example of the prevailing dominant ideology. Baseball, as discussed in Chapter 2, combines both residual and dominant themes, but as we near the end of the twentieth century, it takes on an increasingly residual character. This has been acknowledged by both Michael Farber of *Sports Illustrated* and Stephen Brunt of the *Globe and Mail*, who have described baseball as a dying sport.

Neither the broad culture of groups nor the psyches of individuals are pure types – this one entirely 'residual,' that one completely 'dominant.' We combine within our personalities, our world-views, and our associations various elements of 'feeling-ideas' associated with each of these ideological streams; and these elements coexist in our consciousness more or less easily. At the same time, in individuals, just as in society as a whole, one of these streams will tend to be more influential than the others. With respect to gender, there are differences and tensions in ideologies, not only between those of mixed social classes but also between those of distinct gender cultures. *Men's culture* is generated by and around the activities performed exclusively by men and blends into those spheres populated by both sexes but dominated by men. *Mixed culture* ranges from realms where men outnumber women to spheres, such as nursing and childhood education, where women far outnumber men but men continue in leadership and executive positions. *Women's culture* is about childrearing and caregiving, as well as sexual display and the beautification of the female body. In our society women's culture is a much smaller and clearly subordinate realm, though this need not necessarily be the case.

The core institutions of sport fall squarely within the realm of men's culture, but extend widely into mixed culture: as education, as spectacle, and as a practice supported by the family. The practices and genres of men's culture are the dominant terms of culture as a whole. They successfully set not only their own points of reference but also the permissible and indeed the transgressive contours of mixed and even women's culture. Theirs is not an easy, static, or uncontested dominance, for the gendered cultures are in many ways very different from one another. One contemporary political example of this is the 'gender gap' – a term used to refer to gender–differentiated voting patterns during elections in North America. Such a gap was one of the key factors that returned Bill Clinton to office as president of the United States, and could probably be found to exist in most other realms of human activity.[46] But with respect to power relations and social institutions – for example, the U.S. Congress, the Senate, the Pentagon, the CIA, and so forth – the values of men's culture still predominate. Indeed, in the late 1990s, with the exception of Britain under a new Labour government and the Scandinavian countries, women's numbers in national politics have been in serious decline.

Modern sport, as a masculinist culture rooted in a superseded 'separate-spheres' gender division of labour, has succeeded because it has been able to literally embody forward-looking values associated with emergent, then dominant, industrialization and national formation while basing itself in archaic, residual values associated with the highly differentiated, ranked gender order of tribal male warrior culture. As Donald Mrozek notes, twentieth-century sports leaders 'were ... the inventors of a mythology that outlived the real world that created it.'[47] Sport is an important part of the dominant ideological culture today, and is one of the most important agents of the 'co-opting' ability of the dominant culture with respect to men as a group and gender class.

Approaching Power and Sexuality in Relation to Sport Culture

'The body is directly involved in a political field,' wrote the French historian and social theorist Michel Foucault. 'Power relations have an intimate hold upon it; they invest it, train it, and torture it, force it to carry out its tasks, to perform ceremonies and emit signs.'[48] Sport is the approved dominant physical culture – ceremony in Foucault's sense – in our epoch, setting standards ('emitting signs') for beauty and performance. Sport is a set of practices and institutions that involve the bodies and imaginations-within-bodies of billions of people in extended interactions of ritual training and elite display. For this reason, sport is a very direct form of what Foucault calls 'biopower.' This concept refers to the way a political order organizes the physical lives and experiences of its members through practices of and constraints on the body. Members then internalize within their own personalities the values and conventions of their culture, and monitor and deploy their own bodily actions *voluntarily* in accordance with the system's needs, rules, and regulations – from sexual behaviour to national conscription.[49]

For Foucault, bourgeois power is above all the power of a system based on self-surveillance and self-regulation toward social conformity. Though Foucault coined the term biopower and brought a unique perspective to some of its fluid and multifaceted aspects, he is in fact only among the most recent of the major thinkers on the subject. The leftist psychoanalysts (such as Reich, Ferenczi, Fenichel, Fromm, and Marcuse) and the feminist psychoanalysts (such as Horney, Klein, Mitchell, Dinnerstein, Chodorow, and Irigaray) all to an important extent addressed many of the issues involved in biopower. In their discussions, issues of gender, sex, and sociopolitical identity were central features.

While appreciating the Foucauldian contribution, I part company with him and his followers in seeing power only as fluid and multifaceted. I see power as embodied, institutionalized, and instrumentally wielded to promote the interests of specific groups of people. In the late 1990s, when 358 individuals have personal wealth equivalent to the combined wealth of the poorest 45 per cent of the world's population, when 50 of the world's 150 largest economies are corporations, and when weaponry and systems of war consume more than a trillion dollars a year, it seems absurd to argue that power is not condensed in enduring structures and economies that are based in staggering inequalities of power and privilege. Social science scholars working in the poststructuralist and postmodernist paradigms, taking their cues from Foucault and other French theorists (Derrida, Baudrillard), have gone on to suggest that along with the 'de-centering' of power, the 'master-narratives' of the enlightenment and modernism – rationalism, humanism, nationalism, capitalism, socialism – have fragmented and lost their ability to animate and cohere human thoughts and actions. Without the coherence of these master narratives, there is no commonly perceived reality, no coherent system of gender and sexuality. There is only a multiplicity of socially constructed 'identities' – self-assembled pastiches cobbled together from the discursive offerings of postmodern culture.

Many of the master-narratives these writers have identified have lost their animating and cohering powers. This is evidenced in the global crisis of progressive political ideology, as well as in the deep cynicism about other great '-isms' and about politics in general. But precisely in this context, one master-narrative – the one of hypermasculinity – survives and thrives through the culture of sport and its erotic, heroic, masculine idealizations. The physical deployment and display of the body in sport has an erotic dimension because bodies are not merely collections of muscles, bones, and will; they are also animated by sexual drives, which are biologically based and socially shaped. For many reasons (some of which I explore below) the treatment of sexuality in contemporary human life and culture has been distorted and, in many cases – including that of sport – its presence has been minimized or entirely disavowed. Yet sexuality, particularly as it relates to power, is a subject that deserves much more attention and understanding in our analysis of sport, gender culture, and the social order.

The erotic dimension is a ubiquitous and powerful one in human existence, one bequeathed to us as part of our physical makeup, powerfully active in our consciousness. In *The Arena of Masculinity*, Brian Pronger writes:

Sex is a special interaction between mental and physical experience. The physical dimension transforms the mental and the mental transforms the physical ... When the physical and the mental come together in sexual activity, they are intensely and pleasurably merged. This is a process in which the abstract nature of thinking becomes incarnate in actual physical experience.[50]

Few would contest the power of sexuality in human experience. But there is no consensus about its origins, nature, or effect. My own views have been strongly influenced by the progressive psychoanalytic schools (left and feminist), who took from Sigmund Freud a view that characterizes the unsocialized, undifferentiated drive of sex or Eros as one of 'polymorphous perversity,' a term that emphasizes how labile this drive is and how little its subjective experience is limited to procreative ends and activities. In this view, the *objective function* of Eros as a fundamental instinct, drive, or biological principle is to cohere new units in the service of propagating and maintaining life. Thus Eros functions in small and large social groups, among people of all ages and both sexes, as well as between adult individuals in heterosexual dyads.[51] The *subjective experience* of the drive on the other hand – the way an individual *feels* it – resides in the desire to 'obtain pleasure from the zones of the body.' This psychoanalytic view intentionally designates the whole body, not simply the reproductive organs, as erogenous. It is important, when considering sport and eroticism, to recall that when Freud spoke of sexual 'repression,' he was speaking of the repression of the sensuality of the whole body – of polymorphous perversity – not only of particular genital sexual acts or zones or possibilities.

Just as sexuality is not physically confined to a few designated sexual organs, Eros is not chronologically confined to adulthood, but is generalized throughout the body from birth and is involved in many different kinds of intense emotional relationships: those between parents and children, those between teachers, coaches, and children, those among children, as well as to those among adults in small and large groups. Sport, much of it based on physical engagement and intense emotionality, is a powerfully sexualized arena. Yet our cultural mythology presents it as an asexual or nonsexual arena, especially for its young participants (for historical reasons discussed in Chapter 3). Athletes do not have sex when they play or compete, goes the usual view. Because athletic activities are not officially oriented to achieving genital heterosexual union, sport is not about sex. I disagree.

I assume that the force of Eros – driven biologically, experienced sensually, and organized socially – is an in-built drive that is present and seeking expression, at both individual and social levels, within sport and its culture. I assume that sexuality is as present a drive in women as it is in men, but that the paths for its satisfaction are physically and socially gender-differentiated. Because of the inbuilt nature of this drive, I assume the erotic is omnipresent as a potential and inevitable dimension of human activity, including sport. I therefore accord it an instrumentality and effectivity of its own. I assume that sexuality cannot simply be 'put away' if it is inconvenient. This is especially true if a given practice that officially renounces sexuality actually functions to provoke and incite it – as I argue in Chapter 3 that sport does with homoeroticism (eroticism between men). I assume Eros has many ways of achieving expression even where it is not officially welcomed, through effective displacements, elaborate masquerades, and unspoken subtexts in physical culture. I also assume that no analysis of any social practice, but especially a physical practice such as sport, can really account for the phenomenon it purports to explain if it does not address the presence and shape of sexuality within it.

For children and youth, sport is the earliest organized school for the 'intense interaction between mental and physical experience.' In this sense, sport invokes and affects the eroticism of its participants. Yet we still deny this aspect of sport, and with this denial, turn a blind eye to its central role as sexual socializer, preferring to focus our attention on pornography and sexually explicit images as the sexual bad guys. Meanwhile, we iconize images of the Schwarzeneggerian body and idolize the rituals that produce it, unaware how much this too affects the development of men's sexuality and personality. It is regrettable that influential feminists such as antipornography crusaders Catharine MacKinnon and Andrea Dworkin have led the demonization of explicit sexual imagery.[52] Inadvertently perhaps, they have contributed to the sanitation-by-default of nonexplicit yet very sexual cultural practices and discourses within men's culture and mixed culture in sport. For them and their followers, the 'special interaction between mental and physical experience' of sexual engagement makes pornography a uniquely dangerous cultural industry. But consider how late in life, relatively speaking, we engage with sexually explicit imagery; and how early and how extensively in life we engage in other intense physical experiences – first those of unsupervised play, then those of 'organized play,' or sport.

Far from being juxtaposed subcultures and practices, sport and pornography have a series of significant similarities and mutually reinforcing relationships in society today. Both are cultural source points for the commercial production of sex-symbol icons (sport/male, pornography/female) that function archetypally and normatively across society. The gladiator on the cover of *Sports Illustrated* is the symbolic warrior, the ideal male. The sex worker on the cover of *Penthouse* is his symbolic lover – his reward. The women in the *Sports Illustrated* annual swimsuit issue look very much like those in *Playboy* and *Penthouse*, and in *Cosmopolitan*, *Glamour*, and *Elle*. Sport, pornography, and fashion are industries of spectacle and imagery; both sell the images of the bodies they employ, and the equipment to fashion them. The arena of sexual display is an important one in gender and sexual relations, and sport is a crucial site for men.

Power, forceful instrumentality, and control, up to and including the use of violence, are the terms of hypermasculine sexual display within heroic masculinity in the sporting arena. They are the elemental components of a language of heroic masculinity that all members of society understand, even if all do not speak it. Robert Brannon has identified the four traditional rules of American manhood as follows:

(1) No Sissy stuff: Men can never do anything that even remotely suggests femininity. Manhood is a relentless repudiation of the feminine; (2) Be a Big Wheel: manhood is measured by power, wealth and success. Whoever has the most toys when he dies, wins; (3) Be a Sturdy Oak: manhood depends on emotional reserve. Dependability in a crisis requires that men not reveal their feelings; and (4) Give 'em Hell: exude an aura of manly daring and aggression. Go for it. Take risks.[53]

Because our society is composed of three major classes – owning/governing, managing/professional, and labouring/soldiering – these rules of masculinity are interpreted or grouped in three broad styles of heroic masculinity, with their associated erotics, and are universally recognized and utilized in cultural representation. These types or styles correspond to the specializations of the men of the three main classes. Far from trivial, style is a meaningful code that communicates important messages – so much so that we can think of these styles as three different dialects of a larger language of masculinity, based on the four assumptions above. It is with these differing dialects of masculinity that different subcultures play, though often the games of men are played in deadly earnest.

The first heroic style and associated sexuality is linked to executive power stemming from wealth and/or high office. The eroticism associated with this type can be summed up in Henry Kissinger's formulation 'power is the greatest aphrodisiac.' Associated with the men of the owning and political classes (presidents, prime ministers, corporate directors, generals, network czars) in popular cultural representation, this eroticism also characterizes the big-time villains against whom such characters are pitted in fictional narratives. These would-be gangster bosses, dictators, drug lords, corrupt politicians are typically shown as extremely exploitative of women. Where the line blurs between the 'good' and 'bad' versions of this type, so do the erotic connotations.

The second style of heroic masculinity is associated with intelligence and technique, and its avatar is the middle-class hero. His erotics are related to conceptual performance (as in 'he dazzled me with his mind') and are connected to his skill with technologies – scientific, cultural, sexual. Science fiction and the mystery genre, the great collective escapes of the twentieth-century middle–class, feature men of this type. They are good at 'detecting' what is happening in a confusing and unstable world, and succeeding by their wits.[54] Joe Montana exemplified the hero of this type in football, Wayne Gretzky in hockey. Harrison Ford exemplifies him in film; his evil doppelganger would be a deranged scientist, an equally harassed professional in an enemy system (Karla in John le Carré's work), or a master-mind murderer (Hannibal Lecter in the film *The Silence of the Lambs*).

Finally, the masculinity and associated eroticism of physical bravery and muscularity is associated with working and soldiering heroes, whose bodies wrest raw materials from nature and whose sacrifices in war defend us from the predations of others. They put their lives on the line for us – a sacrifice we justly see as heroic. This type resonates in the unconscious as the archetype of the good parent/champion who symbolizes energy, strength, and protection. In its 'bad' incarnation, however, this type can suggest mindless rage and revenge – the thug, the brutalized beast. Either way, the erotics of this style of masculinity are directly embodied on the carnal plane, rather than mediated by technology, wealth, or intelligence, and rely on physical display of muscular and sexual strength. Sport is the place where this style of masculinity is spoken most comprehensively.

The erotic importance of the physical body in ideals of hypermasculinity is attested to by the power of sport itself – a spectacle of that body – and by the extraordinary importance of physical prowess in all the popular men's fictional genres, from westerns to espionage. Even when the obviously middle-class hero must employ his wits, he must always show his sexual competence by taking part in lethal, gruelling physical assaults. In this sense, the erotic importance of the athleticized, proletarian male body is a major trope throughout twentieth-century literature, drama, and visual art, both high- and low-brow. Pornography written by or for men reveals preoccupations with physical size, staying power, and ejaculatory strength – the signs of potency in ideal hypermasculinity. Gay pornography features the working-class hero – a truck driver, sailor, or construction worker – as its premier erotic icon.

Athletes embody, the spectacle of sport celebrates, and fans tend to emulate primarily the third form of heroic masculinity and eroticism. Athletes embody both the 'good hero' and the 'bad boy' variants – from Ty Cobb to Michael Tyson, rough, sexually charged, and aggressive athletes have always been very attractive for the media and for many fans, and have affected professional standards. For example, 'Night-Train' Lane, a defensive back for the NFL Detroit Lions in the 1960s, pioneered the 'clothesline tackle,' an extended arm across the throat that swept ball carriers off their feet, which is still in use today. NBA stars Charles Barkley and Dennis Rodman are particularly popular because of their macho antics and in-your-face attitude. Many of today's super-athletes – with brains, money, and physical skill – embody all three forms of masculine power.

From the most particular movements of the body, to the broadest dynamics of territorial and sexual appropriation, sport and sport culture are sexual. As a practice and as a spectacle, sport organizes, aestheticizes, represses, and incites sexuality in ways commensurate with its obsession with competition, ranking, and pain – that is, in ways that integrate hyperaggressivity and violence into eroticism and deliberately cultivate these qualities.[55] Sport encodes a gendered, historically created style of masculine eroticism – a sadistic, hypermasculine eroticism – and celebrates a *masculinist* sexuality based in a surplus of culti-vated aggression.[56] Further, because it is a homosocial practice, sport inevita-bly produces homoerotic dynamics, and these are widely characteristic of its culture. Yet the sport world, along with that other site of male-exclusive, prowess-oriented activity – the military – is also a site of intense, profound, and institutionalized homophobia: the hatred of homosexuals and the fear of femininity.

Approaching Violence, War, and Competition

Violence against women is an inescapable part of our culture. However, as psychiatrist James Gilligan puts it,

statistically, most lethal violence is committed by men against other men ... [Lethal] violence, in every nation, every culture, and every continent in which it has been studied, and in every period of history, has always been violence by men against other men ... Men constitute, on the average 75 percent or more of the victims of lethal physical violence in the United States – homicide, suicide, so-called unintentional inju-ries (from working in hazardous occupations, engaging in violent athletic contexts, and participating in other high-risk activities), deaths in military combat, and so on. And throughout the world, men die from all these same forms of violence from two to five times as often as women, as the World Health Organization documents each year. Women, on the other hand, according to best available evidence, seem to be the victims of sex crimes (such as rape and incest) more often than men are ... Virtually every nation that has had a military draft has decided either that only men should be drafted, or that only men should be sent into combat. Again none of this should surprise us, given the competition between men for status, valor, bravery, heroism – and honour – in patriarchal societies.[57]

Military historian John Keegan shares the same evaluation. 'Women may be both the cause or pretext of warmaking,' he writes in *A History of Warfare*. 'If warfare is as old as history and as universal as mankind, we must now enter the supremely important limitation that it is an entirely masculine activity.'[58]

There are important qualifications to this statement. Men belong to families and social groups, and they wage war on behalf of their communities. When men are victorious in war, their affiliated women and children also benefit; when men lose, their entire families, communities, and classes pay the price. In societies consisting of stratified economic classes, privileged men select the targets of aggression in war, direct the war effort, and benefit from it financially while relying on the bodies of less privileged men (foot soldiers) to fight and fall. The more developed the technologies of war and the specializations of labour within a society, the more marked this tendency of elite control and direction of war. In all these respects the men's wielding of organized violence – be it in civil or international strife – is marked by tribal, ethnic, national, or class dynamics, not only those of gender. Yet the rule of the great expansionist civilizations of the last ten thousand years has been that organized violence and war have been masculine monopolies. Men have been foot soldiers and generals, women have minded the home fires or followed the camps. The spoils of war including the right of conquest over women themselves, have been differentially greater for men than for women. Women have generally been excluded from the social bodies that make the political decisions to prosecute war, as well as from the organized bodies of combatants who wage it.

There have been exceptions to this general rule in the historical record. Quite a few societies, also heterogeneous in nature, give evidence of women trained to be warriors. In all societies women have fought to the death to protect themselves and their families in war; in our own century they have taken on combat roles in defensive struggles, especially in wars of resistance against aggressive invaders.[59] Women's inclusion or exclusion from active physicality and/or the administration of lethal force, however, has differed significantly from culture to culture, and from conjuncture to conjuncture. Complex societies have existed in which women had rough and ready equality with men and participated in decisions to prosecute war (for example, among the Iroquois, with their women's war councils). But these societies were over-run or annihilated by other societies with male-dominant gender orders, or destroyed by natural catastrophe (Minoan Crete). In contrast to the lost Minoan civilization in the European region, 'what did survive, what did vanquish circumstance and stamp its mind set on Europe,' as Camille Paglia has noted, was patriarchal warrior culture.'[60]

Evolutionary biologists have attempted to locate the origins of war and war culture in the evolutionary specialization of the primate male in defence of territory, sexual competition, and sexual aggression. These qualities are seen to have been honed by generational selection, and handed down through surviving and thriving male genes.[61] From the early attempts of Konrad Lorenz, Robert Ardrey, and Lionel Tiger, to the work of writers such as Edmund O. Wilson and Robert Wright, attention has been drawn to the prehuman nature of differential male aggression and its function in territorial protection and sexual competition. Since the spread of male genes is thought, in this view, to be maximized by multiple couplings to produce numerous offspring, primate males fight other males for sexual access to a maximum number of females. Males are, by natural selection – and hence by 'nature' – aggressive, competitive, and promiscuous. Females, on the other hand, are thought to need the commitment of a mate to raise the few offspring in which their energy is of necessity invested. So women are, by natural selection, cooperative, passive, and monogamous.

There are some who dismiss the argument that genetic maleness may confer a greater predisposition toward aggressivity. However, I think it possible that through genetic selection and inheritance there is among some males a greater predisposition for aggression, competition, and violence than among females. But this should not blind us to the fact that females are also aggressive, and that aggression need not always be acted out directly. It can be displaced, projected, symbolized, and achieved through passive and vicarious means. Women employ all these tactics in cultures where physical aggression is off-limits to them, and most cultures have stories and myths about annihilating, as well as nurturing, women. As well, we have seen cooperative, sexually responsible human males in human societies without endemic warfare or rape. Finally, the evidence of interpersonal experience shows that many men are both socially peaceable and inclined toward cooperation in gender relations.

Among primates, we see tremendous variation in aggression among individual males and between primate species. Male Bonobo chimpanzees – perhaps our closest genetic relatives – show very little aggression. Instead, a great deal of sexual interaction, including homosexual interaction, diffuses tension and aggression and promotes social harmony. Even among baboons, where males have long been thought to be much more aggressive than females, closer examination has revealed that many males choose associations of friendship and cooperation with females, rather than violent intramale rivalry, as their primary modus vivendi. In other words, aggression and domination are not the only male path to survival, even among the most aggressive and distantly related of our primate ancestors.[62] As well, notions that male hormones are the biological agents of inevitable male aggression were challenged in the 1990s, when research into the relationship between the physiology of hormones and social position among baboons and chimpanzees indicated that activity and rank may well stimulate hormonal response, not vice versa.[63] For example, male primates begin to secrete certain dominance-associated hormones after they assume dominant positions, and stop secreting those hormones when they lose those positions.

Whatever greater predisposition for aggression may reside in human males, war is not hard-wired into genetic maleness. Contemporary research in human brain development shows that during the first ten years of life, the brain sends out scores of neuronal pathways, representing many different possibilities, within the developing brain. After ten years of age, the undeveloped pathways wither away, leaving in place the pathways that were developed by – selected for – the individual's environment. For humans, the prevailing order of society embodied in its culture, not chromosomes or genes, is the most important factor in the selection for, and development of, poly-gifted individuals, and the most important factor in gender socialization and the cultivation of male aggression.

Leading American essentialist feminists such as Andrea Dworkin and Catharine MacKinnon also ascribe aggressive violence to men by nature, just as evolutionary psychologists do. The 'essentialist' brand of feminism they articulate sees women as naturally tender, cooperative, and nurturing, in contrast to men, who are seen as aggressive and appropriational. Though given a more 'politically correct' inflection than the ideas of the evolutionary biologists (who are tainted with patriarchal neo–Social Darwinism in the minds of many), this view still provides a reading of human and gendered nature that locates antisocial aggression primarily in the biological legacy of 'maleness,' not in the unequal social relations that select for male aggression.

In addition, this view flies in the face of the evidence. Consider the dramatic increase in the numbers of sexual partners young women have today compared with the 1950s. Women can behave in sexually promiscuous ways previously thought to be 'male,' particularly when these are culturally validated. From the violent and abusive mother, to the increasingly common female perpetrator of violent crime, to more-aggressive-than-thou political leaders such as Margaret Thatcher, it is clear that men have no biological monopoly on individual violence or social aggression.[64] A proposition that attempts to turn women into cream-puffs and men into monsters is untenable, and in recent years Camille

Paglia has emerged to debunk it. Paglia has brought some much-needed corrections to the idealization of women found in the essentialist feminist approach. Demonstrating a much less benign view of women's ability to nurture, so beloved of essential feminists, she writes that 'there is an element of entrapment in female sex, a subliminal manipulation leading to physical and emotional infantilization of the male.' Nevertheless, she too seems dangerously close to the evolutionary biologists. Paglia wants to accept, even celebrate, aggression and its supposedly unalterable fusion within sex, especially 'male sex.' 'Sex is not pleasure principle but the Dionysian bondage of pleasure-pain,' according to Paglia. 'There is an element of attack, of search-and-destroy in male sex in which there will always be potential for rape.' Paglia proposes that real feminism would accept the sex–aggression, pleasure–pain fusion, and that women should embrace the aggressive quality of sex, or at the very least, stop whining about it.[65]

The problem with all these essentialist readings is that they drastically obscure the role of human social choices and the influence of culture in the cultivation of aggressive specializations for individuals, for men as a group and for societies as a whole. In the following chapters, I work from the premise that humans as a species are a highly sexual lot with capacities for both aggression and cooperation that cultures reinforce differentially. While there may be differences in physiology between males and females that incline more males to somewhat greater aggressivity than more females, I believe it is women's primary responsibility for children – the nature and conditions of women's work as a gender-class – that most pacifies women by the logic of its practical necessities, and not some biologically based lack of aggression and capacity for cooperation.[66] A society's choice to divert human and male aggression to peaceful social relations or to cultivate and enlarge this aggression is the most important factor in the matter of personal and social violence. Such choice includes how to distribute social wealth, how to value and raise children, how to play and worship, and how to relate to the biotic environment. In complex societies consisting of a number of different social classes and ethnic groups, the choices of the most powerful will be the choices that are most promoted and for which incentives are most available.

Historically, there are strong links between the masculinist or patriarchal nature of a society, its physical games, and its military orientation and specialization. The culture and values of the masculine sphere of organized violence – the sphere of armies, war, and warriorhood – I refer to throughout this book as the 'the cult of the warrior' or the 'warrior cult.' Adapted from John Keegan, these terms refer to a common core of practices and beliefs about men, manhood, and masculinity, that are centred on men's specialization in administering force and death, transmitted through mythic ritual and narrative, and enacted by armies, police forces, and gangs. Modern sport has very strong links to this ancient cultural stream of mythology and draws on it in constructing numinous practices and ideals of manhood and masculinity in the industrial age. Athletes have been constructed as symbolic warriors or warriors-in-training.

Central to the contemporary warrior culture within sport is the ideal of *competition*. Competition, often praised as one of the most important lessons sport teaches, is at bottom a hostile dynamic based in a mentality of scarcity. It can be seen as rationalized hostility because it is based on a zero-sum equation, a process of 'mutually exclusive goal attainment.'[67] The victory of one party entails loss by the other. The competitive relation, embodying hostility, is rehearsed over and over again through the rituals of childhood and youth sport. It is validated for young people by important adults, and celebrated by culture and the mass media. The message is simple: doing one's best is measured in doing *better* than others and in getting more (love, respect, stuff) as a reward. In the core men's sports, doing better usually means being more physically aggressive.[68] Children's empathic and cooperative impulses are thwarted through the culture of physical competition, and their narcissism and aggression rewarded.

The rhetoric of competition has been tied up with the rhetoric of the market since Adam Smith proposed his invisible hand. Most recently, it has been pressed into service to aid in 'globalization' and the removal of national barriers to capital. But where the idea of competition once represented the aspirations of bonded individuals against a fixed feudal order, today it cloaks the interests of huge transnational corporations, many times more powerful than the old monarchies and aristocracies. As the mechanism seen to guide the market, the idealization of competition by sport has approached sanctification. Does this athletic culture of competition 'build character,' as it has long been touted to do? This depends on what kind of character we are talking about. Much research indicates that athletic competitiveness does not produce ease and self-esteem – the keys to personal well-being; it often produces high levels of pain and anxiety.[69] In *No Contest: The Case against Competition*, sociologist Alfie Kohn argues that the 'chief result of competition ... is strife.' He points out that 'hostility is practically indistinguishable from intentional competition, so an individual with this orientation will likely seek out competitive encounters.'[70] Kohn writes of the work of renowned sport psychologists Bruce Ogilvie and Thomas Tutko that the authors could find

no empirical support for the traditions that sport builds [constructive] character. Among the problematic results they discovered were depression, extreme stress, and relatively shallow relationships. Ogilvie and Tutko also found, as mentioned before, that many players 'with immense character strengths' avoid competitive sports. Finally, they discovered that those who do participate are not improved by competition: whatever strengths they have were there to begin with.[71]

In fact, far from enriching our interactions, a unifocal celebration of competition, particularly when linked with sports that promote violence, poisons our relationships and encourages antisocial qualities. According to Ogilvie and Tutko, 'the win/lose structure inevitably affects the priorities and temperaments of the individual players.' A personality profile they administered to 15,000 athletes revealed 'low interest in receiving support and concern for others, low need to take care of others, and low need for affiliation.' This is a personality profile of a narcissistic individual who will have a difficult time understanding the importance of prosocial public policy, or what it takes to build and maintain strong communities. 'Such a personality,' these researchers concluded, 'seems necessary to achieve victory over others.'[72]

In the competitive rites of sport, as in war, 'it is men who are expected to be violent, and who are honoured for doing so and dishonoured for being unwilling to be violent,' writes James Gilligan.[73] As a gender, men have been able to ritualize and conduct war because of their lack of direct responsibility for maintaining individual human life within the domestic unit on a daily basis. It is the resulting relative leisure of men within a gender order, coupled with their control of armed state and protostate structures and resources, that has permitted the flowering of apparently autonomous male-dominated and male-defined spheres of politics, culture, and religion centred on war.[74] And the ideology that supports men's entitlement to dominate these spheres still runs deep. A survey for the European Union found that more than two-thirds of Europeans (ranging from 60 per cent in Denmark to 85 per cent in Germany) 'thought it better for the mother of a young child to stay at home than the father,' *The Economist* reported in 1996. 'Mothers should take care of nappies, clothes and food; fathers are for money, sport and punishment.'[75]

Because masculinity, war, and sport have had close relationships from the beginning, and because the exercise of organized violence is so central to social and biotic hierarchies, these issues form themes I pursue throughout the following chapters.

With these terminological and conceptual clarifications in mind, then, it is time to turn to the nineteenth century, and the spectacular growth of sport to which it gave rise.

'To Raise the Wolf in a Man's Heart': Sport and Men's Culture in the Nineteenth Century

During the nineteenth century, adult males left the family household en masse and abandoned their traditional roles in socializing children to take up duties in far-away places. Sport emerged as an institution of social fatherhood to provide training in manly pursuits – war, commerce, and government – and a stepping stone out of the family of women and into the world of men. Today's major sports were elaborated, codified, organized, and institutionally consolidated over the course of the nineteenth century. They were part of a dynamic cultural response to the changes and challenges of industrialization, urbanization, nation-building, imperialism, and gender order flux.[1] Anglo societies – Great Britain, Canada, and the United States – were epicentres for the development of sports that eventually grew to global proportions: football in its several forms, cricket, baseball, basketball, hockey, and track and field (Olympic athletics). These sports found an enthusiastic welcome in industrializing Europe and in all the colonial centres – Asia, Africa, and the Americas – where English, European, and American men gathered to conduct the business of expansion and empire.[2]

The remarkably rapid growth of sport rules, associations, economies, and cultures in the nineteenth century was part of a radical redrawing of work and leisure. In preurban, agrarian-based cultures, the diurnal cycle, seasons of work and rest, and the calendar of religious holidays had governed labour and respite. Both the folk and aristocratic games from which our sports are derived were played in contexts governed by these rhythms and customs. By the end of the nineteenth century, along with the seasonal fluctuation of work and public holidays on saints' days, the folk games had withered away and had been displaced by sport on a mass scale. There had been a tremendous variety to the activities and games of precapitalist Europe. As these crystallized into modern sport forms in the nineteenth century, the variety persisted: team and individual sports, sports for summer, sports for winter, sports with racquets, sports with bats, sports with bicycles – all were part of the larger phenomenon of sport culture that exploded in the latter half of the nineteenth century. There was, however, one major element that the new sport forms had in common with each other and with the old folk and aristocratic games from which they evolved: the vast majority of these were performed by men, even when audiences were mixed. It was men's sports that grew, during the course of the nineteenth century, from participatory pastimes to large-scale public spectacles and lucrative industries. Under the tutelage of upper-class English, Canadian, and American educators, the athleticization of society was effected: 'a virile union of intellectual discipline and athletic prowess.'[3]

This chapter begins a discussion of the consequences of the gendering, indeed the virilizing, of athleticization that marked late nineteenth-century society. I trace the athleticization of Anglo-American society in relation to the issues important to understanding gender. First, I set the larger scene by reviewing the links that scholars have drawn between the growth of capitalism and particular sport forms. I then discuss changes in family and parenting arrangements and in feminism and gender struggle in relation to the growth of sport and sport culture. This is followed by a discussion of the gendered dimensions of industrialization, imperialism, and militarization as they related to sport. I complete the chapter with a case history of nineteenth-century football that seeks to show how the themes I discuss were expressed in the most influential of all nineteenth-century sports.

The Emergence of Sport in Capitalist Culture

In the preindustrial, agrarian British countryside, the physical culture of peasants and farmers centred on local communities, and their seasonal holidays and festivals. Feats of strength, wrestling, and foot races were widely enjoyed, and many variants of field hockey and football were played by farmers and artisans. The games always took place out of doors, tended to be rowdy, and were often violent.[4] While the aristocracy and landed gentry regularly attended these games, they had their own physical culture, played on their own lands and in their own buildings. It was centred on horses, the martial arts of sword-play and archery, and, increasingly in the seventeenth and eighteenth centuries, on golf and tennis.

The aristocracy by and large retained their estates – and thus the sites for the practice of their favourite pastimes – as capitalism evolved during the long process of urbanization that preceded the great burst of nineteenth-century industrialization. Indeed, the sports associated most directly with the upper classes – notably cricket, tennis, golf, and horse-racing – had been standardized and codified as early as the eighteenth century.[5] But this was not true of the physical culture of the labouring masses. Enclosures and land seizures, often combined with church prohibitions in the countryside, and migration to cities where space was nonexistent, pushed the physical games of the popular classes into decline over the same period. Early-nineteenth-century urban working-class physical culture, robbed of village greens, sunshine, fresh air, and holiday merrymaking, became impoverished.[6]

By contrast, the second half of the nineteenth century saw the proliferation among all classes of many new ways of organizing physical culture in the industrial cities. From both British and American institutions of male learning, particularly those of the wealthy classes, rationalized, codified sports emerged and were progressively embraced by all the institutions that had traditionally taken their distance from popular games. Educators, the clergy, and employers all had a hand in repressing folk games through law and custom in precapitalist England. The turn to sport in the 1860s by the Young Men's Christian Association, in their project of constructing the 'Muscular Christian,' signalled the official shift in attitudes toward physical games. Far from being disreputable and hedonistic, they grew to be regarded as respectable and productive.[7] Appropriately reconstructed in the middle- and upper-class athletic associations and educational institutions of the last decades of the nineteenth century, sport colonized public education and recreation, military training, church sociality, civic pride, and public spectacle.

Between 1860 and 1900 national sports bodies for cricket, shooting, soccer, swimming, rowing, cycling, lacrosse, skating, Olympic athletics, lawn tennis, and ice hockey were all established in Great Britain, Canada, and the United States. Between 1881 and 1913, international sports federations were established in gymnastics, skating, Olympic sports, cycling, football, weightlifting, yacht racing, shooting, swimming, ice hockey, boxing, and tennis, and the International Olympic Committee (IOC) was founded.[8] The IOC Olympic games, first mounted in 1896, have set the terms for track and field and many other individual sports in the twentieth century. The athletes were so powerful as symbol bearers that by the 1860s and 1870s, politicians such as William Marcy Tweed, the boss of Tammany Hall, found ways to put baseball players (the New York Mutuals) on the public payroll. In these decades of growth, the activities that were at once popular pastimes and lucrative spectacles prompted collaborations between wealthy businessmen, politicians, and sports figures (discussed in Chapter 4) for such capital-intensive ventures as land development and facilities construction.

The links between the development of popular sport associations and specific features in the burgeoning commercial, professional, and political spheres in the nineteenth century have formed the focus of study for many sport scholars. Sport is often seen as an expression of this phase of capitalism, and its many different forms or branches, a reflection of the specialization, standardization, and organization of work and life in industrial society. For traditional political science, what most distinguishes capitalism from traditional agrarian/ artisan societies is capitalist ownership of the means of production and the industrial organization of work; these dimensions therefore have drawn a great deal of scholarly attention in relation to the evolution of sport. This paradigm has been used to address the different vocabularies and meanings spoken and conveyed by different sports. Different activities model different gestures, values, and relationships, including divergent and oppositional ones, within the larger sport world. Take, for example, the quintessentially nineteenth-century game of baseball, often proposed as an example of a kinder, gentler team sport and style of masculinity than the other team sports. There were many European and Native American versions of stick and ball games before the nineteenth century. The venerable British game of cricket enjoyed wide popularity on both sides of the Atlantic during the nineteenth century, and throughout the British empire in the late nineteenth and twentieth centuries. However, the most popular form of the stick–ball game in the world today is American baseball. This form emerged in the 1840s, when the United States was making the transition between a hand manufacture economy of farming, trade, and artisanal production, in which the individual producer played a key role, to a fully industrial economy within a colonial and neocolonial empire, in which workers and managers became subordinated to the needs and imperatives of large, impersonal corporate structures.[9]

The form of baseball that emerged in American cities in the second half of the nineteenth century spoke to both its past and future. Writing of the nature of baseball's attraction in 1883, *Metropolitan Magazine* stated that the 'delight in exercising the physical and mental powers ... over a game of baseball' is the 'same delight a workman takes in laying bricks handsomely ... or finishing an ingenious piece of machinery, or doing a neat piece of carpentry.'[10] Remembrance and nostalgia took their place in baseball's mythology from the inception of the sport. But baseball was not, as its apocrypha would have it, a game of rural origin. From its earliest days, it was played by urban men: merchants, tradesmen, artisans, professionals, and white-collar workers. With its emphasis on individual achievement and its more leisurely pace, baseball did evoke memories and fantasies of rural landscapes and pastoral days. At the same time, its team work reflected the industrial organization of labour then in the ascendance.

By the end of the nineteenth century, baseball appealed to a collective memory of preindustrial life and a longing for sunnier, more relaxed cadences and gestures than those offered by the rapidly industrializing world. Baseball became 'the national pastime' during a prolonged period of violent, indeed squalid, industrialization and violent territorial expansion, from which the game served as a welcome escape for players and spectators alike. However nostalgic and bucolic it was, baseball also reflected the fundamental changes taking place with the demise of the small businessman and the rise of corporate capitalism. As Stephen Gelber writes,

when baseball began replacing individual and rural pastimes in the late 1840s it was America's first widespread team sport, and as such was a machine that reproduced within the leisure context an environment analogous to the world of [industrial] work ... The game retained important elements of personal accountability ... But inevitably, as a team game, baseball subsumed the individual into the collective ... The rise of baseball as an adult sport was the result of the broadening acceptance of this corporate ideal.[11]

If baseball (and cricket throughout the British Empire) embodied, by the end of the nineteenth century, elements of residual ideologies, other sports functioned more or less straightforwardly as a celebration of the dominant trends and values associated with developing corporate capitalism. The last section of this chapter seeks to illustrate this point with respect to one important sport: football.

Writers have made much of the particularities of different sport forms, and their unique connections with specific communities, defined by locale, class, ethnicity, nation, and race. Despite these important differences, all the major team and individual sport forms to emerge from the nineteenth century also had something in common with one another, and with many traditional precapitalist games. That commonality lay in their definition of who was permitted to 'play the game' (men), what the participants were expected to do (aggress), and what such participation signified and conferred (power and privilege). For many of the founding sport associations of the late nineteenth century, 'amateur' athletics meant 'gentlemen's athletics.' Women, workers, and people of colour need not apply. While class and colour barriers were to prove permeable by the social and economic developments of professionalism in sport in the twentieth century, gender barriers have been more resistant.

This is not to say that women did not participate in the great athleticization of late-nineteenth-century society, for they did, many as supporters of their affiliated males, many others as active participants in physical culture in their own right.[12] By the last quarter of the nineteenth century, Anglo-American women – particularly affluent women – were participating in the more general mania for organized physical exercise through sports such as golf, tennis, curling, and bowling. Women also walked, hiked, and cycled. But, as we shall soon see, women were not encouraged to take on most of the team and individual sports that were performed so enthusiastically by men and were forming an increasingly important part of men's and mixed culture.

Despite the emergence of many talented female athletes in the late nineteenth century, the integration of sport-based physical education in a number of upper-class girls schools, and even the growth of a more active mixed culture in certain of the 'softer' sports, the major team and individual sports of today emerged practically, economically, and mythically as the rites of men, marking out symbolically and literally the attributes and activities of an exclusively male terrain. If the game forms of sport reflected key features of a changing class order, they also reflected key features of a gender order in massive flux.

Filling the Father Gap: Sport and the Crisis of Paternity

From the point of view of gender and manhood in the nineteenth century, capitalism severed the site of daily and generational reproduction (the home) from the primary site of economic production (the factory, the office) and radically changed the place of the familial father in the daily childhood experience of children, particularly boys.[13]

In precapitalist patriarchal economies, the site of production and reproduction had been the same – the family household, however extended. The power of the landed classes was organized through family networks and their alliances. Boys were expected to assume the same class position and duties as their fathers when they grew up. Fathers, uncles, and older brothers were present in the lives of children, especially boys, throughout their childhood. In the colonial period in the United States, boys had lived, as Mark Carnes puts it, 'under the palpable influence and control of their fathers' from early childhood to adulthood.

The colonial father stood firmly at the center of a 'well-ordered' Puritan domicile. Every day he was expected to lead the family in prayer, scriptural study, and the singing of psalms. His dominant position within the family was affirmed by common law, which gave him custody of children in cases of marital separation. Furthermore, if he died, the family as a legal entity was dissolved; no such circumstance attended the death of his spouse. The proximity of the workplace to home facilitated his management of domestic matters ... [Fathers] could be summoned easily whenever household matters required their supervision. During the long winter, moreover, farmers and other seasonal workers had plenty of time to exercise the authority that had been conferred upon them as fathers by the church, the courts, and enduring patriarchal traditions.[14]

Although care of infant boys in the seventeenth and eighteenth centuries was provided by mothers, Carnes catalogues the ways in which the raising of children from an early age was very much the domain of the father. Childrearing manuals, for example, were addressed to the father, who was considered the ultimate authority in family matters. Fathers were expected to assume responsibility for the moral supervision of male children beyond toddler age, when children were thought to be capable of reasoning. From this early age, boys began to help their fathers in the shop or fields. More formal vocational training began between the ages of ten and fourteen. Even then fathers held on to the reins.[15]

In these families, the omnipotence of the family father could be oppressive. Regardless, his presence and involvement in the socialization of children, especially boys, was an important feature of traditional agrarian and artisan family arrangements. Both the slow pace of change and the fixed class positions of traditional agrarian society meant that people in precapitalist societies knew who they were by virtue of who their parents were. Through a formal and informal gender-specific apprenticeship based on gender and class divisions of labour, which in turn formed the basis of communities, people learned the gender and class orders simultaneously.

By contrast, for the emerging urban classes in the domesticated nuclear middle- and working-class families of the nineteenth century, working fathers became absent figures – authorities to be feared but not intimately known. Throughout much of the nineteenth century, the father's involvement in domestic and childhood life became limited largely to matters of authority and discipline. It was not only the distances that men had to travel between work and home and the long hours they worked that made parenting difficult, but also the nature of their work and what it did to shape the quality of attention and energy men had available for interacting with their children.[16] Soldiers, sailors, or merchant mariners were gone for months or even years at a time. Instead, women presided, often with terrifying authority, over the childhood of boys and girls. Without a father and older brothers or uncles working at or near the domestic site, young boys were either left with their mothers, sisters, and nannies (if middle-class) until puberty or sent to boarding school, where they were thrust into the authoritarian and punitive culture of elite pedagogy. In my discussion of football, we shall see the central role elite boys' schools played in generating the forms, codes, and associations of modern sport.

The absence or remoteness of the familial father in turn created an emotional and pedagogical need for extrafamilial social fatherhood to prepare boys for the competitive, public world of men. This is the first and most important function that sport came to fulfil so effectively for men as a group in the nineteenth century. Sport provided a mass form of surrogate fatherhood and male socialization, as the place of the family father underwent massive change.

With the maturation of capitalism in the nineteenth century, the father-headed family was growing inadequate as an organizing system for the tasks of industrialization and empire. Throughout the century, the growing bodies of government and military bureaucracies abroad expanded far beyond the reach of the original family household. Instead, the professions, armies, and bureaucracies emerged, organized on principles of utilitarian affiliation, exclusively male and profoundly gendered. 'One might think it could go without saying by now that European men were the most direct agents of empire,' writes Anne McClintock in *Imperial Leather: Race, Gender, and Sexuality in the Colonial Contest*. 'Yet male theorists of imperialism and postcolonialism have seldom felt moved to explore the gendered dynamics of the subject.'

Even though it was white men who manned the merchant ships and wielded the rifles of the colonial armies, white men who owned and oversaw the mines and slave plantations, white men who commanded the global flows of capital and rubber-stamped the laws of the imperial bureaucracies; even though it was white, European men who, by the close of the nineteenth century, owned and managed 85 per cent of the earth's surface, the crucial but concealed relation between gender and imperialism has, until very recently, been unacknowledged or shrugged off as a fait accompli of nature.[17]

The remoteness of the father and of older males within the nineteenth-century family produced as well a necessary corollary: the 'overpresence' of the mother and women in childhood life. In the second half of the century, aided and abetted by doctors, scientists, educators, social reformers, health professionals, and popular culture, middle-class women participated in the creation of a veritable cult of domesticity. This phenomenon was to dominate the last quarter of the nineteenth century and profoundly shape twentieth-century ideals of family and femininity. Indeed, McClintock argues that the creation of empire and the emergence of the forms and obsessions of Victorian middle-class domesticity were two intertwined and related phenomena.

The middle class carved out the domestic as a realm structured on principles of paternal and class wealth and authority but dominated in everyday life by mothers and female servants, who devoted themselves to the physical, emotional, and social needs of their families.[19] The creation of the domestic sphere as a distinct territory of emotionality eventually gave women expertise and authority in those matters. By the last quarter of the century, based in that maternal authority, significant numbers of women were mobilizing in social-reform and social-purity movements as well as in the feminist movement for women's rights.

Nineteenth-century women, particularly those of the middle class, focused greater attention on family members at home, and on matters associated with their care and welfare in church and educational work – the two extradomestic realms that reflected and extended their maternal role, and were thus considered legitimate fields for feminine, and feminist, effort.[20] Historian Anthony Rotundo, among others, has suggested that the fanatical social projection of middle-class women's attention onto their children, especially their sons, in the service of sexual ideologies may have produced an experience of motherhood that could be invasive and overwhelming.[21] In addition, Rotundo hypothesizes that the asexuality expected of middle-class mothers vis-à-vis their husbands during the nineteenth century might have been translated into increased sexual overtones in their relationships with sons, augmenting sexual as well as other gender anxieties in the domestic site.

More recently, Anne McClintock has introduced important new insights into the sexuality of the middle-class home and the sexual anxieties of middle-class men. She reminds us that middle- and upper-class children, boys included, were most often raised by servants – nurses, governesses, cooks, maids – who served as actors in their socialization and early sexual formation.[22] The evidence of gender and sexual anxieties among adult men at the turn of the twentieth century was so clear that Freud, in his theorization of the Oedipus complex, read these historically specific anxieties and their overcoming as constitutive of culture itself.[23]

The contours of maternal and paternal parenting, and the challenges in gender identity formation arising from the parenting arrangements of the nineteenth-century middle-class family produced, according to some historians, a virtual 'crisis in masculinity' in the nineteenth century.[24] The cleavage between domestic and economic sites made the psychological task of learning how to be a man more difficult for boys left without men – or with only their remote, often punitive, presence – in this new family system. This challenge would predispose, if not compel, boys to indulge in more fantasy constructions and to seek alternative sites of paternal and masculine identification in the evolution of their own ideals of masculinity and personal identity. This social fantasy, or 'fictive scenario,' of masculinity – expressed in men's literature, theatre, and above all sport – would take on a much greater role in the development of modern masculine consciousness and create, in capitalist terms, a huge and hungry masculinity market.

At the psychodynamic level, then, the impulse to develop ritual institutions with exceptionally strong and dominant masculine models that idealized physical activities 'at the extreme possibilities of the male body' was fed by twin drives: to compensate for the absence of close fathers and men (a weak male imago), and to defend against the inner (and outer) residues of 'overpresent' mothers and women servants (powerful female imago). These twin characteristics of compensation and defensiveness led to particular patterns in gender-identity formation that found expression in changes in religious life, fictive culture, and physical culture. It is no coincidence that sport flourished in this context, for it captured and spoke to all three dimensions.[25] Sport responded to and fed the attraction and power of hypermasculine symbols, ideals, and fields of endeavour and thus lead to the valuing of excessive instrumentality and aggressive physicality. This in turn had vast consequences for public as well as private life.

Sport and the Stabilization of Masculine Entitlement

The received ideology of women's inferiority, expressed in preindustrial religion, law, and custom, and women's relative political powerlessness coming into the nineteenth century, meant that women's economic and social paths were blocked by a variety of traditional, patriarchal laws and customs that constrained them socially, economically, and physically and rationalized their delegation to the domestic, educational, and religious spheres. On the other hand, nineteenth-century men, particularly but not exclusively of the middle classes, were creating new male-led and usually male-exclusive public domains: new trades and professions, and increasingly vast institutions of business, higher learning, and government that multiplied decade by decade as imperial capitalism grew.

The ways in which a woman's gender narrowed her social options were profoundly shaped by the economic class of her affiliated males. There was a tremendous difference between being a domestic servant and having one.[26] Life was grim for nineteenth-century working-class, slave, and colonial women. They suffered extreme sexual harassment in factory, agricultural, and domestic work. They were driven from many new male trades as these consolidated over the century and, when they still worked alongside men in factories or pits, were paid only a fraction of the starvation wages male workers received.[27] By the last quarter of the nineteenth century, things grew so bad for working-class women in urban England, for example, that over 90,000 of them worked either full- or part-time as prostitutes in the city of London alone.[28] Women's paid work – factory work, domestic service, and, toward the end of the century, work as teachers and nurses – did not provide even subsistence wages, let alone a family wage. The additional miseries of the women of their class as well as the exploitation and poverty they experienced as men were devastating and contributed greatly to the working-class crisis in masculinity as well as the complementary and unfolding crisis in femininity that together created the crisis of the working-class family described by Friedrich Engels.[29] With children and parents of both sexes working under appalling conditions in the 'satanic mills,' the working-class family came under extreme pressures during the nineteenth century, as did parenting and sexual life. Among the affluent classes – from the growing middle class of male professionals, bureaucrats, and businessmen and their households to the expanding military sectors and the great families of the upper classes – life was very highly gender-differentiated. The domestic–public split was an ideal to which all these classes aspired, with the activity of generational and class reproduction presided over by women, supported entirely by a remote and structurally separate economic sphere presided over by men. Men and women interacted within a narrow band of mixed culture that overlapped these two very distinct, yet interpenetrating, spheres.

While large numbers of middle-class women adapted to and even promoted the cult of domesticity, significant numbers of them, by mid-century, also began to challenge some of its grosser inequalities and the systemic subordination of women on which it was based. In the late 1840s and 1850s, in Great Britain and the United States, women abolitionists and social reformers began meeting to discuss the injustice of women's condition. Thus began a long wave of feminist organizing – for the vote, for sexual, legal, economic, educational and athletic rights – a long wave of overt challenge to women's subordinate status at the political level that crested and dissipated by the 1920s. The struggle for women's rights was fierce and often bitter. It divided husbands and wives, parents and children, as well as communities and legislatures, although a number of men supported and allied themselves with the early feminists.[30] But at the institutional level, as well as in kitchens, sitting rooms, and bedrooms, resistance over multiple decades was often ferocious, and anxiety often rampant. Every right was won through decades of long struggles against resistance by fathers, employers, educators, physicians, politicians, trade unions, and government officials.

It is logical to conclude that much of the political anxiety felt by the men who fought consciously and politically against democratizing gender and granting women equal social, economic and political rights from the 1850s to the

1920s was internally fuelled by a sense that the overwhelming mother had escaped her domestic constraints and now demanded attention and obedience even in public life. Clearly, the political rejection by some women of their subordinate gender assignment during these years provoked a massive outpouring of masculine anxiety and resistance not explainable in other political or economic terms. In response to women's determination to have the same political and physical rights as men, men organized themselves in many different ways. The moulding of physical culture into sport as a set of exclusively masculine institutions was a crucial means by which men could reconstitute and reassert masculine entitlement to public power and the domestic service of women.

While the traditional patriarchal form of masculine dominance was being reshaped into a more modern form of industrial masculinism in the latter part of the nineteenth century, it continued to be characterized by extreme inequalities among men. The horrors of the Industrial Revolution provoked concerns among workers' organizations and middle-class social reformers alike about the harsh realities of working-class life: long working days and lack of basic sanitation, shelter, and recreation. It became clear that working men, shattered by life in the industrial slums, had neither the physical nor spiritual energy to defend and extend the nation and empire. 'Yankee intellectuals such as Thomas Wentworth Higginson and Oliver Wendell Holmes repeatedly lamented the state of 'stiff jointed, soft-muscled, paste-complexioned youth,' writes W.J. Baker. Upper-class reformers perceived working-class urban culture – centred on pubs, mass amusements, gambling, and pugilism – as 'tasteless and soulless dissipations which are called amusements.'[31] They feared that such pursuits could lead to slacking off in the factory and rebellion in the streets.

In the minds of many, 'public playing fields promised to better the situation.'[32] Middle-class reformers and employers needed to offer activities that could compete with the popularity of working-class culture, while improving the fitness and reliability of workers, soldiers, and clerks and minimizing political dissent. Sport had the ability to deliver on all counts. The creation of public education and recreation systems and the incorporation of sport into social reform programs in the mid- and late-nineteenth century was promoted by the middle classes, and was embraced by many in the working classes. Sport-related facilities and activities were promoted for boys, youths, and young men. In Canada, for example, a 'playground movement' for inner-city children, centred on sport, was advanced as a preventive strategy against physical and moral turpitude. 'The basic principle upon which this committee is founded is prevention,' said Mable Peters, convenor of the Committee on Vacation Schools and Supervised Playgrounds in Toronto. In explaining the philosophy of her committee, Peters used words typical of the discourse of the day: 'Its work is formative as opposed to reformative. It seeks to eventually dispense with the curfew, the juvenile court, the jail and the reform school for the young of our land. Educationists are now agreed that the public supervised playgrounds and recreational Social Center stimulates and guides a child's life in a way which no other actor of modern life can do.'[33] The playground movement in Canada, as in the United States and Great Britain, was led by middle-class women reformers who extended their maternal function and class views into the public world. Their efforts met with success because the working class shared the belief that parks and play were important, for both overlapping and diverging reasons. For working people, the winning of playgrounds and parks was a victory, a statement of their entitlement to public space, active physicality, and social resources.[34] For the dominant classes, the extension of sport into working-class cultures and communities meant that the codes of the prevailing social order would be observed in those public spaces.

The women reformers who promoted athleticization understood the need for and supported the strategy of surrogate parenthood, particularly fatherhood for boys, through physical education. With this conviction they lent their considerable moral weight to the athleticization of children's and youth culture. However, in supporting the gender values of sport culture and its gender ideologies, men and women alike also supported the infrastructure, values, and activities of masculinist and imperialist culture. Women's absorption and replication of imperial ideology through their support for sport can be seen in the words of Marion Stevenson, a Scottish missionary in Kenya, who '"played her small part in the diffusion of British games" – in the interests of discipline and more importantly of purity. "Soccer," she alleged, "distracted boys from dances and fistfights."'[35] Her discourse was replete with allusions to the fetishes of discipline and cleanliness so important to the creation of nineteenth-century domesticity and middle-class racism, and with indications of the ways in which sport was thought to purify its participants.[36]

Where late-eighteenth-century folk games had been seen as symptoms of unruliness by the late nineteenth century, sport was perceived as an effective way to civilize hordes of urbanized working-class male youth, to culturally unify them, and to help maintain stable relations among adult men. British reformer Montague Shearman claimed in 1889: 'Since football became popular with all classes there have been less wrenching off of knockers and "boxing of the watch," and fewer "free fights" in the streets.' According to historian William J. Baker, who cites Shearman, statistics supported the proposition that criminal activity declined in the last quarter of the nineteenth century in England. Though education, economic opportunity, and more efficient law enforcement were undoubtedly important to this development, Baker agrees with Shearman's assessment that 'football has its national uses quite apart from the cheap enjoyment it has given to thousands.'[37]

Yet whatever 'criminality' football was preventing, its games were also creating a new kind of social violence, especially within the working-class. This violence provided outlets for the rage and frustration of working men, not against the people or institutions that exploited their labour or conscripted them for war, but against other working men, supporters of other teams, or people designated as Other by racism and other forms of prejudice. This form of social violence – football hooliganism – was organized and lived around the ritual spectacle of territorial struggle unfolding on the pitch. 'What are we to do with the "Hooligan"?'lamented the editors of the *Times of London* in 1890. They remarked with alarm that 'School Boards and prisons, police magistrates and philanthropists, do not seem to ameliorate them' and concluded that 'The hooligan is a hideous excrescence on our civilization.'[38] Through this intermale, and in most cases interclass, culture of gang combat, energy that might have gone into social organizing and political contestation was diverted into an apolitical channel. The violence was bad, even deadly, for those who got caught in the mayhem. But it did not at any time threaten to become revolutionary. On the contrary, it promoted suicidal violence among same-class victims rather than a common front against common enemies.

More politically attuned trade union and social democratic leaders and some members of the 'low' churches supported the inclusion and diffusion of sport through their respective organizations because they were concerned with the physical and social well-being of their own people. In addition, they wanted to offer pleasurable activities that would recruit young men. Sport answered both needs. Thus, the idea of entitlement to a recreation period – a time of 'not-working' – became politicized in the late nineteenth century, along with demands by workers' organizations to shorten the working day and provide publicly funded facilities for sport recreation. The movements for the twelve-, then ten-, then eight-hour workdays, won through privation and struggle, were part of a violent interaction between social classes about the minimum conditions necessary for working people to live and reproduce themselves within the new economic order, and thus about the distribution of industrial wealth. Contests between teams of different classes provided much drama in the sport culture of the time. Successful working-class athletes were perceived by many communities as working class heroes.

A vehicle for exuberant physical release, easily learned by men from many different places, and a focal point for community celebration, the world of sport functioned to regroup working-class men into their own associations and to create new social ties among them that both expressed and mediated class. Because sport provided so much pleasure and cohesion to the men who played it, because it was one of only a few spectatorial diversions available to working-class families, and because it was so important in forming popular, extradomestic affinity groups in urban working-class neighbourhoods, sport provided one of the most effective forms for both working-class social organization (a popular and lateral process), and middle- and upper-class social control (a top-down, vertical process, based on the power of elites). In the sense that sport provided for popular games, it became an agent of social organization within distinct communities, and laterally within classes. At the same time, the commanding institutions that governed its diffusion were firmly those of the affluent and political classes.

Perhaps even more important to the dimension of social control that sport promoted is that whatever class or community it organized, sport emerged fundamentally as an associated system of men. Through and around the new athletic associations, working-class women found themselves in new positions as well, though these had a very different character from the rural women's networks of bygone days, and were fundamentally different in their content from the activities of their affiliated men. Men's sport organized women in relation to their children and to each other as a system for physical support and sexual approval for men's activities.

Indeed, there are grounds to argue that the growth of men's sporting associations in the nineteenth century – particularly their proliferation in the last decades when feminist organizing and social conflict about gender was a constant feature of the political landscape – constituted the unnamed masculinist movement of that century, a practical and ritual gender response to women's political challenge to the patriarchal gender order. In the service of this function, sport drew on the authority of science to rationalize its patterns of gender segregation and exclusivity. And science presented sportsmen with the concoction of 'facts' and hypotheses that constituted the Victorian version of sociobiology. Historian Lesley Hall, in her treatment of Victorian notions of gender differences, describes the widely circulated work of scientists Patrick Geddes and J. Arthur Thomson:

Underlying all their arguments was the belief in 'the divergent evolution of the sexes,' which they expressed in terms of 'anabolic' or constructive and conservative energies, assigned by them to the female, and 'katabolic' or disruptive and destructive energies, assigned by them to the male. To illustrate this thesis they drew examples from all of organic creation, in order to prove that 'what was decided among the historic protozoa cannot be annulled by Act of Parliament' (therefore women should not have the parliamentary suffrage).[39]

Nor, according to this construction, were women fit for athletics. As science had inherited from religion the task of defining what was 'natural,' its views on the 'nature' of women carried enormous social weight. In an address that expressed views typical of the broader reaches of science and medicine – though contested by many of the few women in those professions and by women who had become athletes and athletic educators – Dr Chandler Gilman told the New York College of Physicians and Surgeons in 1898: 'In women, inferiority of the locomotive apparatus, the apparatus of physical labour, is apparent in all parts. The brain is both absolutely and relatively smaller than in men. Women have an abundant supply of soft and semi-fluid cellular tissue which creates softness and delicacy of mind, low power, non-resistance, passivity, and under favourable circumstances, a habit of self-sacrifice.'[40]

The largely successful exclusion of women from sport in the late nineteenth century reinforced the idea of separate gender spheres and masculine entitlement to public power by naturalizing this paradigm of the gendered body and its rightful activities. The practical creation of male-exclusive clubs and associations, and the design of sport forms to celebrate the 'most extreme capacities of the male body' were vehicles of this naturalization. Rationalizing men's organized resistance to women's demands for equal social and political rights, this conviction of gender dimorphism was reproduced deep in the institutions and traditions of men's sport and celebrated in its spectacles. Even as a Greek woman, running alongside the official male competitors, completed the marathon course at the first Olympic Games in Athens in 1896, defying incontestably all such ideas, and even as women physical educators protested such notions to be ideological and not scientific, views such as Gilman's prevailed among, and were aggressively promulgated by, the male elites throughout large segments of society, where they effectively protected the masculine space of sport.[41]

In answering certain problematic issues in masculinity and gender identity for nineteenth-century men, sport developed as the corollary institution of social fatherhood to the institution of domestic motherhood within the family wage system. Sport augmented or replaced remote and absent family fathers, then provided a ritual of masculinity for fathers to share with sons when those of trade, religion, ethnicity, and locality became obsolete. Sport served to regroup men as men, to reassert their gender privilege, to reclaim and extend their entitlement to leisure and public space, to celebrate aggressive physicality, and to symbolically place themselves, both in their own experience and in that of women's, at the heart of community myths of prowess, valour and heroism.

Warriors versus Mothers: The Fraternal Lodges, Sport, and Men's Religion

Sport developed as part of a widespread antifeminine and antifeminist social impulse on the part of men. The evidence for the existence of this impulse can be found in other fields of men's culture as well as in sport. Historian Mark Carnes studied one of the most popular and influential forms of men's culture in the late-nineteenth- and early-twentieth-century United States: the fraternal lodges. His work shows that a widespread reaction against the world and codes of women, and to the remoteness of family fathers, underlay the growth of a variety of ritual practices meant to distance men from women. Women's activities as nineteenth-century mothers, educators, and religious instructors tended, some historians have argued, to elevate liberal and compassionate values into official recognition within educational and theological discourse, and from there, to influence the political discourse of liberal egalitarianism.[42] Yet 'most boys would recognize the extent of the disjuncture between maternal precepts and the values of the masculine world when they went to work, usually after they had stopped attending school at the age of fifteen or so,' writes Mark Carnes of nineteenth-century male youths. 'The repeated childhood admonishments to 'place less value upon the shining dollar in the pocket than upon a shining grace in the heart' must have seemed incomprehensible. If they chose to adhere to the moral maxims of childhood, then, they ... could not marry and establish their own family. They could not become men.'[43] Without adult men to serve as guides to the profoundly competitive, not cooperative, world of adult manhood, young boys drew on fantasy and imagination to construct games – informal rituals – by which to rehearse their destined masculinity. 'In the absence of fathers and of adult male models more generally, they [nineteenth-century boys] contrived a 'boy culture' which in its territorial disputes, cruel pranks, and stylized aggression provided an unconscious caricature of men's roles in business and politics.'[44]

As grown men negotiating the contradictory shoals of home and work with their competing value systems, however, these individuals evidently continued to need ritual practices that combined very specific elements of fantasy and spirituality to address deeply felt gender issues. In the second half of the nineteenth century in the United States, one form such practices popularly took was the male secret order, or fraternal lodge. In 1897, W.S. Harwood, writing for the *North American Review*, described the final third of the nineteenth century as the 'golden age of fraternity.' The men's fraternal lodges began to proliferate dramatically in the mid-nineteenth century, and by the turn of the twentieth century, their membership was enormous. Because many men joined more than one order, Harwood estimated that every fifth, or perhaps third, man in the United States belonged to at least one of the nation's 70,000 fraternal lodges. Indeed, Harwood claimed that by the early twentieth century, lodges outnumbered churches in all large U.S. cities.[45]

It was in the ritual life of these fraternal orders, according to Carnes, that American men 'repeatedly practiced rituals that effaced the religious values and emotional ties associated with women.'[46] Clearly, these fraternal orders addressed deep-seated and widespread needs among American men at the time. From a careful study of their rituals, Carnes concludes that these needs included distance from women and the creation of an alternative reality to the one they projected at home and in church. 'Fraternal orders built "temples" from which women were excluded, devised myriad secret rituals and threatened members with fearful punishments if they should "tell their wife the concerns of the order,"' and they 'created rituals which reclaimed for themselves the religious authority that formerly reposed in the hands of Biblical patriarchs.'[47] The rituals celebrated violence, danger, pain, death and rebirth, filial-paternal-tribal figures, and a male-exclusive, seniority-ranked brotherhood. These rituals prepared young men to live by values – clearly antiliberal values – which they kept secret from women and which they often officially repudiated in mixed discourse.

Despite their enormous popularity in the second half of the nineteenth century, the fraternal lodges began to lose membership in the first decades of the twentieth century. By the 1930s their scope and social role had diminished. Those that exist today represent a residual, not dominant, form of men's association. Carnes suggests that a reduction in intensive mothering and increased involvement of fathers with their children in the early twentieth century were the key underlying factors for the decline of the lodges. These changes bred a new generation of men who, Carnes argues, no longer needed primitive, overcompensatory religious rituals to demarcate themselves from and defend themselves against women.

Carnes writes with insight about nineteenth-century America's changing family system and the competitive world of commerce, placing the religion of the fraternal lodges in the mediating space between them. But he does not devote much attention to other forms of men's culture that were also evolving – for example, sport and militarization. These were alternative, more resilient sites for the same values of woman-distancing ritual, masculine bonding, and intergenerational socialization that the men's lodges cultivated. Carnes compares the men's lodges to other forms of male initiation rituals, and the familial conditions of nineteenth-century society to other societies where such ritual plays an important cultural role. Carnes cites psychologist John Whiting's study of sixty-four societies where such rituals were found. Sport displays the same functions and context of male initiation rituals as those identified by Whiting.

Whiting hypothesized that in societies where the father is absent or plays a minor role in child rearing, the male infant perceives the mother as all-powerful, envies her role, and then adopts a feminine identification. Yet when he begins to notice the world outside the home, at about the age of five, he will in most societies perceive that men control resources and clearly occupy an enviable position. A secondary identification with the masculine role thus becomes superimposed on the female identification. Male initiation ceremonies serve psychologically to brainwash the primary feminine identity and to establish firmly the secondary male identity.[48]

Nineteenth-century men raised in father-absent families would have had strong childhood attachments and identifications with the women who cared for and socialized them, and poorer primary attachments and identifications with the remote or absent men. But they were expected as adults to adhere to a style of masculinity that devalued women and the qualities associated with femininity (qualities such as sensuality, receptivity, compassion) because these clashed with the qualities needed to survive and get ahead in the public, male-dominated world. The new principles of imperial government and capitalist business that reorganized Anglo–North American societies in the nineteenth century required emotional as well as physical and technical abilities from their personnel. From men, they required the predisposition to affiliate – that is, to form new bonds of association with extrafamilial groups, in aggressive pursuit of economic and military goals – and the ability to break emotional affiliations for economic reasons. In youth socialization, sport functioned as a transitional vehicle that could move young men away from their primary identification with and libidinal orientation to the mother and her sphere to the male institutions of the public world – to the fatherhoods. Heads of state, magnates of industry, military officers, and the various clergies figured as senior patriarchs in the great imperial Family of Man.[49] Sport served as an embodied ritual of remembrance and confirmation of men's gender identity and close gender associations, across families, communities, and classes.

More effectively than the fraternal lodges or the 'feminized' churches, sport addressed the socialization needs of younger boys and adolescents for the kind of 'rough' surrogate fathering that the preparation for manhood required. Secular in symbology and in access, and therefore more inclusive of different groups of boys and men, sporting rites far outstripped the historic relevance of the lodge ritual, which appeared increasingly archaic in the twentieth century. By calling on ideologies of masculinity rooted in a secular and increasingly commercial warrior culture and its value system, rather than in a ritual based in Judaeo-Christian symbology, sport succeeded in socializing boys into manhood despite the absence of the family father, and superimposing a masculine template (identity) over the feminine one established in a mother-dominated childhood.

The ritual physical contests of sport answered the need for an arena in which to practise and display unmistakably 'manly' qualities, and for the communal validation (religious worship) of these qualities within the larger culture. Sport provided the kind of rituals of conquest and aggression that men with a weak (because not primal) sense of masculinity needed to symbolize, to make physical and palpable, the difference between a 'man's man' and a 'mama's boy.' Sport created an extensive, institutionalized network of social surrogate and symbolic fathers and brothers-in-arms in close and arduous physical contact – points of 'libidinal cathexis' (sexual bonding) to use the Freudian phrase – that could provide alternative masculine points of identification against women, their sphere of domestic intimacy, and their morality.

Writing of the late nineteenth century, Donald Mrozek observes that as

religion had earlier undergone a 'feminization,' sport now was largely masculinized; and the two different institutions were not antithetical in role. In its pretense toward regenerative functions, it approximated a religious sensibility for men albeit material and secular ... As hero, the sportsman became the symbol of masculine sacrifice ... [a] champion whose largely self-generating character assured his successes. Sport was, to a considerable degree, the masculinization of the regenerative myth.[50]

Sport fits Whiting's definition of male initiation rituals (rituals that turn on male regenerative myths) not only in the nineteenth century but today as well. It is certainly possible that, as Carnes argues, nineteenth-century middle-class American mothers were more obsessed with their children's welfare and more emotionally and sexually invasive than twentieth-century mothers. There have been very important changes in styles of parenting over the last 150 years. Today, it is more accurate to speak of a remote-father than an absent-father family system, and in the last twenty years we have begun to approach a remote-mother family system as well. However, childhood is still presided over primarily by women. There is a major gap between the hours spent with children by mothers and fathers.[51] Males are still the dominant gender; and social life as a whole is structured by principles of strength and domination and a culture of hypermasculinity.

Sport in mid- to late-nineteenth-century America unfolded against a backdrop of what Carnes calls the 'feminization' of childhood: of the family, the growing school system, and the Protestant churches. With respect to the church, the rise of liberal (including antislavery) theology was associated with an increased role for women within Protestantism during the nineteenth century, including their ordination and formalized authority. With women gaining ground in the church, and with the clergy associated with them stigmatized thereby, the majority of men left Protestantism behind as a primary source of interest and power and moved to other spiritual institutions that could address their very different needs. The religious institutions that could respond to these economic as well as psychological needs were the fraternal lodges and the sport associations – both fundamentally religious in their intent and ritual. Military life – the arena where the values of these rituals find their purest practical expression – was also constituted as male-dominant and male-exclusive as it expanded throughout the nineteenth century.

What are the costs to society when the dominant gender order requires boys to disavow the 'feminine' qualities and relational values in themselves – qualities linked with their early identifications with women? Different theoretical and practical approaches to the psychology of gender indicate that adult men who are internally driven to compensate for deficits in actual fathering and to defend against maternal identifications tend to be uncomfortable with qualities and modes of interaction that are reminiscent or expressive of the 'feminine' and that this is reflected in values and standards for personal and public behaviour. What this study of the fraternal lodges suggests is that when parenting conditions produce defended, fragile, overcompensatory masculine character structures, the social result is a gendered men's political subculture that encourages aggressive, violent, atavistic values, even if in secret, and even when official political values are cloaked with the rhetoric of liberal, egalitarian, and compassionate sentiment. When such a hard, instrumental culture is strong and vital among men, the soft, liberal values that are more often favoured by women tend to lose political effectiveness, regardless of the prevailing egalitarian rhetoric. Thus an egalitarian and democratic nation, such as the United States or Great Britain, can wage imperialist war abroad while congratulating itself for its democratic, civilized politics at home.

Sport crafted a streamlined, abstracted, quantifiable version of the manly, antifeminine warrior and succeeded in creating a form of male ritual with great cathecting power and historical adaptability. Thus it should not be surprising that a number of the key ideals that sport pushed to the fore in masculinity were taken from the most unmistakably masculine field of all: combat and organized violence.

Nation-Building, Imperialism, and Militarization

It is important to note that while mothers and servants socialized young males in the domestic and educational spheres, the tenor of male–male relations outside that sphere set the program for masculinity in childhood and adolescence and provided the basis for the growth of hypermasculinist gender styles. For the intensity of men's inner, gender-based needs and conflicts were both cultivated and recruited by outer conditions, particularly the role of force and organized violence in capitalist expansion and imperial colonization.

During the nineteenth century, the scope of human military and paramilitary organization expanded rapidly, and increased the weight and importance of this male-dominated power apparatus within society, government, business, and culture – that is to say, the nation-state. According to John Keegan, this increased militarization was achieved primarily through the construction by nation-states of huge military networks that combined mobilized and reserve forces.[52]

The regimental system was based on a model developed by the French state in the wake of the French Revolution, when it sought ways to bring under its control large bands of men considered dangerous to the social order (semipoliticized brigands in the countryside and dissident, semicriminal gangs in the cities). The French authorities regrouped these men and co-opted their energies in state-friendly directions through the regiment. The regimental model brought together men of several generations, and organized both their active service and their reserve preparedness. This system also had the effect of organizing their civilian life around the military interests and activities of the nation-state. As both wartime and peacetime formations, the regiments were highly successful at integrating men of all social classes into the military realm and its commanding structures and culture.

By mid-century, Great Britain and most European states had such a regimental system in place, and it served as a major gendered social network of power throughout the latter part of the nineteenth century and into the twentieth century. As a result, the regimental experience also came to play an important part in the experience of scores of nineteenth-century men with respect to their ideals of manhood. 'The best of a nation's young men and ... older reservists ...

looked back on their conscript days as the rite de passage which ushered them from boyhood to manhood,' writes Keegan. 'This *rite de passage* became an important cultural form in European life, an experience common to almost all young European males and, through its universality, its ready acceptance by electorates as a social norm and its inescapable militarization of society.'[53]

By the turn of the twentieth century, European nation-states (national fatherhoods) were capable of using this system to mobilize millions of men for 'total war' almost instantaneously, and finally did so in 1914. Warring governments were able to augment the number of men in uniform from four million in July of that year to more than twenty million by the end of August and to draw on the political support of all the men – and their families – who were implicated in the military culture of regiments for the war effort.[54] Against this system, pacifist ideologies and movements were powerless.

This militarization of European and British society went hand in hand with the codification and diffusion of the core men's sports. Military and athletic institutions overlapped and interpenetrated, and their cultures evolved in tandem. While the wars fought in and by the United States in the nineteenth century were different from those fought in Europe and the British Empire, the relationship between the militarization of American society (via the growth of expansionist, state-supported armed forces and armed private enterprise) and sport culture was the same. The last decade of the nineteenth century – a decade of professionalization and commercialization in U.S. sport, the first daily press sports section, much stadium construction and increased sports celebrity – was also the decade of Wounded Knee, a four-year depression, the Pullman strike, and the Haymarket massacre at home, and the Boxer Rebellion and Spanish-American War abroad. The leading members of the New England genteel classes (who played a prominent part in U.S. politics) and robber baron industrialists alike embraced sport, openly and aggressively, as a way to succeed in the noble enterprise of nation-building and nation-extending war.

'The time given to athletic contests and the injuries incurred on the playing field,' Henry Cabot Lodge said in his address to Harvard in 1896, 'are part of the price which the English speaking race has paid for being world-conquerors.' Just as victory on the playing fields of Eton was seen as crucial by Lord Wellington, Mrozek observes that

for Cabot Lodge and Theodore Roosevelt, secretaries of war such as Elihu Root, Army Chief of Staff Leonard Wood, and Rear Admiral R.D. Evans who commanded the North Atlantic Fleet – winning at sports was a prelude to winning the world ... Numerous political leaders, particularly those emerging from the genteel tradition, and a growing cadre of Army and Navy officers were captivated by the psychology of victory; and they linked sport to a general program for renewing their society and reordering world affairs.[55]

Forming, in Mrozek's estimation, 'a highly visible and reputable constituency strengthening sport's grasp at institutional permanence and importance,' military leaders urged Americans to emulate the support the British extended to sport. The costs of promoting sport on a wide scale would be high, American sport advocates cautioned. The British, for example, spent an estimated $200 million per year on sport during the 1910s. But the price was worth it for combative, war-oriented societies. The leading political, military, and pedagogical authorities saw in sport a direct and important role in socializing young males. 'Through athletics,' Mrozek writes, 'the students would ... get an early start in acquiring the combative virtues; and the influence of the military, which was itself much affected by genteel values, would intermix with civilian leadership.'[56]

Mrozek outlines the mutually reinforcing relationships between sport, the military, politics, and what he calls American 'mentality' in late-nineteenth- and early-twentieth-century America. What emerges from his work is that a militarization of ideals and norms in civilian political leadership took place through the athleticization of politics and military life. And this operation also accomplished the naturalization and validation of combat and war:

The system itself [was] touched by confidence in the worth of rough and strenuous experience. Notable was the commitment of the Army and Navy, and by the latter part of the nineteenth century both services had accepted sport as part of their training programs ... During the 1880s, the secretaries of war concluded that physical training conducted in advance of specific, pertinent military drill would make the latter easier and more efficient ... Exercise in the gymnasium, according to [Lieutenant C.D.] Parkhurst, would bring the soldier to 'quick and unthinking obedience to orders' ... In the Navy as well, ... Rear Admiral Robley D. Evans ... promoted baseball, football, track and field, boxing and fencing and ordered that these sports be considered 'part of their drill.' In this way, athletics literally became a military duty.[57]

The close relationship of sport to combat and imperial war in the late nineteenth century was reflected in the antics of the 'great white heroes,' who were featured in popular literature, and in the preferred physical type(s) of Victorian men. In his study of changing family forms and ideals of middle-class masculinity in the nineteenth-century United States, Anthony Rotundo points to a growing obsession with the aggressive male body as the site of provable masculinity for men. Eighteenth-century definitions of ideal manhood had been centred on 'usefulness' – good work, lively citizenship, and 'a favourable relationship with God.' By the end of the Victorian and imperial era, Rotundo contends that 'aggressive physicality' had become the hallmark of masculinity:

[A] true man was ... a physical creature, full of animal qualities and primitive urges. Men took nicknames like 'Toronado' and 'Savage' that connected them to basic, natural forces ... In fact, Theodore Roosevelt [who had been a sickly youth] thought it a good thing to "make the wolf rise in a man's heart."'[58]

Football, Masculinity, and Militarization

Football in all its variations (soccer, rugby, and American, Canadian, and Australian versions) is the most popular sport in the world today. Throughout its history and geographical spread, football has changed radically according to the cultural preferences of the groups and nations that have adopted it. Football has a special place in popular culture worldwide, and for this reason has played a key role in forging cross-class and cross-cultural ideals of strength and masculinity. The two variations of football that have most influenced global football culture – soccer and rugby – crystallized in imperial England in the nineteenth century. As an example of the way in which trends in nineteenth-century life were involved in the emergence, codification, and institutionalization of sport, football makes a particularly comprehensive and enlightening case study.[59]

According to David Riesman and Reuel Denney, the earliest recorded version of a football-like game in the British Isles was called the 'Dane's Head,' in which a skull was used as the 'ball': 'It was played in the tenth and eleventh centuries as a contest in kicking a ball between towns ... In some cases, the goals were the towns themselves, so that a team entering a village might have pushed the ball several miles en route.'[60]

In the small towns and villages of agrarian medieval England, folk foot and ball games had taken place around festivals of the religious or pagan calendar in the common land or territory of each community.[61] But throughout the seventeenth and eighteenth centuries, in increasingly cramped and tense urban conditions, and in a countryside embattled by struggles over land enclosures and bankruptcies, public officials and church authorities came to regard such games as opportunities for rowdyism and unruly behaviour, capable of leading to riots. Many municipalities officially banned the games, or severely restricted opportunities for playing them. Early in the nineteenth century, many young men still played, but illicitly, in defiance of the ban.

While the folk games of football retreated among the labouring classes, they continued to be played by boys in the public schools – the institutions of education for the aristocracy and, with increasing frequency, the rising bourgeoisie. Beginning in the eighteenth century, the public schools suffered from a severe and protracted authority gap. The boys of the aristocracy did not believe they should submit to masters who were their social inferiors, and regularly rebelled against school authorities. These rebellions, which involved rough forms of folk-style football, were the product of an elaborate boy culture in which the older, stronger boys brutally lorded it over the younger, weaker ones. (This was called the prefect-fagging system.)[62] The rebellions were so serious that they often required the intervention of militia and army, and provoked the reading of the Riot Act. As Eric Dunning notes, 'more than twenty-two rebellions are recorded as having occurred in the public schools between 1728 and 1832. [That] is probably the best index of the relative powerlessness of the school authorities in that period.[63]

There are many accounts of the development of team sports in British upper-class boys schools in the nineteenth century.[64] Eric Dunning's is especially good in explaining the complex links between broad trends of industrialization and modernization, the need of the leading classes to create educational institutions adequate to their requirements, and the development of modern sport as a tool for reforming the traditional brutal school-boy culture that stood in the way of educational change.[65] Instead of banning football, as had been done for working-class males, educational innovators (Thomas Arnold of Rugby is usually seen as the leading force) adopted football, made it part of school life, and, in so doing, established the dominance of the headmaster and staff over prefects and fags. This process 'civilized' some aspects of football culture by ridding the old game of its worst brutalities and by generally creating an atmosphere of greater order and learning. But, at the same time, these reforms served to rationalize the violence and dominance of that boy's culture and institutionalized these values.

By mid-century, the public schools were actively cultivating football to help them express the interests of the social stratum they directly served. As sport historian and sociologist Alan Tomlinson remarks,

Through soccer, through team games in schools, these young men of the new ruling generation were being taught very specifically certain codes of leadership alongside codes of loyalty, the ability to accept defeat, the ability to group together to get a particular result, sometimes without asking too many questions about the sense of what you were doing. And so soccer was very much a breeding ground for the new generation of the established elite.[66]

The public schools had codified two major forms of football in mid-century: soccer and rugby. In the last quarter of the century, both forms spread far

beyond the bounds of private schools and clubs: from middle- and working-
class communities and organizations to growing public systems of education
and recreation, to the realm of professionally mounted spectacle. Working-
class communities opted primarily for the soccer form, which went on to
worldwide popularity in the twentieth century. But the rugby form continued a
lively existence, and in Australia and North America gave rise to popular new
American and Australian forms. Crucially, the athleticization of military culture permitted 'sports such as football and boxing that had once been the realm
of children and ruffians' to enter the cultural mainstream.[67] In England, the
Football Association Cup final of 1872 drew only 2,000 spectators, but by
1892 the Crystal Palace grounds accommodated 42,500 spectators for the same
event. By 1901, the event drew 110,000 fans, matching the size of late-twentieth-century crowds. Early but powerful trends to professionalization and commercialization, particularly of men's team sports such as soccer, rugby, cricket,
boxing and weightlifting, were a dynamic part of this growth; paving the way
for a sport-related bureaucracy in public infrastructure, public education, and
recreation.

The game of rugby, the other of the two dominant forms of football to
emerge from the nineteenth-century British public schools, is the direct prede-
cessor of American, Canadian, and Australian versions of football. It was
named after Rugby School, which, in the early nineteenth century, was a
favoured institution for the sons of the aggressive merchant and manufacturing
families of Great Britain. At that time, Eton and Harrow were still favoured
and controlled by the landed and monied aristocracy. It is no coincidence,
therefore, that it was at Rugby School where the radical innovation of adding
arms and hands to a game that had previously allowed the use only of feet and
head occurred.[68] The addition of appendages for possession was an extremely
significant symbolic inclusion that never gained popularity among working-
class players and popular audiences, who, outside North America, have generally preferred the 'poetry in motion' of soccer to the 'grasping game' of rugby.[69]

In the mid-nineteenth century the newly codified game of rugby football
travelled with British citizens and immigrants to Canada and the United States.
Here it encountered a series of dynamic cultures, rich in games and contests,
that were also in the process of codifying their own game forms – notably,
baseball.[70] Rugby-rules football first became popular in upper-class institutions
– the male-exclusive recreational clubs and universities of central Canada and
New England. For some years, this form of football was known as the McGill
game, after McGill University in Montreal, then the pre-eminent institution of
higher learning for the sons of upper-class Anglo-Canadians. Football fever for
the Rugby game quickly spread to the Ivy League schools in the United States,

and most especially to Yale University, where it began to metamorphose.[71] Yale's pedagogical relationship to the new rich paralleled that of Rugby School's. Both were favoured institutions of education for the sons of new industrial capital. It is not surprising, then, that the Yale game took after the Rugby game – hands included.

The Yale game became the basis of modern American football, and it too bore the stamp of those who had adopted and nurtured it – the Harknesses, Paynes, Whitneys, and Vanderbilts. 'The new rich of America's gilded age had no established body of custom or tradition to prescribe appropriate sporting behaviour,' notes Allen Sack in his article 'When Yale spirit vanquished Harvard indifference.' The equable, genteel sportsmanship of Harvard and Boston did not interest them.

For those who amassed fortunes in the cutthroat competition of the period, sport may have reflected the same acquisitive values that permeated the rest of their lives. Money-making, fierce competition and an intense desire to win at any cost became major themes of play as well as of work ... Rules and regulations became barriers to be shrewdly circumvented. In sport as in business, the most rational use of men and resources meant victory in the long run.[72]

The Yale game grew and crystallized under the tutelage of head coach Walter Camp. Camp's take on football and sport was clearly ideological, as evidenced in his analogies between football and business: 'Football has come to be recognized as the best school for instilling into the young man those attributes which business desires and demands.'[73] The style Camp favoured in business and sport was equally instrumental, and inspired by strategies of combat: 'Finding a weak spot through which a play can be made, feeling out the line with experimental attempts, concealing the real strength til everything is ripe for the big push, then letting drive where least expected, what is this – an outline of football or business tactics? Both of course.'[74] In contrast to genteel conventions of 'sportsmanship' ('it's not whether you win or lose, but how you play the game'), Camp passionately shared the late Vince Lombardi's belief that 'winning is not the most important thing – it's the only thing.'[75] The Yale game celebrated the values of the robber-baron patrons just as the game of rugby bore the stamp of Rugby School's clientele. Both games valued extreme aggressivity. William J. Baker describes the football game that emerged during Camp's heyday as 'a mild form of trench warfare, a game of brute force with little finesse.'[76]

What did this American game ritualize? 'It's a celebration of territorial conquest by physical violence' is how David Meggyesy summed up football's formative characteristic.

In the 1870s, when it came to this country, against the backdrop of Social Darwinism which was the rampant philosophy at the time, the British game transformed itself into an even more militarist system, wherein territory was defended and taken through violent means, through physical aggression as such. And as such, [football] mirrors the cultural experience of this country. During the formative years of the American game the U.S. lived the philosophy of manifest destiny, becoming an imperial power in its own right. We settled the west, with the genocide of native people that entailed, we went to the Philippines, we developed a sense of ourselves as entitled to conquest. That was the crucible out of which American football was born ... Major sports are a microcosm of their country's world view and football illustrates this proposition in every detail. You have to do violence to others to win.[77]

Just as the basic values and relationships of traditional agrarian society had been reflected in the folk football that soccer, rugby, and North American football replaced, so in the three dominant forms of football at the end of the nineteenth century we see the basic values and structures of militarized, masculinist, corporate capitalism in its early-mature phases. In 1917, as the United States was about to enter the First World War, physical educator Raymond G. Gettell of Amherst College summarized the specific merits of football. Along with the chance for 'physical combat' and satisfaction of the 'primitive lust for battle,' the game also 'satisfies the higher and distinctly civilized interest in organization, cooperation, and the skilled interrelation of individual effort directed to a common purpose. It typifies the highest achievement in its unusual emphasis on discipline and obedience, on the subordination of the individual to authority and law.'[78]

In a comparison of traditional agrarian football with the modern American NFL version, there are striking differences that are meaningful for players, their communities, and their cultures – differences that were institutionalized in the nineteenth century. While modern football is played on a small, consecrated space, folk football was played over real territory, which the game delineated as collective property: the town and its surrounding lands. The folk game included most men and boys of age; the modern game is elitist, and includes only specialists of a limited age range. American football's elaborate rules and command structure contrast dramatically with the spontaneous, fluid, and egalitarian character of preindustrial football. There were no functionaries outside the participants in the folk game – no coaches, no managers or owners, no doctors or sport psychologists, no board of commissioners – the participants themselves determined the course of the event.

The game of contemporary soccer is closer to the folk football games than the U.S. or Canadian versions of football, which are directly descended from rugby. With two teams of specialized equals, divided into offensive and defensive functions, soccer players work together in an improvisational game that covers territory quickly and spontaneously. This form of football is characterized by a division of labour that is almost free from internal stratification. Games can get rough because they are fast, but brute force is not built into them; coordination, speed, and stamina are the most important factors for success. Soccer also appears structurally democratic – all body types can and do play well. Both the intrinsic pleasure of achieving group coordination among equals, and easy access to the sport (little equipment, basic facilities) have made soccer exceptionally popular among working-class audiences and young people of all classes around the world. Because of its inclusive properties, it has also become, in the last twenty years in North America, a very popular team sport for girls, although its spectacles remain largely male-exclusive, as do those of professional U.S. and Canadian football.

While these differences are important, I want to emphasize the one great similarity among the precapitalist folk games, the sports that had become established at the end of the nineteenth century, and the modern North American sports that are their contemporary descendants: all include men and exclude women from the game itself; all three forms are rites of men. The differences in the three game forms correspond to historical variances in the organization of men's work and property ownership. What they have in common is their gendered constitution, and their function of bringing men together as men.

The athleticization, industrialization, and militarization of everyday life were parallel, interconnected developments that unfolded within the economic and cultural life of the second half of the nineteenth century. Sport was successful in replacing the absent father because it trained males in the values and conventions of the workaday world of factory or office, and prepared males for exercising violence in the service of nation and empire. As Anthony Rotundo has argued, by the end of the nineteenth century, the dominant gender ideal for men had changed from the moral and measured being of the eighteenth century, to a physically dominating and hypermasculine creation. Linked to militarization and business, sport emerged to capture and provide expression to this gendered social impulse and served as its most extensive and popular, institution. Against the spread of liberal-democratic rhetoric in theology and politics, the major men's sports kept alive the ritual and celebration of territorial appropriation and physical domination.

Having looked at the way parenting arrangements in a changing gender order coincided with turmoil and change in economic, political, religious, and military arenas, I now turn to a consideration of the intense relationship between sexuality and sport in the latter part of the nineteenth and early part of the twentieth centuries. This relationship has constituted a large part of sport's massive appeal and cultural triumph.

3

'Taming the Beast': Sport, Masculinity, and Sexuality in the Late Nineteenth and Early Twentieth Centuries

The athleticization of nineteenth-century society was part of a larger movement of material secularization in which science and medicine displaced theology as the most authoritative accounts of the cosmos and nature, virtue, and sin. The popularity of sport expressed this shift from belief in a pregiven, mysterious, and immaterial world of God and spirit, to the man-made, knowable, and material world of human endeavour and the body. In providing a symbolic cosmology of quantifiable, perfectible, physical achievement, sport brilliantly animated the values of maturing capitalism in Anglo-American societies and, increasingly, throughout Europe and the colonial world. Indeed, sport provided an embodied mass cultural practice that, while 'secular' in its worldliness, succeeded in making numinous the mundane, material, and monetary values that were replacing traditional religious ones. This numinous quality was clear to many. For example, in speaking of the popularity of cricket in early-twentieth-century England and throughout the empire, the president of the Marylebone Cricket Club, P.F. Warner, explained that the sport 'has become more than a game. It is an institution, a passion, one might say a religion. It has got into the blood of the nation.'[1] Similar analogies were drawn to soccer football in England regarding its connection with the working class. 'It was no exaggeration for some to describe football ... as a "religion,"' writes Nicholas Fishwick. 'The football grounds of England were the Labour party at prayer.'[2]

'Sport's growing capacity to carry myth itself suggested the shifting emphasis toward the body over the soul,' Donald Mrozek observes of life in the United States: '[The body] was secularized ... and the body was treated as if it were the triumph of the industrial age – a machine. The rationalism of the age and the mystery of religious belief, each pulled some distance away from its originating institution, seemed joined in the attribution of regenerative functions to sport.'[3]

Sport was remarkably successful in fusing these apparently contradictory impulses; and, like the men's fraternal lodges, did so in ways that provided emotional and spiritual sustenance to its participants. The evolution of sport was at once complex, multilayered and multiclassed, appealing for various reasons and in various ways to different groups and communities; and singular, insofar as it demarcated gender uniformly across these groups and communities. Quantification, specialization, rationalization, the obsession with records, and bureaucratization – these qualities set the world of sport apart from other forms of physical culture and clearly exemplified 'the rationalism of the age.' At the same time, the 'mystery of religious belief' became attached to the celebrated athlete-heroes, who, thanks to professionalization and the growth of a daily sport press, became major figures in the cultural landscape of the late nineteenth and early twentieth centuries. In uniting (or at least seeming to unite) these starkly different impulses, the culture of sport effected highly ideological social operations that both engendered and classed their participants and their surrounding cultures. In this chapter I explore how sport promoted particular ideological projects by linking them to the physical, emotional, and sexual needs of men and boys around the turn of the last century, needs that had been trammelled and pummelled by the social changes of industrialization and imperialism. In particular, the sexual dimensions of sport – the 'erotics' of sport, in Anne McClintock's term – were central to its ability to deliver the emotional goods, and hence to its phenomenal success as a secular religion.

In this discussion of sexuality and sport I assume enough similarities in sexual mores and trends between British and Anglo-American societies to make certain generalizations. Despite some important differences in political and sexual attitudes, similar patterns and philosophies with respect to sex and gender were evident on both sides of the Atlantic, in both official (medical, scientific, legal, political) and unofficial (fashion, art, sexual literature and pornography, the formation of communities of sexual minorities, prostitution) discourses on sex. Meaningful generalizations about both societies are possible due to their common religious legacies (Christian Puritanical, Anglican, and Catholic), the influence of British ideas in all fields in nineteenth-century North America; the exercise of colonialism and slavery by both Britain and the United States; and the similar dynamics and problems in heterosocial life that industrialization created for both British and North American men and women. The sexual ideologies of the late nineteenth century in both societies promoted a set of sexual norms within a clear template of what has come to be called 'compulsory heterosexuality.' In this template, marital, heterosexual, procreational sex was validated as 'good' sex and other forms of sex (extramarital, homosexual, pleasure-oriented) were stigmatized and labelled 'deviant' and 'bad.'

Physicality, Materialism, and the Dangers of Sex: Sport in the Spermatic Economy

Between 1850 and 1920, the major sport forms we know today were promoted by the professions, churches, commerce, and the state's growing public sector as a remedy for a variety of 'deficiencies observed, imagined or predicted' throughout American society.[4] In the late nineteenth century, sport lost its negative associations with rough popular games, and took on tonic qualities that were linked philosophically to the traditional 'producer values' – making, saving, acquiring, investing – in Anglo-American society. These values, inherited from the hand-manufacture period, but still vital due to the forces of uneven economic development and cultural lag, were promoted by church as well as secular leaders, in sexual life as well as in economic conduct. Restraint and productive investment were overarching imperatives of dominant, official sexual values.

As a variety of writers have pointed out, the paradigm of the body and its sexual capacities that emerged and then dominated the official discourses of the mid- and late-nineteenth century combined both the new veneration of the miraculous machine and the concern with limited amounts of energy – or fuel – for both the human body, the engines of industry, and for the body politic. In the developing official view, physical and sexual capital, like finance capital, were seen as clearly limited, and were not to be squandered in trivial or 'wasteful' pursuits, such as fornication, masturbation, and sodomy. Steven Marcus has painted a convincing picture of how Victorian notions of the economy shaped ideas about the body and sex. In addition, Anne McClintock describes the close relationship between money and sex during this period.[5] Donald Mrozek has labelled this paradigm of sexuality and the sexual body the 'spermatic economy,'[6] a term that aptly conveys the idea of a closed economy of human energy requiring disciplined, renunciatory practices for success in extrasexual endeavour, as well as sexual energy figured as male.

In the early and mid-nineteenth century, as the tenets of the spermatic economy were being articulated, sport was first promulgated as a way to divert the sexual energy of males from deviant ends. By the end of the nineteenth century it was hailed as 'an activity that would actually regenerate the body ... making the body a renewable resource.'[7] The shift of interest to the body and, through the practice and spectacles of sport, to the forceful, self-regenerating, high-performance male body, was related to the sexual regulatory projects of the late nineteenth century in which the middle classes sought to address sociopolitical issues through sexual means. As Michel Foucault pointed out, these projects involved seeking to define and control 'the hysterical woman, the masturbating child, the Malthusian couple and the perverse adult' – in other words, uppity women, feminists, sensual children, homosexuals and other gender outlaws, and the overbreeding working classes and colonial peoples.[8] Thus, the growth of sport can be read as a sexual practice that advanced all these projects, involving men of all social classes, simultaneously.

Problematically for the authoritative proponents of the spermatic economy and its ideals of sexual restraint, however, the official discourses on sex were by no means the only such discourses. Advances in printing technology and the development of photography, posters, and commercial art produced an unprecedented and qualitative growth in the media of popular culture late in the nineteenth century. Alternative 'discourses' on sex, including such topics as birth control and the 'perversions,' competed more openly, offering contradictory ideas and possibilities to those presented by church, school, and science. Such discourses as sexual folklore, art, literature, the burgeoning realm of illicit sexual imagery, the mass daily presses and sex-oriented yellow journalism, fashion, the formation of communities of sexual minorities, and a thriving sex trade were also powerful influences in the lives of boys and men and in the cultural life of communities. Kevin White observes that through late-nineteenth-century popular men's cultures in the United States, 'the infusion into the mainstream of male toughness and aggression of a sort that had been confined before to the lower orders' was achieved, and 'the logic of the challenge that had always been posed to respectable Victorian manliness by primitivism began to work itself out.'[9]

Many of these unofficial discourses and practices contained ideas that flatly contradicted the dictates of a 'sex for procreation only'/'spermatic economy' morality. Those who did not conform were criminalized and associated with the underworld. (Homosexuality, prostitution, and 'pornography' were all relegated to underworld networks as a result of their criminalization by the growing nation-states.) Indeed, it was the perceived need to counteract such underworld ideas and practices that justified an official, energetic, middle-class debate on sexual matters. This debate began in the middle of the nineteenth century, and accelerated in scope and breadth during the early decades of the twentieth.[10]

From medical doctors and psychologists to politicians and middle-class women mobilized in social purity and social gospel movements, the affluent and influential layers of society elaborated their ideas about sexuality in the 'spermatic economy' paradigm.[11] They then sought to apply these ideas rigorously within the home, the growing school and recreation systems, in religious education, and in public and state life. The paradigm informed their evolving bodies of sexual knowledge, law, and technology. Their sex-related political campaigns, public policies, and jurisprudence developed in ways that were differentially gendered and 'classed.' Divergent views about sexuality – such as those of John Stuart Mill, Havelock Ellis, and Marie Stopes – enjoyed a lively existence. But most members of Victorian professional and political life looked to authorities such as Lord William Acton in matters sexual. According to Lesley Hall, Acton viewed sex as

a dangerous force which had to be held in check; any indulgence might, probably would, lead to enslavement in sensual habits which were not only morally bad but physiologically dangerous ... [Acton] warned against the waste of the vital spermatic fluid by whatever means. Overindulgence (even in legitimate marriage) could lead to the wasting disease of spermatorrhea. (Spermatorrhea was a factitious ailment, the symptoms of which were involuntary seminal emissions waking and sleeping, causing disability and worse.) ... He also feared sexual pleasure was too debilitatingly intense to be experienced safely with any frequency.[12] ... In the later nineteenth and the early twentieth centuries ... this fear of unbridled male sexuality led to the rise of anti-masturbation literature and other propaganda in favour of male purity.[13]

Hall argues that in the writings of many Victorian authorities, it was the male's exercise of control over his own sexuality that formed the crucial key to personal and social health. This appreciation of male sexuality included a belief that men are inherently aggressive as well as constantly randy, and that the two go hand in hand. This view was broadly shared, even among relatively progressive advocates of sexual diversity such as Havelock Ellis. He felt little need to interrogate male sexuality, 'if only because it is predominantly open and aggressive.' Ellis noted, however, that 'since the constitution of society has largely been in the hands of man, the nature of the sexual impulse in men has largely been expressed in the written and unwritten codes of social law.'[14]

Despite the juridical and political expression of men's 'natural' sexuality that Ellis saw around him, men were by no means sexually contented. The emergence of birth-control movements, sex and marriage manuals, a growing sex trade, and the growth of urban homosexual communities, attested that many men suffered as a result of prevailing beliefs and information about sex and sexuality. Suffering could take the form of feelings of deprivation, depravity, and performance anxiety. Not all Victorian marriages were characterized by wives who 'closed their eyes, opened their legs, and thought of England.' But the ideal of passive, chaste womanhood – the counterpart to the aggressive, sexual man who must learn to discipline his eroticism – was very influential, and affected the lives and relations of both sexes in all classes in very important ways.[15]

There can be little doubt that prevailing fears of masturbation and other forms of nonprocreational sex produced by the ideas of the spermatic economy in the late nineteenth and early twentieth centuries were responsible for many troubling experiences for children raised under their aegis, and produced perverse and unhappy results in adult life. Some of the more sensational of these results were chronicled by, among others, Krafft-Ebing, Ellis himself, and Freud. As Lesley Hall notes, 'remedies prescribed by the Victorian medical profession for self-abuse and spermatorrhea are supposed to have been brutal in the extreme.' Medical journals such as *The Lancet* provided detailed prescriptions for ways of mortifying the penis, even recommending cauterization for 'over-sensitivity' of the organ.[16] It is not difficult to understand that male children subjected to such antimasturbation measures may have developed some phobias, anxieties, and unusual sexual preferences.

Contemporary scholars have written about gender and sexual anxieties among late-nineteenth and early-twentieth-century men living through the battles over sex and birth control information, sexual representation in mass culture, sex work, and sexual orientation.[17] Much earlier, Sigmund Freud identified one particular sexual anxiety, which he labelled 'castration anxiety.' Freud located its origins in the childhood socialization of young males in the households of the affluent European classes, in which fathers had sexual access to domestic servants as well as their wives, and exercised power over all members of the household.[18] Freud noted castration anxiety in the preoccupations of culture and art, and observed it at the individual level in the symptoms, stories, and dreams of the men whom he attended as a psychiatrist. He found that anxiety about losing the penis was usually associated with childhood experiences in which the father, older boys, or other adult men generated feelings of competition, inferiority, and physical threat. Freud observed that men's anxiety about their penises seemed to be connected to anxieties about their sexual life and social position. Fear of failing to live up to masculine expectations was equated with the fear of being without a penis – castrated literally and socially – in other words, with being a woman. This seemed to be the most frightening prospect of all, for it threatened to return boys to their primary identification with the woman (mother and nurse), an identification that the men's religions and sport worked to break and to replace with a secondary paternal identification.

Part of the aetiology of castration anxiety among these men doubtless lay in the need of males raised in the Victorian family to find distancing mechanisms from 'over-present' women. As well, the 'brutal' remedies of the masturbation phobia, often administered by mothers and nannies backed up by paternal authority doubtless contributed to fears for the safety of the masculine signifier itself. Widespread sexual abuse in childhood – of boys as well as girls, by men and by women – also likely played a part in the development of castration anxieties.[19] Yet, as important as these factors are, they do not alone account for the particular inflections of the fears Freud described and on which popular imperialist and expansionist culture thrived. The socialization of boys by women in family, church, and school unfolded within a larger and more powerfully determining context: the requirements of manhood and masculine sexual performance demanded by men of boys for life in the public world. Marrying and setting up a household was the expected norm for all classes in this era, even though extramarital sexual arrangements were common, especially among the affluent classes. Manhood entailed success in the economic, political, and military world of men, where physical injury and financial ruin were always possibilities. Aspiring to such success involved sexually charged anxieties and encounters with older, more powerful males, as well as negotiating relations with women. Among junior males entering an 'intermale pecking order'[20] built on principles of inequality, stratification, exploitation, and domination, this evoked, in the emotionality of public life, the imago of the punitive, castrating, familial Father.

Even during the period of the family-wage system, when men made up a gender-exclusive workforce in most trades and professions and monopolized religious leadership and political life, they were experiencing painful feelings about their gender and their sexuality. Kevin White suggests that American men experienced a full-blown 'masculinity crisis as the Progressive era dawned after 1900.' Although painful feelings about masculinity have likely accompanied patriarchal requirements for centuries, it is only within the last one hundred years that we have begun to conduct an analytic conversation about such feelings and what they might mean.[21]

It is not difficult to see how the development of the masculine culture of sport – first within school and church-sponsored muscular Christian organizations of the nineteenth century, then within the commercial youth-oriented urban leisure cultures of the early twentieth century – both assuaged and exacerbated castration anxieties and other fears of men. In the rituals of sport, a sense of strength and position, at least with respect to women and femininity, was continually reinforced, thus providing a sense of relief from castration anxiety (being like a woman). Yet the expectations of the surrogate fathers – the network of coaches, officials, and educators who presided over sport and represented the larger national or ethnic Fatherhood – for a violently instrumental masculinity tended to fuel internal fears of an aggressive, rejecting father among boys and to normalize intermale violence. Thus, whatever its origins, and whatever name we give to the sexually saturated fears and obsessions males had (and have) of other males, the identification of such wide-spread anxieties among men lays bare just how much fear structured the experience of boys with men, in familial and extrafamilial contexts, and motivated the construction of masculine identities and hypermasculine cultural practices and ideals.[22]

Eroticizing the Other: The Politics of Sexual Displacement

The evolution of the idea of male sexuality as dangerous and 'primitive,' as conceived by Anglo-American Victorians, unfolded within the development of empire, in which technologically enhanced aggressive physicality opened up possibilities of sexual access and exploitation in far-off lands, and fed the fantasies of such possibilities at home. These fantasies in turn shaped the way knowledge itself was articulated. Anne McClintock writes that Victorian 'knowledge of the unknown world was mapped as a metaphysics of gender violence, not as the expanded recognition of cultural difference – and was validated by the new Enlightenment logic of private property and possessive individualism.' Examining the imagery and conventions of legends about colonial lands in British Victorian culture, she concludes: 'In these fantasies, the world is feminized and spatially spread for male exploration, then reassembled and deployed in the interests of massive imperial power ... In the minds of these men, the imperial conquest of the globe found both its shaping figure and its political sanction in the prior subordination of women as a category of nature.'[23]

Colonial lands were figured as sexually feminine in the imperial imagination, and the imperial force as assertively masculine. The gendered playing of sport as a mass and increasingly national spectacle during the last half of the nineteenth century and the first decades of the twentieth century symbolized all fields where men engaged with men in the struggle over the feminine territory and all its riches. As a mass ritual, sport literally and symbolically delineated for English and American men and their communities abroad fields of physical power that simultaneously represented fields of battle and fields of knowledge, on which they reigned supreme.

For men of the affluent classes in the late nineteenth and early twentieth centuries in British and American imperial centres, to be the globe's economic masters meant to be its sexual masters, with access to women of other classes, other colours, and other nations being part of the reward for those who conquered them. Even for the white, working-class man conscripted into the armies, navies, and merchant marines of expansive capitalist nations, empire-building was made more attractive by the exotic promise of 'native girls' and sexual access without responsibility. Enormous sexual energy was harnessed in the making of capitalist supremacy and the creation of empire.[24] Rooted in the myths of early exploration, mercantile capitalism, Christianity, and the slave trade, the prevailing ideas of empire in Victorian Great Britain were saturated with what Anne McClintock calls 'a long tradition of male travel as an erotics of ravishment.'

For centuries, the uncertain continents – Africa, the Americas, Asia – were figured in European lore as libidinously eroticized. Travelers' tales abounded with visions of the monstrous sexuality of far-off lands, where, as legend had it, men sported gigantic penises and women consorted with apes, feminized men's breasts flowed with milk and militarized women lopped theirs off. Renaissance travellers found an eager and lascivious audience for their spicy tales, so that, long before the era of high Victorian imperialism, Africa and the Americas had become what can be called a porno-tropics for the European imagination – a fantastic magic lantern of the mind onto which Europe projected its forbidden sexual desires and fears.[25]

This 'pornotropic' tradition ascribed and ranked sexual impulses differentially according to class and race, and these were articulated through gender. 'The gendering of imperialism took very different forms in different parts of the world,' McClintock observes. Different colonial sectors were linked with different erotic fantasies about the colonized. Virgin images were associated with the Americas, for example, but 'India, for one, was seldom imaged as a virgin land, while the iconography of the harem was not part of Southern African colonial erotics. North African, Middle Eastern and Asian women were, all too often, trammeled by the iconography of the veil, while African women were subjected to the civilizing mission of cotton and soap.'[26]

In these associated traditions that linked race, class, gender, and sex in Victorian culture and mores, middle-class men and women were regarded as differentially sexual and asexual by nature. However, women who were excluded from membership in the reputable classes escaped membership in the class of women who were considered passive, weak, and chaste by the dominant classes. Working-class women and black women, all those who performed paid domestic service, factory and agricultural work, were targets of sexual exploitation and sexualized through inferiorization in cultural discourse. Middle-class culture dealt with the contradiction of their sexual exploitation by proposing that working-class women were different in nature from their 'betters.' Anne McClintock writes that women of the lower orders

figured as the epitome of sexual aberration and excess. Folklore saw them, even more than the men, as given to lascivious venery so promiscuous as to border on the bestial[27]

... Surely no other culture has divided female sexuality so distinctly along class lines. Working class women were figured as biologically driven to lechery and excess; upper-class women were naturally indifferent to the deliriums of the flesh ... The Victorian splitting of women into whores and Madonnas, nuns and prostitutes, has its origins, then, not in universal archetype, but in the class structure of the household.[28]

The ideology that constructed lower-class women and women of colour as inherently sexually degenerated and degraded – 'dirty' in both senses of the word – served middle-class women as well as middle-class men. It permitted the politics of antiprostitution and sexual delinquency campaigns to be seen as prosocial insofar as they involved moral 'uplift.' This ideology also encouraged a politics of displacement: a tendency to split ideas about women and sex into bipolar, morally ranked categories; to disavow the 'bad,' then displace and project this dangerous, conflicted sexuality onto Others – women, the poor, colonials – of imperial Victorian society.

The economic, sexual, and political power imbalance between the genders that this Madonna/whore mythology both attested to and sought to reinforce meant that, at the practical social level, the dangerous sexuality of women, especially that of poor women and colonial women, was stigmatized and juridically punished in the mid- and late nineteenth century. However much men's 'dangerous' sexuality was problematized in the official debates of the new professions, and however strongly this notion affected the norms of sexual socialization of children, in public life men bought women whose poverty compelled them to sell sex, and in political life these same women became targets of sexual control and repression. The sustained political attack on working-class prostitutes who were thought to 'prey' on the vulnerable young men of the affluent classes was one of the major ways this took place.[29]

Employing a rhetoric of protecting women and preventing venereal disease, legislators, businessmen, clergymen, and middle-class social reformers in the 1860s and 1870s launched a moral panic over prostitution ('white slavery').[30] Their campaigns swept across British, American, and Canadian society in the last quarter of the nineteenth century and into the first decades of the twentieth.[31] Many women social reformers, predominantly middle-class, argued the virtues of sexual moderation and supported antiprostitution campaigns out of a desire to protect their own relationships with men and the domesticity of the home.[32]

An important minority of politically active women – the feminists – articulated different views on prostitution and a host of other sexual topics. Many rejected the political focus on prostitution as well as Victorian ideas about the relative sexlessness of middle-class and working-class women. In their own ways, women as different as Ida Craddock, Emma Goldman, Marie Stopes, and Margaret Sanger all fought for women's rights to pleasure and respect in sexual relations. Many feminists who advanced such minoritarian views paid dearly for their beliefs, some with jail terms.

The possession or exchange of erotic material and information about sex – whether educational, artistic, or straightforwardly prurient – became increasingly stigmatized late in the nineteenth century in an attempt to control the circulation of sexual ideas. As sexual expression was criminalized, a sexual police was created, just at the time when photography and mass printing techniques made sexual material increasingly accessible to the masses. However, the depiction and discussion of sex, by feminists as well as others, could not be stopped.

Nineteenth-century preoccupations with women's sexuality were coupled to a very specific appreciation of women's different natural physical capacities. In the words of two contemporaneous authorities:

It is generally true that the males are more active, energetic, eager, passionate and variable ... The more active males, with a consequently wider range of experience, may have bigger brains and more intelligence ... being usually stronger, have greater independence and courage ... The stronger lust and passion of males is likewise the obverse of predominant katabolism ... greater cerebral variability and therefore more originality ... Man thinks more, woman feels more.[33]

For late-nineteenth-century experts such as Patrick Geddes and J. Arthur Thomson, women who 'wasted' their limited ('katabolic') energy in activities other than procreation – sexual pleasure, extradomestic work, and sport – were 'masculinizing' themselves, contrary to their essential natures. (Working-class women who took paid work were often described as 'unsexed,' or 'manly' by official and popular culture, presumably because their hard, dirty work defeminized them).[34] Further, by diverting procreative energy to sport or nonprocreative eroticism, such women were 'committing race suicide' (to use the phrase of the day),[35] neglecting their class and national duty to bolster the numbers of the superior folk.

Oppositional views rejected this paradigm, including with respect to sport. A number of women and some male physical educators, for example, pointed out the similarities in the bodies of the genders, and argued that sport could regenerate women's bodies as well as men's, that women's energy was a renewable resource that could be greatly developed by sport. Views such as these, which are dominant today, gained more currency in the early twentieth century, especially among women educators of the upper classes and active women of all classes. For the most part, however, even advocates for active physicality for women recommended milder forms of exertion for the 'weaker' sex. And, what is much more important, sportswomen remained a distinct and powerless minority within the early sport nexus, unable to either command equivalent resources for women or change the evolutionary course of male-oriented sport.

The Working Class and Colonial Peoples

Clearly, the involvement of sexuality with economics, morals, and identities was not limited to a simple dynamic between women and men, nor even to that dynamic as powerfully impacted and variegated by class factors. In addition, an erotics of racism was also important. The privileged position of middle- and upper-class men in Anglo-American societies depended on their ability to maintain their dominant position in a set of dichotomized and potentially explosive social relationships: between men and women (subsets: wives and whores), the upper and lower classes, imperial and colonial peoples, Christians and pagans, white and coloured, master and slave. Each of these social polarizations required complementary psychic splits on the part of those who aggressively expanded and benefited from imperialism. As a result, while poor women and women of colour were cast as whores, and politically and juridically scapegoated, and while white middle-class women had to bear the burden of chastity and institutionalized infidelity, men too were struggling with the sexual requirements of their gender assignment.

In the late nineteenth century, to be 'white' was to represent civilization, to be 'higher' than the culture of colonials by virtue of sexual restraint – to be, in Kevin White's typology, the 'Christian Gentleman.' To be dark, on the other hand, was to be the 'Underworld Primitive,' dirty, savage, and sexually insatiable. Paul Hoch writes of the tendency to project 'bad' sexuality onto an eroticized, dark, masculine Other in Christian folklore from precapitalist religious apocrypha – a tendency in keeping with the 'pornotropic' tradition of an 'erotics of ravishment' that evolved in the sixteenth, seventeenth, and eighteenth centuries:

The Devil was often depicted as a lascivious black male with cloven hoofs, a tail, and a huge penis capable of super-masculine exertion – an archetypal leering 'black beast from below.' Thus, in white civilization which considers many forms of sexuality to be immoral – and consigns them to the dark dungeons of the unconscious – the 'devil,' dark villain or black beast becomes the receptacle of all the tabooed desires, thereby embodying all the forbidden possibilities for ultimate sexual fulfilment and becoming the very apotheosis of masculine potency.[36]

Though the Victorian Christian Gentleman ideal of masculinity was rhetori-
cally supported in mixed culture, men of the affluent and military classes were
called on to be both gentleman and 'underworld primitive,' Dr Jekyll and Mr
Hyde. They were to be chaste family fathers and democratic national citizens
as well as violent, aggressive, sexual conquerors. Toward the end of the nineteenth century, the men's subcultures increasingly supported such sexual norms,
alongside the culture of the Christian Gentlemen. 'The male middle class not
only visited prostitutes,' writes Kevin White,

> they could also indulge in male social life as spectators of boxing and baseball and
> participants in gambling and drinking. As men, they had access to the entire public
> world, and so they could enjoy themselves how they liked. The underworld also incor-
> porated those whom we would call today 'homosexuals,' for whom there was no option
> but to enter into this society, since the Victorian public morality of manly love pre-
> cluded consummation of homoerotic desire. The mood and tenor of the underworld,
> according to one writer, was summed up in 'crude nineteenth century potboilers which
> dealt with moral insanity, monomania, sex and sadism.' Pornography was rampant.[37]

As Anne McClintock and Paul Hoch have both pointed out, middle-class
ideology linked the sexual with the bestial (associated with labouring, as in
beast of burden), and projected it outwards not only onto working-class and
colonial women – their objects – but, in its most menacing form, onto working-
class and colonial men, who blocked sexual access to their women. In the class
and colonial systems of the late nineteenth and early twentieth centuries,
intermale ranking and competition took place both literally and symbolically
over the terrain of women's bodies, the prize when geographic territory was
conquered, or economic success achieved.[38] Privileged access to the bodies of
colonial women, however, implied the defeat of colonial men.

Working-class women and women of colour were vulnerable to sexual pre-
dation, yet figured in ideology as lazy, rebellious, and hypersexual. Working-
class men and men of colour, especially black Africans, with their supposedly
overwhelming sexuality, were both bad and dangerous.[39] Indeed, it was with
respect to ideas of phallic supremacy that colonial males were figured as most
threatening. Class, imperial, and colonial rivalries among men as a gender
were sexualized and politicized and gave rise in adult life to racialized sexual
fantasies and castration anxieties. Thus the erotics of late-nineteenth- and early-
twentieth-century racism were generated by intermale as well as intergender
developments.[40] Indeed, in the politics of intermale competition – issues of
envy (of sexual prowess) and fear (of physical prowess) – lent the racialized
culture of sport an intensely homoerotic quality.[41]

By the end of the nineteenth century, racism was organizationally embodied in sport in many forms. Practically, the segregated nature of both community and professional sports was an accepted norm in the United States and established patterns of race discrimination that were thrown over only slowly and partially later in the twentieth century. The diffusion of sport took place under the ideological, organizational, and financial leadership of the British and American upper classes even as they utilized the powerful engagement of the urban working classes and colonial men with these physical games. From the private schools and universities of the rich, to the public playgrounds and rinks of the urban working classes, men's sports were rehearsed as rituals for distinguishing males of white, athleticized civilization from those of the dark, nonathleticized heathens. For while the rules of the games spread across classes in England and North America, sports organizations and associations formed inside class and race lines. This was true not only of private athletic clubs, but, in the latter decades of the century, of public recreation and professionalizing organizations as well.

This was the case abroad, as well as at home. One of the most important functions of sport in colonial societies was the regrouping of British (and, later, American) men on foreign soil, to ensure their contact with one another and their preparedness to assume their colonial roles – military, financial, or administrative. For this reason, colonial sport clubs tended to be exclusive. The network of late-nineteenth-century sports associations that became the model for twentieth-century sports were both classist and racist from their inception. For working-class or colonial men, on the other hand, who saw sport as a possible 'level playing field' in the great class drama of intermale rivalries, being able to beat the masters at their own game – as happened when professional working-class players grew to dominate soccer, baseball, hockey, and football in the late nineteenth and early twentieth centuries – was deeply satisfying. Thus sport created a symbolic class and race battlefield, where the stakes were sexual as well as political.[42]

The story of the black American heavyweight Jack Johnson, who was permitted to fight white men in 1905, and then beat James J. Jeffries, the 'great white hope,' in 1910, is one example of the sexualization of intermale racist dynamics:

The [1910] fight was no contest. Johnson taunted, jeered, and jabbed, controlled the tempo from beginning to end, and finally knocked out his exhausted opponent in the fifteenth round. News of the black man's victory provoked ugly racial conflicts in no less than fifty American cities. Eight deaths were reported as proud blacks and humiliated, frustrated whites lashed into each other ... The editor of the *Chattanooga Times* observed that the spectacle of 'a powerful negro knocking a white man about the ring' would maliciously 'inspire the ignorant negro with false and pernicious ideas as to the physical prowess of his race.'[43]

Johnson's athletic superiority was only one of the issues that sparked the conflict that unfolded around him:

Huge and handsome, black and proud, [Johnson] dressed flashily, drove the finest cars, and violated the most rigid taboo of his society: he openly courted and married white women. His first wife committed suicide, but within the year, Johnson found another. Although he lived in Chicago, free of southern state laws banning interracial marriage, massive stacks of hate mail and threats of assassination greeted him daily. For some blacks, such as the aged, mild-mannered Booker T. Washington, he was an embarrassment to his race; for younger, more assertive blacks, he was a hero of epic proportions, a 'bad nigger' who refused to bow and scrape to please white society.[44]

From the point of view of sexual culture, the events that unfolded around Johnson show that contests of prowess between men of different races carried explicit sexual anxiety, and thus represented an erotic spectacle and social drama of their own, with reverberations in the broader culture.

Kevin White argues that by the end of the 1920s, the qualities of 'underworld primitivism' – violence, sexual promiscuity without responsibility, and aggression – had moved into the centre of American cultural idealizations of masculinity, displacing the previously dominant 'Christian Gentleman.' Through men's homosocial cultural institutions such as sport, dance-halls, newspapers, men's fictional genres, and pornography, these qualities had an accompanying erotics. According to White's hypothesis, men's culture (and sport as an important actor in men's culture) acted as a site and conduit for the idealization of hypermasculine qualities. However, his thesis regarding the class provenance of these qualities is problematic.[45] Because of the exploitative nature and rapaciousness of upper-class and imperial sexuality, often practised by imperialist men of all social classes abroad in British and other empires, it seems insufficient to credit the increasing violence of men's culture and masculine idealizations in the late nineteenth and early twentieth century to a simple 'trickle-up' effect from the rough culture of the labouring classes to the refined middle classes and the cultural mainstream. For, at the same time, the imperially motivated militarization of society – promoted very much at the top – was equally 'trickling down.'

Whether in the American West or in Africa, Asia, and Latin America, the imperial project and its attendant masculinities and erotics were approved of at home through all forms of culture. White captures one important phenomenon as the dominance of the nineteenth-century Victorian Christian Gentlemen waned and the twentieth-century 'Underworld Primitive' waxed, but he misses another. The class provenance of the linked ideals of violence and sexual aggression that came to constitute core ideas of masculinity was not only the lower social orders with their rough amusements, but the militarized masculine orders, dominated by senior and powerful men. For the same reason, I do not agree with those, such as Eric Dunning, who see in sport primarily a 'civilizing' impulse that 'contains' physical violence.[46] Rather, I see in the sport that emerged from the nineteenth century a *rationalization* of violence. And this is not the same as its attenuation.

Sport: 'An Inner Balance between the Civilized and the Primitive'

In the official middle-class mores of the nineteenth century, to be a 'good' man was to be a man of 'character,' one who met the rigorous standards of masculine and class duty. This ideal included being robustly active and exercising sexual restraint according to the dictates of the spermatic economy. 'The good man was not a victim of his own physical impulses,' Rotundo writes of the Victorian Christian Gentleman: 'He took pride in his powerful will which vanquished laziness and lust. Parents held up this standard of inner control to their sons, calling on them to practice "Spartan" self-discipline and live "pure in heart" ... A minister from upstate New York preached a funeral sermon over a four year-old boy, praising him for his "self-control."'[47]

Yet, as we have seen, the sexual program was not so straightforward. For at another level, a successful man was also a sexual predator, a prolific sower of superior seed, an imperial pasha. Victorian imperial status called on men to be primitive warriors physically and sexually with lower-class and colonial women, yet to be constrained, almost asexual with women of their own class. 'The good [Victorian] man had to walk a fine line,' Rotundo observes. 'He was a person of physical strength and primitive energy, and yet he was also the master of his own impulses. How to achieve an inner balance between the civilized and the primitive was an urgent problem.'[48] Sport purported to answer that problem, and its advocates successfully argued its merits.

George M. Beard, a physician and writer of guidance manuals, believed that sport cultivated in urban youth the virtues he saw in the lives of '"savages and semi-savages,"' American blacks under slavery, and 'the strong, healthy farming population in all civilized countries' [who] triumphed over the annoyance of sexual desire "when they have no opportunities for gratification."'[49] Of the representative 1872 book *Our Children*, written by Dr Augustus Kinsley Gardner ('an innovator in gynecological surgery and an author of moral and sexual guidance literature'), Donald Mrozek notes that 'the survival of the traditional stock, the re-creation of conventional morals, and the balanced development of the body ... merged in the thinking of the day, and sport was grasped by all three.'[50]

Bodily exercise began gaining advocates among ministers and doctors as an antidote to unwanted (bestial) sexual urges even in the ante-bellum period in the United States:

Few institutions so persuasively promised to 'tame the beast' within man without losing the benefits of the beast's great energy. Whether conceived as a kind of repressed sexuality or used as a curative for both lassitude and overindulgence, sport addressed Americans' concern over sex during the Victorian age and grasped at a naturalistic solution that retained the primitive while aspiring toward social progress.[51] ... Thus the Reverend John Todd, a prolific and influential writer of sexual guidance and anti-masturbation literature at mid-century, advocated body exercise and hard manual labour as remedies for the dreaded 'disease' of 'secret vice.'[52]

Leading activists and ideologues in the reform movements of the latter part of the century applied this philosophy to class relations. 'Get them off the streets and they won't riot or strike' was paired with 'Send them to the gym or playing field and they won't masturbate or fornicate.'[53] Muscular Christianity, a quaint term to late-twentieth-century ears, was the dominant philosophy of the last half of the nineteenth century. Its proponents viewed athletics as a way to build strength, create habits of dominance, teach abstract principles of group effort and common goals, promote the values of nineteenth-century Christianity and thus to harness and control men's sexual impulses in the service of worthy social enterprises. The value of sport lay in its ability to create the civilized male animal. In this sense, sport was a perfect example of the larger trend toward Kevin White's 'underworld primitivism' in ideals of masculinity at the turn of the century.[54] 'Primitivism' was a cultural movement that celebrated and cultivated the energy and aggression of the 'lower' orders in men, while using it for 'civilized,' 'Christian' goals. Properly bowdlerized and highly competitive, sport was sold as a safe, nonsexual activity for men, and an acceptable celebration of the strong male body among men thirsting for unqualified symbolic expressions of visible manhood. At the nonverbal level, however, male athletes, radiating physicality and all the energy of the displaced and aggressive eroticism sport actually carried, became idols and icons of masculine sexuality.

In their advocacy of sport, influential nineteenth- and twentieth-century sport enthusiasts emphasized the sexual restraint and responsibility it developed in men. But these admonitions were dramatically contradicted by the visible physicality and sexuality of the activity and its surrounding cultures – especially the photographic and filmic – and by the values of masculine exclusivity, force, and appropriation sport celebrated, particularly in its elite and increasingly commercial aspects. White shows how the ideal Christian Gentleman was displaced in the early twentieth century by an ideal who 'rejected [Victorian] repression and suppression of desires and abandoned respect for women in a flurry of aggressiveness associated with a violent homosocial culture.'[55] Sport became a privileged site cultivating aggressive masculine sexuality through masculine sexual display in industrial society.

This phenomenon can also be traced through the evolution of fashion. In *Fashion and Eroticism*, Valerie Steele makes an excellent case for understanding fashion as a practice of eroticism and sexual display. Because fashion is about personal presentation, including sexual presentation, its trends tell a lot about the erotic preoccupations of its surrounding culture. In the Victorian case (the focus of her work), Steele argues that, for women, fashion provided a means to live eroticism that did not correspond in any simple way to the dictates of the official, male-dominated, late-nineteenth-century discourses on appropriate feminine (a)sexuality, even as fashion developed within their constraints. Victorian women's fashions were exemplified by the corseted, full-bodied woman who reigned as the century's ideal beauty. While we can read this style as emphasizing women's reproductive parts and, hence, maternal social role, the emphasis on breasts and hips is also erotic. While early feminists rightly criticized this ideal as causing considerable damage to women, Steele argues that many women embraced the ideal themselves precisely because of its sexual emphasis. Fashion could – and did – provide a way to play out women's eroticism, in flagrant refutation of the maternal and asexual ideals of womanhood in official discourses, or the moralistic critique of feminists. This embrace of the erotic dimension of the hourglass ideal was especially evident in evening wear, which bared women's skin and moulded their form. Furthermore, in general and across classes, the accoutrements and elaborations of this ideal in women's fashions tended, decade by decade, to borrow most from the styles of courtesans and prostitutes.

Though Steele writes primarily about women's fashion in the nineteenth and early twentieth centuries, she notes some major changes in men's sartorial culture in the same period that have great relevance for the erotics of sport. To begin with, in the middle of the nineteenth century the clothing of the affluent classes underwent a radical shift:

In the mid-eighteenth century, both men and women of the elite wore clothing of similar ornamentation and novelty, and with a parallel emphasis on the sexual body. By

the mid-nineteenth century, vivid colours, luxurious fabrics, decoration, and change-
ability were essentially restricted to women's dress, and most men wore some version
of the plain, dark, uniform three-piece suit ... The only vestiges of men's earlier elaborate costumes remained in military uniforms and very formal evening dress. The clear
sartorial distinction between men and women is a primary characteristic of Victorian
fashion.[56]

What is striking here is that the separate spheres ideology of the nineteenth
century shaped men's fashion in relation to gender and sexual display to such
an extent that 'class distinctions, while important, were nonetheless secondary.'[57] Because gender differentiation was of primary concern, men adopted the
suit, eventually across all classes, to underline their differences from women.
Where women's fashions emphasized the erotic through ornamentation and
sexual emphasis, 'the ordinary man's suit of the second half of the [nineteenth]
century tended to conceal any possible physical attractions or evidence of
physical strength, other than sheer size and bulk.[58] ... Apparently the man's
dark suit was intended to express both masculinity and the social position of
the gentleman.'[59] As Kevin White observes, 'the respectable Victorian man
must look the part of the Christian Gentleman: dignified and self-controlled,
asexual and commanding.'[60]

As men took their sartorial and erotic distance from the feminine, short hair
also came into fashion. 'Symbolically, long hair seemed to represent femininity and short hair masculinity,' writes Steele. According to the French writer
Gabriel Prévost, 'short hair is virile and perfectly appropriate to the role of
man in our epoch. It leaves the head free for struggle, movement and thought.'[61]
The transformation in men's clothes emitted very clear signs: 'producing, serious, not frivolous' and tended to emphasize the sexually repressive. Women's
clothing said 'consuming,' 'using up,' 'pleasurable,' and tended to emphasize
the expressive and sexual.[62] Fashion was women's unofficial road to eroticism
and sexual display. Men's workaday and even evening fashions retreated from
such a display.

But men's sexual display did not disappear completely from public life.
Rather, it shifted ground to sport. Sport uniforms emphasized the carnal male
form or left large parts of it naked. Sport offered up the male body to the male
as well as the female gaze in ritual display and entertainment, just when men's
fashion was closing this body down.[63] (By the late twentieth century, sport was
to leave an indelible mark on 'leisure' fashion for men and become a hugely
lucrative market.) The erotics of the 'new virility' of the late nineteenth and
early twentieth centuries was most clearly displayed in the spectacularized
athleticized male. In *Hard to Imagine*, a study of gay male eroticism in photog-

raphy and film, Thomas Waugh uses a wealth of visual and analytical evidence to show the popularity of athletic beefcake when it emerged in the late nineteenth century, as well as the central role it eventually played in the evolution of twentieth-century gay and straight male eroticism and culture.[64] As Waugh relates, athletic body-builders such as Eugen Sandow and Bernarr Macfadden made considerable fortunes distributing photographs of themselves and in promoting the erotic spectacularization of the male body:

The circulation and consumption of the male nude and the nude in general automatically constitute a sexual articulation in our culture, no matter how vigorously disavowed ... Like most of the emerging cultural forms of mass production, the institution of looking at the male body at the turn of the century was male – overwhelmingly so in terms of its control, its operation, and its constituency ... The beefcake industry was in tandem with the companion cheesecake industry. The musclemen emerged alongside their female analogues – actresses, models, fan dancers and burlesque queens – and were depicted in equally brief costume ... Male bodies ... were marketed in exactly the same way to the same male gaze in every medium from mail-order photography and postcards to vaudeville. There is some record of a female following for such figures as Sandow, but the audience for both beefcake and cheesecake was overwhelmingly male ... An obsession with male sexuality was an explicit part of the larger discursive environment of Physical Culture.'[65]

The association between hypermasculinist sport and certain types of physical sexual ideals was also evident in *The Police Gazette*, a very popular men's publication of the late nineteenth century that combined risqué pictures of women with coverage of pugilism and the rougher men's sports. 'The underworld ethos after 1880 was captured in the *Police Gazette*,' writes Kevin White, 'where spoofing of homosexuality went hand in hand with sports reports and pictures of scantily clad "ladies."' It was through cultural vehicles such as the *Gazette* that hypermasculine ideals spread throughout the culture, and linked men across other socioeconomic divisions: 'One hundred and fifty thousand men of the working and middle class read this publication: in this way, it represented a pivotal point, connecting in its darker and seamier side a standard of underworld primitivism that united American men across classes. Here male primitivism, the very antithesis of the high ideals of the Christian Gentleman, ran rampant and unchecked.'[66]

In this capacity of display and affirmation of violent physical and sexual prowess, highly eroticized yet strongly antihomosexual, sport was able to address, if implicitly and tacitly, a variety of gendered sexual anxieties. As we have seen, by providing heroic figures and masculine heroics, sport created a mass ritual activity of counteridentification with women and the feminine – it conferred masculinity. More, it emerged to provide a field of 'clean' masculine physicality, offering physical release while warding off anxieties about 'dirty' sexuality. Indeed, sport ritually tamed dirt and the sexuality and exploitation it stood for. Through its rough and filthy contests it evoked memories of childhood 'dirt' as well as the messes of colonialism and class exploitation, harnessing dirt to worthy, glorious symbolic ends. The clean uniforms before the event, the clean clothes and ritual homosocial ablutions following the athletic event, the customary libations that accompanied play, and the ovations from the spectators all performed the alchemical conversion of men's dirt into cleanliness. And cleanliness – condensing ideals of class status, asexuality and imperial whiteness – was a towering Victorian middle-class obsession.[67]

At the turn of the twentieth century, sport animated the myth of the great, clean, athlete-warrior and his band of fellow adventurers off to build nation and empire. In presenting spectacles of physical strength and group appropriation, the game forms and physical activities of sport rehearsed the imperial drama on 'domestic' (in both senses of the term) frontiers and in far-away lands. Sport bound up anxieties about the masculine as well as the feminine sexual Other, and valorized as moral and attractive the actions and beliefs of sexual as well as territorial and economic appropriation. 'Militant force had supreme value as the "primordial element" governing the formative process of a nation, and all activities that cultivated this primordial force shared its high esteem,' Mrozek writes of sport and American expansionism.[68] Particularly important was the cross-class unifying function of sport. Through manly rituals of sexual display that celebrated 'militant force' – hypermasculinity – the nationally celebrated athletes drew men of lower social classes in the metropole to identify with the men of their upper classes instead of with the men in the colonies who were potential class and even sexual allies. Thomas Waugh notes that it was during this period that the dominant ideal of man as authoritative *paterfamilias* was replaced by the ideal of the 'champion.'[69]

In addressing, expressing, and containing classed and racialized intermale issues of fear, hostility, and sexual competition, Victorian sport was able to provide eroticized, gendered, and racist 'strategies of renewal' for its participants. Centred in and focused on the sexually problematic masculine body, sport was an inspired way to capture this body's sexual energies and divert them into the antisensual, nongenital physical activities considered socially constructive for males and for the gendered economic order of the times. For privileged men, sport initially was their masculine proving ground. But by the First World War, all team sports and many individual ones had been flooded by athletes from the underprivileged classes, who proved their physical and sexual equality – if not superiority – with their economic betters through their victories in sport.

Sport succeeded in becoming a site in which the male sexual beast was harnessed, then celebrated. It also was able to divert men's physical and sexual attention from women and focus it more on the violent, competitive, homosocial world of men alone, a world profoundly linked to armies and war.

The Militaristic Homoeroticization of Sport

In the previous chapter I traced the coterminus ways in which nineteenth century society became militarized and athleticized. These same trends also had consequences for sexual life and culture. Most importantly, athleticization and militarization functioned to create extensive and intensive male-exclusive arenas for physical interaction between men, with norms very different from those that were supposed to regulate middle-class heterosocial life and comprise the sexual life of the restrained 'Christian Gentleman.' In these rugged homosocial sites, middle- and upper-class boys and men, as well as those from the lower classes, engaged in the 'primitive' (in White's usage) behaviour of 'criminals,' but in sanctioned ways. Through spectacle and heroization, centrally through sport, during the last part of the nineteenth century, and increasingly into the twentieth, the resultant eroticism of these overlapping and reinforcing men's cultures was then promulgated more widely throughout the culture at large.[70]

As we have seen, sport and war were pursued with similar enthusiasm and vigour, often by the same people, in the nineteenth and early twentieth centuries in Britain and the United States. As Mrozek notes: 'The language with which military theorists spoke of the need for national unity to guarantee success in war paralleled that which many physical educators used to describe the quest for victory in sport; and they shared a common concern to prevent excessive civilization from corroding the militant, dynamic, primitive impulses of the people.'[71] Like sport, military life was often promoted as a good way to keep the masculine, aggressive, sexual 'beast' alive, but appropriately harnessed, disciplined, and obedient. Nevertheless, official glimpses into military life on both sides of the Atlantic, indicated what art and popular culture had long suggested: that men's military culture was actually quite bestial, and, harnessed or not, did not subscribe to the dictates of official mores at all.[72] We have seen how the men's religions provided a site for the ritual renewal of paternalistic, anti-egalitarian values as against the maternalistic liberalization of public political discourse during these decades in North America. Now we see the same political function played by the military and sport, in which males lived out the aggressive sexual ideals and behaviours that imperial and class ideologies encouraged. All the institutions of men's homosocial activity – military life, athletic associations, bars and dance-halls, and the world of prostitution – sustained sexual subcultures that were more or less violent, masculinist, promiscuous, and, in their 'underworld' qualities, in contradiction to the 'official' masculine idealizations of the Victorian middle-class gender order. While these men's subcultures clearly generated the conventions and economics of heteroeroticism (sex with women), the primary practical and spiritual quest of male-exclusive military and athletic experience – consciously pursued by its organizers – was homosocial interaction. And this homosocial interaction produced, paradoxically if not surprisingly, a strong, though denied, homoerotic dimension in athletic and military cultures. In effect, nineteenth-century sport stimulated – in Foucault's word, incited – a great web of homoeroticism.

The physical and symbolic homoeroticism of sport culture lies in the experience and spectacle of intense physical interaction between male practitioners. Thomas Waugh chronicles how in the late nineteenth century the aesthetics and iconography of homoeroticism offered up the sporting male for the male gaze, and provided a nonverbal language of desire for all men about each other.[73] The revival of Greek athletics via the Olympic movement in the late nineteenth century recalled contests that had been rigorously homosocial, had been conducted in the nude, and had involved direct homoerotic appreciation and idealization of male athletes. The fig-leaf added by late-nineteenth-century athletic heroes such as Eugen Sandow drew attention to the tabooed genitals, even as it officially hid them from view.

In rare written testimony, a gay man of the same period noted the presence of actual homosexuality (beyond simply the presence of homoerotic feeling) in sport:

Let us note that similisexualism is widely manifested in professionally athletic occupations. It is common to circus-riders, tumblers, acrobats, to men who are devoted to sports and professions of high physical dexterity. The 'super-virile' theory may be recognized here, the male so emphatically masculine as to repudiate instinctively the feminine ... In athletic circles of all social grades, there is more or less uranianism.[74]

However, the combined prevailing ideologies of separate spheres/compulsory heterosexuality and the spermatic economy meant that the extensive experience and spectacle of homoeroticism within sport could not be translated into open or acknowledged homosexuality. Indeed, homosexuality was increasingly studied, isolated, and stigmatized by official discourses of 'deviance,' even as it became increasingly visible in the growth of homosexual communities in urban centres in the late nineteenth and early twentieth centuries. Distorted by its repression, homoeroticism fed instead into a vast matrix of institutionalized homophobia within sport. In this case, homophobia reflected an obsession with and fear of homosexuality, disavowed and projected onto designated male Others: queer, effeminate 'she-men.'[75] The category of 'homosexual' crystallized at this time, as Foucault points out, 'when it was transposed from the practice of sodomy into a kind of interior androgyny, a hermaphrodism of the soul'[76] – that is, when it came to represent femininity in men.

Ideas of homoeroticism and male/male sexual relations are not static, and differ from culture to culture. Nevertheless, many cultures – including our own – draw a similar line between being masculine (randy enough to screw anyone or anything), and being queer (being screwed). In this arrangement, only the sexually receptive person really transgresses the gender order. 'Real men,' writes Brian Pronger in his treatment of sport, sexuality, and the gender order, 'that is, men who fulfil the masculine requirement of the myth of gender, are assertive with both men and women because assertiveness is basic to the myth of masculinity.' The distinction based on who penetrates whom in a sexual exchange, rather than on same-sex engagement per se, has an accompanying value system.

Men who are not assertive are failures in this myth. Men who are receptive are worse than failures, they have betrayed their dominant position and made themselves 'like women.' For a man to be like a woman in our culture is considered contemptible because it is a step down; the greatest insult one can give a man is that he is like a woman. Getting fucked, therefore, is the deepest violation of masculinity in our culture. Enjoying being fucked is the acceptance of that violation, it is the ecstatic sexual experience in which the violation of masculinity becomes incarnate ... it is the experience of being subordinated; it is feminine.[77]

Pronger thus conveys how masculinity and sexual assertiveness through penetration (appropriation) are fused.

This understanding is common to many societies.[78] 'Answering the question of who penetrates whom is a pretty standard means of testing masculinity cross-culturally,' notes anthropologist Allen Dundes in his studies of American football.[79] This attitude expresses a widespread male phobia of being 'in the feminine position,' but no such fear of being in the masculine position. Hence a culture can accommodate homoerotic sexual behaviour – especially active, penetrative behaviour – and hold homophobic ideas at the same time.[80] (Thus athletes can accede to fellatio from male as well as female fans, yet not consider themselves in any sense homosexual, while considering the men who

provide the service to be queer.) In the homosocial, homoerotic, and homophobic cultures of sport and military life, there are long-standing traditions in
which homosexual penetration signifies mastery over those penetrated. Pronger
notes:

In wars, rape is a traditional occupation of the victors, a sign of their conquest. This is a
tradition that even crosses some cultures. The Ancient Egyptians, when victorious in
battle, had a ceremonial custom of buggering defeated troops, thereby asserting sexual
and political mastery over them. The homosexuality of the ancient Greeks was pedo-
philic. The older man, being superior by virtue of his age, was, upon entering the anus
of the youth, imparting symbolically his learning and manliness. It was quite unacceptable for a mature man to be the willing recipient of another man's penis, because this
would be placing himself in a position of inferiority to another man.[81]

The fear of femininity and the equation of femininity with homosexuality
became established in the popular imagination and cultural production in the
late nineteenth and early twentieth centuries. As Kevin White observes, 'in
many ways, by the 1920s, men's fear of effeminacy, which had characterized
the "masculinity crisis" of the progressive era, was diffused into a fear of the
new category, the homosexual.'[82]

The notion of a structural homoeroticism in sport, in service of the fear of
femininity, may seem to contradict directly the idea that one of sport's primary
social functions in the nineteenth century was to create and establish dominant
styles of heterosexual masculinity in extreme opposition to the qualities society
had ascribed to women and femininity. But the sexual cleavage between men
and women – their 'separate spheres' and cultures, the need to resist the internalized 'overwhelming' mother, and the need to achieve male bonding outside
the family – could not have been maintained without some successful redirec-
tion of eroticism away from highly constrained heterosexual relations into
homosocial ones. The shift of energy and eroticism to the homosocial men's
terrain via sport involved the linkage of eroticism to the violently instrumental
(hypermasculinist) values of men's culture. In Melanesian societies, characterized by constant warfare, ritualized homosexuality creates 'a strong common
bond ... that cements the men together into a close warriorhood,' writes anthropologist Walter Williams. 'Just as heterosexual intercourse cements a marriage, Melanesian homosexuality cements a warriorhood ... Rather than somehow threatening masculinity, homosexual behaviour ensure[s] it.'[83] Ancient
Greek homosexuality was understood to play the same role as the homosociality
and homoeroticism of modern sport. Through sport's homosocial, sexually
charged template of competition, inequality, authority, submission, sacrifice,

and continual change, the basic necessary reflexes and patterns for life in capitalist culture were reinforced within participating individuals and their public supporters. These reflexes and patterns coloured sexual ideals and behaviours and the patterning of erotic desire.

'Men's violence against other men is one of the chief means through which patriarchal society simultaneously expresses and discharges the attraction of men to other men,' Michael Kaufman writes of the function of intermale physical conflict in culture.[84] Sport rationalized and provided for such violence, and hence became one of the most important arenas for this double-edged engagement.[85] Late in the nineteenth and early in the twentieth century, football and boxing, long regarded as the rough sports of boys or the lower classes, became integrated in the sporting mainstream. Kevin White writes that by 1890 'the popularity of boxing grew beyond the underworld as John L. Sullivan became the first folk hero of the sport, and helped make popular with a mass audience the Irish male style of aggressiveness.'[86]

The consequences extended far beyond the playing fields and locker rooms. When the aggressive eroticism of military and athletic male subcultures moved into the centre of ideals of masculinity and into the lived practice of mass physical culture, the resultant effect on wider norms of eroticism was a fusion of aggression and eroticism: sado-masochism in a word. When the giving and/or receiving of physical pleasure is accompanied by, or even transmuted into, the administration of pain; when dominance and submission are ritualistically confirmed through the respective rewards and penalties assigned to 'winners' and 'losers'; when affection and respect are associated with competition and suffering in men's culture, there will be consequences for women and heteroeroticism too. Rotundo described the 'new virility' of the 1890s as characterized by its 'aggressive physicality,' and quoted one young woman as commenting that it is 'very strong and mistrustful; and relentless, and makes you feel as if somebody had taken you by the throat; and shakes you up, awfully, and seems to throw you in the air, and trample you underfoot.'[87]

The erotic (including homoerotic) dimensions of sport are not a 'bad' thing. Eroticism is inevitable in sport.[88] Any practice of intense physical engagement will by definition have erotic elements or erotic effects, since the body is a sensual and sexual entity, not simply a collection of muscles and reflexes. When bodies of the same sex interact intensely in homosocial contact, sexual feelings will be provoked. Delight in sensual and sexual experience is part of the human constitution, and men's delight in each other could conceivably be a force for bonding and solidarity. What was deeply problematic in the formative period of modern sport, however, was the way this delight was mobilized: to divide men from women; to devalue sexual activity per se; to develop antisensual, aggressive, and violent norms of masculine sexual practice (sado-masochism); and to stigmatize open, explicit homosexuality, thus reinforcing divisions among men themselves while at the same time uniting men against women. The homoerotic athlete in his homophobic athletic culture became society's ultimate masculine icon. He was an embodied celebration of the qualities required by a masculinist industrial society, a bulwark against the claims of women for social rights and sexual practices that could reflect the attributes society so insistently assigned to femininity, and so implacably de-valued.

In the late nineteenth and early twentieth centuries, the sexual dimensions of sport were based, as they are today, on the physically embodied nature of sport practices – the physical experiences of playing, training, and competing. At the same time, eroticism was also involved in and mobilized by the social experiences of sport, including the many benefits of athletic camaraderie; the symbols and rituals of the spectacle; the adulation attained by nineteenth-century sport heroes; and the privileged status attained by sport itself – a status that, as we have seen, made sport the worthy recipient of support from politicians, public officials, and the clergy. Nineteenth- and early-twentieth-century authorities explicitly discussed the merits of sport in relation to sex. Most tried to construct sport as an asexual and even antisexual field of endeavour, one that restrained or neutralized dangerous male sexuality. This had a great deal to do with the acceptance of sport as a respectable venue for male physicality and socialization and with setting the terms for what have become masculinist sexual traditions in sport and sport culture. It also created a profound and abiding hypocrisy about sport and sex that is still with us to this day.

The erotics of sport underwent a massive change beginning in the early decades of the twentieth century, as we shall now see, when sport, media, and commerce came together. But we are still dealing with the erotic legacies of the sport that emerged in the nineteenth and early twentieth centuries: notably, the aggressive, sado-masochistic, and homoerotic qualities that still character-ize contemporary athletics. Sport still aims to cultivate, if not to tame 'the beast,' to bring out the 'primitive,' to 'make the wolf rise in a man's heart.'

With these historical notes in mind, then, it is time to move into our own century. We begin by taking a look at the marriage of sport and the mass media: the central phenomenon of twentieth-century sport and its culture of hypermasculinity.

4

Delivering the Male: Sport Culture, the Mass Media, and the Masculinity Market

In 1993, *Sports Illustrated* dedicated a special issue to the forty individuals its editors judged to be most important to sport since the magazine began publishing.[1] Of these, four were women athletes who, as tennis players, figure skaters, and gymnasts, were practitioners of 'gender-neutral' and 'feminine' sports. The thirty-six men selected for honours were a more varied group. Eight were media innovators, sports medicine pioneers, and athletes' agents. Seven were auto racers, golfers, tennis players, and cyclists. Twenty-one individuals came from the six key sports – football, baseball, basketball, hockey, boxing, and track and field – the sports that constitute the practical, financial, emotional, and symbolic heart of the sport–media complex and the sport nexus as a whole. In the words of a 1980s advertisement by ESPN (the American sports network that broadcasts sports to more than 60 million homes) to prospective sports sponsors, these sports 'deliver the male.'

Hypermasculinity was bequeathed to twentieth-century athletics by the consolidation of sport rules and organizations late in the nineteenth century. At the same time, however, dynamic gender struggle was also underway. New gender ideologies were emerging in political organizing (feminist, socialist, utopian) and in cultural production, including sport, which was taken up by large numbers of women in early twentieth-century North America. Conditions were ripe for sport to change toward greater gender egalitarianism. Yet, as this and subsequent chapters contend, the hypermasculinist dimensions of sport and sport culture grew over the course of the twentieth century. Late in the 1990s, women's participation in sport notwithstanding, the core men's sports and the culture that derives from them remain prime sites for the regeneration of masculinist mythologies – fictive master narratives of heroic manhood that homogenize in fantasy and symbol a reality of diverse, contradictory masculinities that are often far from the ideal.

With this chapter, I begin my extended examination of the hypermasculinization of twentieth-century sport culture and its political consequences. This analysis involves a number of thematic accounts of interacting trends and developments in the growth of sport and its institutions over this century: the evolution of the core men's sports; their relationships to the growing communications industries, which have taken these sports to a new level of spectacle and mythological power; and the emergence of larger social issues that both animated and framed the triumph of the culture of sport, particularly during the century's latter half. Some of these issues are discussed in detail in later chapters. In Chapter 6, I look at issues of sport and hypermasculinity in relation to violence, war, and neoconservative politics. In Chapter 7, I consider sport and hypermsaculinity in relation to the politics of class, race, and sexual orientation. In Chapter 8, I address hypermasculine sport's relationships to heroic biotechnology on the one hand and to national and corporate politics on the other, through Olympic athletics. But because the media marketing of men's sport as men's culture and as hypermasculine spectacle for society as a whole has been so central to the weighty influence of sport's values and ideals in society, chapters 4 and 5 consider the way in which corporate capitalism and masculinism became twinned, mutually supporting pillars of the sport–media complex.

Accordingly, the first two sections of this chapter present an overview of the development of the sport–media complex in North America from the 1890s to the 1990s. This sketch seeks to identify the main structural features of ownership and financial control that evolved within and shaped the sport–media complex as it matured, while tracing the media's 'discovery' of the power of sport to sell commodities to men. Then, by locating the history of the sport–media complex within gender relations, I outline the key ways these relationships changed, and the issues in gender identity provoked by these changes, particularly in the post–Second World War period. Chapter 5 looks in more detail at how sport, media, and gender have interacted by providing an analysis of three important ways in which hypermasculinity (and hyperfemininity) have been constructed in the fusions between sport and media from the 1960s to the 1990s.

While I will discuss certain relevant issues in women's involvement in sport in chapters 5, 8, and 9, a comment on the subject is in order before I embark on a description of men's sport in the twentieth century. Women with the means and/or the access to sport and other forms of vigorous activity practised by men have always pursued, enjoyed, and excelled in many forms of athletics. The massive growth of the core men's sports and their influence on culture in the twentieth century have not precluded the growth of a smaller, but not insignificant, sector of the sport nexus that includes women as athletes and as spectators of women athletes. My account here of the relationships between the dominant men's sports and the mass media is not meant to ignore, still less demean, all that women's athletic accomplishment represents. Rather, it is an effort to better understand why, for all its achievements, women's sport remains so limited, and why it has had so little qualitative impact on the sport of men.

The Emergence of the Masculinity Market

The influence of sport as a gendered cultural practice and spectacle is a result of its marriage to the communications industries. The foundations of today's sport–media complex were laid in the 1890s, and took more substantial shape in the first half of the twentieth century. During these decades a new urbanized culture of amusements emerged for North American working-class and middle-class youth. The growth of sport and the sport press were part of this larger phenomenon.[2] Many popular magazines and newspapers had reported on baseball, horse racing, boxing, track, rowing, and billiards during the nineteenth century as sport became an increasingly popular activity to perform, to organize, and to watch. But it was the mass proliferation of the daily sports section of North American newspapers in the 1890s that opened up a new a relationship between sport and the mass media of communications. In the United States, according to Sut Jhally, between 1870 and 1900 the number of newspapers increased from 387 to 2,326, and circulation rose from 3.5 million to 15 million. At the same time, advertising revenue jumped from $16 million to $95 million.[3] As Jhally notes in his essay on the development of the sport–media complex, the growth of the advertising-dependent mass press and the consolidation of men's sports – especially team sports – went hand in hand in the latter decades of the nineteenth century and the early decades of the twentieth.[4]

Key to this growth in mass newspaper circulation was a bonding process between the daily press and sport. By the first decade of the twentieth century, most of the large city newspapers had initiated sports sections, acknowledging the powerful draw of sports for their readers. 'It was the metropolitan and then the smaller city dailies which sponsored teams, promoted contests and brought the lingo of the diamond, the turf, the links and the gridiron to the great American middle class,' writes historian J.R. Betts.[5] Because sport sold newspapers and newspapers sold sport, many newspaper owners in the early years of this century began investing in athletes, sports teams, and sporting facilities, and then in the advertising that promoted them. This marked an early stage in the trend to the corporate integration of ownership of athletes, teams, parks, arenas, stadiums, and newspapers.

In the late nineteenth and early twentieth centuries, highly influential citizens – press barons, business leaders, property owners, and construction developers – played a central role in persuading local municipal and state politicians to fund and facilitate the arenas that would house the teams whose fans bought newspapers and voted for politicians.[6] From the beginning, construction of mass athletic facilities involved substantial public subsidies and friendly civic policies toward professional sport. In the early twentieth century, in specific jurisdictions, some stadiums were undertaken along with an expansion in public recreation; just as often stadium construction took place instead of public recreational facilities.[7] The alliances between sport and commercial communications created an enhanced role for politicians and the state in promoting sport culture. By the turn of the twentieth century, governments were already dispensing public funds to underwrite the land and construction costs of sport venues. At the same time, by including sport as a feature of public recreation systems and as a compulsory component of expanding public education, the state acted as a promoter of sport in direct and instrumental ways. In this sense, the state was involved early as a partner of commerce and a pro-active agent of masculinist men's culture.

From the beginning of the twentieth century, the growing importance of sport in North American life was consciously promoted and exploited by dynamic economic and political interests originally external to it. As we have seen, sport had been instrumentally developed and utilized for education and socialization by specific social forces in the nineteenth century. But its marriage to the mass print media (and electronic media when radio was introduced in the early twentieth century) permitted its energies to be harnessed much more directly than ever before for commercial and political projects such as world fairs, Olympic festivals, and international and civic exhibitions.[8]

As noted in Chapter 2, a number of the core men's sports, particularly the team sports, began an aggressive campaign of professionalization in the last quarter of the nineteenth century. This was central to the early commercial relationships between sport and the media, since professional teams organized much larger audiences for the wares of concessionaires and expanded the readership of newspapers. The sport media wanted dramatic performances that would increase paid attendance. These performances in turn required a higher standard of skill than was possible to achieve or maintain on a part-time ('amateur') basis. Hence, professionalization was both a precondition and a beneficiary of the turn-of-the-century sports press. The payment of athletes permitted runners, boxers, weight-lifters, and tennis players to devote their full time to perfecting their skills and talents. It also augmented the broad popularity of football, which had been widely implanted in the college and university system, but now expanded to become the sport of choice in the homosocial male subcultures around which the early-twentieth-century, primarily middle-class, youth culture formed.

With the emergence of fully professional teams, the importance of professional sport within sport associations and leisure culture grew. Colleges, universities, men's clubs, city streets in working-class neighbourhoods, vacant lots, and urban recreation centres all felt the pull of the professional games. (Some sports associations – notably those of Olympic athletics – chose to maintain official 'amateur' status until well after the Second World War, thus creating the basis of a different rhythm and pacing to the commercialization of these sports. I trace this theme in Chapter 8.) In the increasingly pyramidal sports networks a wealthy elite owned male athletes – a mixed-class lot, but increasingly working class – and men of all classes engaged with their spectacles. Standards and conventions of play and training in the 'lower,' more local and participatory levels were profoundly affected.

At the turn of the century upper-crust publications such as the *New York Times*, *Harper's*, and the *Atlantic Monthly* decried commercialization for degrading sport's capacity to serve as a wholesome and character-building enterprise. But the trend was irreversible. Paying fans wanted the games and working-class players wanted the financial and social rewards made available to them through sport. For working-class audiences, the promotion of working-class men as social heroes through sport was irresistible. For whatever defeats they might regularly have suffered at the hands of upper-class men in their daily lives, working men could regain their lost masculinity on the playing fields, as their professional representatives bested their class opposites. Thus, in bringing contestants of different classes together, sport provided a forum for symbolic equality with, and even revenge on, the upper classes.[9]

The popularity of sport continued to grow rapidly at the beginning of the twentieth century – the early days of consumer capitalism – aided and abetted by the newspaper industry, then radio. In the United States, baseball and football entered the century in crisis. Baseball professionalized early, and was characterized by cutthroat competition between players and owners, and among owners. Football, still largely a college game, was marked by extreme violence.[10] Due to a series of struggles and reforms in both sports, by the 1920s each had addressed its respective problems with a variety of strategies, and grew again in reach and popularity. Baseball enjoyed enormous interest. 'During the decade fifteen of the sixteen major-league clubs made a profit,' notes

Baker. 'The New York Yankees led the list of moneymakers. Their prime attraction was, of course, "the Babe," whom they bought from the Red Sox in 1919.'[11] President Calvin Coolidge recognized baseball as 'a real moral and physical benefit to the nation.' As an elevated occupation, different from 'trade or commerce in the commonly accepted use of those words,' (Oliver Wendell Holmes), the Supreme Court in 1922 gave baseball club owners carte blanche in shaping and protecting their investments, and acquitted them of an antitrust suit brought against them by the players. In this way the juridical arm of the state in effect foreclosed on the possibility that the leagues could be organized to benefit players and spectating communities rather than owners and the moneyed elites.[12]

Football too extended its scope and deepened its cultural role. Writes Baker:

College football became a national mania in the 1920s. The autumn game spread as a mode of mass entertainment for Americans east and west, north and south, rural and urban, rich and poor – for everyone near a college or university campus. Huge football stadiums, larger even than their baseball counterparts, sprang up across the nation. Football attendance doubled within the decade. Marching bands, majorettes and cheerleaders took the field as supporting casts for the athletes. College football in the Roaring Twenties became an autumn ritual, a fiercely competitive game wrapped in tinsel and bathed in fervent partisanship. A system of football scholarships was established. 'It is at present a religion,' *Harper's* observed toward the end of the decade; 'sometimes it seems to be almost our national religion.'[13]

Even boxing, 'a favorite means of preparing American service men for the rigours of hand-to-hand combat, emerged from World War I cleansed of its seedy, back-alley image.'[14] As well, swimmers, golfers and tennis players (of both sexes), and jockeys, captured the public imagination and turned athletic skills into lucrative careers.

All this was unfolding as advances in electrification and industrialization made possible the early-twentieth-century rise of both huge corporations, such as General Electric, General Motors, and Westinghouse, and huge new distribution networks, such as the department store chains. These enterprises needed markets for their wares. According to Jeremy Rifkin and others, it was not easy during the early decades of this century to part the traditional American worker from his or her hard-earned wages for manufactured commodities, or from the time it would take to earn more money to buy them. Consistently, people preferred to trade work hours for leisure hours rather than for additional paid labour; and unemployment, created by technologization, created shrinking pools available for purchasing.[15]

One possible response to the discrepancy between the need for consumers and the growing unemployment of the 1920s, as Rifkin notes, was to share the profits from industry through higher wages, shorter work hours, and the higher employment these would produce. But this option was generally discarded in practice. With a few important exceptions (such as Ford Motors and later Kellogg's Cereals), wages did not keep pace with production or profits in the 1920s, and technological innovations continued to create successive waves of poverty-producing unemployment. Eventually, this structural contradiction would provoke the Great Depression. During the 1920s, the industrial class favoured a different strategy to promote consumption: they utilized commercial propaganda – advertising – to appeal to those who had resources to spend them.

The economic imperative of 1920s corporate consumerism set the stage for a qualitative intensification of the mobilization of fantasy, desire, and anxiety via advertising and the mass media of communications – newspapers, comic books, pulp fiction, radio, and film.[16] In order to get citizens to spend, 'the American business community set out to radically change the psychology that had built a nation – to turn American workers from investors in the future to spenders in the present,' writes Rifkin. Charles Kettering of General Motors said 'the key to economic prosperity is the organized creation of dissatisfaction.' In a phrase he summed up the mandate of the new advertising industries and the new approaches to publicity.[17] His program guides Madison Avenue to this day.

In working toward the organized creation of dissatisfaction, 'it was not long before advertisers began to shift their sales pitches from utilitarian arguments and descriptive information to emotional appeals to status and social differentiation,' Rifkin notes.[18] The sources of status themselves were affected by this campaign. It was 'no longer the ability to make things, but simply the ability to purchase them' that really began to count.[19] Kevin White points out how advertisers of men's clothing and other products in the 1920s appealed to men's gender identity:

While claiming their products would give men individuality and personality, they also imposed a kind of wholesome, crass, corn-fed, clean-cut conformity on young males that may have fitted in perfectly with the peer-led, other-directed youth culture but that boded badly for the genuine individualism of the Victorians – for 'character.' For success as a man now turned on the superficialities of dress and appearance.[20]

The consuming mentality was temporarily replaced during the Depression of the 1930s by a return to the producer values of frugality and conservation – values that would certainly mark the generation who came of age during those years. But even during this decade, the reach of advertising through newspapers and radio, and the production of extravagant images of wealth and plenty from the new Hollywood film industry, kept the dream of consumption alive. And sport, despite a five-year retreat in the early 1930s, came back stronger than ever in mid-decade, to surge ahead powerfully into the 1940s. In the United States, the New Deal, in which government-funded public works produced 'new parks, playgrounds, athletic fields, gymnasiums, swimming pools, ice-skating rinks, ski trails and public tennis courts and golf courses,' further secured sport's popularity in the 1930s. The New Deal also expanded the role of the American state in the physical culture and recreation of its citizenry.[21] And the 1930s witnessed a major revival of college football, the establishment of the National Hockey League, and the appearance of women's professional softball and basketball leagues. Internationally, the World Cup in soccer was established, and international sport came to the United States in 1932, when Los Angeles hosted the Olympic Games.[22]

Beer companies were notable among the sponsoring industries that took a special interest in sport during this period.[23] In addition, since the late nineteenth century, a whole industry of sport novelties and sport equipment had developed in association with the growth of professional sport. Entrepreneurs such as Albert Goodwill Spalding promoted their products through sport, and supported sport through advertising and political lobbying.[24]

As we have seen, in the mid-nineteenth century, sport became accepted as the clean, manly, 'character-building,' Christian way to have physical fun and avoid bad forms of sex. In this mould, sport primarily exemplified the dominant restrained sexual style expected of middle-class Victorian men, at least in their relations with women of their own class. We have traced how in the early twentieth century, as sport became a central subculture within the homosocial and heterosocial youth leisure cultures, a rougher, more sexually aggressive ideal began to appear. This trend continued into the 1930s. As sport was increasingly harnessed to the task of marketing other products, it began to show just how well it could adapt to serving a new ideological function – the physical, often overtly sexualized, exemplar of a culture of consumption – by constructing and drawing on the rough sex appeal of sport.

When radio came on the scene, sport broadcasting acted initially as a powerful inducement for buying radio sets. According to Sut Jhally, between 1922 and 1925, RCA sold over $83 million worth of radios to the enchanted American public. 'Sports events played a crucial role ... By 1925 sports broadcasts had become an integral part of radio programming – they seemed to appeal to a common denominator.'[25] However, when the market for radio sets became saturated in the 1930s, commercial radio interests worked to find other products they could market.

Sport had already shown that it could bring together large numbers of people into stadiums and arenas, sell them refreshments and souvenirs, build large facilities and infrastructures, and take the game to millions of people via newspapers and radio. What became clear during the 1930s was that sport could sell much more than just tickets, beer, hot-dogs and souvenirs. In 1939 the true profitability of the sports–media relationship was revealed to prospective advertisers. In that year Gillette paid $100,000 for the privilege of exclusive sponsorship of the World Series through single-network coverage. This enabled Gillette to have exclusive access to the baseball audience. The results were stunning. 'We couldn't believe our eyes,' Al Leonard, Gillette's public relations manager, later said of the experiment. 'Sales were up 350% for the Series. It wasn't even a new product and here were these fantastic records coming in. We didn't wait, we went running all over the country to buy every major event we could find.'[26]

With the realization that the most lucrative 'product' or commodity that sport could deliver to media owners and commercial sponsors alike was its own audience, two other crucial developments followed. First, teams began to negotiate direct contracts with radio networks. By 1938 all but three major-league baseball teams were selling radio rights. By 1939, players for the Brooklyn Dodgers were receiving average salaries of $70,000 per year and the New York Yankees and Giants over $100,000 per year as a result of their radio affiliations. College and professional football soon joined the baseball players in developing comprehensive radio contracts. Second, the primacy of advertising surged even more powerfully to the fore, particularly after the Second World War. With the Gillette experience, sport had demonstrated its ability to promote the consumption by men of sport-associated products. And so, as the cultural and political emphasis shifted to renewed industrialization and economic expansion after the war, the media sport spectacle became one of the principal conduits for gendered commercial propaganda for a growing stable of major industrial corporations. In the 1950s that spectacle was developed through the new and influential medium of television.

The convergence of radio and sport changed crucial relations of ownership, power, and accountability in the sport world. As a direct result of the dollars flowing from radio, team owners and top athletes in the 1940s and 1950s grew increasingly interested in advertising-generated media revenues and less concerned with the local game and audience. Successful sports teams had previously been owned either by individual businessmen, often press or beer barons, or had been supported by their communities (or some combination of both). But in the middle of this century, the teams that had featured local heroes and had relied on gate receipts and concession revenues for their principal funds began to look toward the national, advertising-driven electronic media for increasingly important funding sources. The media no longer covered sport and benefited from it indirectly; they now began to control sport.

The mythic power of sport – made more numinous than ever by television – was a radiant feature of the 1950s. Fuelled, streamlined, and reorganized by the Second World War and the Korean War, the industrial economies of the United States and Canada turned to the production of consumer commodities. Television was an unparalleled promotional device. At the same time, North American industries expanded their production of capital goods for domestic use and export, and a strong military-industrial complex was maintained and expanded in the service of fighting the Cold War with the Soviet Union and preserving neocolonial ties with countries across the developing world. Men such as Mickey Mantle and Joe DiMaggio were not just athletes. They were national heroes of unequalled admiration and affection, masculine and American in identical measure. Sport was firmly established throughout the public school system and formed the core of university physical education curricula. It was entrenched in both private and public recreation, and valued in military life. Little leagues located boys firmly in the matrix of masculinity and patriotism forged by the Cold War. Where a boy might have attended the local stadium to see a game once or twice a season with his father before the advent of television, now Sunday afternoons watching football or baseball around the television set became a weekly family ritual with Dad and the boys glued to the tube. Just as Mom and apple pie were the American signifiers for patriotic femininity in the 1950s, the American athlete signified patriotic masculinity.

Television, Sponsors, Sport, and Gender

The 1960s were the high-water mark of American imperialism and a time of consolidation for international corporate capitalism. At the same time, they were a decade of remarkable ideological challenge to the politics and moralities of the 1950s. They produced a very broad radicalization that resulted in the civil rights movement, the antiwar movement, the women's movement, the gay movement, environmentalism, and the beginnings of First Nations mobilizations. The 1960s also witnessed the beginnings of the disintegration of the family wage system. During this decade, the relationship between sport and television consolidated, as sport became a North American cultural site that presented a univocally masculine and patriotic front that was increasingly challenged by those it marginalized, especially black and women athletes.

The expansion of sport during this decade was qualitative, by virtue of its maturing alliance with television. Total receipts for regular season major league baseball, for example, rose from $2 million early in the decade to $9.6 million at its end. Professional football's yield increased even more dramatically: from $6.5 million to $43 million over the same period. Television deepened its links to sport itself (to teams and individuals), to other sport media (via media concentration) and to sport-associated industrial companies as it consistently expanded its own 'coverage' of sport. Corporate integration and alliance-making created new and much more powerful economic constellations in which the older interests, such as the beer companies, were able to retain and expand their stake.[27] Another result was the qualitative expansion of passive sport time around the televised spectacle, within men's and national cultures. In short, the 'athleticization' of North American culture and ideas and styles of masculinity continued apace.

It is important to note here that the large-scale monopolies increasingly characteristic of the sport–media complex would not have been able to develop to the next stage of corporate concentration and interlock without political intervention at all levels – from the 'friendly' actions of municipal governments in subsidizing arenas and stadiums (see Chapter 9) to the legislative behaviour of the federal state. Until 1961 in the United States, only individual teams – not leagues – could sell rights to broadcasters. This was not profitable for either party, for each had to compete with other teams and stations for the same audiences. The solution to the conundrum was effected by the U.S. government, which, in 1961, passed Public Law 87-33. The Celler Sports Bill in effect allowed professional sport teams to pool their broadcast rights to sell to the highest bidder, permitting them to become monopolies.[28] No local station could possibly afford the costs of the pooled teams; only the major networks had those resources, and political intervention permitted them to utilize them.

Corporations selling cars, electronic appliances, insurance, clothing, sports equipment, and cigarettes had, by the 1960s, joined the beer companies and men's grooming industries on the sport bandwagon, bringing their advertisers along with them. Drawing from the ranks of postwar graduates in economics and the social sciences, advertising agencies brought increasingly sophisticated techniques to the business of sport advertising, refining the demographic technologies begun in the 1950s.[29] Demographic methods allowed broadcasters and advertisers to identify precisely who was watching each program in terms of age, sex, region, income, and product preferences. With this information, the networks could systematically develop programming and advertising strategies in tandem with advertisers, to group, subdivide, and exploit specific audiences.

From television's inception, specific programming and advertising were targeted to women, who watched the game shows, situation comedies, and soap

operas of daytime television and bought domestic items such as laundry deter-
gent. Both sexes and all ages watched 'prime-time' television – public affairs,
entertainment, variety, sitcoms, urban police dramas, and westerns. The large
prime-time audiences made advertising worthwhile to companies with family-
oriented products to sell. But research revealed that prime-time programming
was watched by a sixty percent female audience, and held men's interests
considerably less than women's. It was the sport broadcasts, first and foremost,
that attracted solid male audiences and proved to be the most lucrative. Long
before the Dream Team, men watching men's sport were the Dream Audience.

Not surprisingly, demographic research revealed that men between the ages
of eighteen and forty-nine had the highest disposable income of any group, in
terms of decision-making power for major purchase items. In addition, men
were seen to have additional resources available to them as they began to leave
the family home as divorcing adults through the 1960s and 1970s (a process
described by social historian Barbara Ehrenreich in *The Hearts of Men*).[30] This
trend freed even more of their income from the family orbit, creating an expanded market for nonfamily, male-oriented products. By the end of the 1970s,
men's standard of living had increased by about ten percent on average upon
divorce, while women's fell by 30 percent.[31] (This process has played an important part in what has come to be known as the 'feminization of poverty,'
whereby women, and the children who are dependent on them, have become
differentially poorer than men in the overall fall in the standard of living in
North America since the late 1970s.)

With the rise of television, the male sporting audience became a gold mine
that television and sport enthusiastically developed. Having determined just
how lucrative such audiences could be, the North American television networks boosted their advertising rates for sports events consistently from the
sixties to the nineties. This made access to the sport-organized television masculinity market an expensive and therefore exclusive proposition, possible only
for extremely wealthy individuals, large corporations, and national (and international) brands. The sponsors who could afford a stake paid up, however,
convinced of the selling power of sport. As John Delorean, a former general
manager of Chevrolet, said in 1971: 'The difference in paying $7.00 a thou-
sand for sport and $4.00 a thousand for 'bananas' [prime time] is well worth it.
You know you're not getting Maudie Frickert [women]. You're reaching men,
the guys who make the decision to buy a car. There's almost no other way to
be sure of getting your message out to them.'[32]

Men's relative wealth and leisure have made them the richest target audience of choice for many sponsors and a key reason these sponsors have chosen
to ally themselves with sport throughout the postwar period. What held true in
the 1960s continues to apply in the 1990s, despite the increase in the number of

women earning wages and salaries in the intervening years. In 1992, for example, *Sports Illustrated* noted that the typical ESPN viewer 'is a male high school graduate somewhere between 35 and 49, with a household income of more than $60,000.'[33] Throughout the postwar period, sport has given the networks an unfragmented, high-income male audience that could be sold to advertisers for enormous sums. By 1964, magazines such as *Advertising Age, Broadcast, Editor and Publisher,* and *Business Week* carried a plethora of articles dealing with sports, corporate sponsors, advertising, and network television. The paired monopoly of major-league teams and major-league networks that came into being at this stage became the driving force of the sport nexus, and has produced a vast, aggressive economy with masculinist spectacle at its core.

As advertising revenues for sport continued to diversify and grow, the de facto power of television sponsorship over athletes and teams expanded. In 1961, for example, early in the marriage between U.S. television and football, fourteen NFL teams, negotiating separately for television rights, earned an average of $332,000 each in yearly broadcast revenues. Just three years later, this time negotiating as a league in the context of burgeoning television advertising revenues, teams averaged $1.1 million each. Thirty years later, in the early 1990s, television rights with NBC brought the NFL teams a collective purse of $3.6 billion. Meanwhile, each of the twenty-six major league baseball teams received $17 million per season from 1990 through 1994, as a result of a $1.2 billion contract signed with CBS in 1988, with an additional $480 million from ESPN to carry 175 games per season over four years.

In the 1980s and 1990s, as larger television revenues poured into the professional teams, star athletes who drew the audiences went for a larger share and began signing contracts with team owners and sponsor-advertisers for millions, sometimes tens of millions of dollars. Hockey superstar Wayne Gretzky, known to most Canadians simply as 'The Great One' and *Sports Illustrated*'s 'Athlete of the Decade' in 1990, was sold from the Stanley Cup champion Edmonton Oilers to the weak, poorly drawing Los Angeles Kings in 1988 for the then-breathtaking sum of $18 million. It was a national scandal in Canada, debated in the House of Commons, and a heartbreak for Edmonton. Many press commentators thought it was a crazy gamble that would never pay off. But in twenty months, the Kings' increased revenues had almost paid for the deal: ticket revenues climbed from $129,000 to $420,000. But most significant for the owners was the gain in advertising revenues, which tripled to more than $4 million a season.[34]

In the 1990s, baseball, basketball, football, and hockey players have signed multiple-year contracts in the $20 to $30 million dollar range. Even for these athletes, the revenue they receive from playing is dwarfed by the money they earn from endorsements. For example, while basketball superstar Michael Jordan earns $31.3 million a year playing for the Chicago Bulls, he earns much more from his endorsements and other business ventures: 'an astounding $47 million in endorsements.'[35]

Figure 4.1 shows the structural importance of television in the larger sport–media nexus. It shows the enabling economic links between sports organizations, television, and the other component sectors in the nexus. What this chart does not show, however, is the extent to which the apparently distinct and independent enterprises that make up the sport–media complex are parts of much larger corporate constellations with integrated business interests and strategies. In its June 3, 1996 edition, *The Nation* published a chart showing the corporate linkages in four major corporate constellations in communications in the United States. The chart sketched in and grouped the corporate players and many of the sports to which they are linked. Time-Warner, for example, is one of the big players, with (to name only a minority of its corporate holdings) *Sports Illustrated, Sports Illustrated for Kids, People,* HBO Home Video, Little, Brown and Time Life Books, The Atlanta Braves, World Championship Wrestling, the Goodwill Games, Warner Brothers motion pictures and Warner Brothers Animated, Hanna-Barbera Cartoons, CNN, CNN sports, and Turner Retail Group and Home Entertainment Licensing and Merchandising. In this description of Time-Warner's support of the 1996 Warner Bros. Michael Jordan–Bugs Bunny film *Space Jam, Toronto Star* columnist Naomi Klein illustrates the symbiotic and mutually interested actions of the corporate constellation's different parts:

For parent company Time Warner-Turner, *Space Jam* – with its link to the big money markets of kid's cartoons and professional sports – provided the perfect opportunity to flex its new synergy muscles and blow the Disney-ABC merger out of the water ... [With a] $70 million marketing blitz ... [*Space Jam*] was promoted through every orifice of the Time-Warner Empire. There are behind-the-scenes television specials on the Turner-owned Cartoon Network, and when NBA games play on Turner Network Television, they are interrupted with ads for *Space Jam.* Warner Bros. has used the movie to launch a new toy division and to open a Warner Bros. store in New York, filled with *Space Jam* promo paraphernalia. When Michael Jordan cut the ribbon at the store's opening, it was broadcast on the Atlantic Records website – a division of Warner Music, a division of Time Warner. The current issue of *Entertainment Weekly* – owned of course, by Time Inc. – plugs the *Space Jam* website and the Warner Music *Space Jam* soundtrack ... Seal, another of the *Space Jam* crooners, represents synergy within synergy for Warner Music, who not only produced the *Space Jam* soundtrack but also distribute and market Seal's other albums ... Seal's new video is intercut with

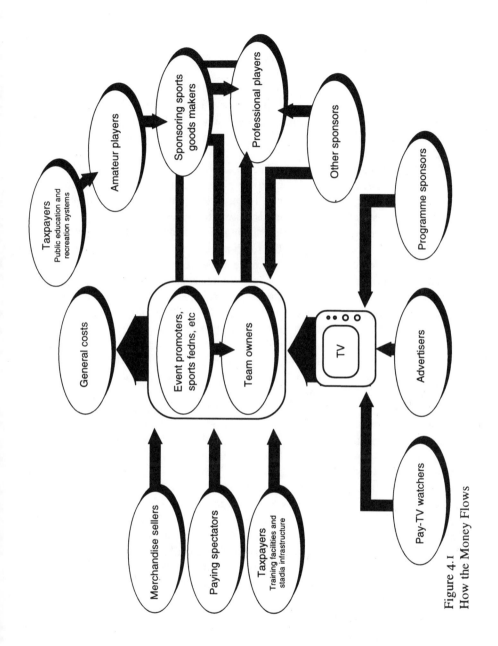

Figure 4.1
How the Money Flows

scenes from the Warner Bros. movie ... *Sports Illustrated for Kids* has published a 'special collector's edition' with all 64 pages devoted to *Space Jam*.[36]

At the same time, *The Nation*'s chart revealed that the chief constellations within the sport–media complex are themselves embedded in a much larger set of corporate constellations that include the heavy-hitters of the economy: the automotive, electronics, arms, aerospace, agri-food, pharmaceutical, chemical, insurance, and finance industries. So, for example, the four major multi-industry conglomerates identified by *The Nation* are: NBC–General Electric, CBS-Westinghouse, Disney-ABC (linked to petroleum, natural gas, and insurance interests), and Time-Warner-Turner (linked to Seagrams, Capital Group of institutional investment managers and Houston Industries).

Late in the nineteenth century, the meeting of sport and the daily press had expanded the place of sport in public life. Similarly, the marriage of sport and television – above all in terms of their male audience reach – made possible a new stage in the organization of sport and the mass media, and a larger place for both in the culture as a whole. The profits generated by sport and television together have been, by all accounts, astounding. They multiplied so many times in the sixties, seventies, and eighties that in 1986 *Sports Illustrated* predicted a devastating crash of sports television due to market glut, sport overextension, and a rebellion by even the richest corporate advertisers against the costs of sponsorship.[37] In fact, no such thing happened; the costs of sponsoring sport on television continued to grow.

Corporations are willing to pay a great deal to get exclusive access to the male sporting audience. For example, they are prepared to pay the $1.2 million rates for one thirty-second commercial spot for the NFL Super Bowl because they know their ads have a significantly better recall rate than during other programming.[38] This quality of attention justifies deals such as the one for $20 million concluded in 1995 between Coca-Cola and the NFL – one of the largest single-sponsor sports marketing contracts ever. The package, which involved all five of the networks that broadcast NFL games gave Coca-Cola worldwide rights to all marketing and promotional programs including the Super Bowl and NFL theme events. Coca-Cola, also the 'official drink of the Olympic Games,' gained the right to call itself the 'official soft drink of the NFL.' As a result, Coke's budget with the NFL came into line with that of the beer companies, with automobile companies ranking third in football sponsorship.[39]

Magazines play a smaller, yet important, role in creating the sporting audience, the mythology and culture of sport, and the masculinity market. *Sports Illustrated*, called 'America's sport bible' because of its centrality to sport as well as sport publishing, is ranked number three for top magazines in advertis-

ing revenues in the United States, drawing on the same advertisers who spon-
sor television sports. *SI* was well ahead of *Newsweek* and *Business Week* (by
over $60 million), in the mid-1990s, and is perhaps the single most important
sport communications medium. In addition to *Sports Illustrated*, a whole industry of specialized sport-related magazines – from *Runner's World* to *Muscle
Mag* – provide detailed coverage of sport stars, copious self-help information,
and advertising for sports equipment and nutrition. *Sports Illustrated for Kids*
plays an important role in developing a younger and younger audience for
sport heroes and the products they sell. 'We believe children make brand
decisions very early that they will carry into their adult lives,' said Ann Moore,
publisher of *Sports Illustrated for Kids*.[40]

The aggressive marketing of sport in the commercial mass media has created
a large economy of sport-related products. Writing for *Sports Illustrated* in
1994, Steve Rushin describes this in a vivid account of his trip to the largest
indoor shopping mall in the United States in Bloomington, Minnesota. He
begins his excursion in 'America's Original Sports Bar' where patrons watch
games on the fifty-five televisions beaming action in from around the planet.
'But,' he notes,

the most telling snapshots of sports and society today are to be seen in the Mall's more
that 400 stores: in Kids Foot Locker and Lady Foot Locker and World Foot Locker, in
Footaction USA and The Athlete's Foot and Athletic X-press, Sports Tyme and Team
Spirit and The Sportsman's Wife, in No Contest and Golf For Her and MacBirdie Golf
Gifts, in Big Leagues and Going to the Game and Wild Pitch ... I follow my nose to
Oshman's Super Sports USA, a sporting-goods concern so breathtakingly vast that one
hardly notices the basketball court, the racquetball court, the batting cage or the archery
range on its premises. Not far away, the 11,000-square foot World Foot Locker is tiny
by comparison. Every NFL, NBA and major league baseball jersey is available here.
World Cup jerseys are on display. Every icon of international sports appears to be
represented ... A friend once counted two dozen megamall stores in which you can
purchase a Starter jacket ... There are meanwhile two bookstores in the place.[41]

Today, the interdependent relationships between the athletic, industrial, and
media sectors of the sport nexus are wide and deep.[42] In 1990 the WEFA
Group of Pennsylvania, a private economic-forecasting firm, estimated the
total revenues generated by sport and sport-related activities of all types in
Canada and the United States in 1989. According to their estimates the North
American sport economy (ranging from ticket sales to the purchase of sports
equipment) was worth more than $88.5 billion annually.[43] (Compare this with
the pulp and paper industry, which earns about $50 billion annually.)[44] Over

the next ten years WEFA projected the figure to rise to $160 billion. By the year 2000 WEFA predicted that Canadian and American firms would spend $13.8 billion on advertising through sport alone, and that global sports advertising would top $30 billion. None of these figures included salaries to public education and recreation personnel involved with sport, or the huge infrastructural costs involved in sport-related public education and recreation systems. It is difficult to determine the exact size and extent of the sport nexus because appropriate statistics are not collected by public agencies and because corporations tend to keep ownership and investment information secret, refusing to disclose the nature of their holdings.[45] Still, it is clear that the money generated by the sport nexus is equivalent to the gross national products of small nations, or the budgets of large states, provinces, and cities. The public pays heavily through 'leisure' dollars, through taxes for sport training and infrastructure, and through sport-related consumption that benefits a small layer of owners, sponsors, and star athletes far more than the public itself.

Second-Wave Feminism and the Gender Crisis

Using the propagandistic power of sport to create engaging symbols and narratives of masculinity that hooked men to agendas outside and beyond sport became strategically important for the manifold interests involved in the maturing sport–media complex and the larger nexus that grew up around it in the postwar period. Through the mass media, sport culture spoke to successive cohorts of twentieth-century males as they contended with booms, busts, wars, and migrations. As a master narrative of masculinity, sport was able to provide points of identification, masculine regroupment, and symbolic affirmation in a social landscape with constantly changing gender, class, racial, and ethnic relations. Here, then, I want to locate the evolution of the sport–media complex within one of the most important social dimensions with which it interacted: the shifting gender order.

Just as the second half of the nineteenth century produced both the first wave of feminism and the consolidation of masculinism in sport, so the second half of the twentieth century, with its crises of gender, has produced another great wave of feminism and several new stages in the evolution and hypermasculinization of sport and sport culture. I argued in earlier chapters that sport evolved as an institution of social fatherhood in the nineteenth century, filling the gap left by the exodus of men from the home. I also contended that the constitution of sport as a set of masculine associations celebrating masculine bodies *in extremis* represented a cultural and political backlash against the claims and demands of first-wave feminism, which overtly politicized sex and gender issues. Sport formed a countermovement of men that took ludic and ritual ('cultural') forms – and hence escaped perception as 'political.' But it was powered by impulses to exclude women, weave a masculine generating myth, and create patriarchal identifications and values. Such impulses have substantial political implications.

During the early decades of the twentieth century, when sport's relationship to the media was widening with the reach of the daily press and radio, the father-provider family-wage system enjoyed broad social support as the ideal family form for both middle and industrial working classes in North America. While working-class women never ceased to work for wages outside the home, the higher wages of some industrial workers and skilled tradesmen provided a family wage for the upper layers of the working class, and made possible the extension of the ideal through the class as a whole. At the same time, in the context of urbanization, a developing youth culture, feminism, a world war, and a postwar boom, the Roaring Twenties, sometimes called the golden age of American sport, saw the emergence of the slender, androgynous, antimaternal gamine – the flapper – as a mass sexual ideal for women. She had a more serious counterpart – the feminist 'new woman' – who favoured a companion-ate marriage with economic independence for women. During this decade, this idea of marriage took substantial root in North American life.

Styles of masculinity were shifting as well. As we have seen, in the early decades of this century, with a global war and the first great surge in consum-erism, the Victorian ideal of the genteel, moral, but muscular Christian Gentle-man began to lose ground to a much rougher, more sexually aggressive ideal.[46] Kevin White notes the overt sexualization of this ideal with respect to manli-ness in the shift in emphasis from 'character' to 'sex appeal.' He also notes that violence, including that against women, went hand in hand with this sexualiza-tion, and that the desires and anxieties this produced among men themselves were addressed and manipulated by advertising. He notes too the expansion of pornography and sexual literature in which men figured as phallic heroes. He sees this trend to validate promiscuous, aggressive, and nonprocreative sex as more rewarding for men (who had economic and social power) than for women, but at the same time more anxiety-provoking. For it created expectations of sexual and masculine performance that were difficult to meet. Sport and its culture were prime terrains on which those expectations were forged.

The ideas of urban intellectuals, popular cultural producers, and feminists had an impact on ideas of heterosocial relationships well after the 1920s, when organized feminism subsided. Growth in educational opportunities for women, and their establishment in educational, nursing, and white-collar support jobs ensured that new ideologies about social and sexual possibilities for women as well as men continued to be generated through the Depression and war years. The hardships of the Depression brought about a revival of familial ideology, a shift to union and community organizing by working-class women, and reclamation of the poor through voluntarism and state welfare work for middle-class women. Women were organized in many different formations, from church groups to union auxiliaries. But from the 1920s to the 1960s – the forty-year nadir of feminist organizing – these organizations no longer expressed the proactive politicized inflection of feminism. As well, the generalization of ideas from the liberal discourses – sociology, psychology and psychoanalysis, sexology and family therapy – became a way in which society discussed gender issues that had been privatized by Victorian mores. And the explicitly erotic trends in literature, art, and popular pornography within a growing consumer culture over the century made erotica accessible to women as well as men.

Advances in transportation and a shorter working day brought the middle-class family father back home sooner and for potentially longer periods. But while they retained economic authority in the family, in general, fathers remained remote from their children's socialization in the domestic realm. For boys, the family remained an institution dominated by the emotional presence of women and the punitive power of men, while adult social power remained achievable only through institutions dominated by men and their values, relationships, and ideas. This emotional contradiction between a mother-dominated early socialization and a male-dominated adult life is one of the main emotional engines of hypermasculinity, and the institution that gave rise to it remained essentially intact until the Second World War. Continuing the Victorian obsession with ritually purging feminine influences from boys raised in remote-father families, American gender culture in the first half of the twentieth century continued to construct homosexuals as feminine and to fear homosexuality as a fundamental compromise of masculinity. Concern about the 'sissification' of boys was a consistent theme of both clinical and popular psychologizing. While paternal involvement in domestic childrearing remained small, sport increasingly became a main activity fathers shared with sons, and was generally understood as a tonic against effeminacy. Solidly implanted in educational and recreational systems and public spectacle, sport provided terms for masculine interaction between generations, and supplied points of engagement and transfer with educational and corporate systems.

The Second World War brought rapid and dramatic changes to the organization of the North American family and to the experience of both sexes. Hundreds of thousands of men vacated households and jobs and took up life in the largely homosocial societies of the military. Being stationed abroad opened up geographic and cultural horizons for many North Americans, and often resulted in sexual liaisons. As well, new possibilities for homoerotic life were created by mass mobilization.[47] Notwithstanding new experiences and associations, however, for the men fighting far away from home and struggling to survive in combat conditions, the war most often meant hardship, suffering, and trauma. On the home front, women grappled with the deprivations and challenges of the war. Called on to take over industrial jobs and family responsibilities and assume a new family leadership role, many women found this new independence to their liking. Both sexes found it difficult to adjust to the more limited and prescribed domestic life they were asked to resume when the war ended and governments sought to restore the previous family order – that is to say, a father-headed family-wage system as the correct and necessary complement to a booming corporate economy.

The campaign was intensive and highly politicized. In addition to economic policies in both public and private sectors that actively demoted or fired women to make way for men, historian Geoffrey Smith notes that 'medicine and psychiatry, the clergy, J. Edgar Hoover and the Federal Bureau of Investigation, the civil defense establishment, and groups like the American Social Hygiene Association all contributed to determining proper gender roles and acceptable sexual activity.'[48] Men had to contend with economic dislocation and uncertainty, and with severely limited avenues for political expression and dissent (in the form of anticommunism and McCarthyism), at the same time as they confronted lovers and wives who had changed in their absence. Women were asked to abandon jobs, their own wages, and the new sense of self-reliance and freedom that had come with them. Along with reconfinement to the home and the private sphere, they were also asked to return to repressive ideals of feminine chastity. In keeping with the official reassertion of separate gender roles, those who broke the mould were demonized in culture and in politics. 'The gendered subtext [of official policy],' writes Smith, 'marginalized middle-class white women who aspired to careers and identified non-heterosexual activity with perversion, disease, and social decay as threats to national safety.'[49]

In keeping with the paradoxical principle that repression often acts as a form of incitement, and with the possibility of maintaining ideological monolithism in the face of both history and new realities – subcurrents of nonconformist ideologies – of crime, politics, and sexual 'transgression' – also characterized the postwar period. These current of transgression were evident in both popular and bohemian culture: in films and pulp novels, in the illicit economies of crime and prostitution, in the beat movement, in women's fashions, in the movies. All of these forums provided a running counterpoint of dissent to the themes of wholesome familism validated in the dominant cultural and social policies of the era.[50]

The Hollywood films of the late 1940s and early 1950s provide examples of these tendencies.[51] In the up-beat, profamily musicals and melodramas, traditional familist values were openly celebrated, indeed dictated. But in films that have since been dubbed 'film noir,' another reality was revealed. The male characters are uprooted and adrift, or struggling to survive in dead-end jobs and stifling family obligations, or they are portrayed as unscrupulous criminals. They resent the 'good woman' – the asexual, confining wife figure (a.k.a. Madonna) – and are attracted to and fear the 'spider-woman' – the dangerous, sexualized femme fatale (a.k.a. whore), who tempts men from their familial duty, only to discard them in her selfish and instrumental ('masculine') manipulation of others. The women in these films are trouble personified, the source of men's problems, the ones to blame for their unhappiness. 'The popular image of the "bombshell" helped imbue female sexuality (and non-heterosexual, non-monogamous and non-marital sexual behaviour) with its threatening character,' writes Geoffrey Smith. 'A photograph of Rita Hayworth was actually taped to one of the H-bombs dropped in the [Bikini Atoll].'[52]

The sexual stereotypes and narrative conventions of film noir – also familiar in the works of such writers as Raymond Chandler and Mickey Spillane – were symptoms of a massive emotional-ideological trend in postwar North America: the displacement of attention from problems of class and race in the McCarthyist public world of economic and political life onto the gendered, interpersonal, domestic, and sexual terrain and onto the women – sexual or maternal – who represented that terrain.[53] Yet while this form of denial and displacement served effectively to obscure some large social fissures in uniting the nation against the Communist threat, it also spilled over into and permeated the very political life it cloaked. Thus the Cold War National Security State that emerged after 1947 in the United States carried with it great anxiety and much admonition on gender and sexual matters.'[54] As in the nineteenth-century imperial British state, gender was the organizing metaphor for world and class domination:

The specter of the Soviets as regimented he-men (and she-women) ... underscored the need for American women to take distance from their Soviet counterparts, to become as feminine as the latter were mannish, and for the nation's leaders to brandish more power than their adversaries. This perception shaped the self-image of a generation of American Cold Warriors, even as it legitimized popular cultural archetypes like Humphrey Bogart and Marlon Brando ... as well as the real life 'men' like John Wayne and Joe McCarthy ... Above all, this Cold War subtext clarified that an image of manliness, of toughness, was a *sine qua non* for American presidents and national security managers – and for dad himself.[55]

In the 1950s' masculinist social policy – from discriminatory laws against women and work to a government-approved 'production code' in Hollywood that proscribed the depiction of behaviours seen as threatening to the father-headed family – multiple authorities attempted to restore the family-wage system. At the same time, sport was approved as the sine qua non of patriotic American boyhood and masculinity. Yet, while all this was taking place at the cultural and political levels, key features of capitalist economic development – inflation and consumerism – were already eroding the very base of this family form. Never fully recovered from the war experience, the family-wage system began to unravel through the 1960s. In the late 1960s, when consensual divorce was finally legalized, divorce rates increased dramatically in North America. Consumerism and the supporting culture of advertising raised expectations of what constituted minimum acquisitions, while inflation diminished buying power. In addition, marriage breakdown compelled more and more women to work as primary family supporters.

All these trends, within the expansive world of postwar capitalism, pushed women to seek education and work outside the home in ever larger numbers. In the 1990s, women form 45 per cent of the paid workforce, a tremendous change from the 1950s, when their participation rates were below 20 per cent. The barriers that women encountered as they were compelled to compete with men in the labour market were perhaps the most radicalizing of all the underlying structural factors responsible for the rise, in the 1960s, of the second great wave of feminism. However, as participants in the sexual revolution, issues of sexual rights and sexual representation were also crucial to the women who were part of second-wave feminism. Feminists grew critical of the values of the new (heterosexual) male-oriented culture of consumer sexuality divorced from family and children that had emerged into the cultural and economic mainstream in the late 1950s and early 1960s. *Playboy* magazine blazed the trail, then *Penthouse* and many other, less slick, pornographic publications began to appear on corner newsstands, full of images whose explicitness had previously been found only in sleazy downtown stores. Today, a multibillion-dollar publishing and video industry exists to market sexually explicit material whose points of distribution are the local mall or corner store.

The ideal women pictured in the mainstream pornography of the 1960s and 1970s were different from those in earlier pornography: the obvious 'whore' in older works gave way to a young, acquiescent, sporty girl next door as the appropriate partner in the single man's life of 1960s and 1970s sexual hedonism. At the same time, leading athletes such as Jim Brown and Joe Namath were figured as overtly sexual and promiscuous 'bad boys.' Similarly to the 'underworld primitive' style of masculinity in the 1920s, the bad boy was depicted as increasingly more attractive than the good in cultural production from the 1960s on. Women's magazines such as *Cosmopolitan* and *Glamour* instructed young women in how to become the sexual playmates favoured by this new, and affluent, male culture. Meanwhile, the wife and mother, caricatured in cartoons and attacked by editors such as Hugh Hefner, Al Goldstein, and Bob Guccione, was constructed as the primary menace to this way of life.[56] In detaching sex from commitment (as well as from procreation) the men's magazines sought to extend permissibility for nonmarital sex for men, and therefore to secure the sexual availability of appropriate sexual partners. This meant social and political proselytizing on issues that would extend support for nonprocreational sex to women as well: hence the 'liberalism,' indeed radicalism, of these magazines' editorial policies on abortion, birth control, sexual orientation, and free speech. In the 1960s, they gained energy from the willingness of a whole cohort of young women to explore their own nonprocreational sexuality with the aid of the birth control pill.[57]

Questions of sexuality moved into the cultural foreground due to a number of factors: the increasing tendency to deal explicitly with sex in mainstream culture; the tendency to quantify sexuality (Kinsey, Masters and Johnson); the further popularization of psychoanalytic ideas; and the social weight of the preoccupations of the youth culture. This cultural emphasis on the sexual was, in part, commercially stimulated and nurtured. But commerce was also working with and responding to the feelings and ideas created by broader tendencies in gender relations and masculine identity that were linked to the changing place of men and women within a consumer-capitalist society, marked by deep economic fissures and internal political disagreements.[58] As the identity-anchor of the provider role weakened for men in the 1950s, 1960s, and 1970s, the importance of sexual performance per se – as much of it and with as many women as possible – grew in significance in masculine self-definition.[59] It was no longer good enough to be a success in financial terms; now a man had to become a tireless sexual achiever. Elaborate tales of phallic mastery filled the pages of mass market pornography, establishing standards of performance bound to provoke anxiety in the hearts of even the most enthusiastic sexual athletes at the same time as they fed a seemingly inexhaustible need for sexual stimulation. The phallus, a symbol of masculinity since ancient times, took on even greater mythic proportions.

But where Victorian men were able to resort to the dogma of conservation of sexual energy and the privacy of the bedroom to justify or obscure sexual reluctance, inadequacy, or idiosyncrasy, now sexologists studied every penile nerve and impulse, and the pornographic culture demanded in sex ever-increasing levels of consumption. Hendrik M. Ruitenbeek, in his 1970 book *Sexuality and Identity*, wrote that 'men, heterosexuals and homosexuals alike, are tortured by the very thought of not being considered virile; their sexuality seems much more in peril than that of women, who still seem to be able to hold on to established concepts of femininity.'[60] But when masculinity is in crisis, it follows that femininity will also be unstable. As it turned out, both sexes have been struggling with gender and sexual definitions ever since.

This crisis of masculinity was further exacerbated by the strains of trying to construct a masculine identity in families headed by remote fathers. The boys of the Depression, the war years, and the postwar period (the influential male cohorts of the 1960s, 1970s, 1980's, and 1990s) not only had to cope with the challenges of differentiating themselves from the women who had been their primary parents and teachers throughout childhood; they also had to assimilate and position themselves within the contradictory definitions of masculinity that had been generated by their culture. In response to the traumas of depression and war, the mass media – films, comic books, and, eventually, television – offered hypermasculine fantasy figures embodying exaggerated ideals of performance within the larger American myth of limitless success. In the 1940s and 1950s, the superheroes of boy's culture – Batman, Spiderman, Superman – joined national athletes in a new pantheon of American boyhood.[61] Their continuing revival in film in the 1990s attests to the imprints they left. As well, we can plot their evolution, via the rite of passage of Vietnam, into the musclebound, violent hero of today's men's action genres.

For boys trying to construct their individual identities, cultural ideals of masculinity that emphasize antifeminine instrumentality create, in the words of sport sociologist Michael Messner, 'a very fragile and ambivalent gender identity, which results in the development of ... psychosocial boundaries which make closeness and intimacy difficult.'[62] Such a gender identity would be responsive to the growing trend to legitimate nonprocreational sex. For such men, the sexual practices of the 'new virility' and the consumer-pornographic culture could deliver on two important levels: they valorized 'uninvolved' sexual exchange, thus reducing periods of intimacy, and, through the traditional coding of gender differences, provided symbolic confirmation of men's difference from and superiority to women. Geared to appease certain deep, underlying psychosexual needs, however, these cultural expressions also incited men by presenting a cultural field of constant sexual activity. Finally, the cultural expressions exacerbated men's sexual needs by setting up impossible expectations of sexual behaviour that corresponded badly to men's, as well as to women's, capacities and needs. Whatever his real failings, the *Playboy* man became the ideal male representative of the 1960s capitalism and its world political order. He was behind 'the most pervasive male image' of the 1960s cinema: James Bond, of whom Joan Mellon notes:

As portrayed by Sean Connery, [Bond] could relate to women only on a comic-book level by transferring to the screen the pubescent distaste for women disguised as lust for female objects like those flaunted by *Playboy* magazine ... Bond never doubted that women were sex objects eternally ready and grateful for his use; nor did he doubt his mission as a secret agent holding together the empire of the 'free world.'[63]

But while James Bond linked Anglo-American global dominance and sexual conquest in the popular imagination, the social order he represented was facing massive challenges to its legitimacy. The political hyperconformity of the 1950s gave way in the 1960s to a left-leaning youth radicalization in the industrialized nations that expanded through the decade, developing side by side with national liberation struggles in Africa, Asia, and Latin America, and taking the Chinese and Cuban revolutions to be exemplary political models. In many European countries, mass left-wing student movements led huge social mobilizations, resulting in moments of political crisis for governments of the day. In France, in May and June 1968, this wave crested in a near-revolutionary situation. In the Unites States as well, the sixties were a decade of turmoil: antinuclear demonstrations, civil rights marches, student protests, and antiwar rallies expressed and heightened the key tensions of the decade. And for Americans, the 1960s were a decade of political executions: John F. Kennedy and his brother Bobby, Malcolm X, and Martin Luther King. Malcolm's and King's deaths left the Black civil rights movement without its most mature and charismatic leaders, as city after city succumbed to ghetto riots and destruction. Young, middle-class antiwar protesters organized in every community, and were gassed and beaten on campuses across the country, even as their cause continued to win adherents. These were key features of the turbulent context in which the new feminism emerged, put the sexual myths of the gender order into question, and politicized intimate life.

In politicizing sexual life, women assumed a new agency with respect to their own sexualities, as well as to those of men, which did not fit well with the patriarchal sexual legacy and the sexual identities this legacy had helped to construct. By the later 1960s and early 1970s, young women who had been raised and come of age in the newly 'open' culture of sexual hedonism and participated in it both more and less enthusiastically had deconstructed the bedroom and revealed it to be a place of considerable unhappiness for women.

Best-selling works such as Ann Koedt's *The Myth of the Vaginal Orgasm* and Shere Hite's *The Hite Report* indicated that the penis was not an instrument of endless pleasure for the majority of women, but a fetish for men, in whose gratification female pleasure was very often sacrificed. Feminists called for an end to the double standard in sexual behaviour (based on the maternal/sexual dichotomy), sexual satisfaction for women as well as men, and the same autonomy as men in choice of sexual partners. The masculine anxieties provoked by the intense social, political, and gender tensions of the times became evident at the cultural level in a qualitative heightening of male violence in cultural production: in film, television, publishing, video games, popular music, and sport. Albert Broccoli's choreographed ballets gave way to Sam Peckinpah's ejaculatory gun fests. Stylized, elegant, and urbane sixties hero James Bond gave way to the gritty, mean, parochial *Dirty Harry*. This phenomenon, which I explore in Chapter 6, expressed an increasingly defensive and explosive sense of masculinity, challenged by the contradictory, not to say irreconcilable, demands and possibilities of ideal manhood and real life in the late twentieth-century.

Another crucial area of gender conflict and feminist analysis was the more mundane, but ultimately equally important, issue of domestic labour and 'free time' – time spent doing neither paid nor unpaid (household and childrearing) work. Tracts from this period such as 'I want a wife' and 'The politics of housework' showed how, far from being a trivial matter, such time is at the heart of men's and women's differential capacity to perform economically and politically – that is, to support themselves and their children in the world, and to control that world for their benefit. The struggles between men and women over housework and time away from family responsibilities bitterly divided millions of couples, only some of whom considered this issue from an overtly political perspective. What was often at stake in these arguments was men's right to spend time away from mate and family, not only to be 'at work,' but also to be 'with the boys,' playing sports or watching the game at the local bar or at home on weekend afternoons, while women tend to laundry, cleaning, shopping, and childcare.[64] Women are rarely encouraged to be physically active and enjoy their chosen activity in homosocial company at similar times and in similar ways. As I have argued at length in my critique of Engel's theory of women's oppression, men are the leisured gender.[65]

Thirty years after the beginning of feminism's second wave, almost twice as many hours of paid labour are required to earn a standard of living equivalent to what an average male salary could purchase in the mid-1970s. Compared with the 1950s, the figure is more than twice as much. The forty-hour work week is a thing of the past in North America. As women have increasingly been drawn into the workforce and men have declined to take on equal responsibility for unpaid domestic work, the gendered inequities in time and resources available to pursue sport and other 'leisure' activities (it would be better to think of these activities as those of 'self-care') have grown acute. The sport–media complex is complicit in this situation, because it has competed through a gendered promotional discourse for men's attention and resources in ways that generally promote men's continuing leisure privilege and sexual exploitation of women. As *Playboy* magazine, a major exploiter of the masculinity market, has said of itself: 'What a man does with his own time is our business.'[66] And this applies equally to commercial sport culture as a whole. Instead of encouraging an equal division of paid and unpaid work to resolve the problems between men and women within the family in late capitalist society, commercial men's cultures – both erotic and sporting – have proposed ways to keep men's economic, social, and libidinal energies tied up away from home, in nonprocreational sex with young women, in homosocial relations with men, and in a 'lifestyle' based on the consumption of commodities produced by the large corporations that enthusiastically exploit the masculinity market. This idea is illustrated in a two-page ad by *Playboy* in a 1992 issue of *Advertising Age*:

Clear Blue skies. Six inches of fresh powder. New skis, boots and bindings. This is the payoff. The reward for the hard work that earns the average *Playboy* man a household income of more than $35,000. And an indication of the kind of balance *Playboy* readers want in their lives. That's what makes *Playboy* the best-selling men's magazine on the planet. Its pages are packed with the things men truly enjoy. From sports to films, from gorgeous cars to beautiful women, from the pleasures of HiFi to the joys of mountain highs, *Playboy* helps men who want to take time out make the most of that time. If you have a product that appeals to this side of men, put it in the environment that takes it out of the office – and into their lives. *Playboy*. We're tuned in to men.[67]

Men's sexualized, liberal, consumer culture, of which sport has been an important component, is the characteristic new development in masculinism since the 1960s. Despite the tenaciousness of the double standard, it has, along with the struggle of feminism for sexual and reproductive rights, opened up a limited space for women's experience of nonmarital sexuality. In this sense, the new men's culture is different from traditional patriarchy, which ties women's sexuality to their husbands. However, it has not in any other ways challenged men's entitlement to sex and 'leisure' or to the larger prerogatives of masculine dominance.

The dominant quality of ideal hypermasculinity in late-twentieth-century North American mass culture has been successfully established despite the emergence of many different types of 'femininities' and 'masculinities.' Since the 1960s, the women's and gay movements have affected all spheres of society in important ways. Women, whether or not they have self-consciously identified as feminists, have assumed tasks and qualities in the labour market previously regarded as 'masculine.' Communities and subcultures of gay men and lesbians represent de facto possibilities of living gender, at least in part, beyond the constraints of compulsory heterosexuality. From the 1960s on, a politicized vocabulary emerged that made the power imbalances in gender and gendered relationships more transparent and amenable to political struggle. Some legal and political barriers to equality have been taken down (more in Canada than in the United States) and the principle of gender equality established in jurisprudence and political discourse. These developments have explicitly and implicitly challenged masculinist gender values and hypermasculinist ideals, showing that they too are not seamlessly hegemonic. Yet many of these values and ideals remain dominant and powerful.

The dominance of ideal hypermasculinity in the culture of our changing gender order has resulted from a dialectical process in which the sport–media complex has used constructs and identifications of gender, combined with those of community, country, class, ethnicity, sexual orientation, and race, to market sport and sport-related products. Marketing and promotional discourse have proceeded in interactive response to the measured 'needs' of the consuming audience of sport, both reacting to and affecting ideas of gender. Ideas of gender, in turn, respond to changes in actual economic and political relations, and to dominant ideas in popular culture, even when these are highly contradictory. The next chapter examines in greater detail some of the ways in which the sport–media complex, as a gendered entity, generates ideologies of hypermasculinity and the ways in which gender and marketing are intimately connected.

5

Spectacle, Commerce, and Bodies: Three Facets of Hypergender in the Sport Nexus

From 1981 to 1996, I lived in an economically, ethnically, and racially diverse Toronto neighbourhood, through which I developed several jogging and walking routes. As I tended to take my exercise at the same time as school let out (three to four o'clock in the afternoon), I was able to make my own informal survey of gender participation in unsupervised play in my neighbourhood's public school grounds. At the public schools serving the lower-middle- and working-class components of the neighbourhood, only boys played sports on school property after-hours and on weekends. Sometimes the boys grouped themselves along ethnic-racial lines, in groups that were often sport-dependent (West Indian boys played cricket, Italian boys soccer). But just as often, in common sports such as hockey, basketball, and baseball, the impromptu teams were ethnically and racially mixed. Though girls might sometimes come to watch and socialize with the active boys, in general their absence from the scene was striking. For the most part, once the school crowd dissipated after the final bell, the girls vanished. The boys stayed on, occupying the playing fields, concrete terraces, and tracks, and hanging out at park benches and street curbs in boisterous groups. In these ways, young males were staking their claim to physical control of public space without even knowing it.

At schools serving the upper-middle-class components of the neighbourhood, there was generally less unsupervised activity in the school grounds after school hours and fewer young people playing in the streets. As well, some supervised girls' sports were in evidence on some weeknights, notably baseball and soccer. But the unsupervised sports activity that took place in these schoolyards showed the same gender composition as in the schools serving the less affluent parts of the neighbourhood: boys only. Road hockey, the universal sport played by Canadian boys of every ethnic origin and all social classes, was strikingly male-only in all parts of the neighbourhood. At the local high school, the outdoor track and playing fields were dominated by teenage boys from a variety of class, ethnic, and racial origins, though some young Black women of West Indian origin could sometimes be seen training.

This snapshot of one urban neighbourhood turns out to be representative in many ways of the larger North American experience. Organized attempts to include girls in sport by increasing resources at all levels of public education and recreation systems since the 1970s have made a significant difference in the supervised integration of girls and young women, especially in the more affluent classes. But the spontaneous expression of sport culture implied in popular, unsupervised, childhood neighbourhood sport remains male terrain. This is true of adult recreational sport as well, with similar class variations. The public tennis courts in my neighbourhood – located in the parks in the professional and upper-middle-class sections – were always in use, by people of all ages, though more young than old. Males outnumbered females roughly seven to three, and they played in single-sex and mixed pairs. In the lower-middle- and middle-class parts of the neighbourhood, there were soccer pitches and a cricket field, where men, often ethnically organized, played in gender-exclusive teams. Women were absent from these games except as spectators. Organized sport exhibits similar symptoms. Public skating rinks, basketball courts, baseball diamonds, football fields, and indoor and outdoor tracks are all still overwhelmingly given over to boys' and men's sports.

There are many facets to the engendering qualities of contemporary sport culture and its larger role as a dominant, masculinist institution. For reasons outlined in the last chapter, it is impossible to account for the gendered evolution of sport without acknowledging the profound partnership it has forged with the commercial mass media of communications in the twentieth century, especially television. This chapter focuses on three very distinct ways in which the sport–media relationship has addressed and influenced gendered ideals, expectations, and behaviours in the latter part of the twentieth century. First, I look at how sport has evolved from a local, active, and participatory experience to one that is largely abstract, passive, and spectatorial. Second, I look at the manipulation of gender anxiety and sexual desire through sport and advertising. Finally, in my discussion of the athleticized body aesthetics for the two genders, I consider the various strategies of symbolic disqualification of women athletes as complementary to those of overqualification of men athletes.

From Participation to Spectacle: Sport, Entertainment, and Hypermasculinity

Some sport scholars, such as Michael Novak in *The Joy of Sports*, maintain that sport is a special kind of cultural practice that transcends the limits of its social and economic origins. Nonutilitarian play, the pleasure of the body and group expression, the development of solidarity, and the expression of creativity have a special role in providing a space that is free from the harsh constraints of industrial society. Novak writes:

> The basic reality of all human life is play, games, sport; these are the realities from which the basic metaphors for all that is important in the rest of life are drawn. Work, politics, and history are an illusory, misleading, false world. Being, beauty, truth, excellence, transcendence – these words, grown in the soil of play, wither in the sand of work. Art, prayer, worship, love, civilization: these thrive in the field of play. Play belongs to the Kingdom of Ends, work to the Kingdom of Means. Barbarians play in order to work; the civilized work in order to play.[1]

In this view of sport as pleasure, sport is distinct and apart from all those alienating activities that are compulsory, demanding, and painful – working, studying, fighting. The 'sport as joyful play' approach equates the functions and effects of sport with play, art, and spirituality. Many passionate sports writers, such as *Sports Illustrated*'s Frank Deford, William Oscar Johnson, and Steve Rushin, share this approach. They deplore the attachment of instrumental commercial and political agendas to sport. They see these agendas as corrupting, smothering, or displacing sport's intrinsic transcendent rewards and values.

   Though it shares some commonalities with this view of sport, the Marxian wing of sport studies sees this as an idealized position, a belief that sport can transcend utilitarianianism and alienation, rather than a true perception of its ability to do so. These scholars believe that what makes sport unique is not the generic physical activities that it shares with other cultures, but how it organizes, ritualizes, and ascribes value to these activities, and how it mobilizes physical energy in keeping with the economics and politics of industrial societies. From the Freudian-Marxist ideas of J.M. Brohm and the writers of the French 'anti-sport' journal *Quel corps?*, to the historical English readings of British class cultures by John Hargreaves, Alan Tomlinson, Paul Willis, and others, to Canadian and American historical reconstructions and sociological analyses – all sport scholars who work to any extent with Marxist ideas emphasize the powerful ligatures between sport and the organization of labour. Likewise, scholars who approach sport from a feminist perspective, and/or from a perspective concerned with understanding the workings of racism, also stress the close relationships between sport and social stratification. Many of the writers in these broad groups agree that sport, particularly popular activity, can and often does deliver a number of positive outcomes: physical exercise and release, group coordination, a sense of play, and occasions for various forms of spiritual communion and community bonding. But these experiences are seen as framed by, not separate from, a matrix of social structures, ideologies, and possibilities.

Yet many of these critical writers, in their attachment to and love of sport, share with the idealists a sense of the liberatory potential of sport and physical culture. Much of their affection for sport stems from the play, pleasure, and bonding that sport is capable of delivering. Indeed, physical games and ritual culture, if changed, could and should be major sources of pleasure and solidarity for both sexes and all ages. Concerns with the negative effects of commercialization, commodification, and media control of sport and physical culture are often voiced in terms of the 'degradation' of sport – a phenomenon with many different facets.[2] The way in which the positive qualities of participatory sport have been replaced by the values of sport as spectacle is one of the most troubling of these.[3] The rule changes, extra-athletic 'packaging,' star focus, and loss of player control characteristic of late-twentieth-century sport have resulted from the ever-growing weight of the spectacle within sport. From participation, 'a manifestation of the play element in human activity,' sport in the twentieth century has undergone a qualitative shift to become spectacle, 'played for and shaped into a form which will be "consumed" by spectators searching for titillating entertainment.'[4]

John Sewart analyses the series of changes made to football in the early 1970s, by agreement of network executives and team owners, to boost football's falling gate receipts and diminishing television ratings. For example, games were rescheduled to Mondays, Thursdays, and Saturdays for a wider television audience, disrupting a seventy-year tradition of high-school games on Friday night, college games on Saturday, and professional football on Sunday afternoons. This dislocated community-based activities and increased the overall weight of the professional game within the larger football system. In 1976, the Super Bowl was played at night for the first time to get higher television ratings. In addition, numerous entertainment devices were introduced by the networks to attract viewers: microphones on officials, slow-motion and stop-motion videotape, instant replays, and isolated cameras and split screens. These had the effect of altering the perception of the game as a flowing continuity, creating a heightened focus on brutal as well as skilful plays, and magnifying the status of the individual player out of the context of the whole game. As Sewart points out, many fans now prefer the recorded replays to live action.[5]

Other professional sports underwent similar changes. In professional basketball, zone defences have been abolished, and a three-point shot and the twenty-four-second clock have been added, all to increase action, scoring, and ball turnovers. In professional baseball, the pitcher's mound has been lowered, reducing the speed of the ball and giving the batter (seen as the offence) greater advantage; the strike zone has been enlarged to encourage more hitting; fences in some parks have been moved closer to home plate in order to increase home runs; relief pitchers have been given fewer warm-up pitches; managers' trips to the mound to talk with the pitcher have been limited; umpires have been instructed to keep the game moving at a faster pace; artificial playing surfaces and night games have been added. In hockey, the NHL has expanded into the southern United States, and the Stanley Cup Final is played in June.[6] Major changes have been made in these sports to abet their function as entertainment and spectacle, even when these changes have not benefited the majority of players (those who toil in the feeder systems of the major leagues and those who play sport recreationally). The packaging of sport spectacles now includes paid cheerleaders and 'mascots' – people dressed as cartoon creatures, who often make their appearances in helicopters or parachutes; giant video screens showing replays and advertisements that dwarf the live players; wall-mounted television screens in bathrooms and at concession stands; and public-relations programs in which famous athletes make public appearances at media and community events that have nothing to do with their sport but increase the perception of professional athletes as culture heroes, and act as free sport advertising.

Communications and sport sociologist Richard Gruneau notes that 'the media favour a highly visible, star-studded, personality driven form of sport because they've discovered that this sport form best organizes and exploits their audiences.'[7] Yet if the individual star athlete has risen in importance, all those who play these sports, as a group, have progressively lost control of the game as revenues from sport spectacle have been used to fund an enormous superstructure of officials and entrepreneurs. In 1966, for example, the ratio of athletes to nonplaying employees in the NFL was eight-to-one. By 1986, it was thirty-to-one. With the growth of a huge superstructure of coaches, managers, owners, and media in the core men's sports came a loss of player control, along with many of the intrinsic pleasures and benefits of sport. The power of coaches, managers, and owners increased exponentially.[8] Despite the big salaries earned by the stars, 'it's pretty much an authoritarian, militarist kind of system,' David Meggyesy noted in 1986.

In *Out of Their League*, I talked about the system as being essentially dehumanizing to the athlete. You're a professional athlete, you're thirty years old. You have a wife and children and the coach says you have to be in at 11 o'clock and comes and bed checks you. It's like checking twelve year olds in summer camp. It's symbolic, but symbols have a lot of meaning. You have to wear a certain kind of uniform on the road. You don't talk back to the coach, you don't have any feedback into the system as an employee. I think you're more than an employee. It is a system almost of neo-slavery; as employees we're in a similar position to that of employees in the 1860s in this country, in terms of workers being able to protect their jobs or any kind of job security. That doesn't exist in professional sports. It's a very ruthless, competitive system, where athletes are pitted against each other to make the team.[9]

A story entitled 'Maximum Exposure,' in a 1990 issue of *Sports Illustrated* brought Meggyesy's point home. The main photo for the story featured Mike Elkins, a 'big young quarterback,' standing exposed in his briefs on a harshly lit platform, while an older man took his measurements in front a crowd of 150 owners, general managers, head coaches, assistant coaches, personnel directors, and scouts of the college football scene. This gathering is what *SI* called 'the most revealing part of the college football draft process – a ritual dubbed the Meat Market.' Elkins was one of seventy-five players who would 'parade around in their underwear' under their watchful eyes. In the words of reporter Jill Lieber, 'until he was drafted on April 23, Elkins was under a powerful microscope ... he was poked, prodded, interrogated and graded by a number of NFL teams.' 'I felt like a prize bull at the county fair,' Elkins said of his experience, which he found embarrassing and painful.[10]

The physical objectification of male athletes that takes place in commercial sport is not dissimilar to the sexual objectification of women. The difference however is that its erotics stress the potential of the male body for strength and domination rather than for curves and acquiescence. 'You look at size potential,' George Young, general manager of the New York Giants, told *SI*.

Can the player add weight? Is he fragile? You worry if an offensive lineman has thin hips, because he won't be able to explode well through his legs. A defensive lineman with skinny arms will have to prove he can muscle somebody. And how many running backs with small calves run fast? ... It's a livestock show, and it's dehumanizing, but it's necessary ... if we're going to buy 'em, we ought to see what we're buying.'[11]

From the athlete's point of view, the potential for earning more than most corporate presidents is a big incentive to put up with this sort of treatment. But only a few of those who train ever reach this pinnacle. Further, even as an incentive, money does not dissipate much of the day-to-day alienation among professional athletes, alienation that seriously erodes the pleasure that could be delivered if sport were organized differently, that is, with less emphasis on competition and pain. In former Notre Dame player Allen Sack's estimation, even for professional players, the rewards of playing football are extrinsic to the playing of the game itself:

I think if you asked most players, you would probably get this answer, whether they love the game or not. I think they'd all admit that [the college or professional game] is not much fun, that it gives little intrinsic satisfaction. Generally speaking, football is brain concussions, it's contusions of your thigh, it's the cartilages which are being operated on, it's blood, it's pain. So what do you get from it? It's an outer-directed game rather than inner-directed. You get accolades from the public. You get big cars. When I was at Notre Dame, I flew from coast to coast by jet. The airlines diverted their flight plans so that the Notre Dame football team could fly over the Grand Canyon on the way to California ... One hundred thousand people came to see us play. Now, was that fun? I got kicked in the groin twice in that game. It was the last game of my life. It was kind of a symbolic way for me to end my career, bent over on the sidelines. No, that was not fun, but certainly in the locker room afterward, with Bill Cosby and all the other celebrities walking through, the extra money that I would get, and so forth – the extrinsic rewards were overwhelmingly gratifying. I think that is the 'fix' that the modern day athlete gets on. And I think that's to the impairment of their ability to enjoy their sport.[12]

The commercialization and commodification of men's sport in the television era have played a large role in turning professional athletes into modern-day gladiators, exchanging alienation, injury, and pain for material and social rewards. Chapter 8 takes a detailed look at the performance-enhancing drug culture in Olympic sports – one of the most perverse ways in which athletes' physical sacrifice is required by the sport–media complex. Olympic athletics involve a form of gladiatorial violence that is primarily self-inflicted (in the form of extreme training regimes). In numerous men's team sports and in boxing, training regimes are equally extreme and punishing (steroids are endemic to football, for example, as well as to track and field). But in these sports, exercising physical violence against others is also mandatory.

Inescapably, the value assigned to the size and violence of the athletes has transformed certain elements of the way sports are played. For example, some violence has always been present in men's hockey in Canada and the United States.[13] But in the high-combat spectacle that the NHL has cultivated in the last twenty-five years, violence has become central to the heart and meaning of the play. The star and his 'enforcer' have become the two most important trend setters and high earners. 'One factor contributing to the high level of violence in the NHL is that the players are bigger, faster and more skilful than in the past,' *Sports Illustrated* commented in the early 1990s, reversing the causal relationship (players are bigger and faster because of the premium on violence). Still, the following observation is true: 'The undersized player with fair-to-middling handling ability no longer occupies the 16th, 17th or 18th spot on a roster. That spot may well be taken by a player with no redeeming social skills or social value – your classic goon.'[14] For hockey writer William Houston, the NHL's emphasis on violence has produced a serious 'decline in skills evident at all levels.' In a four-part series for the *Globe and Mail* in 1997, Houston traced the reasons for the waning of Canada's superpower status in hockey. He identified the NHL policy of cultivating aggression, and its consequences as it filtered down into the minor levels, as most culpable for the present state:

Today, Canada's best junior players are aggressive and hard-working. They skate with strength and speed, and they shoot the puck with as much force as anyone in the world. But even among the most talented prospects it is rare to see a flashy show of stickhandling, a slick move or a fancy pass ... the skill players are all coming from Europe.[15]

Almost a decade ago, *Sports Illustrated* noted that 'if the NHL were to make the penalties for fighting *and* high-sticking costly enough, both forms of mugging would stop, and all the more swiftly if teams were banned from bringing up replacement fighters from the minors when the resident pugs receive suspensions.'[16] However, as Houston points out, violence was the way to hook new audiences in expanding markets, a way to deal with the thinning of the talent pool after league expansion, and it continued to be promoted. Wayne Gretzky, from his unassailable position as the greatest hockey player of his era, opposed fighting in hockey for a long time. But when he took on the mantle of ownership in 1994, he publicly withdrew his opposition to violence, to the dismay of millions of hockey parents all over the continent. He explained his action, stating that fighting 'is good for the sport.'[17]

The emphasis on larger, tougher players in increasingly violent games is evident throughout men's professional sport. In the case of football, the extent to which this emphasis is commercially driven and media promoted is illustrated by two all-star games that NFL players put on for themselves and the public during their 1982 strike against the NFL owners. There was very little money at stake for the players, about $2000 each between winner and loser. 'The most amazing thing happened,' David Meggyesy recalled:

You had all these tremendously skilled professional athletes out there from across the league, and they played hard. There was respect, they played very tough football. But nobody got hurt. Nobody was out there under the coach's whip trying to kill someone, or maim somebody, or trying to take somebody out of the game ... Our all-star games showed that you can play football aggressively and well, but you can eliminate this notion that you have to hurt other players. Football can celebrate sportsmanship at its very best. But what you have now is a celebration of avariciousness and greed.[18]

To drive this point home, Meggyesy recalled what Jack Tatum, the player responsible for paralysing opponent Daryl Stingley, had written about the instructions he had received from the owners. 'In his book,' said Meggyesy, 'Tatum talks about the fact that the owners told him he had to maim people or he wasn't going to get a better contract the following year ... They actually told him that. Most players face similar pressure, even though most owners don't put it so bluntly.[19] Clearly, for professional athletes the big dollars, as well as the accolades, provide the incentives to play under authoritarian and violent conditions.

What many sports enthusiasts value in sport is the way it can practise and model group solidarity. But the heightened emphasis on the violent dramatics of TV spectacle and the focus on individual athletic stars cancel much of this valued team experience. The commercially driven spotlight trained on these star athletes inevitably casts their teams and the symbolic and existential significance of egalitarian group play in deep cultural shadow. The effort and necessity of team work, the valorization of each component as essential to the whole, the valorization of collective spirit based on dynamic cooperation, fades from cultural view. Because of the enormous impact professional sport has on amateur and youth sport, young athletes and coaches look increasingly to a style of play that makes the star the focal point of the game. This has consequences for how we view and experience sport, and, thanks to the place of sport in our culture, for how we measure success and failure, and what it takes to 'win.'

Today, many salaries for professional athletes are on a par with or greater than those of major film stars and top corporate executives. It is not surprising that these salaries should become a major point of contention between players and owners, as the baseball strike and hockey lockout of 1994 showed. Having expanded and commercialized these games, owners found they could not maintain profit margins, keep the small-market teams alive, and pay limitless salaries to the players. For their part, the players felt that owners' profits, not their salaries, should subsidize the expansion. These disputes were, in fact, feeding-frenzies of avarice on both sides. They displayed a sense of entitlement to the proceeds of major league sports that never considered the interests of the community or the younger players whose apprenticeships sustain the upper stratum.

In fact, while the earnings of the top players glitter at the top of the sport pyramid, the economic reality for the majority of boys and men who play and train in the broad feeder systems of professional sport is generally grim. There are many accounts of successful athletes who have had to neglect their education and personal development.[20] Even among the most famous and highly paid, the unifocal intensity required to make it in sport has often had negative consequences for the quality of many athletes' lives. One consistent motif in sport reporting is the story of the broken-down former pro athlete who, poor and suicidal or strung out on steroids or alcohol, turns assaultive and murderous.[21]

College sport scholarships – the basis for the entire football and basketball systems in the United States – do not, as a rule, provide good college educations for young athletes. Instead, the athletes are temporarily employed, exploited, and then discarded.[22] The system makes money for some colleges and their sports departments, but it does not profit most of the young athletes who exit the system with no sellable skills, and often without basic competence in anything other than sport. In baseball and hockey, a system of minor league and farm teams supplies the major leagues with their players. But though the feeder systems are officially separate from the educational system, the reality is the same: young athletes who want to make it to the major leagues have to devote their entire lives to the development of their skills, leaving many of them stranded and resourceless when they fail to score with the pros. For the vast majority who never reach the major leagues, low wages, short playing careers, and postcareer trauma are a common lot. The harshness of these realities is particularly acute for black men. A black man has a greater chance of becoming a doctor or a lawyer than a professional athlete.[23] Despite this fact, many talented young African Americans devote their most important years to acquiring sports skills. Despite their outstanding athletic records, African American athletes still have to outperform white athletes to win scholarships and positions. But when the system finally cuts them loose after high school or college, they may find themselves without resources in a racist labour market full of structural barriers.

Sport is everywhere in contemporary society: in schools, community centres, summer camps, public recreation systems, country clubs, union halls, and corporate offices. As a result, the identification spectators feel with the spectacle is based to a large extent on personal sports participation in childhood and adolescence, especially for boys and men. In this sense, the spectacle of modern sport is not, as some would have it, only a passive and nonparticipatory experience. There still exists a shared, common experience between players and their legions of fans. Still, the nonprofessional athletes who comprise the vast majority of sport's active participants, have no determining role in defining the rules and conventions that govern the way their games are played and displayed. The sport–media complex has shaped sport and its culture in the service of mounting a spectacle of elite/professional performance, driving the evolution of sport forms and affecting the nature of mass sport participation.

This practical loss of control by people of their games is mirrored in the loss of connection between professional athletes and the communities they are paid to represent. Throughout most of sport's history, teams were composed of local heroes, young men of the community, who played for and directly represented local audiences with their various class, ethnic, racial, and national characteristics. But today, professional sports teams are made up of men who might have been raised anywhere in the world. Hockey players trained in Moose Jaw, Saskatchewan, end up playing in Anaheim, California; African Americans play professional basketball in Europe; Japanese men play professional baseball in the United States. Spectators, however, still want to identify these athletes as representative of their communities. When the Toronto Blue Jays won the World Series two years in a row in 1992 and 1993, Torontonians were thrilled to have broken the U.S. hold on baseball's highest honour, despite the fact that the whole team consisted of Dominicans and Americans. Professional athletes' first loyalty, however, is not to the local audience, but the vast electronic audiences who have no strong geographical or social links to the individual players. The international market in athletic labour has done away with heroes who speak the same language, know the same countryside, live by the same mores, and fight the same battles as their spectators. As these older identifications with athletes fall away in the ultramobile global sport economy, the only passionate identification that endures is with masculinity itself, which has become the central axis of sport organization and promotion.

Our athletic tastes and physical aesthetics, like other cultural preferences, are not timeless, universal, or inherent. There are powerfully shaped by the structures of ownership and economic control that influence the media of athletic diffusion.[24] The dimensions of sport that are valued and encouraged by the sport–media complex and its emphasis on gendered display are often counterposed to the values conferred by participatory events.[25] As Sandra Curry Jansen and Don Sabo observe: 'The value and standards of performance within these [North American contact] sports are not only androcentric, they also embody instrumentalism, aggression, and the zero-sum concepts of competition that dominate corporate capitalism.'[26] Because of the importance of gender and sexuality in animating sport spectacle and its promotion, the next section of this chapter is devoted to analysing some of the ways in which the sport-associated advertising industries use gender and sex to sell their products.

The final section will look in more detail at the aesthetics and iconography that these techniques, along with other sociocultural developments, have produced.

Psychodemographics and Hypermasculinity

In the 1950s and 1960s, advertising relied on demographic measurement to help design effective campaigns. In the early 1970s, the industry took a major step forward in enhancing the power of their appeals by introducing a technique called 'psychodemographics.' A product of the impact of psychology and neurology on the advertising industry, psychodemographics could evaluate the effects of given visual-auditory messages on the feelings and behaviours of demographically grouped viewers, and then aid in producing tailor-made advertisements to stimulate particular responses. 'According to the new model of communications that emerged,' Joyce Nelson writes in *The Perfect Machine*,

the human receiver is by no means an empty vessel waiting to be filled with a potent message. Rather, the human receiver is a bundle of needs (many of them unconscious or below the threshold of awareness) and a compendium of emotional experiences (many of which are common to all of us as members of this society) ... The receiver is a highly involved participant in the communication. The goal is to shape the message so that it matches the unconscious needs, emotional experience, and coded expectations of the desired audience – so that it speaks to, or resonates with, their deepest feelings and beliefs. This isn't putting something into the receivers, it's drawing something out of them and attaching it, or labeling that emotion with the product being advertised.[27]

In this view, what makes people buy products is not the rational or utilitarian information in an advertisement (for example, 'Gillette razors shave better than others') that is normally processed by the left brain hemisphere. Instead, what makes people buy products is the emotional message ('Gillette products will make you sexier than other products'), normally absorbed and responded to by the right brain hemisphere. 'We don't target a market to a demographic,' a Nike public relations director told *Sports Illustrated*. 'But we do sell to a psychographic segment – such as people who love only basketball. We sell to passions and states of mind.'[28] The key to selling, then, lies not in making a logical argument, but in activating a series of sometimes irrational associations geared to stimulate the emotions that drive people to buy, notably desire and anxiety. As John Berger explains in *Ways of Seeing*, these two emotions are manipulated in tandem.[29] The overt associations (the text) suggest that a product will deliver something desirable – say, a great body or an attractive sexual partner or male friendship. The undercurrent beneath those images (the subtext) suggests that without this product, the sexual partner or desirable friend will be unattainable. This process creates a tension that is relieved by consuming behaviour. In short, this form of advertising is the 'organized creation of dissatisfaction.'

Budweiser beer commercials are ubiquitous in sports advertising. They currently feature either highly sexualized young women with men or rugged young men doing manly activities, or a combination of both. 'This Bud's for you' appeals both to the desire to be like the people in the ads, and to the anxiety provoked by not being like them. Being like them is 'having what it takes' (i.e., the Bud, the Toyota, the Nikes). Some ads concentrate on stimulating sensual pleasure through music, colour, rhythm, or sex. Other ads appeal directly to fear. Most office hardware commercials, for example, play to the terror of falling behind one's competitors, recreating and intensifying the anxiety of a fast-paced, competitive workplace, then suggesting the security and prestige their products will assure. The camera techniques (distortions, angles, filters), fast cutting, the deliberate evocation of nostalgia, all function to exploit emotions rather than provoke rational decisions.

Within this understanding, then, it is crucial to remember that the most important emotional associations in the media are not those in the advertisements as such, but, rather, the implicit links between the commercials, the programming, and the actors themselves – in our case, between the ads, sports events, and athletes. The programming that forms the larger context for the advertising becomes a form of advertising in its own right. As Nike boss Phil Knight noted of key trends in sport in 1993, 'retailing and entertainment are moving together.'[30] In the ideal match between ads and programming, the associations evoked by the program should merge with those aroused by the commercials, to create a larger reality of desire, anxiety, and identification in which we are prompted to consume. Once again, these associations are profoundly gendered.[31]

Around the heroic figure of the male athlete, such a match has been consummated in the marriage of sport with television and advertising. Steve Rushin's story about his visit to the Mall of America in Bloomington, Minnesota, gives countless examples of the spectacular commercial success of mobilizing the power of identification between consumers and athletes. His examples demonstrate dramatically how much the male sport hero is the quintessential force that turns the key on buying behaviour. To begin with, the hero is highly profitable in himself:

On display at Field of Dreams, a sports memorabilia store, is the cover of *SI*'s 35th Anniversary issue. Framed – and autographed in the enfeebled hand of Muhammad Ali

– the cover can be yours for $149. A 1954 Topps Hank Aaron baseball card from his rookie year goes for $900. The same week, on a home shopping channel, I have seen Stan Musial peddling his signature for $299.95, 'or three monthly payments of $99.98.' Children once got Musial's signature on a game program. Now they get it on the installment plan.[32]

The male sport hero is unsurpassed at selling the products of others. During the 1989 Superbowl, for example, Nike wowed television viewers with a fast-paced, $1.5 million commercial featuring many of the most famous stars in professional sport. According to Nike, this strategy was largely responsible for their soaring sales: $1.4 billion in 1989, increasing by 25 per cent every year since.[33] A subsequent campaign featuring Michael Jordan outdrew even this initiative, and played a key role in creating the phenomenon of sports-shoe fetishism, at its height when Nike released their 'Air Jordans.' So successfully did the advertising campaigns transfer a sense of power to certain athlete-identified shoes, that young men, white and Black, urban and suburban, re-sorted to robberies, assaults, and killings to obtain them.[34] In 1996 similar incidents were reported in Japan and other Asian countries, showing that as the NBA and other U.S. sports organizations have expanded aggressively into these markets, along with equipment, they have effectively transported an American culture of masculinity into these societies.

No matter how appealing shoes and jackets may appear to be, it is the idea of the athlete the equipment represents, not the equipment itself, that is so passionately emulated and identified with, and so carefully cultivated by the mass media. Constructing these athletes as larger-than-life figures is the meat and potatoes of sport journalism as well as sport advertising. Indeed, in many cases, the two have fused. Take, for example, a story about NBA star Charles Barkley in *Sports Illustrated* in which writer Leigh Montville ostensibly set out to describe the relationship between Barkley and his new team, the Houston Rockets. In reality, the story was a pure publicity piece for the athlete himself. The graphic featured a huge close-up of Barkley, gleaming in a sheen of sweat, striking a sarcastic, bad-boy pose. The headline read 'Listen Up!' The text recounted in detail Barkley's dressing-room soliloquies (on the subject of soft white players) and concluded by describing how the Rockets' coach waited in vain for reporters to come to his postgame press conference because they had all gone to the dressing room to wait for Barkley. On emerging, Barkley 'is surrounded. Television broadcasters kneel at his feet. A reporter from the *Houston Chronicle* stands inside his locker. The crowd is maybe 30 people, maybe more. Those at the edges strain to hear Barkley speak ... The writers jot down his words. "This is the easiest job I ever had," one Houston reporter says. "I just write down what he says."[35]

Steve Rushin's description of the Mall of America illustrates how powerfully an athlete's image functions as a selling device. Here are his observations on an experiment he conducted, 'to count the stores in which one can purchase an item bearing the euphonious name of the seven-foot spokescenter' NBA superstar Shaquille O'Neal:

> When the toll hits 19 [stores] I realize the laughable inadequacy of my count: I have not looked in video-game stores or department stores. A pasty fat boy wearing an O'Neal road jersey pads past me in Shaq Attaq shoes by Reebok. I have even neglected, somehow, to count the shoe stores. How could I have forgotten? An unmistakable size-20 Shaq shoe stands sentry in front of World Foot Locker. One cannot handle the autographed shoe, for it reposes under glass like the Star of India. What the shoe really is, is the star of Bethlehem, drawing Mall-walking magi into the store ... Sam Goody stocks the rap album, Shaq Diesel ... At Toy Works, I adore the Shaq action figures by Kenner. Shaq's film debut, *Blue Chips* has come and gone at the movieplex. *Shaq Attack!* and *Shaq Impaq* beckon from bookstores. Shaq-signature basketballs line the shelves at Oshman's. Field of Dreams stocks wood-mounted photos of O'Neal: Shaq-on-a-Plaque. I stagger to the Coffee Beanery, Ltd., looking for Swiss Shaqolate Mocha, Vacuum-Shaq-packed in a Shaq-Sack.[36]

Even as we analyse the magnetic draw of the heroic male athlete, it is important to note that the industries benefiting from their association with him also benefit from an unequal gender and class order. For example, the mid-1990s anti–sweat shop campaign of international garment workers made it publicly known that Michael Jordan's endorsement contract for Nike shoes was larger than the combined pay of all the women workers in the Southeast Asian factories that produced the shoes.[37] Typically, a pair of shoes costs $5.60 to produce in Asia. The same shoes are sold for over $100 in North America. The women who make Nike shoes and sew Nike clothes are paid about $1.35 per day, for an approximate annual wage of $500 for each worker and the family that depends on her earnings. Michael Jordan's promotional fee from Nike, on the other hand, was $20 million in 1993.[38] Today Nike is a five-billion-dollar-plus corporation.

Anne McClintock writes that 'advertising's chief contribution to the culture of modernity was the discovery that by manipulating the semiotic space around the commodity, the unconscious as a public space could also be manipulated.[39] Though they do not use the same language as McClintock, sport entrepreneurs and the sport journalists understand this. 'The work of drafting, balancing and maintaining the Nike endorsement team,' wrote Donald Katz in *Sports Illustrated* in 1993, 'requires a particular, almost metaphysical vision of the sports landscape.'[40] Nike executive Howard White told a gathering of sports market-ers: 'When I scout and draft a Nike basketball team ... I'm looking for attitude and style ... A player we draft has to represent something. We consider ele-ments of style. Does he excite anyone? If he can't move people and offer a certain attitude, then he just won't do much for us as an endorser.'[41]

Such instrumental processes of psychological manipulation, conducted on mass levels through advertising, have consequences for culture and for culture-driving mythologies as well as for sports and sports equipment. *Sports Illus-trated* has attributed Nike's success to its 'keen sense of the power of sports and a genius for mythologizing athletes to help sell sneakers.'[42] Marion Woodman writes that, 'as watching television replaces all other social rituals, it becomes the unacknowledged ritual container; triggering archetypal responses and tagging them with brand names, consumer mores, celebrity faces, as catch-phrases of the marketplace. These TV mediations become what we have in common.[43] Woodman's points are especially true for commercial sport, where the commercial propaganda associated with it has many 'side effects.' For example, the conclusions of a study undertaken by a number of academics for the American Automobile Association's Foundation for Traffic Safety in 1988 raise important questions about the larger cultural and gendered impact of beer commercials, a ubiquitous feature of sports broadcasting.[44] The authors of the study were most concerned with the effects of beer ads on children because 'between the ages of two and eighteen, the period in which social learning is most intense, American children see something like 100,000 television com-mercials for beer.' Through these commercials, the study points out, children are presented with 'a particular view of what it means to be a man' as well as attitudes toward drinking and driving. The report concludes that in beer com-mercials, men's work is mostly physical – 'felling trees, loading hay, welding beams, rounding up horses.' As for play, 'the men of beer commercials fill their leisure time in two ways: in active pursuits usually conducted in outdoor settings (e.g. boat racing, fishing, camping, sports) and in "hanging out," usu-ally in bars.'

'We found no sensitive men,' the authors report, 'nor any thoughtful men, scholarly men, political men, gay men or even complex men.' The women are 'largely reduced to the role of admiring onlookers. Men appear to value their group of friends over their female partners, and the women accept this ... they become the audience for whom the men perform.' (Since the time of that report, many women in beer commercials have become much more sexualized, though unchanged in other respects.) The men and women of these ads, the report states, are 'almost laughably anachronistic ... a peculiar set of figures to offer the young of the 1980s as models of adult females and males.' In addition to the very general messages about gender conveyed by beer ads, the authors of the study also conclude that by associating masculinity with beer drinking and linking both to high-risk behaviour, beer commercials 'promote an association between beer drinking and driving,' and recommend that broadcasting policies prohibit such commercials.

Advertisements are not meant to be rational communications, nor are they meant to be socially beneficial. They are carefully constructed symbolic manipulators of desire and anxiety, reaching deep into the psyche to stimulate the kinds of feelings that will motivate us to buy certain things. Hence, though much of the sport audience is middle-class, images of strong, physical, working-class men (especially potent in provoking sexual desire, as I discussed in Chapter 1) are used to represent an energetic, physical, sexual masculinity, evoking among the 'softer' men a wishful, sometimes anxious and envious identification. These thoughts from a respondent in a 1980s survey of American men's sexuality give a sense of how this process takes place:

My number one sexual fantasy is hitting a home run in Fenway Park, preferably against the Yankees. Mind you this is from someone who in little league batted .083 ... As a boy becomes a teenager and then an adult, he learns to associate his sexual identity with his physical prowess and with corresponding psychological qualities (competitiveness, aggressiveness, the ability to 'take it') that are associated with athletes ... What I'm really talking about regarding the traditional roles of men is not the physical attributes of the athlete, but the psychological ones. After all, most men can't try to be football players, but most men can try to be competitive, dominant, rational (in a manner that implies non-emotional), aggressive.[45]

While the majority of men grow up with patriarchal, racist, and xenophobic cultural legacies, they are also generally more complex and thoughtful than the men in beer commercials and the larger commercial sport discourse. For many men, women are real partners, even if the partnership may be difficult. Whatever underlying anxieties they may have about their masculinity, many men are trying to work out different ways of relating to women and releasing the influence of macho ideals in their lives and relationships. But the qualities associated with masculinist consumerism generally work against other qualities that would be helpful in challenging macho ideals.

Many writers have pointed out how the reification of products characteristic of the capitalist age – consumerism as a way of life – impoverishes human relationships, diminishing our capacity for emotional and intellectual experience. Karl Marx prophetically called this investment in things 'commodity fetishism.' Commodity fetishism, nurtured and cultivated by the mobilization of sexuality and sexual fetishism for marketing purposes, affects the organization of desire, and therefore our sexualities.[46] The persistence in advertising of highly sexualized images featuring the heroes of sport spectacle is the clearest evidence that the psychodemographic approach is effective in influencing our behaviour as consumers. It is also clear that in numerous ways, this form of advertising appeals to and affects our sense of identity and social location. The promotional discourse of sport builds narrative myths about heroism and masculinity: 'being tough,' 'being competitive,' 'taking it,' 'dishing it out,' 'God-given talent,' 'backbreaking work,' 'winning against all odds,' 'going down fighting,' 'making a sacrifice play,' 'sudden death,' and 'winner take all.' Condensations of ideology, these myths soak through the membrane of critical consciousness and take hold at the emotional and unconscious levels. As promotional sport culture builds myths about masculinity, so it weaves a complementary construct of femininity. These myths take carnal form in both the ideal and actual athlete's body, as it changes under rigorous conditions of training, to meet the requirements of high-performance professional sport.

The Aesthetics and Iconography of Hypergender

Today, we are surrounded by an aesthetic of the athleticized body, and an iconography of its ideal forms. Like sport forms and conventions of spectatorship, these are also social texts written by sport. This section explores in more detail how the production, aesthetics, and iconography of the male and female athletic body in contemporary sport culture embody gender ideologies – a discussion continued with respect to men in chapters 6, 7, and 8. Here, in discussing the evolution of sport culture in heterosocial terms, I consider specifically the way in which bigness itself has become crucial to the signification of masculinity in relation to femininity. Then I discuss a number of important ways in which, despite women's involvement in sport, this same culture has struggled to diminish women and to make smallness a signifier of femininity.

The Enlargement of Men in Sport Culture

In the ideal male bodies that have been cultivated in the last thirty years or so, massive muscularity and visible strength have become obsessive hallmarks of masculinity and power. Olympic swimmer and 1950s television Tarzan Johnny Weismuller would be considered flabby by comparison with the 1990s' Jean-Claude Van Damme, Wesley Snipes, or Sylvester Stallone. The terrain for the modern athleticized male includes not only the athletic field, but also all the fields of physical action characteristic of men's fictive genres: westerns, spy, science fiction, war, horror, and crime. As Joan Mellen argues, the period from the 1950s to the 1970s (the decades in which sport and television coalesced and transformed each other) saw a marked trend toward the hypermasculinization of film genres, narratives, and actors.[47]

In film, the mid-sixties James Bond movies linked a fantasy of techno-sexual finesse to Cold-warriorhood. While clearly preoccupied by phallic themes, in puerile ways (boys with their toys) their hero at least retained a soft edge of charm and chivalry. By the early 1970s, however, a new ejaculatory realist violence appeared, exemplified by Sam Peckinpah's *Straw Dogs* and Clint Eastwood's *Dirty Harry*. As the representation of violence expanded within film, so did the bodies of the heroes who enacted it. Arnold Schwarzenegger and Sylvester Stallone, products of the body-building gyms, staked out the macho beat in the 1970s and 1980s, bringing big bodies and big weapons together. Today they share that turf with many others. Susan Jeffords in *Vietnam and the Remasculinization of America* and James William Gibson in *Warrior Dreams* provide compelling and wide-ranging evidence of a much more general 'remasculinization' of American culture around themes of violence and warriorhood from the 1960s to the present, propelled by the experience and aftermath of the Vietnam War.[48] Schwarzenegger is the leading exemplar of the trend to bigness and muscularity. His career progressed rapidly from marginal body-building competitions to crude men's action films to top-earning status in mainstream Hollywood films to head of the President's Council on Physical Fitness and Sport in 1990 under George Bush. Schwarzenegger's career as primal macho icon is clearly a result of his appeal to a large population of men, including politicians and decision-makers in the communications industries. His very bigness is attractive, and is certainly central to his own sense of self, as he indicated in this interview for *Muscle and Flex*:

I despised growing up in a little country. That's the reason I left Austria. I did not want anything about my life to be little. What I wanted was to be part of the big dreamers, the big skyscrapers, the big money, the big action. Everything in the United States was big. That's what I enjoy about this country. And there's no monkey business; I mean, you have to make an effort to be little here.[49]

Training for the core men's sports provides ways for men to get 'really big' – literally as well as symbolically. But though the big masculine physique is presented by commercial discourse as supremely healthy ('fit'), as well as supremely sexy, in fact the conditions of its production are often injurious. The use of steroids and human growth hormones by young men to achieve size and strength is a truly deleterious and endemic practice, linked to punishing and injurious training regimens. (These topics are discussed in Chapter 8.) As well, for the really big bodies, unnatural eating regimes to bulk up are mandatory. In *Muscle: Confessions of an Unlikely Bodybuilder*, Samuel Wilson Fussell describes the forced feeding of the serious body-builder, and its earliest consequences:

For breakfast, six poached eggs, six pieces of whole wheat toast, a whole grain cereal mix, a can of tuna. For my first lunch (around ten thirty), a pound of ground hamburger, a monstrous baked potato, a fistful of broccoli, a small salad. For my second lunch (two thirty), two whopping chicken breasts, spinach pasta, two slices of whole wheat bread. And dinner (eight thirty), dinner topped it all. Another pound of hamburger or steak, a super-size can of tuna, another potato, more bread. It also meant drinking ... in addition to a gallon of non-fat milk a day, three mammoth protein shakes – each one consisting of three raw eggs, three tablespoons of BIG protein powder, three teaspoons of lecithin granules (to lower the cholesterol level), a pint of nonfat milk, and a dash of vanilla (recommended by Arnold for flavor) ... [T]he bleeding and the barfing I passed off as minor glitches in the overall program.[50]

While the cult of bodybuilding has been caricatured and criticized, it has, like pornography and fashion for women, become an influential source of masculine sexual ideals and iconography in the last twenty-five years. Body-building magazines are often sold, like pornography, sealed in plastic wrappers and their conventions of body presentation are clearly recognizable as transplants from the genre of athletoporn, which caters to a number of different types of sexual desire.[51] But the dominant eroticism of the practice and genre of body-building is beefcake – the celebration of the huge male body. As Richard Dyer, a British film theorist, noted in his essay on the male pin-up, 'whether the emphasis is on work or sport or any other activity, the body quality that is promoted is muscularity. Although the hyper-developed muscularity of an Arnold Schwarzenegger is regarded by most people as excessive ... it is still the case that muscularity is a key term in appraising men's bodies ... Muscularity is the sign of power – natural, achieved, phallic.'[52]

Massive body-builders, killer football players, and giant basketball players are the leading masculine icons of our age. The ideal of big masculinity, embodied in bulk and muscularity, draws on the historical cultural legacy of men's culture and the warrior cult. But its hyperlarge ideals are also attempts to assert and symbolize masculinity in circumstances – economic, social and sexual – that seem to diminish and undermine its achievement. This has certainly been true with respect to the contradictory and difficult terrain of heterosocial relations, with women surging into the workplace and becoming sexual and cultural subjects. This has also been true, as we shall see in chapters 6 and 7, in the homosocial arenas of men's culture, where men are each other's primary reference points.

The Diminishment of Women in Sport Culture

While the iconography and body aesthetics of sport culture have enlarged men and masculinity, they, like the practice of sport itself, have been more contradictory terrains for women. Women are presented in three distinct aesthetics and iconographies, related to body types and three kinds of sports. The muscled amazons such as Florence Griffiths Joyner and Gail Deevers play the core men's sports. The fluid androgynes – such as Martina Navratilova and Steffi Graf – play tennis and golf, individual, no-contact sports played by both men and women. And the graceful, anorexic waifs with the bodies of barely pubescent girls such as Nadia Comaneci or Tara Lupinski excel at gymnastics and figure skating. Both the amazonian and androgynous body styles and iconographies contain and express genuinely challenging and emergent ideologies about gender and the body. Thanks to the commercialization of gymnastics and figure skating, the anorectic presents a version of female athleticism that co-opts the liberatory potential of women's sports and attaches it to residual and dominant ideologies of gender. The anorexic is the extreme feminine pole in our commercial sport culture's template of hypergender, the perfect complement to the enlarged male.

In the 1970s, women's low levels of participation and absence from leadership positions in sport were noted, along with highly inequitable delivery systems, minimal research on women and physical activity, and scant media coverage of their efforts. Over the last twenty-five years, feminist educators and legislators across North America have worked hard to expand girls' and women's access to sport. Statistically, the results appear less than overwhelming, despite Title IX – the U.S. legislation that requires equality of treatment of women within educational institutions receiving public monies. In 1992, *Sports Illustrated* reported on a National College Athletic Association (NCAA) study indicating that the average Division I school spent twice as much on men's scholarships and three times as much on men's operating expenses as it spent on women's – a trend that persists late into the 1990s.[53] The study also showed that men's coaches received an average salary of $71,511, while women's coaches got $39,177. The gendered contours of participation, marginalization, and exclusion are still evident throughout North American sport.

Nevertheless, under the protection of Title IX in the United States, and of equity legislation in Canada, far-reaching changes have been made in expanding sport for girls and women. These changes have affected many levels of public education and recreation systems, and the sport-scholarship system. As a result, more girls and women have taken an interest in team sports such as basketball, softball, hockey, track and field, and winter sports – previously male turf – as well as in sports such as tennis, gymnastics, and figure skating. Based on the assessment of the interest of women, in 1997 the NBA launched a women's professional basketball league that will begin play as this book is completed. A professional women's hockey league is also in the works. Time will tell whether the fruits of the athleticization of girls and women will produce a permanent television audience for women athletes, but it is certainly possible this will occur. Particularly in the gender-neutral or 'masculine' sports women have practised, they have found a practical ground on which to stretch the physical and symbolic boundaries of sexism.[54]

As well, large numbers of women relate to the core men's sports – up to 30 per cent of television audiences for certain events such as the NFL Superbowl are women. Some women enjoy identifying with the male athletes; others enjoy the masculine spectacle and sexual display. Still others watch or support participation in these sports in order to be with the men (lovers, husbands, brothers, sons, fathers) to whom they are affiliated. Market research has shown that the quality of attention from women spectators at live and electronic games is generally different from that of men. Women less often escape into a fictive scenario of narrative and dramatic pleasure, as many men do, when watching sport on television – still less if they are preparing food and organizing the household in the background.

Clearly there is enough of an athletic culture among North American women that significant numbers of girls become serious athletes who compete in Olympic and team sports. Yet women have still not succeeded in achieving the pinnacles of athletic stardom. Jackie Joyner Kersee may be as talented and accomplished an athlete as Carl Lewis. Martina Navratilova had throngs of admirers in the tennis world. But even these extraordinary women never had the charismatic weight or the economic clout of a Michael Tyson, a Michael Jordan, or a Wayne Gretzky. In 1997, for the second straight year, there were no women athletes on *Forbes* magazine's list of the forty highest-paid athletes; Steffi Graf (tennis) made the list in 1995. The earnings listed include salary, prize money earned, incentive bonuses, licensing money, and appearance and exhibition fees. There were no female football, baseball, basketball or hockey players, no track and field stars, no auto racers, equestrians, or skiers. Not even skaters or gymnasts were mentioned at the time.[55]

The mass media employ a number of strategies and tactics to diminish the appearances of women athletes in sport culture, even as women become more athletic. The power of omission, evidenced in all fields, not just in sport, is the media's single greatest ideological weapon, and it is fashioned and wielded with ideological bias. The dearth of media coverage of women's athleticism is a major factor in the absence of women from the top ranks of athletic stardom. The same bias that omits women's physical heroics also colours and shapes what coverage is devoted to women's sport. Scholars have noted the ways in which its conventions disqualify, and hence distort, impressions of real women's athleticism. In the 1980s, in *The Sporting Woman*, Mary Boutilier and Lucinda San Giovanni described how this distortion acts as a powerful form of what they called (drawing on George Gerbner's work) the 'symbolic annihilation' of women.[56] A decade after Boutilier and San Giovanni's research, Jane Crossman, Paula Hyslop, and Bart Guthrie reviewed the literature on the representation of women in the print sports media in Canada, the United States, and some international jurisdictions and found consistent patterns of gross underrepresentation of women. In the case of *Sports Illustrated*, they reported the following:

For the years 1954 to 1987, 90.8% of *Sports Illustrated* articles were devoted to male athletes (Lumpkin, 1991) ... Furthermore, females were often described in sexist terms ... Kane (1988) assessed whether the efforts of Title IX were evidenced in the coverage given to women in *Sports Illustrated* from years 1964–1987. She concluded that following 1972, there was a significant increase in the proportion of coverage given to women particularly in 'sex appropriate' sports versus 'sex inappropriate' sports.[57]

Evaluating the media's treatment of the spectacularly successful American women athletes at the 1992 winter Olympics, Gina Daddario concludes that 'although women are depicted in physically challenging events that defy "stereotypical notions of femininity," such as mogul skiing, luge and the biathlon, rhetorical analysis suggests that the sports media reinforce a masculine sports hegemony through strategies of marginalization. These include the application of condescending descriptors, the use of compensatory rhetoric, the construction of female athletics according to an adolescent ideal, and the presentation of female athletes as driven by cooperation rather than competition.'[58] The media's desire to frame women athletes as driven by cooperation rather than competition shows the association, within sport culture, of the feminine with empathic, sharing, 'liberal,' or 'socialist' impulses and ways of behaving. Competitive and dominating behaviours are valorized; their opposites devalued. The media's desire to present women athletes in 'nonmasculine' ways results in the coverage we see, and exerts a strong pressure on women athletes competing in sports previously monopolized by men (whether team or Olympic) to prove their femininity – their difference from and vulnerability to the hypermasculine male – regardless of their athletic prowess. Many women athletes who do not wish to be perceived as threatening employ a variety of 'apologetics' to provide reassurance of their femininity – through clothing, adornment, and physical comportment that symbolically code 'feminine.'[59]

In this age of surgical cosmetic enhancement and other forms of physical modification, the pressure for feminine apologetics can be very oppressive. Female body-builders are a case in point. As a uniform group, these women used to be a conspicuously flat-chested lot. Breasts are composed of body fat, the evaporation of which on other parts of the body is the goal of bodybuilding. Thus women's breasts melted away as training brought out articulated pectorals. The result was that women body-builders began to look distinctly more like men. In the 1985 film *Pumping Iron II: The Women*, the clearly superior body-builder in the competition was Australian power lifter Bev Francis, who looked like Arnold Schwarzenegger's younger brother. But she lost the competition to a contestant who was smaller, weaker, and curvier and who adopted feminine gestures when posing. The judges rejected Francis because she was not 'feminine enough.' She had no visible breasts. When I surveyed a number of muscle magazines in 1994, however, I found that a significant number of the featured women were now sporting huge, round, comic-book mammaries. Articles and letters revealed that an epidemic of breast implant surgery among women in the body-building community had occurred, not two years since the silicone breast implant scandal had broken in North America.[60] A similar proliferation of breast implants had taken place in heterosexual pornography a few years earlier. This story illustrates one small way in which the liberatory potential of sport for women is often cancelled out by the gendered requirements of beauty.[61]

Large, powerful women have achieved sensational successes in traditional male sports over the course of the twentieth century, just as women have entered and mastered all previously male-exclusive domains. And their achievements have not gone wholly unnoticed or uncelebrated, either by the media or by various industries. Florence Griffiths Joyner's muscles make a tremendous impact on anyone who sees her, and her notoriously long, painted nails are not so much feminine disqualifiers as they are talons. Martina Navratilova also had an enthusiastic following, and both women had a certain degree of success as icons. Film stars such as Sigourney Weaver, Linda Hamilton, and Bridget Fonda are examples of physically strong women who play heroic roles in the Hollywood cinema, representing the new heroization of women that has occurred since the mid-1980s.[62] These women are significant alternative models that challenge the notion that ideal female bodies need to be acquiescent and pliable. Indeed, in muscle magazines, makers of videos of strong, power-ful women wrestling each other, or overcoming men, advertise to a lucrative response.

Insofar as taking on 'masculine' gestures through sport has encouraged girls and women to reclaim their physical and existential agency, women's involve-ment in sport has arguably been an empowering experience for women.[63] But this building of strong bodies and assertive styles has by no means been the only way in which girls and women have encountered sport. For many, sport has been the royal road to the style of athletic femininity most consistently favoured and promoted by the mass media for superstar status in the last twenty-five years: the anorectic – exemplified by the gymnast and figure skater – who epitomizes 'the construction of female athletics according to an adoles-cent ideal.' Since the 1970s, and with renewed vigour in the 1990s, the sport media have developed the draw of figure skating at the Winter Olympics and women's gymnastics in the Summer Olympics. In the late 1990s, figure skat-ing has become the highest-earning sport for women. Large submarkets of women have grown around these hyperfeminine sports.

Jane Crossman, Paula Hyslop, and Bart Guthrie noted the increased cover-age in *Sports Illustrated* given to 'sex-appropriate' sports versus 'sex-inappro-priate' sports for women. As a result, for many young girls and women, sport and the attempt to conform to the oppressive requirements of feminine beauty go hand in hand. In the mid-1980s, Ann Hall, a professor of physical education and pioneering author and activist in the area of women and sports, noted:

We're seeing thousands more women involved in physical activity, which is something I've been working on for twenty years now. And yet they're doing so in a manner that is very disturbing to me. All the accouterments that go along with that, the television 20-Minute workout, the natty little exercise outfits. People are making a lot of money on this fitness industry. As the fitness industry now seems to be settling in the market place, I liken it very much to the diet industry, the cosmetic industry, the dress industry. All of these industries are there to make women more acceptable to men. Women are taking on muscles but they are doing so in a highly classic 'feminine' way. All you have to do is go to a local news stand and pick up magazines like *Shape* and *Fit*, and there are others which might as well be entitled 'Beauty and Muscles,' 'Muscles for Sex' and so on. And all of these publications portray a particular image of heterosexual femininity.[64]

From the 1950s to the 1990s, the aesthetic ideals for women's bodies changed from curvaceous to lean, and sport culture participated vigorously in this shift. In contrast to the full hourglass figures of Marilyn Monroe and Jane Russell (as

oppressive to women as any other dominant stereotype), the slim body represents the nongestating and nonlactating body – lean, mean, and ready to compete for resources with men in the late capitalist labour market. At least in part,
the thin aesthetic has become popular because women in industrial societies
have had to curtail their childbearing and want models whose bodies imply
limited or forgone maternity. However, women's impulses to idealize a body
that is other than maternal have been powerfully shaped into the current neu-
rotic obsession with being thin by a commercial discourse of clothing and
cosmetics suggesting that thinness is essential to attracting men. Thinness appears to be less threatening to men seeking emotional and erotic distance from
women than large, mature female figures. Yale psychologist Clare Wiseman
claims that 'in 1995, the average weight of *Playboy* centrefolds was 83 per
cent of the average weight for women their height and size.' This figure had
declined from 91 per cent in 1959. According to Wiseman, the current figure is
dangerously underweight.[65] And it is a higher figure than the weight for fashion models.

Two studies presented to the Third London International Conference on
Eating Disorders in April 1997 showed that in Britain, the United States, and
Australia, 'girls who are just a little heavier than their peers are much less
popular.' 'It's the heavier girls who are least popular,' Andrew Hill of Leeds
Medical School commented. Although none of the girls in the studies was
clinically obese, and most did not 'even look fat,' the heavier they were, the
more likely they were to be on a diet. However, dieting, offered to the girls by
'the media and perhaps, their mothers,' did not work; indeed, the physicians
stressed, dieting is harmful to girls during puberty and adolescence when their
bodies are changing rapidly.[66]

The difficulty most women have in attaining fashionable thinness creates a
self-renewing source of needs that can be answered by profitable goods and
services. Hence a 'femininity market' geared toward the physical shrinking of
women has evolved in parallel to the male-enlarging masculinity market, and
is increasingly doing so in association with the 'feminine' sports. The 1997
Nutrasweet Figure Skating Championship, for example, linked dieting, thinness, and 'sweetness' to the feminine icons on skates. In the femininity market,
anxiety about sexual attractiveness plays an even more central role than in
the masculinity market. Especially if they are white and affluent, women
feel tremendous social pressures to be thin. (Black women, who identify less
with the models of commercial discourse, suffer less from food and weight
anxieties.)[67]

Women who want to be lean and physically fit can find women to emulate
in the world of sport if they look for them. The images of athletes such as

speed skaters Bonnie Blair or Catriona Le May Doan appear briefly on a mass scale during the Winter Olympic games every four years. Their bodies, like those of women rowers, softball players, cross-country skiers, and shot putters, are strikingly muscular and strong, nothing like the models in fashion, film, or pornography. But then their images fade, and the images of tiny athletes such as gymnast Nadia Comaneci or figure skater Tara Lupinski join with those of models such as waif Kate Moss on billboards, in the malls, in magazines, and on television. In this role, the most feminine of professional sports have provided moral legitimacy to the ideal of the small, thin woman. Today, under normal circumstances, an anorexic teenager is considered a seriously troubled young person; anorexia and bulimia have been identified as widespread serious disorders among girls and young women. On the other hand, the celebration of gymnasts and figure skaters that has formed the core of Olympic women's sports broadcasting for the last ten years, has placed the small, girlish physique in the adoring media spotlight, and had redeemed the abused, anorexic body. A national gymnast is considered the apotheosis of feminine grace and female athletic achievement.[68] The chances are excellent that today such a champion will be a starving teenage girl.

It was not always like this in gymnastics. In the 1950s and 1960s, most female gymnasts were mature, full-bodied women, many of them mothers, and most of the world-class athletes were in their twenties. That all changed at the Munich Olympics in 1972, when Olga Korbut became the first of the tiny, perfect gymnasts.[69] By the early 1970s, it was clear that the media, especially television, wanted to attract an audience to female athletes working within the traditional gestural vocabularies of femininity, and a newly immature femininity at that, and gymnastics fit the bill. Basic to this vocabulary was size: 'I ate every day, but I ate barely at all,' Korbut has said of the years she competed at 4 feet 11 inches and 82 pounds. The media went crazy for her:

In the Soviet Union, oddly, she was seen only as another part of the sports machine. Here, she was a star. After the Olympics ended, she toured the US. She went to Disneyland and posed with Mickey Mouse. She was presented with a red Chevrolet sports coupe ... She met the Queen of England. She met the Shah of Iran ... She met President Richard Nixon at the White House. ('You're so tiny,' the President said. 'You're so big,' Olga replied.)[70]

By the 1976 Olympic Games in Montreal, Korbut was twenty-one years old and, thanks to the style she had pioneered herself, was no longer capable of her earlier feats. Instead, the media lionized Nadia Comaneci, who, in the words of *Sports Illustrated*, had 'a lean boy's body that responds to all her demands and a valentine face with straight, dark eyebrows that pierce it like Cupid's bow.[71] By that year, the average U.S. female Olympic gymnast was already small – seventeen years old, only 5 feet 3½ inches tall, and 106 pounds. By 1992, she was sixteen years old, 4 feet 9 inches, and weighed only 83 pounds.[72]

The trend toward tininess in figure skating has paralleled that in gymnastics, though it has been somewhat more uneven and contested. The great Katarina Witt and the not-as-great Nancy Kerrigan, for example, have tall, substantial, mature bodies. Nevertheless, skaters such as Midori Ito, Kristi Yamaguchi, Oksana Bayul, and, most recently, Tara Lupinski, have set the trend. In 1997, Lupinski, at fourteen, became the youngest women's singles world figure skating champion. She was described as a 4 foot 8 inch 'minuscule moppet' and looked ten or eleven years old.[73] Women's gymnastics during the summer Olympic games, and figure skating at the winter Olympic games, now constitute the primary Olympic coverage for women athletes; indeed they've become a kind of Tinkerbell Superbowl, fetching huge advertising revenues and conferring on the winners the power to obtain rich sponsorship endorsements. After Kerri Strug's ankle-injury-defying performance in Atlanta, she was immediately signed by agent Leigh Steinberg, who was lining up 'deals for over seven figures' the day after the competition.[74] Women softball players and speedskaters, no matter how good, are never rewarded with deals like this.

The problem is that the apparently effortless grace of the extraordinary girl athletes not only overshadows the achievements of women in gender-neutral sports, but is very often accomplished at great cost to the athletes themselves. We are more than twenty years into the regime of the girlish athlete. We know the methods and technologies used to maintain the prepubescent body, and can evaluate the evidence of their after-effects. The most important of these methods is the deprivation of food. And on this count, the record is appalling. Anorexia nervosa – understood in this context as a self-assumed discipline of smallness – has wreaked havoc with the health of two cohorts of young gymnasts. The most famous example of these is U.S. gymnast Christy Heinrich, who eventually died of multiple organ failure due to anorexia and bulimia in July 1994. But less visible is the harm starvation does to the anonymous young women who have left gymnastics behind and gone on to lead their lives with a legacy of physical and emotional damage. Starvation not only keeps fat off the body; at the crucial time of puberty (through mechanisms that are only now being clarified), it prevents the brain from releasing the estrogen and testosterone that bring about sexual maturity in females.[75] Hence, starvation is usually accompanied by irregular or no menstruation and osteoporosis. Indeed, the combination of disordered eating, amenorrhea, and osteoporosis is so common among female athletes that it is defined by the American College of Sports

Medicine as 'The Female Athlete Triad.'[76] Dr Connie LeBrun, who has studied
the conditions of women athletes, reports that 'there have been cases where
young women with *anorexia nervosa* have had bone densities in their twenties
the same as women in their seventies, and there are actual case histories with
X-rays looking like post-menopausal women. The hunched over spine ...
'dowager's hump,' and in many cases it's due to small compression fractures
in the vertebrae.'[77] Women gymnasts who have starved lose teeth as well as
bone mass at a young age. Some experience ectopic pregnancies and infertility
due to scarring of the fallopian tubes and ovarian irregularities, making them
candidates for more drugs later in life. All of this is on top of the broken bones
and dislocations that both male and female athletes must endure. (In addressing
a conference of Canadian doctors in 1992, Dr Robert Woollard compared the
injuries of gymnasts to those of children working in Scottish coal mines at the
turn of the century. Like those children, young, elite gymnasts put in seven to
ten hours of work a day.)[78]

Studies estimate that one in six adolescent girls has an eating disorder, but
that adolescent gymnasts are more than twelve times as likely as nongymnasts
to have serious eating problems.[79] Smallness and thinness are important, young
gymnasts learn, for purposes far above and beyond sport. As one former national champion has stated: '[The coaches] said, "Oh well, don't just lose
weight for the gym. You want to be that way so that you can impress the boys,
so that you can feel good about yourself, and so that you can look good when
you go out" ... To me that's saying you're not acceptable unless you're smaller.'
Christy Heinrich once recalled that 'five out of six of us that were on the world
team when I was that year ... had eating disorders. One tried to commit suicide
over it.'[80]

The resounding messages that young gymnasts receive about their bodies is
part of a larger set of messages about authority and obedience. (I take up this
theme with respect to the training of children and teens for Olympic athletics in
Chapter 8.) The young girl is expected to obey her coach and her sport uncon-
ditionally, no matter how difficult, dangerous, or senseless the sacrifice. When
Kerri Strug performed while injured, she was heaped with adulation even
though no medal depended on her performance. But, as physical education
professor and former gymnast Margaret MacNeill writes, 'Strug's pursuit of
the gold medal for Team USA was anything but courageous ... It was stupid ...
[This] "tiny teen" made this choice from limited options. An honourable con-
valescing exit was not a choice ... A recent graduate of adolescence, Strug
remains an inmate of an elite gymnastic system that abuses child-adults in
favour of winning at all costs.'[81]

In her discussion of the presentation of women in the Hollywood cinema from the 1950s to the early 1970s, film critic Molly Haskell hypothesized that as women moved out of the private domestic sphere via work and politics to occupy a greater role in public life in the sixties and seventies, the fictive life of mainstream cinema attempted to push women back, to minimize them through a number of narrative, casting, and directorial strategies.[82] In the pruned, stunted, infantilized, or horrific roles created for women in the films of the 1960s and early 1970s, Haskell read a tremendous element of wish fulfilment for restored masculine superiority and control. The emergence of the family- and woman-centred horror film and the woman-terrorizing slasher films of the 1970s and 1980s, originally identified by film theorist Robin Wood as expressions of profound gender malaise and anxiety, can be seen as further extensions of this impulse into our own time.[83]

The athletic hyperfemininity and infantilization of 'women' gymnasts can also be read as an expression of the same wishes Haskell and Wood identified. But it is bought at an enormous price.[84] The discipline of smallness and thinness for women is a major form of their social oppression, for it contradicts the diversity of body types, women's genetic predisposition to accumulate fat with age, and their right to occupy space and share power with men. As such, its ideals demand from the majority of women a fight against their own natures. That discipline is at its most rigorous and cruel in the world of the ideal feminine athlete, and is based on institutionalized starvation.

For Jean-Marie Brohm and others, the capitalist paradigm of the body as performance machine is seen as the key model for the body idealizations of sport. This body is seen as the carnal expression of sport's link to the stratified and technological nature of industrial capitalism and the resultant alienation of its culture. My argument is that this thesis, while important, is not differentiated enough, for it neglects the distinctly gendered nature of the body aesthetics of sport culture. At the gender poles, the ideal athleticized body for males is the big power machine; for women, it is the small, anorexic flower. The supreme machine that sport cultivates as the ideal body is a masculine machine that embodies the qualities of violent instrumentality. The female machine is either modified by mechanical manipulation and fuel deprivation such that her strength is undermined, or reclassified as masculine (amazon, she-man).

The myriad, sometimes perverse, ways in which women try to conform to idealized femininity can be oppressive and wasteful of energy and resources. But some are more oppressive than others. The lotus foot and generalized anorexia are more extreme and damaging, for example, than mascara, nail polish, and depilation. When the requirements of femininity demand not an adornment or refinement of the body but an assault on the physical and psychological nature of women, the aestheticization of beauty passes from play to alienated work, and from pleasure to anguish. The athleticization of body ideals for both sexes transmitted through the dominant sports and their culture contribute in many cases not to self-love and body acceptance – for either sex – but to standards that demand generalized physical self-abuse. The approximately one million young men taking steroids in the United States today are not aiming for the body of Michelangelo's David. And bulimic and anorexic girls are not driven by Botticelli's ideal of female pulchritude. Women have abandoned external corsetry, but for an internal obsession – for 'body cosmetics,' in the words of Margaret MacNeill.[85]

We cannot, however, account for the evolution of ideals of hypergender and hypermasculinity through commercial sport culture only by reference to anxieties and desires in relations between the genders in the domestic realm. From the 1950s to the 1990s, conflicts of nation, class, race, and sexual orientation have equally set the social context for gender anxieties and given them texture and meaning. Due to men's gender dominance in the institutions involved in these conflicts, many of the sharpest antagonisms have been played out not between men and women, but among men themselves in largely homosocial arenas. Thus the focus of chapters 6 and 7 is on homosocial men's subcultures and their relationships with the culture of sport.

6

'Hit, Crunch, and Burn': Organized Violence and Men's Sport

On the afternoon of 17 June 1994, former football hero, sometime actor, and frozen-orange-juice advertising icon O.J. Simpson went for his last touchdown. As he made his way across Los Angeles freeways, a heroic procession of Los Angeles police, cheered on by crowds of spectators, followed behind. The live media coverage of the event rivalled that of the 1969 moon shot. For almost a year afterwards the media force-fed the O.J. Simpson trial to North Americans. From January to October 1995 alone, coverage of the trial accounted for more minutes on ABC, CBS, and NBC prime-time news than Bosnia and the Oklahoma City bombing combined, and thirteen times as much as the debate on Medicare.[1] Part gladiatorial combat, part soap opera, part show trial, part pornography, the trial served as a classic weapon of mass distraction – a lightning rod for social and political disaffection – a massive circus that captured public energy, exacerbated ugly attitudes with respect to race, sex, and gender, and bred cynicism about the police and justice systems.

During the long months of the trial, O.J. Simpson, the black athlete, and Mark Fuhrman, the avowedly racist white police detective central to the prosecution's case, faced each other as consummate antagonists. Simpson's defence team packaged him as representing 'Black civil rights' while Fuhrman's political views were associated with 'white supremacy.' Both men stirred considerable passions among their supporters and detractors. Their personal enmity, linked to differences in colour of skin and ideologies of race, was much publicized, part of the way 'the race card' was constructed and played. In this drama of difference, the strong similarities between Simpson and Fuhrman – particularly the shared ideology of what I have called coercive entitlement – escaped discussion. More colloquially, this ideology is expressed in phrases such as 'might equals right,' 'survival of the fittest,' 'rugged individualism,' 'winner take all.' Simpson and Fuhrman shared this ideology through their gender ideals and behaviour. From Simpson's and Fuhrman's informal speech and from the record of their accomplishments, reported at length in media coverage, it was evident that both men engaged in violence in the sanctioned realms of sports or police work, as well as outside those realms in sexual and family life. Both men expected respect and rewards for their violence. In their own private scripts, both men saw themselves as masculine warriors. Deploying physical violence was part of their gendered self-definition and sense of self-worth. In fact, measured against this ideology of masculinized coercive entitlement, their other ideological differences appear much more superficial and secondary.

For many athletes the deployment of injury, pain, and organized mayhem is a valuable part of what they do, and they are usually rewarded for it. Heavyweight boxer Mike Tyson, who was released from prison in 1995 after serving time for raping a young woman, is an extreme example. As a boy, Tyson was brutalized on the streets of Brooklyn; as a teenager, he discovered his ability to brutalize back.[2] As a boxer, he was rewarded for inflicting violence, and violence became pleasurable to him. But Tyson could not distinguish between the realm where he was supposed to enjoy hurting – the ring – and the place where he wasn't supposed to enjoy it – the bedroom. 'I like to hurt women when I make love to them,' *Sports Illustrated* quotes Tyson as saying. 'I like to hear them scream with pain ... to see them bleed ... it gives me pleasure.'[3] In 1997 that pleasure in pain permitted him to take a bite out of Evander Holyfield's ear as he was losing a fight to him.[4] Judging by the size and nature of the audiences Tyson has commanded for his fights, the hypermasculine ideology of coercive entitlement he embodies links him not only to the sadism of Simpson and Fuhrman, but to millions of other men in the United States and globally.[5] Tyson is in many ways a tragic figure, as are other athletes like him, a gladiator exploited for violence within the 'rules of the game,' then despised when that violence spills over into real life.

The initiation into manhood through violence is not the only purpose or effect of the core men's sports and sport culture. But it is one of the most important of their effects, and deserves critical examination. The ideology of coercive entitlement is central to gender, race, class, and biotic hierarchies. However complex the cultures of these stratified systems may be, all of them are based on the *force majeure* accorded to males of specific groups, and are physically policed by organized groups of armed and violently instrumental men. Linked to the cult of the warrior, the template of this ideology has been actively constructed in the ritual formations of men's culture as well as in military and paramilitary structures, above all in the bastions of men's professional sports. The elaborate media attention given to Tyson and Simpson were grotesque but accurate caricatures of the broader ways in which the mass media exploit the charismatic celebrity of violent, hypermasculine sport heroes.

As we have seen, such athletes are able to stir deeper levels of collective disturbance, desire, and fear than most other men, even famous ones. Had O.J. Simpson been a famous heart surgeon or even a politician, the coverage of his trial would not have commanded nearly the degree of attention it did. With the emotional attachments so many men make to sport and its heroes, however, come profound expectations. The first of these is that the good athlete, the symbolic warrior, our champion, is supposed to turn his trained violence against our 'enemies.' He is not supposed to use that violence against 'us.' For this reason, when a famous and 'beloved' athlete is accused of committing a violent crime, the social contract between symbolic warrior and community is violated. When this happens, the dichotomy between the violent behaviour society approves in sanctioned arenas and the behaviours it condemns in official policy, political rhetoric, and social mores may become transparent.[6] The O.J. Simpson trial provided such a glimpse into this disturbing contradiction. However, the media never acknowledged or debated the complicity of sport in the violent actions of these and other athletes, and of the men who emulate them consciously or unconsciously. No interrogation of the culture and values of the big-time sport that made Simpson a hero in the first place ever took place.

This chapter seeks to explore at greater length some aspects of the enactment and representation of violence in men's sport and other genres of men's culture, particularly war. The following section reviews some of the ways in which violence is institutionalized at present in contemporary men's sport. I then raise certain issues concerning violence against women and the fear of femininity in relation to sport. From there, I proceed to look at certain developments in American masculinity and sexuality in the latter half of this century, as they related to the wars in Vietnam and the Persian Gulf. The last two sections of the chapter explore the impact of violent ideals and practices of masculinity on political consciousness, and the function that sport serves with respect to the politics of coercion and the economies of war.

Sanctioned Violence in Men's Sport

'Sport is the human activity closest to war that isn't lethal,' said former U.S. president Ronald Reagan in 1981.[7] The similarities between sport and war consist of a shared culture of combat and the competitive deployment of force and violence. When I speak of war in this chapter, I refer not only to formal, declared wars such as the Vietnam or Gulf wars; I also include the actions and ongoing 'campaigns' of the more coercive institutions of domestic class and race relations, particularly those of policing, security, and imprisonment. Although we should not simplistically reduce these institutions to the service of war – there are prosocial needs for policing – these apparatus of power do serve as instruments of class and race war.

Speaking of the architecture and ambience of many U.S. prisons, James Gilligan writes that 'the whole system has a military feel to it; it is like a state of civil war that never ends, in which there are no victors, neither side surrenders, and there is not even the possibility of a peace treaty.'[8] 'War culture' or 'military culture' used in this sense would include the ways of life and the cultural representation of police and prison societies, and of 'criminal' as well as 'political' adversaries and conflicts.[9] Along with sport, war is the other arena in which lawful, sanctioned violence (heroism) is distinguished from unlawful violence (villainy) along rules established by cultural conventions and practised on a large scale by men as a gender.[10]

The celebration of the ritualized violence of sport is a staple of commercial sports journalism. Sometimes it is delivered unvarnished, in a tone of admiration. Often its details are delivered along with pious nostrums about how deplorable it is. Perhaps it should not be surprising that sports journalism only rarely acknowledges the darker ideological functions of sport, functions tied to the ritualization and celebration of force, pain, and aggression. Still, from time to time, sport journalists do speak openly about it. Boxing 'allows you the sense of suspension that you get in watching theatre,' reporter Stephen Brunt said in a radio documentary about boxing.

It doesn't look quite real. But the first time someone bleeds; or the first time you see someone hit and you see the pain in their face ... or when one person is hurt and you see the surge in the other athlete trying to put him away, [you see] the killer instinct, the aggression, that's bred out of us. That's absolutely the antithesis of what you're supposed to do on the street. If you see someone who's hurt you're supposed to help them, not finish them off. Boxing teaches people the opposite.[11]

Also featured in this documentary was Vince Bagnato, a former boxing promoter and ex-fighter, an old fashioned, pre-technological gladiator. He was even more succinct: 'It's controlled violence,' he said. 'People go to fights to see someone get flattened. The minute someone tells you "I like to go see the boxing end of it" – that's lying ... Maybe that's a sad comment, but that's the truth.'[12]

Boxing is uncontestably a violent sport, and a masculine sport; it also teaches us about the rewards of violence, and hence about coercive entitlement. Whatever poetic and mythic meanings people attach to boxing, the violence is palpable and unsublimated, indispensable. Although boxing is now our only officially sanctioned 'blood sport,' sport violence spreads far beyond this one sport. 'On Wednesday night, a gang fight broke out in a building in central Toronto,' wrote Bob Richardson, a hockey fan and coach, describing a junior hockey game played in Maple Leaf Gardens. 'Some of the gang members had found themselves in a tense situation they couldn't handle. So they lost control and went berserk. There were several injuries.'[13] Richardson was a member of the Hockey Management Team that acted as the disciplinary watchdog for an Ontario county high-school league. In his comparison of junior hockey games to gang warfare, Richardson was adding his voice to a growing chorus of people concerned with hockey violence at all levels of the game. Richardson's point, one repeated by many officials, parents, and sports scholars alike, is that sport sanctions forms of violence that, outside the arena or playing field, would be considered violations of the law and grounds for arrest and punishment. Though Richardson made his case particularly well, it was not a new one. The issue of violence in hockey – from the NHL to the peewees – is well known, as is the celebration of such violence.[14]

A similar story is true of football. In 1978 John Underwood detailed the far-reaching violence of football at all levels, from junior high school to university and professional teams. According to Underwood, more than half of the non-professional players could expect to suffer injury serious enough to take them out of practice or playing during a given season. In his survey, high-school players faced an 86 per cent chance of injury, and college players a 96 per cent chance. In the late 1970s, thirty-two college and high-school players annually became paraplegics because of the sport.[15] According to a 1994 National Football League Player's Association bulletin,

over the 1983 through 1986 seasons, there was almost one reported injury for every player. There were an average of 1,582 players per season and an average of 1,450 reported injuries. That represents a ratio of .92 reported injuries for every player ... The toll: An average 6.47 reported injuries per game, 91 per regular season week, and 3.3 reported injuries per club per week over the four seasons. Over 20% of the reported injuries fell into the two most severe injury ratings – out (*100% probability the player would not play in the next game*) and doubtful (*75% chance of not playing.*) Fifty five per cent of the reported injuries were classified in categories that meant the player had a 50% or less chance of playing in the next scheduled game.[16]

'Relatively speaking, football is no longer a killer sport,' John Underwood writes. 'The real issue is not dead bodies but wounded ones, the systematic wasting of men and boys within the boundaries of "legal play."'[17]

The brain injuries that often afflict football and other team sport players are similar to the kinds of injuries sustained by boxers. 'It's not a hurt like a pin poke, it's a brain kind of hurt,' explained Tony 'The Kid' Pep (a Commonwealth super feather-weight champion) in describing the pain involved in a knockout punch. 'You're hurt cerebral, like a cerebral damage. You get a tingling in your feet ... Once you get that tingling feeling, if you get hit with another one you're probably going to go down.'[18]

Dr Michael Schwartz, a neurosurgeon at Toronto's Sunnybrook Hospital, examines every boxer knocked out in the ring in the province of Ontario. He led a team studying the force of knockout blows. His study found that 'a professional fighter can punch a person's head with about the force that one would suffer if you were not wearing a seatbelt and hit the windshield in a low speed automobile collision.' 'So the brain which is a bit like jello swirls around inside the skull and actually cracks, or breaks up, and there are little tears in the brain. And the [breaks and tears] tend to be focused in parts of the brain that subserve memory and analytical thought ... controlled murder in a sense.'[19] According to Stephen Brunt, the concussions that football players sustain are equal in intensity and much larger in number than those sustained by boxers.[20] And according to early 1997 findings, sport-related brain injuries and deaths have increased significantly since the 1980s, not only in boxing and football, but in hockey, soccer, baseball, and basketball.[21]

Even in men's professional sports where violence is not intrinsic, violent attitudes and aggressive gestures are validated. Michael Clarkson has written a portrait of Chicago Bulls superstar Michael Jordan, 'the greatest basketball player of his era, the role model who invites us to Be Like Mike.'[22] According to Clarkson, while Jordan is unsurpassed in terms of 'athleticism, grace and championship production,' behind the 'sweet smile' is 'a poster child for ego, pride and revenge.' Jordan is 'the epitome of a contemporary, in-your-face warrior, who develops his skills and then unleashes them against challengers – as much for animalistic survival as for love and money.' As Clarkson notes, Jordan has 'sharpened his vindictiveness to the point where it's the most dangerous weapon in the league today.'[23]

The provocation and cultivation of this useful and strategic anger involve the encouragement of violence by a masculinized individual. 'Players have been conditioned since childhood that every confrontation is a test of manhood,' says [Chicago Bulls coach] Phil Jackson, who calls Jordan a 'peaceful warrior' yet concedes that he sometimes uses rage for points. 'Win or die is the code: rousing the player's bloodlust is the method.'[24] After cataloguing Jordan's questionable behaviour, Michael Clarkson observed that 'the fans don't seem to mind because Jordan is a winner and because sports is one of the few arenas left in our society where physical combat and revenge are acceptable.'[25]

Sport, Violence against Women, and Fear of the Feminine

As well as sanctioning violence between men, there is evidence that sport culture encourages direct expressions of physical and sexual violence against women.[26] Addressing the resonances between sport and men's violence against women in the O.J. Simpson story and in the increasing reports of professional athletes involved in physical and sexual assault, *Sports Illustrated* authors William Nack and Lester Munson noted that 'surely in no other arena – from academia to entertainment, from politics to industry – have more and varied men been exposed as batterers than in the relatively small, if highly visible, world of sports.'[27]

This violence consists of a number of different patterns. One of the most highly visible patterns in recent years is the finding that rapes on college campuses are being performed by team athletes in numbers significantly out of proportion to their presence in the student population. In a newspaper series on rape and college athletes, a Philadelphia reporter found that a college athlete was reported for sexual assault once every eighteen days on average between 1983 and 1986. Some of the rapes involved more than one athlete. 'Football and basketball players representing NCAA-affiliated schools were reported to police for sexual assault approximately 38 percent more often than the average male on a college campus' the reporter concluded.[28] In reviewing the experiences of a number of former athletes, Michael Messner noted that 'whether they liked the sexism and homophobia or not ... when verbal sparring and bragging about sexual conquests led to actual behaviour, peer group values encouraged these young men to treat females as objects of conquest.'

This sort of masculine peer group dynamic is at the heart of what feminists have called 'the rape culture.' Eugene Kanin's study of date rape revealed that college men who have experienced pressure from their current male friends to engage in sexual activity are more likely to rape female acquaintances. Similarly, in a national study Mary Koss and Thomas Dinero (1990) found that 'involvement in peer groups that reinforce highly sexualized views of women,' such as varsity athletics and fraternities, is an important predictor of 'sexually aggressive behaviour' by college males.[29]

Nack and Munson reported on other studies, including one that reviewed 107 cases of sexual assault reported at thirty Division I schools between 1991 and

1993. The researchers concluded that 'male college student-athletes, compared to the rest of the male student population, are responsible for a significantly higher percentage of the sexual assaults reported to judicial affairs on the campuses of Division I institutions.'[30]

With respect to the connection between teams sports and sexual violence, former football player Allen Sack commented:

I played football from the time that I was in seventh grade until the time that I graduated from college ... I think we ... almost learn rape from our young male athletic experiences. In other words, we learn that when a woman in the back of a car is saying no, no, no, I don't want to do this, we learn, on the contrary, to push it further. She doesn't really mean no, she means yes. And I think that oftentimes athletic behaviour, even more than ordinary behaviour, socializes young males to not understand those kind of boundaries ... We dominate opponents, we dominate other athletes, we dominate our friends on the athletic field, and of course, we dominate women.[31]

Nack and Munson reported examples of comments that confirm Sack's view: 'On the occasion when the Philadelphia 76ers barely defeated the New Jersey Nets on Nov. 3, 1990, Charles Barkley said 'This is a game that, if you lose, you go home and beat your wife and kids.' Joe Paterno, a Penn State football coach, after a team loss on Sept. 8, 1990 said 'I'm going home to beat my wife.'[32] Jeffrey O. Segrave, in his study of the use of sport metaphor in sexual relations, observes that 'overall, th[e] data substantiate the common perception that the use of sports metaphors in the language of sexual relations is predominantly a male practice.'[33] The metaphors that make up the core of this language when men speak it to each other link sex, force, domination, and, hence, violence.[34]

The sexual validation athletes get for their athletic violence is an important factor in this phenomenon, part of the eroticization of coercive entitlement. 'Sex itself is incorporated into the athlete's language of hostility and aggression,' Robin Warshaw writes in her chapter on group rapes in *I Never Called It Rape*.[35] Nack and Munson remark that 'an athlete cherishes nothing more than control over an opponent, and nothing lifts him higher than the sense that he has attained that control.' Alisa DelTufo, the founder of Sanctuary for Families, a shelter for abused women and children in New York City, told Nack and Munson: 'The pursuit of dominance lies at the heart of all athletic contests, and it happens to be the animating force behind the men who batter their women ... Men who need to be in control of their environment in order to feel O.K. about themselves often have a problem with domestic violence.'[36] Very often, according to Warshaw, intervention by college authorities and alumni results in light or no punishment for the athletes, a point acknowledged by Nack and

Munson: 'The athlete can usually count on a worshipful public that wants to believe him.'[37] In addition, anti-rape activists are often harassed and assaulted themselves. For these reasons, Warshaw concludes that athletic teams are 'breeding grounds for rape' and 'are often populated by men who are steeped in sexist, rape-supportive beliefs.'[38]

The massive documented occurrence of rape in the former Yugoslavia is the most recent – and clearest – expression of the relationship between intermale violence and wartime violence against women.[39] When men rape in gangs, whether as soldiers or athletes, they are involved in a male–male agenda of orgiastic hatred. Expressed in genital assault, it spills over in a displaced manner onto women affiliated with 'enemy males.' In this sense, as 'rewards' for men, Other women become the receptacles for men's distorted and self-hating behaviours, particularly their disavowal of the 'feminine' within themselves.

Many scholars in many disciplines have noted that in our culture the 'softness' that men must disown in the process of becoming men and conforming to their role in the gender template is projected and displaced onto women. In turn, women become symbols in the masculine imagination of what men are fighting for (the rewards for their sacrifices) and those they must not become like (feminine = castrated). 'Particularly in the contact sports, things feminine have served as symbols of things to be avoided,' write Nack and Munson. As Ted Crosset, assistant professor of sports management at the University of Massachusetts told them, 'Part of the male athlete's subworld is not to be a woman. Women are degraded. You don't want to be skirt-of-the-week. You don't want to be a wimp, a sissy. To be a man is not to be a woman. Women are not to be respected. Women are despised.'[40]

This same gender culture characterizes the military as well. 'A traditional technique for turning American teenagers into soldiers at boot camp,' writes Loren Baritz, 'was for the drill sergeants to accuse slackers of being queer.'

The formula was that only 'real men' could become soldiers, and the military's first job was to teach youngsters manhood, not soldiering. Relying on deep cultural shame, the drill instructors shouted, 'Ladies, attention.' The novelist Tim O'Brien described what happened to him during basic training at Fort Lewis. He and a friend were sitting alone polishing their boots. Their sergeant screamed at them: 'A couple of college pussies ... Out behind them barracks hiding from everyone and making some love, huh?' The sergeant stared at them: 'You afraid to be in the war, a goddamn pussy, a goddamn lezzie?'[41]

'Years after women were integrated into the all-volunteer force,' writes Linda Bird Francke in her 1997 book on women in the U.S. armed forces, 'the services continued to pump up masculinity by tearing down femininity.'

Army drill sergeants in the early '90s humiliated lagging male recruits by calling them girls. 'So are we having menstrual cramps this morning?' a drill sergeant at Fort Jackson, SC, derided a male recruit struggling with push-ups. The same techniques were applied to female recruits to drive out their femaleness. 'You wuss, you baby, you goddamn female,' was shouted at a company of female recruits in 1991, also at Fort Jackson.

Tod Ensign, director of Citizen Soldier, a civil liberties organization based in New York, told Francke that 'one of the most important and guarded myths of the military is the necessity to maintain that hyped-up sense of maleness.'[42]

Donald Sabo discusses this disassociation of the feminine with respect to the culture of men in prison, a discussion that makes links between prison and sport as homosocial environments where men 'do masculinity.'

The hardness-softness dichotomy echoes and fortifies stereotypes of masculinity and femininity. To be 'hard' means being more manly than the next guy, who is said to be 'soft' and more feminine. To be called hard is a compliment; to be labeled soft can be a playful chide or a serious put down. The connotations around hardness and softness also flow from homophobia, which is rampant in prison. The stigma of being labeled a homosexual can make a man more vulnerable to ridicule, attack, and ostracism.[43]

Men deny any softness and prove their hardness by killing other men and women, actions legitimized and rewarded by the apparent blessings of their own women, whom they will defend and then possess. In the ritual of rape, however, whatever personal rage toward women is involved, it is mandatory to prove hardness and masculinity to other men, to disavow the feminine and the expressive values that go with it. As James Gilligan argues, 'the absence or deficiency of self-love is shame; its opposite is pride, by which I mean a healthy sense of self-esteem, self-respect and self-love.'[44] Constant shaming – as in a culture, like sport, that ridicules the 'feminine' feelings – 'leads to a deadening of feeling, an absence of feeling.'[45] According to Gilligan, this deadening is what makes violence both attractive (violence can at least be felt) and possible (violence depends on the absence of empathy). In our culture, when men perceive their emotional wishes as rendering them 'passive or powerless, dependent, helpless, immature and inadequate both sexually and socially,' Gilligan writes, 'those wishes are shameful, and they feel that they themselves are contemptible. When that happens, they are likely to project those wishes onto others, experiencing others as wanting to control them.' And this serves as the justification for their violence against others.

A gender culture that requires men to disavow the feminine is dangerous not only for women but for men themselves. 'Statistically, most lethal violence is committed by men against other men,' Gilligan writes of the incidence of lethal violence in North America and globally. 'Violence is primarily men's work; it is carried out more frequently against men; and it is about the maintenance of "manhood" ... To say that is not to minimize men's violence against women; it is rather, to take the first step toward understanding the etiology of all violence.'[46]

Initiatives to address violence against women are important components of a broader political, educational, juridical, and cultural process needed to change values and behaviours in society. But because violence against women is also driven by conflicts over masculinity that are internal to and between men themselves, it will be impossible to solve the general problem of such violence unless we also solve the problem of organized violence by men against each other, and the fear and devaluation of the feminine on which so much of this intermale violence is based.

Sport, War Culture, and Masculinity from the 1960s to the 1980s

In chapters 4 and 5, I described the evolution of the sport–media complex in the postwar period. I noted that during the 1960s, sport enjoyed its first great expansionary decade since its marriage with television, and that the televised marketing of products through sport sought to appeal to the gendered desires and anxieties of vast male audiences. Having examined the ways in which the emergence of second-wave feminism destabilized gender relations, and how sport, commercial, and media culture in turn responded to these changes, it is important to sketch in the other key sociopolitical developments that had similarly dramatic effects on the consciousness and identity of North American men in the postwar period. Without question, in the 1960s, one of the most difficult developments for American men to negotiate was conscription and mobilization for war in Vietnam, presented in the rhetoric and culture of the times as a test of both individual and national manhood. National politics and gender idealizations fused around the axis of combat and war. The war in Vietnam was rationalized by the most powerful men in the United States as necessary to defend American interests in Asia, and Asians themselves from the Communist peril. It was a war undertaken by a giant nation of huge men against a small country of tiny men – often characterized as 'fags' in American military discourse[47] – in the full arrogance of mature American imperialism. The direct imprint the Vietnam experience left on U.S. service men and the men and women they supposedly fought on behalf of at home, bled into the culture as a whole, affecting, in very disturbing ways, ideals of masculinity, eroticism, and social conduct.

Since the war in Vietnam was a war that the United States lost, and since it came to be seen as an ignominious war, a significant portion of the 1970s, 1980s, and 1990s proliferation of Vietnam culture – 'Vietnam representation,' in Susan Jeffords's phrase – was obsessed with addressing the many agonies and humiliations of the American experience. And, whatever the larger political assessment of failure, the culture also included both celebrating the exploits and restoring the honour of the 'American fighting man.' Jeffords's commentary on Vietnam representation, *The Remasculinization of America: Gender and the Vietnam War*, written in the late 1980s, drew on material from then-contemporary American culture: 'films, novels, personal accounts, collections of observations and experiences, political and social analyses.'[48] Jeffords argues convincingly that these multiple discourses produced a body of representation that was both a collective narrative about the Vietnam war per se, and a collective 'emblematic text' about men, masculinity, and gender in late-twentieth-century America more generally. Jeffords sees this tide of Vietnam representation as having been central in re-creating narrative and symbolic forms that – like those of sport – served to validate what she called 'masculinity' and 'the masculine point of view,' and what I have called 'hypermasculinity.'

Jeffords suggests that 'Vietnam representation is emblematic of the general restructuring and circulation of ideological production in America today.' This general restructuring, she argues, has been taking place around several cross-discursive 'strategies,' all of which were evident in the 1970s and 1980s representations of Vietnam: 'the shift from ends to means, the proliferation of techniques and technologies, the valorization of performance, the production and technologization of the male body as an aesthetic of spectacle, and the blurring of fact and fiction.'[49] These strategies have continued to characterize Vietnam and war representation in the 1990s as well. And they are familiar from sport culture, a partner with Vietnam representation in this larger remasculinization. We shall presently see how sport has been implicated in the violent aestheticization and eroticization of the fighting male body in relation to technology and weaponry. Chapter 8 discusses at length sport's obsession with the high-performance body as such. Most to the point here, however, is that equally within sport and Vietnam representation, as Jeffords puts it, 'the framework through which each of these operations is enacted ... is that of gender.'[50]

With respect to gender, Jeffords notes a number of recurring, indeed structurally central, themes within Vietnam representation. One of these is men's cultural preoccupation with violence and death as compensatory for or parallel to women's ability to give birth. 'War is the enduring condition of man, period,' writes William Broyles Jr in his highly controversial article for the November 1984 issue of *Esquire* magazine about his Vietnam war experiences. In explaining the title, 'Why men love war,' Broyles states that 'war is, for men, at some terrible level, the closest thing to what childbirth is for women: the initiation into the power of life and death.'[51] Our culture has a massive commitment to thinking of war as an essential test of manhood and, like sport, a quintessentially masculine activity.[52] What makes sport and war quintessential tests of manhood is the involvement of danger and violence, actually or symbolically lethal. A similar point was made by NFL lineman Marvin Upshaw, who, when asked by sociologist Michael Messner how he could endure such punishment for so many years, replied:

You know, a lot of people look at a lineman and they say, 'Oh man, you gotta be some kinda *animal* to get down there and beat on each other like that.' But it's just like a woman giving birth ... I think it's something that's an act of God, that's unreal. But she hasn't done nothing she wasn't built for ... Now here I am, 260, 270 pounds, and that's my position ... That's what I'm built for. Just like a truck carrying a big Caterpillar: you see the strain, but that's what it's built for.[53]

The idea that women are built for birth and men for violence and death is one of our gender order's most important organizing principles. Through sport as symbolic war, this idea is not only continuously re-created, but normalized and naturalized in everyday life. It provides an identity anchor for masculine self-definition on both an individual and a social scale, especially if other anchors are melting away. It is also the idea through which sport cultivates our old friend 'the beast' of Victorian masculine sexuality, and harnesses it to violent collective political and economic ends. Today 'the beast,' is called an 'animal,' but his provenance is obvious. In reflecting on his own youthful athletic career in football, Donald Sabo criticizes the bestialization of young football players through pain and injury. 'I learned that pain and injury are "part of the game." I learned to be an animal,' he has written. 'Animals made first team.' 'Being an animal meant being fanatically aggressive and ruthlessly competitive. If I saw an arm in front of me, I trampled it ... The coaches taught me to "punish the other man," and to secretly see my opponents' broken bones as little victories within the bigger struggle.'[54]

The masculine, athletic animal lives to break bones. He is a 'fighting machine,' a 'big caterpillar,' an instrument of violent penetration. Engaging in violence, according to this view of masculinity, actually serves to put men in touch with their deeper, authentic selves. 'War is a brutal, deadly game, but a game, the best there is,' Broyles writes. 'War may be the only way in which most men touch the mythic domains in our soul ... If you come back whole you bring with you the knowledge that you have explored regions of your soul that in most men will always remain uncharted.'[55] The idea that confrontation with death permits a unique exploration of the human and masculine soul has complex sources, and is a feature of masculinity in many different societies. It may well have a physiological basis in the heightened states of awareness that danger and anger trigger through the endocrinological system. These sensations provoke huge cascades of adrenal hormones and neurotransmitters and bring about an intensification of experience. In this sense, they can become addictive as well, especially if other parts of life are devoid of such a quality of experience (alienation), and the action/response of violence/intensification, organized through war, can become a learned response as a pathway to this experiential state.

Our culture has specific obsessions with, and particular interpretations of, this belief in the sacredness of violence in war, not because of hormones or neurotransitters, however, but because of social choices and the influence of mass media culture. The way in which certain types of violence have been institutionalized in the dominant genres of television – from police and detective shows to heroic cartoon characters to sport – heightens both conscious and unconscious expectations that it is only in the masculine encounter with particular forms of violent risk and physical action that personal identity and meaning are possible for males; and that only such males are fit objects of sexual desire for females. Cop or robber, cowboy or Indian, Rambo or 'gook' – these conventions of fictive culture are all ideologically loaded, gendered around the axis of violence, and converge with sport. 'There is a connection between this thrill [of destruction] and the games we played as children,' writes Broyles, 'the endless games of cowboys and Indians and war, the games that ended with "Bang, bang, you're dead." Whenever another platoon got a higher body count, I was disappointed: it was like suiting up for the football game and then not getting to play.'[56] NFL players' representative David Meggyesy further elaborates this connection, proposing that a society's games mirror its historic experiences, that American football is linked to underlying themes of manifest destiny and war, and that, through men's ludic activities that include and ritualize violence, groups both re-enact and rehearse their larger political destinies.[57]

These political destinies are not gender-neutral, however. Boys play cowboys and Indians and football and men wage war. They do so in the pervasive cultural belief that violence is essential to manhood, a belief that has very deep roots in the psyche.

The Erotics of Warrior Culture

'The love of war stems from the union, deep in the core of our being, between sex and destruction, beauty and horror, love and death,' writes William Broyles, Jr, who goes on to say that 'war is, in short, a turn on.'[58] In the last thirty years, within sport and other forms of men's culture, violence and war have been highly sexualized, a process that has been visible in the dramatic eroticization of the athleticized, fighting male body, on its own, and in relation to weaponry and technology. Take, for example, the following excerpt from Don Pendleton's *The Executioner*:

The Executioner moved out, naked, at a low trot toward the riverbank, carrying the pouch containing arms and clothing. These were ... the final minutes before this mission went hard. The American warrior's combat consciousness was already accelerating, jumping ahead to what lay before him. Bolan was a penetration specialist ... He would get inside ... Bolan's motto was 'Live Large, Stay Hard.' His favourite weapon was called the .44 AutoMag, and it was the most powerful going in handguns. It was three and a half pounds of stainless steel ... yeah, stainless steel ... and measured overall, eleven and a half inches. A guy with a small hand wouldn't want to get involved. It took a big, strong hand to cope with the recoil from more than a thousand foot pounds of muzzle energy, and especially long fingers for a comfortable grip and trigger squeeze. Amazing ... yeah ... All silver with ventilated ribs across the top of the barrel.[59]

In this typical example of men's action fiction, the strong, muscled male body, fused with its weaponry, is highly athleticized and eroticized. Bolan is naked, his mission is about to 'go hard,' and his relationship to his gun is transparently sexual. He is a violent, hyperphallic being. However, this form of eroticization increases the hero's sexual interest primarily for men, not for women and, by virtue of its association with violence, is highly sadistic in nature. Susan Jeffords notes that in a heterosexual and patriarchal society it is not acceptable for men to gaze in a frankly erotic manner at the male body.[60] Combat and weaponry thus provide an excuse for such gazing. 'By representing Rambo's body as performance, the otherwise erotically suggestive display of his bare chest throughout the film is diverted as an object of military training, "a fighting machine,"' Jeffords writes of the visual presentation of Sylvester Stallone/Rambo's body in the *Rambo* film cycle. 'Through establishing that body as an object of violence ... erotic desire can be displaced as sado-masochism.'[61]

In Chapter 3, we noted the tendency within late-nineteenth- and early-twentieth-century sport to displace homoerotic interest onto large, strong male bodies engaged in violent physical acts. Jeffords shows the extent to which this tendency is present in representations of Vietnam. Indeed, it is featured throughout the multiple forms of contemporary men's culture. In the men's action genres per se, despite the hero's supermuscular body and (sometimes) the token woman protagonist, all the erotic action takes place between men, and between men and their weapons/extensions. Nakedness is reserved for combat, not lovemaking. Ejaculations are mechanical, not organic. Bonding is intermale but not usually explicitly sexual or genital. Women are present as signs that the soldier is not a homosexual, but in every other respect, they are irrelevant. Sexual energy in violence binds men together in a repressed homoerotic fashion, and only up to a very carefully demarcated point. For in the paradoxical homosocial world of militarized men, as in the world of men's sport, too much affection disrupts the rules of competition, ranking, and aggression that hold the hierarchies together. (I will return to this issue in the next chapter.)

The eroticization of the fighting male body attaches not only to personal weaponry, but to the whole technology of war, inflating it and adding to its appeal and grandeur. 'Through [Rambo] this technology is unchallengeable and its structure of operations seemingly undefeatable,' Jeffords states. 'As the camera's intimate examination of Rambo's body declares, this ideology is seamless.'[62] And while the old army training chant – 'this is my rifle and this is my gun, this is for fighting and this is for fun' – is still being used in the late 1990s, the identification between phallus and weaponry has attached to ever larger systems.[63]

The links between sex, weaponry, death, and war in sport and in men's popular culture are expressions of Eros in an embrace with, not a refusal of, Thanatos.[64] The source of the rage they mobilize may lie, in part, in the claustrophobia boys feel if they are overwhelmed and invaded by women caregivers in a remote-father nuclear family. But another, more obvious, source for this violent aggression lies, as I noted with respect to the program of masculinity for boys of the nineteenth century, largely beyond the worlds and capabilities of women, in the worlds led and dominated by men, where males are often called on, by other men, to sacrifice their bodies and their lives. If boys must create a sense of masculinity largely out of extrafamilial experiences and fantasy construction, one that can serve them during perilous times, many will seize on the most obvious and extreme of masculine associations and masculine symbols. And those symbols and practices that link masculinity to violence, such as sport and military culture, qualify as such.

The period since the 1970s has seen a vast proliferation of men's cultural genres as well as an expansion in the world of sport. In this very broad cultural movement of remasculinization, emotional and sexual intensity have been focused onto men (homoeroticism) and weaponry (lethal technology fetish).[65]

This eroticization of death, worked through the homoerotic 'weaponization' of the athletic male body, represents an antisocial development, but one consistent with the forms of alienation characteristic of this period of history.

Despite its eat-or-be-eaten quality, war, according to William Broyles, still attracts men because its 'enduring emotion, when everything else has faded, is comradeship ... A comrade in war is a man you can trust with anything, because you trust him with your life ... Despite its extreme rightwing image, war is the only utopian experience most of us ever have. Individual possessions and advantage count for nothing; the group is everything. What you have is shared with your friends ... It is, simply, brotherly love.'[66] Of all Broyle's insights, this observation most attests to the bleakness of the contemporary masculine experience for so many men. The 'individual possessions and advantage' that 'count for nothing' are after all what contemporary American society prizes above all other things, the supposedly anticommunist values over which Vietnam was fought. Yet, in men's action genres, as in Broyle's assessment of war in light of his experiences in Vietnam, the material rewards of corporate society do not compensate for a pervasive sense of isolation and meaninglessness, and biting anxieties about economic and sexual performance. Certainly this is the portrait Lewis Lapham paints of the endemically disappointed and miserable 'equestrian class' – his name for the American bourgeoisie.[67] Men's action heroes are always struggling to make their way through a wasteland – jungle, desert, or mountain top – clutching their rigid weapons. As a symbol, their waste lands stand in for all forms of alienation. The dirty, bloody, proletarian work the hero performs appeals to the anger of affluent and powerful males as well as to those less privileged. Across class divisions and cultures, then, like athletes, these heroes and their stories perpetuate the warrior-cult myth that the only place men can have a 'utopian' experience is in combat with other men.

Broyles acknowledges that the desire to wage war is not a constant for all men at all times. 'I am also a father now, and a man who has helped create life is war's natural enemy,' Broyles notes, suggesting, though not pursuing, the allegiance that actual fatherhood and close kinship ties create with peace, and the alliance they potentially create with women, life's 'givers.'[68] War is the time of social fathers – the Fatherhood – organized by men across family ties and divisions of colour and class. For the Fatherhood, individual parenting has been displaced or superseded by the allegiances of collective warriorhood. For many, if not most, boys, the template that prepares them for the demands of the Fatherhood is first cast in childhood by sport.

The sport–media complex both draws on and promotes a militarist response to men's feelings of frustration, isolation, alienation, and rage in corporate society. 'Hit men' reads a typical headline in *Sports Illustrated*, in this case for an article on college linebackers – 'fast, powerful and mean.'[69] On the opposite page, another ad blares 'These two schools are on each other's hit list.' Similar metaphors issue from television: 'Whenever they get together, the fighting is fierce, the tempers are hot ... So you can expect a head on collision this year ... Turn to ESPN. Because we're always putting on the hits.' Militarist terms such as training camp, sudden death, veterans, aerial game, balanced attack, shootout, blitz, bomb, bullet pass, field general, flank, flare, pass, neutral zone, shotgun formation, submarine, and suicide squad suffuse football media and team language, linking and conflating sport and war.

For men who do not fight in wars, or who are preparing for the possibility of fighting or seeking vicariously the lost or never-attained brotherhood of comrade-soldiers, isolation is overcome through sports, which creates a fighting group and supporters with common goals, and promotes common efforts involving physical strength and danger. For players in team sports with risk and violence, a similar experience of trust is established as within the platoon – your teammate is the only one who can pull you out of harm's way when you are under attack by an opponent. It is fascinating to note how often the metaphor of family is applied to the homosocial formations of military and sport culture, and how the idea of the father-headed family is used to legitimize reprehensible behaviours and institutions. For example, in a biographical sketch of former Houston Oiler coach Jerry Glanville, *Sports Illustrated* recalled his response to a 1984 game with Pittsburgh in which the Steelers had 'flattened' the Oilers' quarterback while his teammates stood around helplessly. 'It made me nauseous,' said Glanville, 'I knew then we'd never be any good if we didn't protect each other like family.'[70] In his 'family,' Glanville installed a 'buck-shot four-wideout offensive called the Red Gun and ... a smash-mouth spirit in the defense line,' reports linebacker Robert Lyles, who was prompted to add: 'We're so cocky we'd play Russian Roulette with a guillotine ... Jerry teaches us to expect everything but fear nothing. We go out to tackle them hard on every play. If the sucker's moving, our goal is to get 11 guys on him. Put the flag up. Surrender. He's dead. It's over. He's a landmark. It's hit, crunch and burn.'[71]

Of the origins of Glanville's macho football style, an old friend commented: 'A lot of it has to do with growing up without a father.'[72] The hypermasculine quality of Glanville's approach is explained by his need to compensate in exaggerated terms for the absence of a masculine figure in his own past and in his own psyche. The authoritarian coach is the social father and the emotional linchpin in the hierarchical sport family, just as officers are surrogate fathers (as well as older brothers and uncles) in the homosocial military 'family.'[73] In homosocial combat cultures such as the warrior cult and the core men's sports, women are relegated to a marginal and support position. War organizations and sport create, in fact, a mother-absent family of patriarchs, brothers, and sons. Though both war and many sports put men at risk of serious injury and death, they give men social and symbolic fathers and a sense of security and belonging that seems, at least to many, ultimately more important than the physical risks they are asked to take.

These highly patriarchal cultures communicate that, notwithstanding women's remonstrations about peace and love or the exhortations of social movements for equality, power and domination are the most important goals, and violence is an acceptable way to bring about these ends. Sport sociologist Jay Coakley has concluded that 'repressively organized team structure at least partially accounts for the acceptance and use of violence among players.'[74] Coakley draws an analogy between team athletes and men in prison, whose self-esteem is constantly being challenged and undermined in a variety of ways. The analogy can equally be made with athletes and soldiers. Coakley contends that, like prisoners, an athlete's moral worth is always on the line. 'If an athlete fails to perform, he can be seen to lack loyalty and commitment ... Violent acts become mechanisms through which players' moral worth is demonstrated.' Athletes' adult status, like that of prisoners and soldiers, is undermined by the infantilization of which David Meggyesy also spoke. 'Aggression works to establish adult status in male terms,' Coakley concludes. 'Violence may be the only way to do it.'

Physical well-being, in prison and in the military, depends on the ability to fight. Athletes too have to prove they are not weak or soft. Injuries are 'badges of courage.' By the same token, a prisoner's (and soldier's) masculinity must always be reproven. Violence and domination among athletes is seen as evidence of manhood, the opposite of femininity, just as they are among soldiers, police, and prisoners. 'When violent behaviour is validated as good for the team as a whole, violence becomes the means through which a sense of adequacy is achieved.' Coakley concludes that 'this is one of the ways in which behaviour that is defined as illegal and reprehensible in the everyday lives of most people comes to be defined as normal in at least a portion of the lives of many athletes in some of the most popular sports in North America.'[75]

As we have seen, along with changes in gender relations, the conduct, loss, and aftermath of the war in Vietnam brought a remasculinization of American society that included a heightened emphasis on violence and war in men's and popular culture. Sport and war cultures are related in their underlying ideology of the essentialism of violence to masculinity and sado-masochistic eroticism; in the literary conventions and visual iconography of the athleticized, homo- and techno-eroticized male; and in the way in which these cultures provide a social and symbolic fatherhood that permits the neutralizing of normal morality in the male exercise of force, indeed constructs an alternative morality of coercive entitlement based on valuing force and domination. Now I want to trace more directly how macho athletic patriotism has been expressed in the views and stances of a number of presidents, and the way in which such gendered patriotism has affected the evolution of political discourse and power.

Hypermasculinity, Sport Culture, and the Rise of Neoconservatism

Since the establishment of democratic rhetoric as the dominant political discourse in the nineteenth century, many politicians and officials have sought to justify their actions and policies on the basis of appeals to ideas of equality, fairness, and collective well-being. The idea of democratic rights was created through large, collective struggles of many groups and classes, and produced, at its height, the New Deal and the welfare state. Yet the ideologies of social Darwinism and aggressive individualism have survived among important layers of the population and, in many instances, have overtaken the democratic values in majoritarian political discourse. The triumph of neoconservative politics and neoliberal economics has effected this process in recent times. The political strength of such powerful right-wing ideologies, whether in religious or secular guise, attests to the vitality of underlying ideologies of coercive entitlement, despite widespread social liberalization among other broad social layers. Sport, in partnership with warrior culture, has kept this ideology alive and attractive, and has succeeded in placing its values at the centre of dominant masculine ideals. In this function, it has been crucially abetted by the agents of spectacle – the mass media of communications.

As a shared vocabulary of assumptions, standards, and values, tropes commonly used by the media to express correspondences among sport, politics, war, and gender are powerful cultural agents effecting important ideological operations. Such tropes have had currency in the United States at least since the Civil War.[76] The majority of influential decision-makers in political, economic, and cultural life in the last hundred years have been men whose sense of self was shaped by sport-cultivated expectations for personal and national domination. When a male president or prime minister contemplates going to war or enacting a policy, his character will have a great deal to do with his decisions. And his character includes a certain sense of gender identity, of masculinity. The same can be said for the personnel right across the commanding strata of human society – the male economic, political, military, professional, and cultural elites whose decisions affect large aggregates of people in complex and powerful ways. The identifications of these elites with given groups and institutions are highly gendered as well as demarcated by strong class, religious, ethnic, and other identifications. In the 1960s, this gendering was an important factor in America's imperial conception of itself as a young, virile political force, and in the way its male executive political leadership understood its mission. As historian Geoffrey Smith wrote of the most idealized president of the post–Second World War period,

John F. Kennedy ... entered the White House in 1961, accompanied by 'the best and the brightest' security managers the nation had to offer ... [T]hese ranks included few, if any, females (who might have questioned the Bay of Pigs invasion and Vietnam). The Kennedy men were real men who aimed to get the country 'moving' again and who entreated their countrymen to prepare ... 'to bear any burden, to pay any price' to make the globe safe for liberal democracy. Scholars now note the breadth of that burden, which included Kennedy's attitudes and actions toward women – attitudes and actions apparently shared with male civil rights leaders, black power, and anti-Vietnam protest leaders.[77]

Kennedy was by no means unique in his athletic, aggressive masculinity and gendered political attitudes. Smith calls succeeding presidents Lyndon B. Johnson and Richard M. Nixon 'the two toughest hombres of them all':

Johnson's policies in Vietnam were peppered with sexual references, as the Texan defended his masculinity against adversaries at home and in Southeast Asia. After an American bombing campaign in 1965, he boasted that 'I didn't just screw Ho Chi Minh, I cut his pecker off.' Johnson also had little use for the 'nervous nellies,' persons who questioned his policies, and therefore lacked the necessary sexual equipment. Of one in-house dove, Johnson explained, 'Hell, he has to squat to piss.' Nixon was an even harsher patriarch. His administration nurtured a cult of toughness, underscoring the need to punish dissenters.[78]

This tough, antifeminine mentality toward political opponents among the political cadre was profoundly intertwined with the culture of sport. 'By the time the Watergate tapes were produced during the Nixon administration,' write Sandra Curry-Jansen and Donald Sabo, 'football imagery had become the root metaphor of American political discourse. Indeed Richard Nixon mixed football and political metaphors to the point where the boundaries between the two realms blurred. He selected *Quarterback* for his code name as president and developed the habit of regularly telephoning the coach of the Washington Redskins to discuss strategy before big games.'[79]

Jeffords analyses Richard Nixon's own evaluation of the U.S. loss in Vietnam, and shows how he attributed that loss to 'gutless' and 'feminine' attitudes in the country. 'Emotion, weakness, inaction, negotiation, compromise – all are painted with the palette of blame in Nixon's schema,' she writes. 'Most Vietnam representation ... does not flinch from labeling these as the characteristics and features of the feminine, and does not hesitate to blame the feminine for the loss of the war.'[80]

In my discussion of the men's fraternal lodges in the nineteenth century, I noted how their rituals kept alive an antifeminine ideology of blood and patriarchy with its own rules of participation and entitlement. This was taking place even as political discourse was being feminized and liberalized (notably through church and educational systems, eventually through the welfare state) within mixed culture. Sport, as a bastion of men's culture, has continued to play this masculinist political role in the twentieth century. The labeling of cooperation and compromise as weak and feminine through the warlike ideals and metaphors of sport culture affects broader attitudes to social and political policies of cooperation and collective support. In neoconservative ideology, it leads to a 'feminization,' and thus to a devaluing, of prosocial state policies and services – the redistributive functions of government.[81] Hence, in 1995, public spending on U.S. prisons overtook spending on universities for the first time in history.[82]

The remasculinization of American society was evident in sport and men's cultural genres in the 1960s and 1970s, when the United States was governed by Democratic administrations with a liberal domestic agenda. In the 1980s and 1990s, however, the prosocial (liberal, humanist, cooperative) aspects of government and social policy came to be regarded as feminine, weak, and unmanned, and the antisocial aspects of government and social policy (elitist, militarized, individualist) as masculine and strong. The 'association of the loss of the war [in Vietnam] with the government and the honor of the war with the soldier' that Susan Jeffords found as a theme in 1980s Vietnam representation, 'reconstitutes one of the principal thematics of U.S. culture, in which individual interests exist in tension with those of the society as a whole'[83] – in other words, in which a macho individualism undermines ideas of collectivity.

Thus, the hypermasculinization of American society helped to effect a shift in American political mentality to the right. This was expressed in the election of Ronald Reagan's and George Bush's Republican administrations, in the triumph of the vocabulary of neoconservatism, and in the expansion by the state of large, repressive apparatus and the industries that sustain them, despite the end of the Cold War. Bush himself embodied the hypermasculine ideals: he was a football fanatic and he appointed Arnold Schwarzenegger to head the President's Council on Fitness. Schwarzenegger commented that

[President Bush] loves all sports ... He's very serious and works out everyday in the gym for an hour – barbells, dumbbells, weight machines, rowing, stair climbing, sit-ups, everything. He has a great gym, a complete one, at Camp David and another excellent one at the White House ... Everyone around him – Dick Cheney (secretary of defense), Dr Sullivan, (Louis Sullivan, secretary of health and human services), all his pals – are runners, hikers, basketball players, tennis players, you name it. We're all involved, heavily involved, and Bush insists on that, because he believes you can do a much better job if you're strong, energetic and fit.[84]

This masculinized mentality was a key factor that made it possible for Bush to go to war in the Persian Gulf early in the 1990s. Indeed, the close relationships between war, masculinity, sport, mass media culture, and politics became transparent during that war. Sport scholar Suren Lalvani writes:

On February 27, 1991, at the first press conference held after the invasion of Iraq, General Schwarzkopf, commander of the Allied forces in the Persian Gulf, compared the highly successful flanking move by the allies deep into Iraqi territory to a 'Hail Mary' play in football. 'The desire for a quick and decisive victory that would decimate the Iraqi Army and heal the post-Vietnam national psyche was euphemistically encapsulated in the metaphoric use of the word "touchdown" ... Schwarzkopf's resort to a football metaphor was not the exception.[85] To the contrary. 'During the war, the Pentagon public relations officers seemed to consciously cultivate vocabularies and images of sport,' Sandra Curry-Jansen and Donald Sabo observe. 'The press briefing room in the field closely resembled the set used by producers of television sport media for pre- and postgame analyses and interviews with coaches of professional football teams.'[86] The sport/war metaphors throughout military discourse and media coverage of the Gulf War were so blatant that both U.S. and Canadian networks ran commentary on the phenomenon. War reporting began to use the conventions of sports broadcasts, from instant replays to colour commentary. War became sport and vice versa.

A peak moment in this relationship occurred at the 1991 Superbowl. After international advertising giant Hill and Knowlton, acting on behalf of ruling Kuwaitis, persuaded Congress to wage war rather than exercise economic sanctions against Saddam Hussein or help organize a UN- or Arab-led action, President Bush decided he was going out there to, in his own words, 'kick some ass.' He needed popular support, and so he turned to the NFL. 'The [1991 Superbowl] game between the Buffalo Bills and the New York Giants was ultimately staged as a war spectacle,' write Curry-Jansen and Sabo, 'involving a barricaded stadium, X-ray security searches of 72,500 fans, antiterrorist squadrons in the stands, hand-sized American flags distributed to every seat, a rousing rendition of the national anthem by Whitney Houston, and a rousing half-time speech by President Bush.'[87] The Superbowl was collaboratively produced and cosponsored in truly Orwellian fashion by the NFL, corporate television, and government. In addition to delivering pure pro-war propaganda to a viewership of 750 million people worldwide, it also delivered to the network $800,000 of sponsor fees for every thirty-second spot. The entire five-hour broadcast was one massive infomercial for war, for warlike masculinity and its machines and institutions.

In an influential essay, Richard Grey Sipes investigates the anthropological evidence for two opposing conceptions of the relationship between aggression, sport, and war.[88] In the first theory, which has had the greater currency in both military and sporting circles, aggression is seen to be the result of an innate drive in the human individual, especially male, and this drive generates tension. Tension accumulates in individuals and in society, and seeks an outlet. Combative sports serve to discharge this accumulated tension, thus diverting aggression away from real war and containing it in a ritual vessel. This catharsis theory of sports and aggression is articulated by heavyweight fighter Tom 'The Bomb' Glesby, who said: 'We live in a violent world. It's better to see two guys go in the ring and fight each other legally, with countries going to war and fighting each other like that ... I don't condone violence, but controlled violence is another aspect.'[89] Perhaps the most sophisticated statement of this theory was formulated by sport sociologist Eric Dunning, who argues that

an aspect of the European civilizing process that is of central relevance for the development of modern sport has consisted of a tightening of the normative regulation of violence and aggression, together with a long-term decline in most people's propensity for obtaining pleasure from directly taking part in and/or witnessing violent acts ... Psychologically, this has entailed two things: firstly, the lowering of the 'threshold of repugnance' regarding bloodshed and other direct manifestations of physical violence. As a result, people nowadays tend to recoil more readily in the presence of such manifestations than was the case with people in the middle ages. Secondly, it has entailed the internalization of a stricter taboo on violence as part of the super-ego. A consequence of this is that guilt-feelings are liable to be aroused wherever this taboo is violated.[90]

The accompanying taboo on watching physical violence to which Dunning refers was in part responsible for the kind of emotional reaction groups and individuals had to the war in Vietnam. As film and television cameras brought a spectacle of brutality and suffering into North American living rooms night after night, the images became unbearable. By the same token, however, the absence of such imagery and its replacement by the imagery of technological warfare in the Persian Gulf made the waging of a destructive war seem insignificant. Terms such as 'surgical strikes' and 'collateral damage' went hand in hand with images of planes and missiles, roads and maps. The environmental damage caused by oilwell firestorms, and the pain and privation of huge civilian populations may have been real but were absent from the television screen. Out of sight, out of mind.

The second conception of the relationship between war and sport – the culture pattern theory – sees individual and group aggressive behaviour as a learned response. This view sees a tendency toward consistency in a society, so that similar values and behaviour patterns such as aggressiveness tend to manifest themselves in many areas of culture. War and combative sports are seen to overlap and reinforce one another, rather than substitute for each other. Sipes finds overwhelming evidence for the second model, the 'culture pattern' theory, and virtually none for the first, the catharsis theory. He concludes that 'cross-culturally, war and combative sports show a direct relationship. War and combative type sports therefore do not, as often claimed, act as alternative channels for the discharge of accumulable aggressive tensions ... war and combative sports activities in a society appear to be components of a broader cultural pattern.'[91]

In his book *No Contest: The Case Against Competition*, Alfie Kohn reviews a broad sample of anthropological, sociological, and psychological studies on the catharsis theory, arrives at a similar conclusion, and notes that 'there are few beliefs so widely held by the general public that have been so decisively refuted by the evidence.'[92] He reminds us that ethologist Konrad Lorenz himself told an interviewer late in his life that he had developed 'strong doubts' whether watching aggressive behaviour even in the guise of sport has any cathartic effect at all. Psychoanalyst Bruno Bettelheim also noted that competitive or spectator sports 'raise aggressive feelings of competitiveness to the boiling point.' For George Orwell, sport was 'war minus shooting.' Douglas MacArthur and Dwight D. Eisenhower agreed. Eisenhower declared that 'the true mission of American sports is to prepare young people for war.'[93]

However, in such competitive, warlike training, we equip ourselves poorly for peace. 'Football players are expected and required to be good sportsmen when we are engaged in an endeavour that is hostile and aggressive,' a safety for the New York Giants points out. 'To go from being gentlemanly and following the rules of society to people who play violently and aggressively for two or three hours on Sunday ... It's not easy to do, especially when the people around the line of scrimmage are literally the enemy.'[94] It is not surprising, then, that so many athletes find themselves involved in violent assaults against both women and men outside the legal boundaries of play. Contemporary big-time sport culture, interwoven with the cult of the warrior and a culture of domination, and based on competition, promotes both intermale and male–female violence. This violence can be direct and physical or abstract and institutional. This reality stands in dramatic contrast to the rhetoric of sportsman-like and gentlemanly behaviour regularly trotted out in defence of sport by many of its traditional apologists. The dichotomy between the rhetoric of peace and democracy and the physical practices of violence and domination in sport culture is evidence of the extent to which sport is still a blind spot in social consciousness. Perhaps this is due to the wider refusal to face how American social structures, institutions, and economies promote war. For then the question of how to reorient these is posed, and it is difficult to answer. Nevertheless, the simultaneous cultivation and disavowal of masculinist political violence is deeply characteristic of American society. The cover for an August 1997 issue of *Time* magazine vividly illustrates this schizoid quality. A bold, approving painting of a macho chimera fills up the page. It has a huge, bulging body of Arnoldian perfection, its loins are clothed in briefs made of the American flag, and its head is that of a bald eagle. The headline reads: 'Even its best friends are asking: is America in danger of becoming a bully?'

Because men's genres of entertainment that present violence as spectacle are one of the most important staples of the mass media in North America, one question that has generated considerable debate is whether the media cause violence. Certainly, no single image of violence, however brutal, can be declared a direct incitement to assault on its own. The meaning of a single image depends on context, content, and receiver. But an entire fabric of violent representation – acted out in ways that range from direct modelling to implicit messages of approval through mainstream genres of representation – does present a picture of a violent social world whose categories imprint themselves on social and political consciousness.

The Hollywood apologists for this existing cultural production tell us not to worry about the materials they generate through commercial culture. Portrayals of psychotic snipers, abusive husbands, power-hungry politicians, and corrupt police officers are defended as either 'harmless entertainment' or 'news'.[95] Further, some cultural theorists insist, audiences know the difference between 'actuality' or 'fantasy,' between 'imaginary' and 'real' violence, and can discriminate and choose appropriate meanings. They can watch sport in the same spirit, maintaining a similar ironic, cynical, or playful stance toward what they see.

The problem with stressing the agency of the viewer is that it disregards the deeper-level effects of watching what is offered by the mass media. For example, it is not possible that North American children, watching thousands of television commercials per year, should not be profoundly affected by the main messages and features of this commercial discourse. The idioms of gender, class, race, physical ability, and material possessions of this commercial discourse are the *lingua franca* of youth. By the same token, sport and other ubiquitous forms of men's culture that overlap with commercial or publicity discourse and are taught and reinforced at school, cannot be written off as 'harmless.' Personal and political choices, from personal comportment to voting, are profoundly shaped and constrained by the values and expectations people absorb from their cultural institutions. In the absence of other forms of information – about gender, sexuality, material success, law, violence, political enfranchisement – choices that are outside of or in opposition to these institutions and the cultural genres that represent them are foreclosed as surely as if they did not exist 'objectively' at all. This is especially true if – as happens through the practice of sport – the same values the media are celebrating have taken up residence in the bodies and in the unconscious of very large numbers of boys and men. For this reason, the struggle over the way in which society organizes its physical cultures and its communications is the struggle over what kind of society it actually is and wants to be.

In deploying violence through men's cultural genres, especially sport, the mass media craft particular forms of political consciousness. Legitimizing violence through the ritualization of physical games both validates and mystifies organized coercion by the powerful, a process in which violence is celebrated and censured at the same time. As the force meted out by the possessors of sanctioned violence, violence is constructed as good. As an unsanctioned act outside the rules of the game – the realm of the outlaw – violence is bad. This powerful ideological operation allows for the disassociation from, and the refusal to take responsibility for, violent acts and policies. So politicians pretend that war is an ugly necessity that we engage in for 'defence,' because corrupt regimes force us to, even as they promote a war economy and war itself. We deny our society's responsibility for war and violence, and deny that sport has anything to do with encouraging it.

The ideology of coercive entitlement, based in a view of aggression as instinctual and competition as sublime, a view naturalized by masculinist sport, justifies political conservatism, the support of the status quo, and the violence it embodies. James Gilligan writes:

If the assumption is that violence is an inextricable part of our inborn 'human nature,' then clearly the only way to keep the problem under control is to emphasize just that: control, meaning the control of some people (whose violence is 'bad') by other people (whose violence is ... 'good'). The fact that that 'solution' simply constitutes a perpetuation of violence, a 'recycling' of it, so to speak, among different victims, rather than the elimination or prevention of it, can always be regarded as unavoidable, if violence is instinctual ... The problem with this ... moral, legal framework, which is the existing arena of jurisprudence, judgment, and punishment [is that it] often leads to the aggravation of violence and its perpetuation.[96]

Far from an unwanted, anomalous, and episodic problem in sport, violence is actually central to it and to the hypermasculine dimensions of the culture surrounding it. If the ritual violence of sport is a drama enacted primarily between men, a drama of intermale rivalry, it functions to maintain a whole superstructure of complex inequalities – between genders, classes, races, abilities, languages, and so forth – structured in the characteristic modes of corporate capitalism. And via sport, in the service of the warrior cult, this system of masculinism is maintained through the selective brutalization of males. 'Both men and women seem to feel that men are more acceptable as objects of physical violence than women are,' writes James Gilligan, 'for both sexes kill men several times more often than they kill women.'

Even in experimental studies conducted by psychologists, both men and women exhibit greater readiness and willingness to inflict pain on men than on women, under otherwise reasonably identical conditions. Studies of child abuse in those countries in which reasonably accurate statistics are available find that boys are more often victims of lethal or life-threatening violent child abuse (being treated as violence objects), ... with few exceptions. Virtually every nation that has had a military draft has decided either that only men should be drafted, or that only men should be sent into combat. Again none of this should surprise us, given the competition between men for status, valor, bravery, heroism – and honour – in patriarchal societies.[97]

As others have pointed out before, as well as being a system in which men as a gender have greater privileges than women, masculine dominance is a system in which a minority of elite and senior males dominates, and benefits from, a majority of disadvantaged and junior males.[98] Such a system therefore entails a net loss for the majority of men. They lose as much, or more, to the demands of patriarchy as they gain from the service of women. As an ongoing codification of ideal masculinity, sport plays an important role in maintaining this unequal system. 'Male gender codes reinforce the socialization of boys and men, teaching them to acquiesce in (and support, defend and cling to) their own set of social roles,' Gilligan notes. 'Boys and men are exposed thereby to substantially greater frequencies of physical injury, pain, mutilation, disability, and premature death. This code of honour requires men to inflict these same violent injuries on others of both sexes, but most frequently and severely on themselves and other males, whether or not they want to be violent toward anyone of either sex.'[99]

The ability to endure pain and to risk one's life – the qualities developed in the masculine warrior – are heroic abilities that have historically elicited awe in relation to violence and war. Glorifying heroes who excel in killing others, however, stops us from seeing the socially dysfunctional nature of violence as an individual, social, or political survival strategy. The costs of class, racial, national, and ethnic violence on individuals and communities, the impact of violence against women on women, children, and gender relations, and the ravages of the violent instrumentalism of industrialization on the biosphere all put its viability into question. We need new heroes who model a masculinity constructed along prosocial, not antisocial lines.

I will return to this question in the concluding chapter, when I address the need for change in sport. By way of getting there, I now want to look at the relation of sport to some of the specific tensions that have existed between men in postwar society – tensions rooted in class, race, and sexual orientation, and articulated around specific ideals of masculinity.

7

'Hooligans, Studs, and Queers':
Three Studies in the Reproduction of
Hypermasculinity

Hypermasculinity – the belief that ideal manhood lies in the exercise of force to dominate others – is the prevalent ideology of manhood in contemporary society. While many of the distinctive characteristics of hypermasculinity (notably those related to warrior culture) pre-date our own century, ideal hypermasculinity is not static. Rather, it maintains its contemporary appeal by co-opting ideals and styles of minority and even oppositional men's subcultures and mutating in appearance accordingly. In the 1980s, for example, newspaper and television images of British 'soccer hooligans' conducting gang warfare in European capitals publicized the activities of a small group of British men to the global mainstream. These images glamourized and normalized violent standards of hypermasculinity that had been cultivated in a small, distinct, class- and nation-based men's subculture. Doc Martens, the hooligans' favourite shoe, became fashionable footwear for cohorts of young people around the world. Meanwhile, with the U.S. and global expansion of football and basketball and the commercialization of Olympic sports in the United States, black male athletes went from triumph to athletic triumph. The collective masculine persona the mass media constructed for and around them strongly influenced standards of masculinity. As well, in the same decade, from yet another men's subculture, homoerotic imagery moved from the gay margins into the mainstream advertising and fashion industries.

Poststructuralist and postmodern theorists have argued that because the great master-narratives of the Enlightenment and modernism (rationalism, humanism, progress, liberalism, socialism) have lost their power to cohere society and individual identities, we are witnessing a multiplication of identities, and, with this, of masculinities in contemporary life. Indeed, at the individual and subcultural level we have hetero, bi-, and homosexual, pro-woman, misogynist, nurturing, and destructive masculinities, inflected with national, ethnic, regional, race, and class tones. Postmodernists stress the ways in which this multiplicity of identities complicates, disrupts, and further fragments the modernist ideologies, including gender ideologies. Thinkers working within this perspective are right to note the demise of many of the great modernist '-isms' in this period. Postmodernist writers have done excellent work in detecting and sensitizing us to ways that individuals and communities have resisted prescriptive and oppressive ideologies within their cultures on a daily basis, and helped us understand the dynamics of subcultural community formation.

However, the conditions of inequality that the modernist ideas sought to explain and address have not disappeared, despite vast changes in technology and consciousness. Financial, political, and military power is more concentrated today than at any other time in human history. Hence, I disagree with the postmodernist assessment of the relative power of dominant and emergent/ oppositional ideologies and identities in advanced capitalist societies. While many North Americans no longer believe politicians on either the left or right, and are wary of their rhetorical ideals and promises, this has not translated into a political radicalization, but rather to an overall conservatism, if that word can aptly be used to characterize the combination of mean-spirited individualism, patriarchal gender norms, and antisocial state policies evident in North American neoconservative political culture in the 1980s and 1990s.

Within this ideological climate, the sport–media complex is not a fluid, shifting 'discourse,' but a set of large, powerful economies and institutions. In sport's apparent distance from work and politics, it may be easy to forget the economics that lie behind it. There is a materiality to the conditions and relations of cultural production – sport in this case – that the postmodernist perspective tends to obscure. Further, there is an ideological consistency in sport culture with respect to gender, linked to its materiality, that constitutes a successful master-narrative of hypermasculinity within a fragmented cultural landscape. As I have argued at some length, when traditional identity anchors are shuffled or undermined by the mobility demanded by capitalism, the importance of gender and sex in identity construction expands. Sport culture, working within this dimension, has been highly influential in shaping and homogenizing masculine ideals across, through, and despite the multiple and diverse masculinities of real men.

To make this case for the ongoing power of hypermasculine ideology, in this chapter I examine the three examples already mentioned: British football hooliganism, the cult of the black super-athlete, and the convergence of gay culture with the athleticized body. In all three instances, the body is deployed around or through sport to assert a sexualized and politicized gender identity. In all three cases, sexuality is mobilized in homosocial ways in the culture surrounding sport, as well as within sport practice itself. However, the relationships between sport practices and sport culture differ significantly in these cases. In the case of soccer hooliganism, the athletic match has provided space *outside* the stadium for a sport culture consisting of violent male territorial battles. In the case of the cult of the black super-athlete, the game *inside* the stadium has been the major site for the assertion of racial pride through manly achievement, while commercial discourse publicizes, diffuses, and extols this achievement. In the case of the gay subculture, sport has provided a source of ideals and the training 'lifestyle' to produce the built, hypermasculine body so ardently cultivated in gay gyms from the 1970s to the present, and gay body aesthetics have in turn informed commercial discourse and physical idealization. Yet despite all these apparent subcultural differences, the hypermasculine idealizations of sport culture appear coherently in each case. As in other chapters, I want to explore the political implications for the larger society of the hypermasculinist gendering that takes place through sport culture.

Hypermasculinity and Football Hooliganism

The solidarity-producing qualities of sport have been celebrated at length in popular writing and in scholarship. The xenophobic impulses in the dominant men's sports, on the other hand, have received less attention. The way sport tends to organize around competing identifications, the way it draws lines and divisions, the way its objectives are to dominate and even obliterate the designated Other – all these aspects of sport contribute to the way it often nurtures xenophobia and antisocial behaviours. Xenophobic impulses are obviously not confined to any continent, nor to any one sport or set of fans. Rioting, injury, and death motivated by class, racial, national, and ethnic divisions have occurred worldwide as the result of sporting matches. North America is no exception. In June 1993, four people were killed in Chicago when riots broke out after the Chicago Bulls' victory in the National Basketball Association championship. 'A crowd pulled drivers from their cars at an intersection, shot to death one man and stabbed another,' sportswriter James Christie noted at the time. 'Police arrested 682 people and 164 were charged with felonies – mostly break-ins. Yet this was a quieter, less violent celebration than those that followed the Bulls' 1991 and 1992 NBA wins, and its death toll fell short of the seven recorded in Detroit after the Pistons' 1990 championship victory.'[1] In 1997, three people lost their lives in Chicago after yet another Bulls victory.

While these riots have been episodic in the United States, a subculture of soccer violence has existed in the United Kingdom since the late nineteenth century. In the 1980s, amid Thatcherite monetarism and post-imperial sabre-rattling (the Falklands War), a particularly strong wave of such hooliganism erupted. Over that decade, lethal collective violence was so routinely practised around both championships and weekly games that soccer matches throughout the UK and Europe were regulated by mounted police forces and large army contingents. The riots resulted in many injuries and deaths, making for hot media coverage.

In the fan culture surrounding British soccer, violence had traditionally been incited by local, regional, class, and racial identifications that echoed England's history of colonialism. But in the 1980s soccer hooliganism grew in ferocity and scope in response to a new reality – that of competition with Europe. Even as soccer violence escalated in cities and towns all over the British Isles, it expanded into Europe and targeted other Europeans – that is, white people not traditionally regarded as the Other within British imperialist race typologies. In Europe, the Heyschel Stadium massacre in Brussels in 1986 is the best known of hundreds of incidents in which British football supporters launched campaigns of mayhem on others – in this case, Italians – whom, they believed, threatened the integrity of their identity. In England and Scotland this violence coincided with a dismantling of public funding for recreation and public works, and a crisis of disrepair in many soccer stadiums. Unable to withstand the mass motion of fan participation and rioting, a number of stadiums gave way and increased the number of injuries and deaths. Hundreds of people died and thousands sustained injuries.

Writer and editor Bill Buford spent several years observing and documenting football hooligans in England during the 1980s. He became a participant-observer in football hooliganism in order to better understand the perplexing phenomenon of football violence and the dynamics of violent crowds. Buford reveals that the gangs of violent, organized club supporters, a minority within the broader soccer culture, were also a highly active part of that culture as well. 'In Britain, fifteen million people would watch the match on television – a quarter of the population, a staggeringly popular manifestation of popular culture,' Buford writes.[2] The hooligans knew they had huge audiences for their performances, and the audiences watched them with baited breath. The hooligans revelled in the radical militarization of 'leisure moments,' as country after country brought in heavier security measures to deal with them, and the media devoted more and more attention to their exploits.[3]

Buford's descriptions of violent engagements strikingly convey the sexual thrills of soccer violence. He captures the erotic anticipation of menace and power in his pictures of pre-game and pre-riot rituals. When one 'firm' of supporters finally connects with another and/or the local citizenry in the streets, 'ecstasy' follows in an orgy of mayhem. Buford makes clear that the experi-

ence of football hooliganism is one of astounding violence against the designated Other, as well as an experience of extreme self-mortification. He dwells
on the results of massive over-drinking, bruises, broken limbs, arrests from
street fighting, and, sometimes, death. But the physical and sexual high – the
hormones released by danger, the psychic sense of release expressed by violence, and the emotion of belonging (which he calls one of 'happiness') –
overcomes the pain, or fear of pain, in the riots themselves.[4] 'Violence is one
of the most intensely lived experiences,' says Buford, 'and, for those capable
of giving themselves over to it, is one of the most intense pleasures.'[5] As the
descriptions in Buford's text reveal, the main attraction of hooliganism lies in
the realm of pleasure, lust, and violence, in the clearly sexual pleasure that
seems all the more intense for being rarely genital. This is the kind of sexuality
William Broyles wrote about in 'Why Men Love War.'[6]

Buford considers a number of explanations to account for the draw and
power of football violence. Included in his analysis is the sociological view
that hooliganism originates in the dispossessed or disgruntled members of the
working or lower middle class whose communities have been decimated by
government downsizing, cutbacks, and corporate reorganizations. The thugs in
Buford's book emerge as plumbers, electricians, car mechanics, telephone workers, and petty criminals, but, despite the fact that they seem to have adequate
financial resources, the desperate bleakness overtaking their communities forms
the overarching context of their lives. In this sense, Buford's experience con-
firms many elements of the sociological explanation for football hooliganism.[7]
Still, as Buford spent time with groups of soccer supporters and went on
rampages with them, he concluded that, while important, the class desperation
factor was not enough to account for the love of real violence displayed by
football supporters on a regular and organized basis. Most people Buford interviewed in the fans' communities abhorred hooliganism. Buford thus turned to
the idea of the aggressive crowd itself and its inherent potential for violence,
particularly if its members are desperate enough and 'deadened' enough to
need 'violence to wake [themselves] up.' The 'lad culture' of football hooliganism, he concludes, 'pricks itself so it has feeling, burns its flesh so it has
smell.'[8]

Buford set out to answer the question of why young males engage in football
violence. But he did not fully explore the first term of that question: young
males. Buford frequently uses the word 'crowd' as a neutral, generic term even
though he clearly discusses hooliganism as 'lad culture.' But hooligan crowds
are men's gangs, expressions of men's culture, leaping into the terrain of
mixed culture. They are not crowds of men and women equally laying waste to
neighbourhoods. Gangs of soccer fans are not gender-neutral but hypermasculine
'crowds.' In these crowds, the intense need to feel liked or loved is a driving

force. It is expressed not in the bestowal of affection by supporters on a welcoming town, but in the bonding achieved with brothers-in-arms from one's own town, through assault, ravage, and plunder. Belonging, dominating, and violating during football riots are experienced as one emotional totality. There are generally few rapes, though much sexual harassment, because it is the rape of the city and its whole population that constitutes the orgasmic experience, not an individual sexual act. In keeping with men's monopoly over coercive power, these gangs of threatened men exercise their masculinist right to dominate public space by enacting their rituals of violent rage on city streets.

The most important characteristic of soccer violence – one that class and employment status cannot account for – is the fact that hooliganism is committed by a specific group of men, asserting their manhood through protomilitary actions on public terrain, as male practice. For these men, if a mêlée results in the mobilization of the army and the mounted police, it is considered a success. When one group of supporters had humiliated another, Buford notes: 'The language – rich, as usual, in military metaphors – is important; the firm from East London had entered the city of Manchester and had taken it. They had made a point of showing that they could take whatever liberties they wanted to. They had walked into the city as if it had been their own.'[9]

While Buford provides many useful insights into football hooliganism, he is ultimately unable to answer the question he originally posed about its aetiology because he fails to fully explore its gendered nature. As long as gender itself is not considered a central part of the framework for analysing soccer violence, a satisfactory answer will never be achieved. For soccer hooliganism is a gender-specific way of expressing class- and nation-linked xenophobic and coercive ideologies. For example, in the following passage from *Among the Thugs*, we can see how local, national, gender, and sexual identifications combine to produce aggression. Here, Buford had just landed in Turin on an airplane full of Manchester United supporters who had consumed hundreds of gallons of beer, wine and vodka on the trip over, and were in a riotous mood. Looking out the windows they spotted a contingent of the Italian army. 'The soldiers were funny looking according to Mick, who was sitting next to me,' writes Buford.

Actually the phrase he used was 'fuckin' poofters.' They wore strange uniforms and brightly coloured berets; the soldiers were not English – that was the point; the soldiers were *foreign*. The effect was immediate: these were no longer supporters of Manchester United; they had ceased to be Mancunians; in an instant, their origins had, blotter like, spread from one dot on the map of the country to the entire map itself.[10]

The identifications made by soccer hooligans with city, country, class, and language – the 'honour' of which they are defending – are evident in this

description. What is also suggested is the process by which these identifications become linked in the psyche of the soccer supporter, how they spread
'blotter-like' during the metamorphosis hooligans undergo before each battle,
from a group of individual working blokes to a cohesive, savage crowd flying
national colours. In Buford's many descriptions, it is clear that the local identification animates the general (a neighbourhood team represents a city, a city
team represents the nation). It is equally clear, however, that gender identifications, and the emotions and energy they mobilize, provide the violent thrust
that finally ignites the group into outright assault. On the way to the Turin
game, Buford describes chants such as 'fuck the Pope' and 'kill the poofters'
that sexualized the hooligans' political rage, while in Sardinia chants of
'England! England! England!' established and expressed a sexual driving
rhythm.[11]

The core identification that links municipal and national identifications for
the football hooligan is expressed in a physically palpable 'celebration' of
masculine coercive entitlement on the streets of neighbourhoods of cities affiliated to rival teams. Through the ritual desecration this celebration involves, we
see how the male fan's need to confirm his masculinity and reclaim his manhood impart power to the other traditionally 'political' identifications – local,
racial, ethnic, or national – the athletic contest is seen to represent. The masculine self that is battling on the physical and symbolic terrain of hooligan sport
culture is engaged with the Others (white or black) as aggressors. However,
while ideas of class, ethnicity, and nationalism define the targets of xenophobia
and racism, and while women may hold similar views to those of soccer thugs,
and even provide support services that free men to engage in soccer culture,
the physical violence itself is an action of men, and a phenomenon of
hypermasculinity.

Hence the hooligan or gangster is not a unique expression of a singular set
of circumstances, but a recognizable type who appears when a particular constellation of conditions – dislocation, emotional deprivation, and socialized
brutalization of males – are present. So, for example, the loss of the First
World War and the dislocation, dispossession, and shaming of Germany's
lower-middle and working classes in the 1920s, inflicted by the Treaty of
Versailles and the Depression, produced and sustained similar formations of
males who took pleasure in launching gang assaults on neighbourhoods and
cities. In *Male Fantasies*, Klaus Theweleit paints a profile, similar to that of
the soccer thug, of the men who made up Hitler's early Nazi shock troops.[12] In
the United States, the militias and neo-Nazi organizations, one of which was
responsible for the Oklahoma city bombing of 1995 in which over 250 people
were killed, attract this type of individual: a person who makes sense of his

troubles by blaming and physically attacking people of his own or lower socio-economic status in hypermasculinist ways legitimized by the values of warrior and sport culture.

Psychiatrist and prison administrator James Gilligan sheds light on the psychodynamics of masculine violence within these particular types of social conditions. As we have seen, Gilligan locates violence primarily in the workings of masculine dominance ('patriarchy'), a gender system in which males are emotionally and physically brutalized, and in which many men are disadvantaged by poverty and cultural stigmatization while a minority benefit from wealth and power. The character traits that men socialized by patriarchy find intolerably shameful, are, according to Gilligan, 'weakness, cowardice, impotence, homosexuality, sexual inadequacy, and so on'[13] – the so-called feminine characteristics. Men to whom these qualities are anathema and who are dislocated and disempowered by larger economic and political trends will tend to experience themselves as 'feminized,' 'unmanned' by the workings of society. This emasculation precipitates a response of shame and anger, and of banding together in gangs to reassert gender and community honour. This sense of honour and shame both genders and sexualizes most social divisions and political conflicts. Gilligan sees shame as the inducer of all forms of violence – whether of the individual murderer or the collective gang member or the bellicose nation-state. With respect to most murder and gang warfare (he considers prisons and war to be sanctioned gang warfare), Gilligan sees poverty as the major culprit in creating conditions in which men feel so shamed they must strike out in violence. And he ascribes to gender culture the responsibility for encouraging men to defend their honour through violence.[14]

The political effects of this kind of hypermasculinity are profoundly regressive. For when relatively powerless people are used as targets of rage by other disadvantaged groups, the truly powerful, those far above them in status and power, need never feel the fury of the dispossessed. They escape social and political accountability, and systemic inequalities remain intact. It is not a coincidence that many British hooligans, as individuals and through their clubs, have associations to neo-Nazi groups. The political valence of a culture that supports the idea of all-male gangs who roam the civil landscape and attack the citizenry is a fascistic one. This hypermasculine form of men's rivalry shifts the political dynamic to the right in several ways. As well, it calls for a militarized response to its violent initiatives on the part of the state. In this way, it strengthens the political impulses to develop further the repressive apparatus of the state within society as a whole. And it totally marginalizes women from the real and symbolic 'action.' This is true of its sexuality as well. Within hooligan culture, as in U.S. men's culture (discussed in the previous chapter) sexuality is mobilized primarily in homosocial contexts, as a dynamic among and between men, expressed sadistically through violence. The following quotation from Buford's *Among the Thugs* describes a party ritual in which the homoerotic nature of this subculture is evident:

The air had grown heavy and damp. Sixty or seventy lads were in the middle of the room, clasped together, bouncing up and down, rubbing their hands over each other's heads and chanting in unison: Wogs out! White power! ... They had taken off their shirts and were stripped to the waist, their braces dangling by their sides, knocking against their legs ... covered in perspiration, pressed tightly together. They were bouncing so vigorously that they all fell over, tumbling on top of each other ... they resumed their dancing. They fell over again, wet and hot ... There was a menacing feeling in the air – sexual and dangerous ... I looked at the women, sitting in the dark, smoking cigarette after cigarette, none of them dancing. Something was happening that they didn't understand.[15]

The football hooligan subculture is based on extreme physical behaviour. In addition to kicking and striking actions during a battle, vomiting, defecating, and urinating are common. In psychoanalytic terms, these forms of expression are associated with a stage of infantile character development (anality) that precedes the so-called genital phase, in which the child finally differentiates himself or herself from others and understands the world as separate. (Orality is the first of these stages.) Regardless of whether or not one finds this terminology useful, there is a regressive quality to the explosive, scatological sadism of hooligan culture – a sense that it is a huge temper tantrum thrown by large, dangerous children. At the same time, we might equally ask what social stresses elicit this violent striking out. Why do some periods (such as the 1930s or the 1980s) bring about such dramatic increases in this behaviour? The targets and the forms of violence chosen by soccer hooligans suggest their practitioners perceive themselves to be traduced objects of extreme invasion. Invasion is one of the major metaphors mobilized by anti-immigrant, populist, right-wing political movements thriving all over Europe and North America in times of economic difficulty and dislocation. Invasion implies the penetrated, violated – feminine – position. Hypermasculine soccer hooliganism, and other forms of right-wing gang activity, reassert the penetrating, violent, masculine position. In this sense, this form of gang behaviour can arise whenever groups of men who have been given permission (through idealizations of competition and violence) and social space (the turf around the stadium, membership in the armed forces) to enact their masculinist dramas. Few people from any political perspective would argue that football violence has any socially redeeming qualities, whatever causes they may ascribe to it. In this instance, the cleaving to hypermasculine standards of behaviour by a subculture of men clearly produces a social negative. Now I want to turn to a phenomenon that has been greeted as socially positive – the emergence in the United States of a cult of black super-athletes. Here, as in British football hooliganism, sport articulates with social divisions and an intermale pecking order, and ideals of hypermasculinity are implicated with sport in an interaction between a subculture and the dominant culture.

Sport, Hypermasculinity, and the Reproduction of Racism

In 1997, North America marked the fiftieth anniversary of Jackie Robinson's recruitment by the Brooklyn Dodgers and the breaching of the colour bar in U.S. professional sport.[16] Fittingly, in the same year, young Tiger Woods, son of an African-American father and a Thai mother, won the Master's golf tournament in Augusta, Georgia, the youngest player with the best score ever on the course.[17] Isaiah Thomas became the first black majority stockholder of a major league team (the Toronto Raptors), breaking through another traditional racist boundary in big-time sport.[18] Meanwhile, Michael Jordan continued to excel on the basketball court and in business. The media and the world of sport celebrated these events and the remarkable black athletes who had, in the intervening decades, risen to prominence in all the major North American sports (with the exception of hockey).

However, notwithstanding Woods's and Thomas's achievements, no one would deny that the world of professional sport is still deeply marked by racist stratifications. As Kooistra, Mahoney, and Bridges note:

Racism pervades professional sports. Studies have long suggested that minorities are grossly underrepresented in management positions and in more prestigious player positions that are presumed to require leadership qualities such as intelligence, emotional stability, and greater responsibility. Nonwhites instead are disproportionately located in positions demanding more 'innate' athletic ability such as speed, quickness, or brute strength. Recent data suggest that little has changed.[19]

Indeed, it is not anomalous to find sport and sport culture confirming colour conflicts and racist dynamics, as well as transcending them. In the vast majority of American cities, the playing of popular sport is de facto segregated – in neighbourhood lots, in high-school gyms, and at college games.[20]

The mainstream view, however, contends that despite these well-known realities, sport delivers positive experiences of black achievement and interracial and intercultural collaboration. These are seen to counteract the prejudices of racist culture and to deliver prestige and wealth to successful individuals. For the most part, the phenomenon of black athletes 'dominating' the athletic field and 'representing' black America has been seen as positive – for the individuals involved and for their communities. The black super-athlete has been welcomed as a wholesome, healthy, successful role model. Indeed, the athlete's triumph is felt by many to rehabilitate the image of the black male, so distorted and stereotyped by mainstream, racist culture. As the quintessential meritorious American hero, many have greeted his ascendance as a fundamental challenge to racism.

I agree that camaraderie grows between black and white athletes and that this can be important to individual athletes, their families, and communities. In the 1960s the connections made between white and black musicians animated rock and roll, and went on to affect society as a whole. As well, there is no doubt that the success of black athletes has provided dramatic evidence of equality in athletic and human terms, especially from the 1940s to the 1960s. Further, the power and the beauty of the great postwar black athletes' performances are a tribute to tremendous skill, intelligence, fortitude, and style. At the same time, in less obvious ways, the engagement of sport culture with black athletes has tended to reinforce inequality, rather than undermine it, from the late 1960s to the present.

The new ways in which sport and sport culture have functioned to support rather than challenge racism today are related to the strategies used by the mass media to frame and market successful black athletes. I refer here to television, radio, print, and cyber sport journalism as such, but also to celebrity journalism (*People, Vanity Fair*, television talk shows), news journalism (*Time, Newsweek*), women's and men's sport publications (*Self, Men's Health*), and, weaving its way through all of these, the discourse of advertising. The dominant strategy across the mass media has been to present the black super-athlete as a rebel-stud turned corporate hero.[21] This strategy has had consequences for processes of masculine idealization not only for the black community, but for the larger culture of hypermasculinity where sport heroes are so profoundly influential. In the fifty years between the achievements of Jackie Robinson and Tiger Woods, a tremendous link has been forged both in the black community, and in mainstream culture, between ideals of black pride, black masculinity, and athletic achievement.

Henry Louis Gates, Jr, among a number of other distinguished black intellectuals, has discussed how the gendering and sexualization of politics evolved within the black community, and the kind of masculinity it tended to favour.

While some black artists raised questions about a hypermasculine gender order in the 1960s, Gates nevertheless suggests that evolving black nationalism was based on an idea of manhood that was super-heterosexual and powerfully homophobic:

This is not to say that the ideologues of black nationalism in this country have any unique claim on homophobia. But it is an almost obsessive motif that runs through the major authors of the black aesthetic and the Black Power movements. In short, black identity became sexualized in the sixties in such a way as to engender a curious subterraneous connection between homophobia and nationalism.[22]

I have argued that homophobia is often strongly motivated by men's fear of the 'feminine' qualities – softness, weakness, dependency, sexual receptivity – that are disclaimed in violent sport and displaced onto homosexual men. The exaggerated ferocity of Mike Tyson in the ring, for example, seems a clear repudiation of the vulnerability that had given him so much grief when he was a victimized, fatherless child in the poorest reaches of Brooklyn.[23] It would make sense that cultures experiencing themselves as oppressed and under attack would attach value to masculine styles that repressed vulnerability and other 'feminine' qualities. Black men in the United States withstand spiritual, economic, and physical insults in daily life due to racism.[24] It should come as no surprise that the dominant black ideal is physically tough, socially stoic, and personally cool and detached. In representing and embodying these qualities, the black athlete more closely epitomizes the hypermasculine ideal, not only in black communities, but in the wide mainstream — a key reason for his commercial success. Yet in accepting and then exemplifying ideal hypermasculinity, black styles of masculinity still draw on the legacy of racism. As a result, these ideals of black manhood participate in devaluing not only the reality of the vast majority of black men – who are far from the physical, social, and economic ideals of their athletes – but of all men, regardless of their sexual preferences and colour of skin, whose cultures are affected by this idealization.

In the 1960s, this evolving super-heterosexual ideal was only one part of a larger ideal of black masculinity that contained many more progressive elements.[25] The growth of African-American political consciousness and the great mobilizations of the 1960s propelled community-oriented, politically progressive black men into public leadership and visibility. Men such as Martin Luther King, Malcolm X, and Jesse Jackson provided national political leadership and models of manhood within their own communities. Equally, by virtue of their courage and eloquence, they provided leadership and models of manhood throughout North America. Their examples moved and inspired young men of all colours and classes, many of whom undertook political activism in the service of solidarity with their struggles.

A number of these nationally known black leaders forged important associations with black athletes. Jackie Robinson marched with Martin Luther King; Muhammad Ali bonded with Malcolm X. As Steve Rushin writes,

The night Clay beat Sonny Liston in Miami for the heavy-weight championship in 1964, [Jim] Brown sat with him for two hours afterward in Clay's Hotel, with Malcolm X waiting in the next room, as Cassius confided to Brown that he had embraced Elijah Muhammad and the Nation of Islam and had taken the name Muhammad Ali. Brown was in London two years later filming the *Dirty Dozen* when Ali refused induction into the U.S. Army ... So Brown flew to Cleveland, where a group of fellow black athletes were gathering to hear Ali out in a much-publicized summit meeting. Brown, Lew Alcindor, Willie Davis, Bill Russell and John Wooten listened as Ali said, 'my fate is in the hands of Allah.' The group then announced their support for their friend.[26]

This collaboration between political leaders and athletes had a profound effect on society at large and on black youth in particular. Author and black feminist bell hooks identifies Kareem Abdul Jabbar as important to her in this respect. 'When I was in high school,' hooks writes, 'what was important about Kareem was that he was portrayed in the media as trying to think critically about issues, not simply passively absorbing them.'[27] Courageous gestures, such as the Black Power salutes of Tommy Smith and John Carlos at the 1968 Olympic Games in Mexico City, were profoundly politicized and politicizing.

The murders of Martin Luther King and Malcolm X deprived the black community of living models of manhood as well as symbolic fathers and social warriors. While Jesse Jackson marched along with many others into the 1970s, 1980s, and 1990s, the broader ascendance of commercial culture and the political right caused the visibility and charisma of black political leaders to wane. Sport, on the other hand, married to commerce and the media, grew in scope and prominence, as did the success of black athletes. In the absence of strong public figures to fill the symbolic father gap after the deaths of King, Malcolm X, and other political leaders, successful black athletes took on an important role in the process of identity construction, becoming powerful collective cultural mentors.[28] Jim Brown has said that if he had the participation of the top twenty athletes in the country, 'we could probably create a nationwide gang truce ... These athletes represent such a great amount of resources and influence. These kids would be *flattered* to have their lives changed by them.'[29]

Indeed, the prestige of such athletes has been so great that it has affected many boys and young men who are not black.

The success of these black athletes has unfolded in dramatic contrast to the worsening situation of African-Americans in the United States. Despite the growth of a small black middle class, in the mid-1990s, one quarter of the black male population between the ages of sixteen and twenty-five were either incarcerated or on probation. More African-American men were in prison than in college; more money was being spent on prisons to house them than on universities. The highest cause of death among young black men in the United States was murder. Other major causes of death were early cancer, heart disease and strokes, AIDS, drug overdoses, automobile accidents usually involving drunk driving, and chronic liver disease. Life expectancy for African-Americans in the mid-1990s was six years less than for whites, down three years since 1984. In the 1970s, black Americans had the lowest suicide rate in the United States; today it is the highest.[30]

The poverty of the urban black communities has created increasing violence in the lives of large numbers of black men and greater sociopolitical demoralization among women and men. The pronounced concentration of wealth in fewer hands, characteristic of the monetarist decades, has taken a devastating toll on black communities. As Jim Brown pointed out to *Sports Illustrated*, during the 1970s and 1980s, 'the rich got richer, didn't they?' 'This country has festered; there's an underbelly. Prisons are overcrowded, recidivism is at an all time high, the education system is going downhill, there's this new culture of drugs and gangsters and killing without *any* thought. Kids are shooting each other at 13 and 14, and all of a sudden, it's not going to stay in the inner city.'[31] Cornel West has described a 'state of siege raging now in Black communities across this nation.' It is linked, in West's view, as in Brown's, 'not only to drug addiction but also to the consolidation of corporate power as we know it; and redistribution of wealth from the bottom to the top, coupled with the ways with which a culture and society centred on the market, preoccupied with consumption, erode structures of feeling, community, and tradition.'[32] West has called the culture arising from these conditions in black communities one of nihilism, and believes that 'the nihilistic threat is more powerful now than ever before.'

I believe that the commodification of black life and the crisis of black leadership are two basic reasons [for this nihilism]. The recent shattering of black civil society – black families, neighbourhoods, schools, churches, mosques – leaves more and more black people vulnerable to the nihilistic threat. This shattering spawns a deracinated and denuded people with little sense of self and few existential moorings.[33]

The cult of the black super-athlete, even as it displays 'positive images' of sexually attractive black men, has played an important role in 'the consolidation of corporate power' and the commodification not only of black experience, but of white male and female experience as well. The cult of the black super-athlete has helped elaborate a culture 'preoccupied with consumption,' within and outside the black community. Hence it has participated in feeding a culture of nihilism. The values of the commercial cult of the black super-athlete, even as that cult presents the athlete as a figure of black pride, have contributed to the erosion of structures of 'feeling, community and tradition' so important to collective well-being. This erosion takes place largely through the dynamics of commodification added to those of poverty.

The black athletes who grew rich and famous in the 1980s and 1990s did so in ways unimaginable to those who had came of age in the 1950s and '60s. (Jim Brown's top 1960s salary in the NFL was $65 000.) Much of their income was earned from advertising endorsing athletic shoes and sporting equipment. In the form of corporate publicity, their imagery reached into and saturated every conceivable cultural space where boys came together. Bell hooks recalls giving a lecture in which she critically deconstructed the image of Michael Jordan from a black feminist perspective. During the lecture, 'a young White man spoke up about the image of Black athletes on cereal boxes.' He said 'it was the first time in his life he felt he wanted to be a Black man.' Without withdrawing her critical perspective, hooks comments that her student 'had made a profound point, because for him to see this image as valuable, legitimate, and worthwhile put it in a more humanizing light ... an act which might be subversive, threatening even to White supremacy.'[34]

The appearance of the black athlete on the back of cereal boxes heralds a clear form of success and the broad diffusion of his image – a step forward for African-Americans as a whole in terms of 'normalization.' Yet, in keeping with the kinds of concerns West and hooks (among others) have raised, we must also ask: what kind of person does the young white man, as well as the young black man, want to be when he identifies so strongly with a Michael Jordan, a Shaquille O'Neal, or a Charles Barkley? Does the popular, commodified image of the black super-athlete on the cereal box – or sports jacket, or pair of shoes, or computer – promote anything that threatens the established order, anything that promises to erode the structures and economies of racism, the way images of Muhammad Ali and Jackie Robinson once did? Commodification has laundered the black athlete's image of any progressive meanings it might have had. Where Muhammad Ali in the 1960s made considerable sacrifices for his beliefs, in the 1990s Michael Jordan, as a significant beneficiary of Nike endorsements, declined to support a distinguished black candidate against racist Republican Jesse Helms because 'Republicans buy shoes too.' At the Barcelona Olympics, Charles Barkley, another Nike endorser, said he had 'two million reasons' not to accept a gold medal while wearing a U.S. sweatshirt bearing the Reebok logo. At both the Atlanta and Barcelona games, the U.S. basketball 'Dream Team' declined Olympic accommodation in order to stay in first-class hotels, and many complained publicly that the games were causing them to miss fishing trips and vacations. The sports pages are full of stories about trash-talking black athletes, 'selfish and spoiled players,' according to *Sports Illustrated*.[35] The message of such athletes is clear: be a corporate warrior, not a fighter for equality, justice, or community, and watch out for No. 1.

The consumerist narcissism cultivated by the athlete-based culture of advertising is an important part of what Cornel West has called a developing 'paradigm of market morality.' In this paradigm individuals understand themselves 'as living to consume, which in turn creates a market culture, where one's communal and political identity is shaped by the adoration and cultivation of images, celebrityhood, and visibility, as opposed to character, discipline, substantive struggle.' West sees this paradigm transforming black communities in 'fundamental' and 'very ugly' ways, and corroding a sense of community in white America as well.[36] The marketing of the black super-athlete as corporate culture-hero is contributing to this development of a market morality right across contemporary society, and threatens, not strengthens, the bonds of solidarity. The irony lies in the fact that commercial discourse has exploited the black athlete in his role as a 'rebel.'

In Chapter 1, I spoke of three masculine styles that are recognized by everyone in contemporary Western capitalist society. These styles and their erotics are associated with the three main classes – owning/governing, managing/professional, and labouring/soldiering. I suggested that sport for the most part embodied the third form of masculine sexuality – that associated with the labouring and soldiering classes. Concerned with the forceful assertion of the active male body, this style of eroticism has a greater force of attraction than the other two types (executive and intellectual). By virtue of its association with the exploited classes and races, this masculine sexual type is also imagined and perceived as more disruptive and dangerous than the others, by inciting competitive violence between men or sexual violence against women. The physical, erotic power of the imaginary working-class male produces a contradiction within the larger capitalist construction of male and class power, for it confers on some junior, less privileged, even 'deviant,' men an apparent lever of power over senior, elite men. Although the latter may command sexual services by virtue of their wealth or military prowess, they wish to be desired as though they were physically attractive. Hence envy and competition colour intermale rivalry in both directions on the class ladder. The eroticism of power, associated with wealth, is an object of envy by poorer men; the eroticism of active physicality and strength, nostalgically misconstrued in its association with the labouring, coloured classes, is an object of envy by elite men. This envy accentuates the violence of sport culture in a number of different ways. According to Michael Messner,

Violence among men may ... have important ideological and psychological meaning for men from privileged backgrounds. There is a curious preoccupation among middle-class males with both movie characters who are working-class tough guys, and with athletes who are fearsome 'hitters' and who heroically 'play hurt.' These tough guys of the culture industry are both heroes, who 'prove' that 'we men' are superior to women, and the 'other' against whom privileged men define themselves as 'modern.' The 'tough guys' are, in a sense, contemporary gladiators sacrificed so that elite men can have a clear sense of where they stand in the intermale pecking order.[37]

The black super-athlete is the 'tough guy' par excellence, embodying the physical qualities of the labouring/soldiering ethos. At the same time, due to the heroization of the athlete in North American culture, he now represents and challenges the masculinity and power of the very wealthy man as well. Fans boast of their heroes' earnings as much as they do their playing statistics, finding vicarious gratification for their desire for wealth and fame. This com-bined class appeal of black athletes – who have emerged from among the most impoverished and downtrodden Americans – is both their major asset in com-mercial sport culture, and a supreme irony. For the presentation of the black super-athlete is still, in many ways, continuous with the racist representation of black males in culture more generally. In popular fictive genres, black male characters are often violent and sexually predatory outlaws.[38] 'The danger to the fair heroine of the dark evil apparition was clearly the crucial linchpin in the gothic novel, most science fiction and pornography,' Paul Hoch observes.

Likewise, the threatened assault of the ever erect black buck on the chaste white lady had dominated the mythologies of the American South for more than three centuries ... Almost by definition the villain is threatening and immoral – a representative of the *dark, bestial* forces of lust and perdition, an embodiment of the *lower* and *sexual*, as against the higher and spiritual ties of the hero's conscience ... The conflict between hero and beast becomes a struggle between two understandings of manhood: human versus animal, white versus black, spiritual versus carnal, soul versus flesh, higher versus lower, noble versus base.[39]

Yet, notwithstanding the power of these older racist traditions, the black male outlaw can also be a point of positive identification for those who feel disenfranchised by the social order. His physical and sexual prowess can be associated with, and be seen to represent, the valid anger of the exploited and downtrodden, their just aspirations, and the necessity of their physical self-defence against violent aggression. Malcolm X embodied these qualities in his rhetoric, Muhammad Ali through his sport and his politics. The respect shown for Ali throughout the world exemplifies this identification, and is evidence of the cultural charisma of the 'good' black outlaw – the rebel or revolutionary – and his subversive potential within the social order. Because of the historic links between African-American politics and African-American athletes, most black athletes still carry some association with this politicized outlaw in the popular imagination. If, however, this rebel's charisma is captured and used to support values and behaviours that retard or contradict what it started out to represent – if, in other words, it is co-opted for anti-egalitarian projects – it loses its progressive meaning. In promoting the corporate consumerist order, the commodification of black athletes works indirectly yet effectively to undermine the aims of the civil rights and black movements in their fight for economic justice as well as political enfranchisement.

In dampening the potentially progressive meanings of black athletes' success, commercial discourse has also tended to appeal to and heighten reactionary ideas about black men. It has done so primarily by exploiting the hyper-sexuality and violence embedded in the racist cultural legacy. A significant number of the black athletes glamourized by the mass media today have been presented as irresponsible and even predatory sexual actors. Jim Brown, despite his egalitarian views in matters of race and his own self-definition as 'an activist in the movement for dignity, equality and justice,' has faced charges for assault on young women four times (Brown has denied all the charges).[40] Michael Tyson captured the public imagination when the beast in the ring became the beast in the bedroom. And the O.J. Simpson trial, with its themes of murder and sexual jealousy, revived the associations of predatory black male sexuality linked to brutal violence (this set of assumptions caused a furious backlash in the black community).

Within the media-constructed image of the black super-athlete, violence and danger have increasingly been associated with sexual 'scoring ability.' This has happened with the complicity of at least some black athletes. Without real incidents of violence and sexual abuse, and their own boasts of massive promiscuity, the media would not be able to make these associations with such success. However, we know well that problems of athletes' violence against other men and sexual violence against women are by no means the monopoly of black athletes. So the selective way in which the media make these associations between violence, hypersexuality, and black athletes is an important part of the underlying strategy of representation. For example, in a major feature on domestic violence among professional athletes in a 1995 *Sports Illustrated*, except for one small photo of a white athlete placed low on a page at the end of the article in the back pages of the magazine, all photographs were of black athletes.[41] Anyone casually perusing the magazine would get the impression that sexual violence against women, is, in effect, a problem of black athletes alone.

Contemporary racist beliefs about men of African extraction maintain a view of prodigious, rapacious, and violent sexual instrumentality: the revenge of the oppressed as fantasized by the oppressor, as well as the sexual lever of the working-class hero over males of other classes.[42] For example, consider a *Sports Illustrated* cover photo of baseball players Frank Thomas and Ken Giffey, Jr, standing back to back, holding dark bats in front of them in an explicit sexual gesture, over the aggressive headline 'Top Guns.'[43] Or the photo in a story about Thomas in the same issue, in which he is shot from crotch level up, standing with his hips thrust forward, kissing his bat. The same violent eroticization of the black male athlete, or athleticized male (actors such as Wesley Snipes and Danny Glover), is visible in the way the camera treats his body on television, in celebrity journalism, and throughout advertising (thanks in significant part to the entry of the homoerotic gaze into the mainstream, a phenomenon I shall presently address.) *Vanity Fair* pictured Charles Barkley on its cover, draped in a tiger-skin wrap, wearing wrap-around sunglasses, quietly leering into the camera over the caption 'Bad News Barkley.'[44] Or consider the use of well-known black athletes to sell Right Guard deodorant. Costumed in the incongruous (read usurped) clothing of nineteenth-century gentry and surrounded by numerous sexually alluring women, they deliver the punch line that any other deodorant 'would be less than civilized.' Tactics such as this, even if unconscious, reflect a broader process by which black males are linked with hypersexuality and sexual aggression in North American culture. Particularly in the absence of more positive and varied images, they are highly influential.

This strategy is commercially useful to the sport nexus because the presentation of sex and violence is titillating and shocking. These qualities are increasingly valued in getting and holding the attention of a publicity-saturated public. Sex remains an unparalleled attention-grabber. So shoe stores like Candie's run national magazine ads featuring a model sitting on a toilet, Manager jeans mounts monster-size inflatable sex-dolls on billboards over major highways, and ads for men's underwear have turned into pulse-accelerating displays of masculine endowment. Add a little danger and violence to the sexual mix via sport, and the attention value rises again. As fashion and pornography have sexually objectified women (see chapters 3 and 4), all male athletes are sexually objectified to some extent through commercial sport culture. This culture of sexual display and commodity promotion celebrates and defines athletes – of whatever colour – by their physical and sexual dimensions. However, black athletes are freighted with a double or triple dose of this sexual objectification by virtue of the legacy of racism.

In contrast to the ubiquitous images of huge, aggressive black football gladiators was *Sports Illustrated*'s 1992 article on tennis player Arthur Ashe before his death from AIDS. Ashe modelled a much more constructive masculinity than do the macho dudes, a message implicit in the title of the article ('The Eternal Example') and the cutline ('Arthur Ashe epitomizes good works, devotion to family and unwavering grace under pressure').[45] But men like Ashe are conspicuous by their usual absence from the stage and scripts of commercial sport culture, including the pages of *Sports Illustrated*. In another positive portrayal of a black athlete, the 1996 film *Jerry Maguire* depicted the character of a black athlete (played by Cuba Gooding, Jr) as the sexually and emotionally responsible male, and the character of the white sport agent (played by Tom Cruise) as the childish and dangerous male – a perfectly plausible scenario in life, but a rare one in the mass media.

In effect, then, the corporate glamorization of the black athlete utilizes the charisma of the outlaw (both politically progressive and regressive variants) to heroize the athlete and to attract audiences of consumers to the athletic spectacle. While placing the black athlete at centre-stage, this process of commercialization still manages to suggest that blacks are less than human, hypermasculine creatures, thus perpetuating racism. This creates a double-bind for young black men. As Michael Messner observes:

Ironically, although many young black males are attracted to sport as a milieu in which they can find respect, to succeed in sports they must become intimidating, aggressive, and violent. Television images – like that of Jack Tatum 'exploding' Daryl Stingley – become symbolic 'proof' of the racist belief that black males are naturally more violent and aggressive. Their marginalization as men – signified by their engaging in the very violence that makes them such attractive spectacles – contributes to the construction of culturally dominant (white, upper- and middle-class) masculinity.[46]

For this and many other reasons, young black men would spend their energy and talent to better effect pursuing fields other than sport. But nothing appeals as much as athletics, because of the appeal of the black super-athletes. 'You give the kids athletes to follow, and you give them false hope,' said Jim Brown. 'You take the emphasis off just being a good student, getting a job and having a family. Instead, it's "I want to be Michael Jordan. I want to have those shoes." Kids in this area also look to the drug dealer, the gangster, the *killer* as a hero, which is something we didn't have. So these are the two sets of heroes, and both of them are bad.'[47]

This is a serious indictment of the broad culture of sport and its place in black culture. In writing about similar sociocultural patterns in the UK, Ernest Cashmore summarizes the conditions facilitating the entry of large numbers of black youths into sport: 'Black youths tend to receive particular treatment in sports at school; they develop [extreme] interests in sport that are not curbed by their families; they perceive their alternatives in the conventional occupation sphere as rather limited, especially because of their colour; they adopt models for emulation in the form of successful black sports stars.'[48] In the sense that they discourage young blacks from pursuing other interests and skills, these patterns hurt black youth. Cashmore believes that 'black sportsmen are champions – yet they conceal a failure – the failure of Western societies significantly to disrupt the pattern of inequality that has prevailed for four hundred years.'[49] Cashmore's critical appraisal should provoke serious reflection on the value of black super-athletes as leading cultural mentors and models of masculinity, for youths of all colours, not only for blacks. Gender and sex-related issues are part of the struggle for change in many African-American communities. African-American women have developed their own ideas of feminism and womanism, and have extensively diffused their own views about important issues in black and interracial gender relations and black masculinity, within a framework of antiracist and community-building concerns.[50] Some black men have welcomed their contributions, others have construed them as emasculating and divisive. However turbulent the debates may be, many black men and women are involved in discussions about gender and sex, in their own lives and communities, and in broader American politics and culture.[51] On the other hand, the model of the individualist, hypermasculine corporate warrior is not conducive to the building of strong communities and the movement toward equality.

Mass commodification succeeds in draining a minority or dissident cultural practice of its progressive political dimensions, particularly with respect to black culture. Sport is not the only field of black achievement in which media attention has heightened hypermasculinist and regressive representations. Rap and hip-hop music, for example, developed as widespread, dissident, and often politicized musical practices within the black community, featuring performances that express many different gender stances and possibilities, as well as the better-known hyper-hetero and violent styles of 'gangsta rap.'[52] But the dominant impression of rap by those outside the subculture is one of aggression and misogyny, thanks to the selective commercialization of, and hence publicity for, bands such as 2-Live Crew, and despite commentators in the black community who consider this band to be 'vile, juvenile, puerile, misogynistic guys' who only want to make money.[53] But neither this extensive critique nor the more progressive culture of rap have successfully made it from the margins to the mainstream.

Commodification can thus be seen as a process that tends to cultivate conformist, individualistic, narcissistic, racist, and gendered meanings, selected from the broader offerings of emergent and oppositional ideologies, for the purpose of stimulating purchasing behaviour. The process has worked its logic on black athletes, and on the gay community.

Homoeroticism in Sport and the Athleticization of Gay Culture

The two subcultures of overt *hyper*masculinity described in the previous sections are homophobic – fearful of homosexuals and of 'femininity' in men. I now want to examine a subculture that, in the dominant sexual ideology of the last one hundred years, has been associated with *hypo*masculinity: with, so to speak, the absence of masculinity. This section addresses homoeroticism in sport, and the emergence of a gay subculture in society as it interacts with mainstream sport culture.

As we have seen, ideal masculinity and masculine sexuality in the decades around the turn of the century came to be defined in terms of men's sexual conquest of women and of the repudiation of 'feminine' (expressive and receptive) qualities in themselves and other men. In the mythic logic of compulsory heterosexuality, feeling sexually drawn to or engaging in sex with other men was tantamount to disavowing masculinity and taking on femininity – and hence to a renunciation of power itself. Queerness – implied in admitting to pleasure in the touch and sight of other male bodies – cancelled out what sport had been undertaken to confer in the first place. Compared with most other fields and endeavours, silence about homosexual identity hangs over the world of men's professional sport. We can count the number of professional male athletes who have come out as openly gay on less than ten fingers.[54] 'To call into question the masculine mythos of athletics by asserting one's homosexuality,' Brian Pronger writes, 'is to upset the most fundamental beliefs and deep motivations of many coaches, athletes, sports administrators, writers and fans; it is a break with the established order in sports ... And so those athletes with homosexual desire keep that knowledge to themselves and usually go about their business appearing to be heterosexual.'[55] Athletes are extremely reluctant to challenge these circumstances in today's sport world. The athlete has worked hard to gain approval for his athletic prowess and the masculinity it most powerfully symbolizes, and he is not about to give it up because of his sexual preferences.[56]

Historians have traced how the fear of homosexuality was used from the 1940s to the 1960s to isolate, stigmatize, and damage many people who were identified as threatening or who were needed as political scapegoats. Homosexuality was often equated with disease – an 'alien otherness in our midst' – and simultaneously linked to the political virus that threatened us: communism. Terms such as 'pinko faggot' and 'commie queer' have their origins in these decades.[57] Boys who didn't participate in sports were called 'pansies,' and sport was thought a good cure for 'sissies' and 'mama's boys.' And in keeping with the tendency of national and ethnic conflicts to become gendered and sexualized, these stereotypes went on to play themselves out in the Vietnam war, as well as on North American city streets.

It was into this context of politicized homophobia in the late 1960s that homosexual people of both sexes began proclaiming their existence and their rights in loud, public, and political ways. Those who had been oppressed sexually joined those oppressed by race and gender in a new and militant resistance. Since the Stonewall riots in New York City in 1969, the gay liberation movement has challenged the operative assumptions and prejudices of compulsory heterosexuality on many different fronts. Drawing on the conventions of gay culture and, at least initially, on associations with other politics of resistance, gay men introduced into the cultural arena new possibilities for and inflections of masculinity, at first on its margins, then increasingly into its mainstream.

One consequence of the more open presence of gay culture and gay sensibilities was to make more visible the sexual desires and physical practices of homosexuality. Hence, homosexuality has become better understood as a natural, 'nondeviant' sexuality. Today, homoeroticism has become an acceptable public discourse not only in gay culture (literature, art, pornography) but also in mainstream culture (the arts, fashion, advertising). The accessibility of information about homosexuality also permitted new associations with, and new interrogations of, 'heterosexual' men's culture, including sport. As long as same-sex love was thought by the majority of people to be an aberration, an exception, or a sin, there was no pressure to see the intense physically charged experiences of same-sex physical interactions of sport as homoerotic. The logic went something like this: There's nothing queer about all that hugging, mounting, and butt slapping. It's just good clean fun. Athletes are real men – they don't do what homosexuals do.

Homoeroticism, once thought to be the mysterious province of a few twisted souls, is now visible and recognizable in the actions and rituals of athletics. David Kopay, former professional football player who came out as an openly gay man in the 1970s, describes the homoerotic language used by his coaches:

The whole language of football is involved in sexual allusions. We were told to go out and 'fuck those guys'; to take that ball and 'stick it up their asses' or 'down their throats.' The coaches would yell, 'knock their dicks off,' or more often than that, 'knock their jocks off.' They'd say, 'Go out there and give it all you've got, a hundred and ten per cent, shoot your wad.' You controlled their line and 'knocked 'em into submission.' Over the years, I've seen many a coach get emotionally aroused while he was diagramming a particular play into an imaginary hole on the blackboard. His face red, his voice rising, he would show the ball carrier how he wanted him to 'stick it in the hole.'[58]

This vocabulary, as catalogued and decoded by anthropologist Alan Dundes, affirms aggressive, invasive sexuality with homosexual overtones. Dundes shows that whether such language describes the symbolic territorial 'endzone' or the literal 'butts' of team mates and opponents, eroticism is always expressed in the ranked relations of 'penetrating-penetrated' personnel.[59] Dundes makes a convincing argument for viewing football (indeed, all team sports where the object is to penetrate the opponent's endzone and prevent the penetration of one's own) as a homoerotic ritual for establishing intermale ranking. Victory and defeat are symbolized as homosexual/territorial penetration (victory) or submission (defeat). Dundes suggests that these sports serve a similar function for male relations in our society as certain homoerotic institutions do in noncapitalist cultures: that is, as male initiation rituals that demarcate male preserves (as, for example, in aboriginal cultures in Melanesia, Australia, New Guinea, or in classical Greece).[60] Speaking of the popularity of American football, Alan Dundes draws on the words of William Arens: 'With the lower torso poured into skintight pants accentuated only by a metal codpiece ... the result is not an expression but an exaggeration of maleness. Dressed in this manner, the players can engage in hand holding, hugging, and bottom patting, which would be disapproved of in any other context, but which is accepted on the gridiron without a second thought.'[61]

Locker-rooms and showers are also sites of homoeroticism. Here, for example, in the apparently nonironic words of the authors of *Swoosh: The Unau-*

thorized Story of Nike and the Men Who Played There, is a story of how Bill Bowerman, the legendary coach of the University of Oregon Track Club, established his authority with his athletes:

Back in the locker room after all his lofty talk, he would shower with the team, walk over to one of them – most likely some hot-stuff sophomore – and stand under the running water with his blue eyes riveted on the kid's eyes. 'I want you to go out on that first 220,' he would begin, and go on to outline his strategy for each lap. Then he would finish up with a warning: 'And be real alert not to let guys piss on your leg.' Slowly it would dawn on the kid, and he would look down and realize his coach had been pissing on his leg all along in the warm water. Bowerman, an indefatigable prankster pulled the same routine on most kids at one time or another.[62]

Homoerotic interest is present throughout sport, among athletes, coaching staff, officials, and fans. In the United States, the term used to refer to avid male fans who love to hang out with professional athletes is 'jock-sniffers.'[63]

The emergence of homosexuality into the open permitted a cultural interrogation of sport that, for the first time, put in a different perspective a set of male-exclusive practices that had previously been viewed as super-heterosexual. Brian Pronger utilized and developed such a perspective in his book on sport, homosexuality, and sex. Alan Dundes did the same in his work on football and homoeroticism. Thus, the emergence of gay imagery and gay discourse about sex has been helpful in providing insights not only into gay culture but into many other forms of men's culture as well. Pronger's work stands out because it is one of the few direct discussions in scholarly literature of the libidinal dimensions of sport. These dimensions are a very important part of athletic experience for all males, regardless of their sexual orientations off the playing field. As Pronger notes:

The body contact of football, hockey, boxing, and water polo, the practice of gymnastic routines, springboard diving, and figure skating, the attention coaches may lavish on their athletes, the exposure of naked sportsmen in locker rooms and showers, all proceed under the assumption that no one involved is aware of the erotic potential of these phenomena, and that everyone is heterosexual.[64]

Indeed, the assumption of heterosexuality is the alibi that permits homoeroticism to flourish. But, as Pronger notes, 'only those involved know what erotic inspiration lurks for them behind the ostensible heterosexuality of these situations ... sometimes even they don't know.'[65]

Often males 'don't know' about their homoerotic inclinations, even as they seek out opportunities to experience them within sport, precisely because they are required to deny their existence in themselves and condemn them in other men. As I argued in Chapter 6, this denial has consequences, particularly the hostility and violence used as pretexts for homoerotic interest. In commenting on the role of violence in sport, Michael Messner outlines television and media theorist Margaret Morse's analysis of the use of slow-motion instant replays in football: 'the visual representation of violence is transformed by slow motion replays into gracefulness. The salient social meanings of these images of male power and grace lie not in identification with violence, Morse argues, but rather in narcissistic and homoerotic identification with the male body. Perhaps the violence represents a denial of the homoeroticism in sports.'[66]

Violence is a loud disclaimer of homosexuality. James Gilligan says that 'violence – whatever else it may mean – is the ultimate means of communicating the absence of love by the person inflicting the violence.'[67] In a gender order of compulsory heterosexuality, violence is also a renunciation of femininity, with which homosexuality is identified. As homosexuality has emerged more and more into public awareness, the disclaimers of homophobic men's cultures have gotten louder. Just as feminism has not yet transformed sport in terms of the kind of heterosexuality it continues to construct, neither has the existence of a gay movement changed attitudes to 'femininity,' and hence to homosexuality, in the mainstream of sport.

As gay culture has interacted with the wider sport culture since the mid-1970s, much of its own erotic idealization has tended to reflect – not reject – the dominant ideals of hypermasculinity embodied in the athletic ideal. From the late nineteenth century, the muscled, athleticized male body was an important icon in gay erotics, as Tom Waugh demonstrated in *Hard to Imagine*. Although Waugh's narrative ends in the late 1960s, the trend toward idealizing the hypermasculine body has become even more accentuated in the last twenty-five years. In 1982, Dennis Altman noted that the 'vogue among gay men for self-improvement' had become established among straight men: 'What is striking is that men ... who go to gyms and take up jogging, are increasingly common among straights. There is a fascinating anthropological detective story to be written on the way in which running shoes and shorts moved out of the gay ghettos to permeate mainstream middle-class America with what Blair Sabol called "phys. ed. fashion." '[68]

We have seen how athleticized high-fashion ideals for women have led to unhealthy physical practices. 'Phys. ed. fashion' ideals for men have also had negative consequences. The athleticized ideal that emerged from the gay gyms is unattainable for most men without long hours of training and pharmaceutical assistance. In a 1997 article for *Out* magazine, Michelangelo Signorile noted that large numbers of gay men were using steroids – testosterone chiefly – for cosmetic purposes. 'The use of such drugs appears to be increasing anxieties and pressures on many non-users who are trying to attain the physical ideal. But they're finding it harder than before, often not realizing that at this point the ideal is beyond having "good genes" and working out hard; it's more and more about drug enhancement.'[69] 'Steroids do it,' one 29-year-old Hollywood talent agent told Signorile, echoing the views of the many gay men he interviewed. 'They let you have that cut, defined, lean, but big, *big* look.' Signorile suggests that this phenomenon is a product of both the power of the athletic hypermasculine ideal and the availability of steroids for the treatment of AIDS (testosterone helps to prevent muscular wasting.[70] This is not to say that the story of steroids tells the whole story of gay physical and erotic culture in the late twentieth century. There is a wide repertoire of 'masculine' and 'feminine' acts, roles, and bodies available for gay men in post-Stonewall culture, but the pressure to have a muscular body still persists.

We have seen how sport became a major site for male sexual display in the late nineteenth century, and benefited most directly from the homoerotic interest of the male gaze. That gaze was mobilized in the twentieth century to sell men's fashions and grooming aids. For a long time, such advertising relied on images of women – frequently in submissive and sexual poses. But by the 1980s, the athleticized, sexualized male body became the main lever of consumer prodding for men. The fashion industry (including sports fashion) has been on the cutting edge in the sexualization and homoeroticization of advertising in the 1980s and 1990s. Today eroticized masculine images sell everything from soap to computers. 'Fathers, sons and businessmen have not disappeared from contemporary advertising imagery,' writes Andrew Sullivan of the new iconography that appeared in the 1980s.

But they have been supplemented by someone else: the single male figure, existing in a sexually charged social void with perfect, nautilus-chiseled contours. He exists alone, his body a work of obvious labor in the gym, his lifestyle apparently affluent but beyond that unspecified. The famous Calvin Klein underwear ad began the genre. Last year's Soloflex exercise equipment print ads captured perfectly the way in which the '80s fitness ethic and the new sexuality overlap. A current ad for Calvin Klein's 'Obsession for Men' perfume shows a young attractive man ... in love in the way only an 80s man can be: he is staring straight into a mirror.[71]

The homoerotic, often autoerotic, iconography of fashion and advertising, employing the big, muscled body, has not validated a more balanced form of masculinity than the hypermasculine heterosexual variant. Its men may stand or even languish in apparently 'feminine' sexual display, objects for both the male and female gaze, in their role as symbols for the commodities they promote. In fact, these men are modelling narcissism, which ought not to be confused with 'femininity.' They have not reversed roles with the women whose images often appear with them as disclaimers of homosexuality.[72] They still occupy centre-stage, and their narcissism reminds us of their power in the world. Narcissism in advertising discourse is about male self-absorption, which may be auto- or homoerotic. It is not about assuming an expressive or receptive stance in relation to others. For Andrew Sullivan, the self-absorption denoted by this aesthetic is almost fascistic: 'The central feature of today's ads is the dehumanized uniformity of the bodies they display, a relentless elitism of the flesh.'[73]

The erotic iconization of the athleticized body has become part of a larger movement of consumerist self-cultivation that functions at the social level as self-surveillance and conformity. Writes popular culture scholar Lee Quint:

Instructions, implied or explicit, on how to attain the same look of models on display exacerbates this self-surveillance by inciting us to attain a perfection that is of course unrealizable. In the Age of the Image, the modern health club, with its mirrored interior, regulated diets, improvement charts, exercise classes, and body machines, is today's panopticon [Foucault's primary model of disciplinary power] the architectural structure which most conspires with ads in promising to make us masters of our bodies.[74]

But these bodies, as Quint points out, are themselves the vehicles of social integration. 'The body that carries out the tasks of disciplinary power is a docile body, one that,' in Foucault's words, 'may be subjected, used, transformed and improved.'[75] 'Thus a docile body may be an active one; it may be the epitome of what our society defines as a masculine body; it is nonetheless docile. In fact, according to this definition of power, the more masculinized a body is, the more subjected to disciplinary power it has been.'[76]

For many gay men, crafting a large, strong body in adulthood represents a reclaiming of the masculinity that social prejudice about homosexuality deprived them of when they were young. This tendency points to a preference for, and idealization of, the hypermasculine. Transplanted into the mass media mainstream and taken up by promotional discourse, it has tended to reinforce, not undermine, hypermasculine aesthetic values. This dynamic is similar to the one I noted with respect to the commodification of the black athlete. It is no accident that the political neutralization of progressive meanings in gay imagery should take place via the commodification of the athletic dimensions of gay culture. For advertising is a discourse of social compliance, and flaunting the feminine would be considered an act of nonconformity.

In the late 1990s, there is a more accepting attitude among some men toward their own and other men's homoerotic and homosexual feelings and choices. This attitude represents real social gains for the possibility of a gender order that is not based on compulsory heterosexuality and a bipolar gender order, but rather on the idea that people are unique packages of qualities, regardless of their primary sex characteristics. Among others, however (for example the gay bashers and evangelical crusaders who think AIDS is God's punishment for same-sex love) the more open existence of homosexuality has created an angry social nexus of denial and resistance among men who are very homophobic at the same time as they are very homosocial. The struggle for the right to sexual self-determination, and to new definitions of gender, is far from over. And the role of sport, though re-appropriated by many gay athletes of both sexes as a terrain for the proving of worth (for example, in the Gay Games), has by no means been straightforwardly positive in this arena either, because it requires that gays, like women, take on hypermasculinist values and institutions.[77]

These last four chapters have dealt with the macro-social factors that formed the context for the spectacular growth of the post-war sport nexus. To complete this survey, it is also necessary to understand how sport has evolved in relation to major changes in biotechnology and medicine, and how this, in turn, fits into the picture of gender and politics.

8

High Performance:
Drugs, Politics, and Profit in Sport

When Canadian sprinter Ben Johnson defeated U.S. champion Carl Lewis in the 100-metre race at the Seoul Olympic Games in 1988, cheers rang out around the world. David had felled Goliath. Two days later, Johnson had to forfeit his medal because traces of anabolic steroids were found in his urine, and the 'fastest man on earth' fell from grace in a fiery plunge. The Johnson scandal created a crisis of confidence in Olympic sport, and sent shock waves through the media, governments, and sponsoring industries. The International Olympic Committee (IOC) later admitted that, based on post-game urine analysis, traces of banned substances had been found in many of the athletes who competed at Seoul. It had even been rumoured that one of them had been America's track queen, Florence Griffiths Joyner. But at the time, only Johnson was singled out for excoriation and infamy.

The Canadian government's response was to strike the Commission of Inquiry into the Use of Drugs and Banned Practices Intended to Increase Athletic Performance to investigate Johnson's wrongdoings and their context. Ontario Appeal Court Chief Justice Charles Dubin was appointed to head it.[1] Meeting alternately in Toronto and Montreal, and broadcast live on TSN (the national all-sports television network) to thousands of daytime viewers, the inquiry evoked a show trial as the cream of Canadian elite athletes poured out their confessions of having used steroids and other banned substances.[2] Sports medicine experts had their say, as well as defiant or shamed coaches, and Olympic and government officials. In all, the commission interrogated 122 people and produced 15,000 pages of evidence. It also produced a report which at least began to identify the problems of steroid abuse as systemic, not individual.[3] (Regrettably, compared with the scandal that prompted it, little media attention was devoted to the report itself, published in 1990.)

All these procedures and findings revealed the same information: that in taking steroids and other banned performance-enhancing drugs, the 'Human Cannonball' and his strong and fleet Canadian colleagues were not alone. Johnson had merely been following the norms of elite athletes in Canada and around the world. He may have broken the official rules, but he played by the much more powerful unofficial rules when he took steroids. At least during the months of the inquiry, the flood of evidence made it evident that steroid use was institutionalized in every competitive Olympic nation.

When I use the term 'steroids' in this chapter, I am not referring to appropriately prescribed synthetic hormones that are therapeutically administered by physicians trained in endocrinology to treat a number of health conditions and disorders. Rather, I use the term in the colloquial way it is used in sport culture, to refer specifically to the synthetic high-octane cocktails that have been developed for certain kinds of performance enhancement.[4] These steroids stimulate the development of bone, muscle, and skin. They help athletes override the alarm signals of fatigue, pain, and emotional exhaustion. For all athletes, not just those competing in strength events, steroids permit harder training and aid in rapid recovery from its stresses. The mental state of athletes who use anabolic steroids may include violent mood swings, aggression, explosive temper, and implacable lust. These effects are known colloquially as 'roid rage.'[5] Eventually, loss of sexual drive and androgynization (enlarged breasts for men, hair growth and deepening vocalization for women) are also common results of some of these drugs. Steroids take a toll on the liver, the heart, and the endocrine system. But they do increase the capacity of the athlete to absorb physical punishment. Unfortunately, later in life, as many former Olympic athletes such as weight-lifters, javelin and discuss throwers, and NFL football players have found, the athlete may pay dearly with chronic pain, disability, and even early death.

I have chosen to include the issue of performance-enhancing drugs – and steroids as my case in point – in a book about sport culture, manhood, and politics because I see their institutionalization as part of the hypermasculinization of sport and society. Anabolic steroids are hypermasculine performance drugs par excellence. Derived from or simulating testosterone, steroids extend the physical abilities at the extremes of the male body by hormonally masculinizing the athlete – regardless of her or his biological sex.[6] Female gymnasts are known to use drugs that retard growth – hyperfeminizing drugs – because smallness and thinness are signifiers of femininity. But outside these sports, women as well as men have moved toward the masculinizing performance-enhancing drugs. These are the drugs that have delivered the achievements valued by politicized and commercialized high-performance Olympic sport –

higher, faster, stronger performances – as well as by men's professional team sports. Women's use of steroids as a strategy for competing in the majority of Olympic sports attests to the overall value attributed to masculine sport and culture since the 1960s. Women in significant numbers have taken on hockey, basketball, track and field, body-building, Eastern martial marts, and boxing. But we have yet to see a similar mass incursion by men into sports such as figure skating or gymnastics, sports that provide a more expressive ('feminine') gestural repertoire for men. Thus a case study of the use of steroids in sport is a case study in gender culture, as well as a case study in state politics, corporate commerce, and biomedicine.

In this chapter I examine how steroids became institutionalized in elite and professional sport and turned the myth of the athlete as a model of mental and physical health into pure fiction. I use this topic as a vehicle to explore the systemic nature of the phenomenon of self-injurious performance-enhancing substances; the political, economic, and biomedical factors that brought it about; the effects high-performance culture has had on young athletes; and the negative trade-offs for a society that emphasizes these forms of sport. For as the story of steroids shows, in high-performance sport we pay homage to qualities and attributes that are neither natural nor healthy, but contrived and toxic, and – ultimately – antihuman and antisocial.

The Politicization of Olympic Sport and the Triumph of Testosterone

In team sports in North America, American football represents most closely the social relations and values of American corporate capitalism. On a global scale, the International Olympic Committee (IOC) and Olympic sports express the values of an international, gender-differentiated owning and managerial elite that serves the interests of political empires and transnational corporations. In contrast to the founding Olympic rhetoric of political friendship and economic disinterest, the growth of the Olympic games under the aegis of the International Olympic Committee (IOC) has long been an epic story of economic exploitation and political manipulation.

To understand the physical performance imperatives of the post–Cold War Olympics and to comprehend the effect of corporatism on the goals and practice of Olympic sport and the growth of athlete abuse in the last twenty-five years, it is important to know something about the history of the IOC and its now-planetary networks. Their evolution consists of four distinct stages: the foundation years (1896–1914), when the basic structures and credos of the IOC were established and vied for popular support with large, working-class sport movements; the interwar years (1918–39), when the educational and cultural goals of Pierre de Coubertin and 'amateur' sport flourished alongside distinct working-class and women's Olympic movements that mounted Olympiads of their own; the integrationist Cold War period (1952–80), when nation-states and empires appropriated the symbolic value of the Olympics and Olympic athletics; and the high corporate period (1980 to the present), when corporate culture appropriated the symbolic value of capitalist nationalism and the nation-state itself. This chapter is primarily concerned with the fate of the athletic body in the latter two periods. But some words about the earlier periods are important as background to the points I want to make about more recent times.

The proposal for a 'revival' of the ancient Olympic games had been discussed and attempted in a number of local and national contexts in Europe during the nineteenth century. But it was Baron Pierre de Coubertin, a young, dispossessed French aristocrat, who took up the project and organized the first international games, which took place in Athens in 1896.[7] Because of his upbringing and social position, de Coubertin had the resources and the contacts to animate events on an ambitious scale. And because of his obsession with questions of character, honour, and nation, he had the drive to do it. He had been traumatized by his experience as an aristocrat when Prussia invaded France in 1870. That war culminated in the Paris Commune, the first truly socialist urban insurrection, and serious financial and political setbacks for de Coubertin's class. Through sport, he attempted to find a way to reconcile his contradictory feelings about his own class and nation.

While de Coubertin saw only demoralization in the French upper classes following the war, he was dazzled by the esprit de corps of British society and British imperialism in the 1880s. He attributed British success to the bracing, beneficial influence of their sports. In mounting a set of international 'Olympic' games, he proposed an athletic movement along the lines of the British model that would link men of like mind and status in other nation-states. The movement would be open to multinational 'amateurs' of sport, competing in a spirit of fraternal understanding. The notion of 'amateur' sport, enshrined as an international requirement in the IOC games from the 1890s to the 1970s, spoke about the intrinsic pleasure of athletic exertion and brotherhood among men for whom athletics were part of a larger, balanced life.[8]

But while the IOC was international from its beginnings, it was not in fact fraternal, except within the affluent classes. Olympic competition was open only to amateurs who did not gain financially from sport – in other words, 'officers and gentlemen.' Only people from the affluent classes of society, usually men, had the leisure, economic resources and social approval to explore intensive athletic training in a financially disinterested manner. In the early decades of the century, then, maintaining the 'amateur' standard in Olympic athletics meant excluding talented and skilled men without independent means. Athletically gifted working men, by virtue of their limited financial resources, were compelled to turn professional or to abandon competition in the highly exclusive, record-driven de Coubertin games. Women were systematically excluded from the IOC Olympiads until 1928, then kept in a highly subordinate position. Hence the word 'amateur' was not simply a code for a certain form of athleticism, but also an indicator of gender and class privilege.[9]

In the first two periods of IOC history, the de Coubertin games were for and about the international elite – that is, the elites of nation-states. Their rhetoric of meritocratic democracy denied a reality of exclusivity: Olympic athletics meant rich men's athletics. The result of this was that the IOC games had limited appeal for the more popular classes in Europe, particularly in countries with large trade unions and socialist parties (e.g., Germany, France, Spain, Italy, Great Britain), who organized international competitions separate from those of the IOC. From the late nineteenth century to the Second World War, large sections of the European population become athletically active in a multinational network of sport clubs and associations linked to Social Democratic, Communist, and trade union organizations. Participation in working-class sports' associations included vast numbers of working men and – long before the de Coubertin games – women as well.[9] The 1931 workers' games in Vienna welcomed over 75,000 participants, of whom roughly 25,000 were women. Between 1920 and 1936, workers' sports organizations mounted four international sets of Olympic games each.[10] Over the same period, women based in the United States, Great Britain, and France organized parallel Women's Olympics.

The philosophies guiding these other 'Olympic' games were rooted in their respective values. Broadly speaking, the ideals and practices of both workers and women's sports associations were more inclusive, egalitarian, and participatory than those of the record-driven de Coubertin games. But the 1930s was a bad time for women's organizing and for socialism. Feminism was in deep decline, and the Women's Olympics foundered. The socialist sport movement was annihilated in the 1930s and 1940s, first through the rise of fascism and the suppression of left-wing political culture, then through war and the triumph of Stalinist bureaucratization in the Soviet Union. The last official Popular Olympics were originally scheduled for Barcelona in 1936. On the morning of the opening ceremonies, the Spanish Civil War exploded in the streets and the games had to be cancelled. Many worker athletes stayed to fight on the Republican side. The last Workers' Olympiad was held in Antwerp in 1937.[11]

The triumphalist Berlin games were held in 1936, 'the most ominous pagan spectacle of modern times,' in the words of their historian, Richard D. Mandell.[12]

The 'Nazi Olympics' trumpeted the victory of fascism and the destruction of socialism in Spain, Italy, and Germany. These games unfolded inside Berlin's new Olympic stadium, flanked at both gates by huge statues of naked Aryan men. The stadium was, by the standards of its time, monumental, military in its bleak geometry, built to symbolize German Aryan supremacy to the world. The games were an orchestrated showpiece for fascism, and Hitler presided over them like an emperor, reviewing the spectacle from his dais in the stands. Hitler abandoned his place in rage when Son Ki-Chong, a Korean running for Japan, won the marathon. Nor was he pleased when black American Jesse Owens won four gold track and field medals. Both these athletes emerged as the real *übermensch* of the games, foiling the Nazis' intention to prove total Aryan supremacy on the field. But as former Canadian prime minister John Diefenbaker, who attended the games in a seat directly above Adolf Hitler's, observed of the whole spectacle, 'it was a powerful eye-opener to the tremendous mobilizing power of sport.'[13] Diefenbaker came to believe that sport was crucial in the struggle for the hearts and minds of men.[14]

The lesson was not lost on any of the regimes of the post-war world, least of all on the United States and the Soviet Union, who emerged from their temporary alliance against Hitler as super-enemies – or at least painted as such to their respective populations by their governments and communications organizations. The Olympic games provided a stage on which athletes' performances served to represent American individualism, democracy, and freedom, on the one hand, and Soviet collectivism, care for the many, and democratic centralism (needs informing a planned economy), on the other. In reality, neither picture was accurate. The command economy Stalin built was not informed by need, nor did it care for the many. The mass atrocities that Stalin perpetrated in the name of the Soviet state cancelled out the gains in social security that had been made by working people – a fact that was well understood in the West and used effectively to discredit the credibility of all socialist projects. In the United States, however, virulent anticommunism helped legitimize the construction of an antidemocratic national security state unequalled in size, scope, and secrecy. Hence, as with O.J. Simpson and Mark Fuhrman, despite the apparent irreconcilability of their respective ideologies, the governing strata of both imperiums supported IOC Olympism because of the values they had in common as masculinist industrial powers with huge security states.[15]

In the early 1950s, the popular workers' sport movement was dead in Europe. The Soviet Union had parted from the antifascist and socialist politics of the Western European Communist parties, and their cultural and athletic values, long before the Second World War. By the time of the Soviet Union's debut in Helsinki in 1952, the methods and conventions of its sport had undergone a long period of indigenous development guided by Stakhanovism – a Soviet approach to the industrial organization of time and motion that, like Taylorism in the West, had far-reaching effects on cultural attitudes to the body and its social, sexual, and political, as well as economic, deployment.[16] Stakhanovism was both a tool and an expression of Stalin's masculinist, bureaucratic, industrial totalitarianism, firmly established by the early 1930s. The Stalinist state developed the fundamental structures of the postwar Soviet economy, with its emphasis on military, bureaucracy, and industry, and with a parallel contempt for the needs of daily and family life. It was a masculinist command economy in priorities, structures, and personnel.[17] And it placed great value on high-performance sport as its spectacle and symbol. Under this regime, quantum steps in the intensification and medical technologization of sport were taken. State sport schools were created to sculpt and specialize the sporting body. New disciplines in biomechanical engineering, pharmaceutical intervention, and psychological manipulation were brought to bear on it.[18]

First at Helsinki in 1952, and again in Melbourne in 1956, the East European sport machines were unstoppable. In the only tradition left of the Workers' sports movements, Soviet and East German women were encouraged to participate in strength and speed sports and went on to resoundingly defeat Western, and especially American women. The male athletes of the West fared badly as well. (The Soviet Union eventually outperformed the United States in almost all of the Olympiads until the collapse of the Communist nations in the early 1990s.) The instrumental pursuit of athletic prowess and the techniques developed in the Eastern European and Soviet sport systems gave the Soviets and East Europeans a collective edge over Western athletes and drew the avid, competitive curiosity of the Americans.

John Ziegler, a physician to America's strength athletes in many of the major international competitions during the 1950s, has written that he was only one among many who found himself marvelling at the strength of the Eastern Europeans.[19] In Vienna, in 1956, he had occasion to spend an evening with his Soviet counterpart and heard for the first time about the Soviet's training methods. These included the use of the hormone testosterone, which had dramatically boosted the performances of a number of Soviet and Eastern bloc athletes. But even at that early date it was clear that high testosterone use also had negative consequences: the androgynization of its users, increased aggression, followed by liver and heart damage.[20]

Being of competitive spirit, Ziegler wanted something that would boost his athlete's performances but with fewer of the brutal side-effects testosterone induced in his opponents. In the late 1950s, working with Ciba Pharmaceuticals, Ziegler helped to develop the first anabolic steroids for use in sport, and under his influence a small, elite group of American weightlifters began to use them. The results were dramatic. The first steroid prototypes began to proliferate more broadly among strength athletes in the early 1960s against the backdrop of the Cold War in sport and the hot war in Vietnam. Ziegler was pleased with the results of his work at first, but by the late 1960s, as he has since written, he was a shaken man, appalled by what he had unleashed. Strength athletes were taking huge amounts of the steroid drugs, not the small dosages he recommended, and they were seriously jeopardizing their physical and mental health.[21]

He Shoots Up, He Scores: The Corporate Takeover

If Cold War competition and biotechnological innovation set the stage for the development of steroids in the 1952–80 period of Olympic history, the current period – the high corporate period – has seen their broad diffusion and systemic institutionalization. Two major factors have been responsible for increasing the demand for performances that cannot be delivered without drugs: on the one hand is the professionalization of a cadre of nationally identified Olympic athletes since 1974, linked to a nationalist culture of sport; on the other are the qualitative new relationships between corporate capitalism and Olympic athletes.

In the United States, the growth of a system of sports scholarships at many universities and colleges has provided a network of employment opportunities for would-be Olympic athletes during their apprenticeship. For many years it has permitted young people of various classes (primarily but not only men) to train to a standard similar to that of the East European and Soviet professionals. Steve Rushin, introducing *Sports Illustrated*'s 1997 list of the top fifty sports schools in the United States, refers to these schools as 'jock schools': 'A Jock School is any college or university in which sports are central to campus life, a place where sport-minded students can flourish. Stanford is a Jock School. Princeton is a Jock School. Cal is a Jock School. Which is to say, you can get a world-class education at a Jock School, just as you can get a salad at McDonald's. But that's not why you go there, is it?'[22] The symbolic value of nurturing athletes in the sport system of the jock schools was reaped, until the 1980s, not only by the school-based clubs and national athletic associations involved, but also, most importantly, by the nation-state, which presented American athletes as exemplars of capitalism's strengths and its ability to field national teams without state support.

In Canada, however, with respect to Olympic sport, political leaders were more in tune with the sport policies of European states. Under the leadership of prime ministers Diefenbaker, Trudeau, and Mulroney, the Canadian government increased its support for high-performance sport primarily as a means of shoring up federalism in opposition to Quebec separatism. It was within the highly politicized context of the Quebec crisis of the early 1970s that the Canadian government finally recognized the importance of paying athletes a stipend to train, and instituted a 'carding' system in which Olympic athletes were funded at three different levels, depending on how they ranked in world standings.

These processes marked the de facto 'professionalization' of Olympic athletics across North America, despite the rhetoric of amateurism that still persisted. However, even the best-paid of the carded Canadian athletes received stipends that left them below the poverty line.[23] Of the 1,000 such athletes in 1988 (the year of Ben Johnson's disastrous victory), 66 per cent reported that they relied on their subsidies as their sole source of income.[24] In the United States, sport scholarships vary in their generosity, according to school, sport, and skill of player. But, in general, especially as these scholarships provided for the entry of athletes from lower socioeconomic backgrounds, the system created a layer of poorly paid professionals with strong financial needs to augment their incomes in other sport-related ways. This is where the corporate sector entered the picture, with a new role to play.

In the 1950s and 1960s, when local and national associations looked for financial support, they sought out businesses that would donate funds and services with few strings attached. In return, donating individuals and companies could expect to benefit from the same kind of goodwill they earned when they gave to the opera or the ballet. The relationship of the commercial sector to Olympic sport was still basically patronage at arm's length – at least at the level of local clubs and associations.[25] When athletes competed at track and field meets, they won watches and silver cups. If they were lucky, they might also receive some free shoes and other equipment from Adidas and Puma, the two leading shoe manufacturers of the time.

However, in keeping with their expansive relationships with team sports and the sport media, major corporations turned to Olympic sport in the 1970s. As sport sociologist Richard Gruneau points out: 'Corporations began to want to see measurable returns for their funds. They started to see themselves as investors, not patrons; and they began to shape sport more directly to their own purposes. They wanted value as well as prestige for their money.'[26] The commercial focus by media and sponsors on Olympic sport as investment relied on endorsement contracts with individual athletes. As we have seen, most athletes were economically vulnerable and exceedingly hard working. By the late 1980s, with the help of a major corporate sponsorship, they could become millionaires.

To exploit the possibilities of athlete endorsements, media and sponsors sought alliances with the IOC and national Olympic committees.[27] Making alliances with the IOC turned out to be a relatively easy matter. *The Lords of the Rings,* by British writers Vyv Simson and Andrew Jennings, outlines the development of the IOC's commercial links with a set of key corporations and political figures from the 1970s to the 1990s. It describes the alliances formed between major national Olympic committees, national and international athletic federations, and major sport-associated corporations such as Adidas shoes (initially) and Coca-Cola. The book is a hair-raising account of the venality and right-wing associations of key IOC members who have succeeded in turning the games into one vast infomercial for corporate sponsors and a source of lavish personal gain for themselves.[28]

The IOC had always been dominated by a group of elite men, and it had always been a self-help organization, providing a passport to high living, financial gain, and international power broking for the most select of its select group of members.[29] In fact, the blatant gap between the ideals of Olympic sport and the behaviour of IOC and national Olympic committee members was a constant theme of discussion among athletes and officials during the amateurism and patronage decades. In that sense, the IOC itself (as distinct from the athletes whose performances sustained the games) was never pristine and commercially disinterested. The impression one gets from *Lords of the Rings* – that of a cast of larger-than-life evil-doing individuals and corporations who violated the purity of Olympic sport – is perhaps overdrawn. But the transformative power that Simpson and Jennings describe and ascribe to the melding of the IOC and its network of odious sport bosses, politicians, and military strong men with corporate commercial and media interests from the 1970s on, is accurately and effectively drawn. Since its aggressive turn to commercialism twenty-five years ago, the IOC has allied itself with major corporations in a number of lucrative and successful programs. Most prominent is the TOP program of ten major international sponsors. Membership in the club confers exclusive international marketing rights using the Olympic logo and wording. In 1996, TOP included corporations such as Coca-Cola, Kodak, Visa, Bausch & Lomb, Sports Illustrated–Time, Xerox, Panasonic, and IBM. For 1996–8, the TOP program is expected to yield $175 million for the IOC. Sponsors are estimated to have paid $40 million for the rights and privileges of membership. TOP members also donate major services-in-kind worth millions of dollars: copiers, computer systems, video and audio displays, shoes, clothes, and other equipment.[30] The cost of this largesse is, of course, passed on to IBM's customers.

Television was the key to harnessing the symbolic and emotional energy of Olympic athletics to marketing purposes, just as it was with men's professional team sports. First televised live and internationally in 1956, the Olympic games have since organized ever larger electronic audiences for paying sponsors – between two and three billion people for the Barcelona and Atlanta games.[31]

As we saw earlier, the most important function of sport from the point of view of broadcasters and advertisers is to create audiences. Fees for television rights to the Olympics payable to the IOC have been enormously profitable in the high corporate period. When the IOC charged ABC $175 million for the rights to broadcast the Los Angeles games in 1984, the sport world, including the sport media, was outraged. Yet, despite *Sports Illustrated*'s 1986 prediction that television would begin to lose interest in covering the Olympics, NBC paid $300 million for the Seoul games in 1988, $401 million for Barcelona in 1992, and $465 million to broadcast the Atlanta Olympics in 1996. NBC's 1995 deal with the IOC for exclusive U.S. Olympic television rights until 2008 was signed for $2.3 billion.[32] In addition to the $705 million for Sydney, and $545 million for Salt Lake City, NBC will pay $793 million for the 2004 summer games, $613 million for the 2006 winter games, and $894 million for the 2008 summer games. Only the '98 Winter Games in Nagano, Japan, were broadcast on CBS, breaking NBC's monopoly. (NBC added its Olympic coverage to a 1996 premier sports event line-up that included the Super Bowl, the baseball All-Star Game, the NBA Finals, the U.S. Open golf tournament, Wimbledon, the French Open tournament, and the Breeder's Cup.) The extent of NBC's funding of the Olympic games confers virtual ownership status on the network. This puts NBC journalists in the position of having to cover the Olympics not as independent journalists but as employees of the investors/ owners of the Olympics. One question that arises from this situation is whether their reportage constitutes journalism or advertising. *Sports Illustrated*, which paid $40 million to the IOC to sponsor the Atlanta Games in 1996, has put their journalists in a similar position.

The Los Angeles games in 1984 marked a new stage in the corporate metamorphosis that had begun in the 1970s. For fifteen years before the Los Angeles games, host cities had been terrorized and/or bankrupted by the highly politicized Olympics. Hundreds of rioting students and workers were shot and killed in the streets in Mexico City in 1968; eleven Israeli athletes were massacred at the Munich games in 1972; the RCMP encouraged the entire Québécois Left to leave Montreal for the summer of 1976; the Americans refused to go to Moscow in 1980. But in 1984, a number of factors converged to turn the games from a dubious honour into a commercial field-day. Leading California capitalists, extremely well connected with government on both the state and federal levels, were looking for a major development project. For the first time, the Olympics were viewed as a showcase for what corporate sponsorship could really do. When the Soviets withdrew at the last moment, major security headaches disappeared. And because the real competition stayed home, American athletes cleaned up medal after medal (ABC's coverage was so jingoistic it became a matter of international controversy).[33] The Los Angeles games turned into a huge success for American sport, business, and governments alike, and cast a template for Olympic–corporate organizing and spectacle that has been used ever since. Before 1984, no one would have suggested that the Olympic pool be called the 'Mars Bar Olympic Pool,' or that training facilities should be supported by, and named for, McDonald's. In the old code of amateurism, such hybrids would have been abominable. But the Los Angeles games came to be known as the 'McLympics.' Now the corporations openly joined the IOC in the Olympic driver's seat.

By 1992 in Barcelona, the integration of national-Olympic and commercial forms had proceeded even further, evident in such names as 'Barcelona Bausch and Lomb Olympic Village' and the 'American VISA Relay Team.'[34] Where the nation-state had been the dominant focus of Olympic competition, repre-sented by the Olympic athlete, now the corporation achieved equal representa-tional status. One Coca-Cola commercial that was broadcast during the 1992 games featured a blond, handsome, Slavic athlete who leaves behind his (un-disclosed) war-torn totalitarian backwater and treks over mountains and val-leys, seeking and finally reaching the democratic metropolis of Barcelona. The city, the West, the Olympic games, and the bottle of Coke are all visually associated, and his voice-over speaks of the 'freedom' he has found.[35] Re-sponding to Nike endorser Michael Jordan's refusal to wear a U.S. team uni-form at the games, Frank Deford wrote in *Vanity Fair*: 'At that time, Jordan essentially chose Nike over country, publicly protesting having to wear the U.S. Olympic uniform just because it was made by the evil Reebokian em-pire.'[36] In this case, the corporation's importance had surpassed that of the nation-state within the Olympic framework.

In the service of merging commercial and national themes characteristic of the high corporate period, a new fusion has been created between the athletes and the products they advertise. In 1980s television broadcasting, this became evident in a new visual vocabulary based in the frequent intercutting of pro-grammed sporting events and sponsored messages, and in the mimicking, in the advertisements themselves, of the 'look' of sport. 'Watching the games on television,' sport sociologist Richard Gruneau observed of the 1988 Calgary Winter Olympics, 'I realized you often couldn't tell the difference between the real Olympics and the advertising content. The athletes, the camera sequences, the music in the ads merged right into the athletic events and the media com-mentary. They were one seamless fabric. The athletes and the marketing had fused.[37] In the summer of 1996, leading up to the Olympic Games, *Time* magazine ran a series of photographic essays by well-known sports photogra-pher Bud Greenspan that were virtually indistinguishable from the 'journalism' surrounding them. This new visual conflation expressed the economic association between corporate sponsors and successful Olympic athletes. The endorsement contract became the prize of Olympic competition, and that contract came only with the highest performances, which, for the most part, were made possible only by performance-enhancing drugs.

We have seen how the increased commercialization of men's team sports brought about an accentuation of inter-player violence. In the case of the Olympics, it has also resulted in self- and coach-administered violence in training for the production of ever more sensational sport spectacles. Moreover, commercial interests have strategically structured and framed this spectacle as a struggle in a zero-sum contest. Only 'winners' who bring home the gold are of interest to the marketing departments of the sponsoring corporations. According to Richard Gruneau, in the 1980s the corporate sector sent out the message to the Olympic athletic federations that it was looking for 'winners.' The same message came from governments too, as they increasingly sought ways to limit their expenditure on sport and to accelerate the fusion between sport and commerce. Andy Higgins, head track and field coach at the University of Toronto in the 1980s and an Olympic coach of long standing, noted that this message was simple:

'Winning is important and we don't care how you do it. We don't care if you do it like Ben Johnson or Pete Rose, just go on out and bring us a medal.' I certainly found it objectionable that Charlie Francis was held up by Sport Canada and the Canadian Track and Field Association as an example of the kind of coaching we should be doing to get winners, when the rumours about steroid use had abounded for years.[38]

Winning and breaking records, however, means the systematic breaching of the natural limits of the human body. There has been very little quantitative change in the records for men's Olympic events over the last twenty-five years, even with phenomenal developments in athletic training and technology.[39] It is true that records do not hold for long, but the gains are smaller and smaller, measured in one hundredths of a second. However, the same is not true for women's events. The historical underdevelopment of sport among women has meant that the distance women had to cover over the past two decades to reach a parallel point in relation to their own potential was considerably larger than that of men.[40] But once the gender playing field in sport has been levelled, it is likely that we will see no quantitative breaches in women's records either. As women close the gender gap, their gains too will tend to be lower, slower, and weaker. And women too will be increasingly forced to resort to artificial and harmful performance-enhancing substances.

In the new corporate Olympic regime many athletes and coaches are convinced that without invasive and destructive performance-enhancing drugs, no matter how talented and disciplined the athletes may be, most will never be able to run the faster times or heave the heavier loads needed to win gold and land the endorsement contracts. By 1988, when Ben Johnson won his race and lost everything else, a dangerous point had been reached in Olympic sport: substances that were officially banned were, at the same time, central to victory. This was not a contradiction the IOC wanted the media to explore, as it would call into question the credibility of Olympic rhetoric. Consequently, in the wake of the Johnson scandal, the IOC proclaimed it was going to clean up its act. Testing laboratories were developed, testing protocols were tightened, athletes were caught and sanctioned. Yet in 1997, after a whole new sector of employment for bureaucrats, technicians, and lawyers had opened up in Olympic sport to control banned substances, *Sports Illustrated* reported their widening abuse. Michael Bamberger and Don Yaeger write:

Even casual fans notice that NBA players sport biceps that a Kevin McHale or even a Moses Malone never dreamed of; that Ivy League colleges field football teams with linemen bigger than All-Pro linemen were a few years ago; and that it's no longer remarkable for veteran big league baseball players to show up at spring training having put on 20 pounds of solid muscle since the end of the previous season ... [S]teroid use – and other, more exotic substances, such as human growth hormone – has spread to almost every sport, from major league baseball to college basketball to high school football. It is the dirty and universal secret of sports, amateur and pro, as the millennium draws near.[41]

Steroids have turned up in the urine of Tour de France winners, male and female short- and middle-distance runners, swimmers of both sexes, hockey and baseball players, boxers, gymnasts, weight-lifters, power lifters, and bodybuilders. As Dutch sport physician Michael Karsten told Bamberger and Yaeger, 'If you are especially gifted, you may win once. But from my experience, you can't continue to win without drugs. The field is just too filled with drug users.'[42] Bamberger and Yaeger conclude that despite the Ben Johnson scandal and the consequent determination of Olympic sport to eradicate steroid use, steroids and other banned drugs are even more widespread than they were in the late 1980s.

Though steroids are endemic to sport, they are banned in all official sport competitions. Individual athletes caught using banned substances are punished and vilified in the name of 'fair play,' 'level playing fields,' and the sanctity of 'natural abilities.' But no such level playing field exists in reality, and steroids are only a small part of how the field is skewed. Athletes representing all powerful nations and corporations are supported by a huge infrastructure of personnel and procedures familiar from the old Soviet sport system: sport physicians, psychologists, masseurs, nutritionists, off-season training facilities, sport scholarships, and bursaries. Indeed, within this context, sports associations, governments, schools, and corporations not only turn a blind eye to the use of banned performance-enhancing substances, they provide incentives to use them. Hence the real issue with respect to steroids is not 'cheating,' but the injury these drugs do to athletes, and, via the symbolic significance of the athletes, to our values and ideals.

The commercialization of Olympic sports means that Olympic athletes now face similar pressures to those experienced by other professional athletes, from cyclists to football players. Speaking from the perspective of a team sport player and a representative of professional athletes, David Meggyesy commented in the wake of the Johnson affair that

the capture of Olympic sport by commercial interests is the single most important factor in the creation of working conditions that promote drug use among athletes ... The beauty of the play, the performance you give for your community, even decent wages and safe working conditions for everyone, they're all lost in the scramble for the prize money now associated with elite sport through endorsements and corporate sponsorships. Even in Olympic sport, the highest values are now monetary. That creates the context for steroids. I believe that if sport is going to turn around it needs protection from commercialization.[43]

The Economist, on the other hand, speaking for investors and business, came to the opposite conclusion in a major review of the sport nexus it published in 1992: 'The reality is that today's money-driven sports are faster, higher, and stronger than ever before. That is what top-level sport is all about. Even if the genie of money could be put back in his bottle, let us admit that sport would be worse off if he were.'[44] So much for the ravaged athletic body in the minds of the business elite. But if we attend to the messages about that body circulating in our culture – from art and literature to pulp fiction and its cinematic equivalents – we may wish to take another point of view.

The Nightmare Zone: Bionic Athletes and Popular Culture

The politicization and commercialization of sport within a hypermasculine paradigm, and the high-stakes incentives for steroids and other performance-enhancing drugs, evolved within a broader societal intensification of biomedical and pharmaceutical technologies. Test-tube babies, organ transplants, machine implants, cloning, and 'pharming' of transgenic animals for drugs are just some of the body-related technologies that have developed since the performance-enhancing drugs took root in sport. Sport-related biotechnologies produced not only steroids, but also human growth hormone and human insulin factor, as well as amphetamines, beta-blockers, cortico-steroids, and so forth. Political, commercial, and biomedical interests thus came to be associated with sport.

Distinct sub-branches of medicine and other health professions and new branches of the drug industry became increasingly involved in the sport nexus, particularly companies involved with nutrients, hormonal drugs, and biomechanical engineering. For these companies, training for higher, faster, and stronger results in sports represented an exciting new market – both licit and illicit – in which they could make new applications and new profits for drugs with limited therapeutic applicability. For example, human growth hormone, one of the most widely used banned drugs among athletes today, was developed for children with pituitary dwarfism – a limited market that sport enlarged upon exponentially. Sport also provided a market for growth-retarding drugs. 'Some female gymnasts are said to intentionally retard their growth,' note Bamberger and Yaeger, 'by taking the so called brake drugs, such as cyproterone acetate, a substance sometimes used to reduce the sex drive in hyperlibidinous males.'[45] That same gymnast, often infertile and suffering from osteoporosis in her twenties or thirties, will constitute part of yet another market – for osteoporosis, fertility, and other drugs – later in life.

The bodily ideals generated by the physical culture that came out of Europe and North America in the last two centuries value performances that are, in the words of the Olympic motto, higher, faster, and stronger. These ideals draw on a paradigm in which performance is constantly self-surpassing and delivered by a state-of-the-art biomachine, tirelessly producing ever more power on command. As such a machine, the athletic body is the logical site for more and more biotechnological adjustments. Within the general context of cultural hypermasculinization I have traced over the twentieth century, sport has become a spectacular public showcase for the achievements of biotechnologies as they attempt to produce an ever more powerful biomachine. 'Athletes are a walking lab, and the Olympics have become a proving ground for chemists,' observe Bamberger and Yaeger.[46]

With its team of 'good' sports physicians and sports psychologists lined up behind national athletes, Olympic sport would have us see it as a healthy showcase, providing inspiring examples of the miracles of modern medicine and technique merged with vibrant good health. However, the reality is not so benign. John Hoberman writes

The ... sports physician's intense identification with the ambitions and requirements of his patients can encourage a kind of medical megalomania that disdains limits on performance-boosting treatments as a matter of principle and disparages the competence and devotion of all but a tiny handful of elite practitioners ... Determined to boost their client's performance by almost any means, most have favoured the supervised use of anabolic steroids since the mid-1970s.[47]

As the widespread use of harmful drugs and the incidence of athlete injury and death remind us, there is also a nightmarish quality to the biotechnologies of high performance, the techno-eugenicist values that guide them, and the physical suffering they perpetrate. A reading of cultural production that speaks to and about these elements of the high-performance cult raises some very disturbing issues.

The evolution of our cultural nightmares about the fate of the body as it encounters science, medicine, and commerce dates back to Mary Shelley's novel *Frankenstein*, which problematized the dangers of the wilful fabrication of human beings.[48] In Shelley's story, there were two monsters, the one whose body was fabricated (the creation) and the one who bent the body of another to his will (the creator). Morally, however, there was only one monster – the scientist who attempted to master another human being as an ego extension and servo-mechanism – a theme that has been present in futuristic literature and science fiction ever since. Advances in pharmaceuticals, genetic science, and electronic communications characterized the first half of the twentieth century. In Aldous Huxley's *Brave New World* psychotropic drugs, genetic manipulation, and artificial reproduction maintained a steep social hierarchy and made notions such as democracy meaningless. Huxley was responding to political conditions as well as biotechnological ones, as George Orwell did somewhat later in *1984*, notably the triumph of both fascist and Stalinist totalitarianism. Orwell wrote about televised sport as a powerful weapon of mass distraction, 'war without guns.'

Since the 1950s, dramatic developments in computers and robotics have accompanied astounding breakthroughs in reproductive and genetic science.[49] As a result, much cultural anxiety and attention have collected around the possible gains and losses involved in different types of fusion between humans and machines. In the 1950s and 1960s, writers such as Isaac Asimov, Robert Heinlein, and Arthur C. Clarke explored new ideas and addressed new fears in a much more optimistic tone than Huxley (or Orwell) had done. Asimov, with his 'three laws of robotics,' presented the development of artificial intelligence and strength as an entirely benign enterprise. In the 1980s and 1990s, however, due to the radical interventions made possible by reproductive, genetic, and surgical science, sharp new anxieties emerged, giving shape to a host of imaginary mythic creatures resulting from biological and mechanical manipulation in futurist and science fiction genres.[50]

One group of such mythic creatures, generally called robots, are all machine but often endowed with human abilities and sensibilities (3CPO and R2D2 in the *Star Wars Trilogy*, for example). The term android, by contrast, has been used to refer to creatures that are wholly organic, but often endowed with machine-like abilities and sensibilities (the 'replicants' in *Blade Runner*, for example). Cyberpunks are humans who, pharmaceutically aided, 'jack in' to vast computer consciousnesses.[51] But in popular culture today, in films, television, video games, and comic books, the term cyborg is most commonly used to refer to a variety of fabricated human-like beings whose powers have been enhanced through biotechnological intervention. The importance of the physical body, and of the biotechnical incursions made into it in the service of enhancing and enslaving it, are central to the idea and presentation, the dream and the nightmare of the cyborg. Far from withering, the physical body of the cyborg is improved, empowered, eroticized. Its physical attributes are enlarged in size and in narrative meaning, as are its encounters, sexual and conflictual, with humans. Cyborgs have superhuman physical qualities, are super-embodied, and therefore super-attractive. Cyborgs are often gladiatorial – athleticized, militarized, and oppressed. The honed, tuned, and pumped elite athlete is the closest living counterpart to the fictional cyborg – Arnold Schwarzenegger as *The Terminator*. As James Wolcott writes: 'The definitive Schwarzenegger roles are ... those in which he is a cyborg figure, a hot-wired combination of sinew and circuitry (fulfilling Nietzsche's vision that "the higher man is inhuman and superhuman.") ... His catchphrases ... sound like the bass notes of a witty computer, a butch HAL.'[52]

In retrospect, the optimism and technophilia of writers such as Asimov caused them to vastly underestimate the social costs of automation and the physical pain and suffering involved in using technology to enhance the human body. The physical being of an athlete is organic. Treating it as though it were a machine may produce extraordinary feats in the short term but it exacts high costs. Just how much anxiety exists about the human costs of these incursions in and for high-performance athletes was suggested in the 1987 science-fiction film *The Running Man*, also starring Arnold Schwarzenegger. The film opens in southern California in the year 2010, somewhere in the Greater Los Angeles area. The region is a self-contained, post-apocalyptic fragment of what used to be the United States. Schwarzenegger plays a police helicopter pilot who refuses to fire on a group of ordinary citizens and is sent to prison for insubordination. Along with other inmates, he escapes and makes his way back to the city, a high-rise techno-paradise of climate-controlled, interconnected spaces where the 'haves' live, work, and rule. One big part of how they rule is a special form of spectator sport called 'The Running Man.' This phenomenon is part 'sport' event, part game show, and takes place weekly as a joint enterprise of 'The State Department' and 'The Network.' The show features a bloody gladiatorial chase, where athlete-mercenaries (gladiators) pursue 'criminals' (dissidents) with the intent of killing them. Sports reporters provide locker-room coverage of pre-game jitters among the gladiators for the television audience. In the derelict neighbourhoods outside the city, large groups of impoverished men stand outside newsstands and watch the spectacle at huge outdoor television screens, as the rain falls incessantly.

Schwarzenegger and his allies are caught by the police and forced to 'compete' in the event. They are to be pursued through a deadly athletic obstacle course by the team of State–Network gladiators (whose leader is played by Jim Brown). As it shows their ensuing ordeal, the film reveals athletic training and performance to be hellish torment. Gladiators and dissidents alike are prepared for combat in a state-of-the-art sport medicine lab, used as an outright torture chamber for the dissidents. The marathon obstacle course the dissidents must 'run' is a succession of highly stylized and lethal sporting events: a terrifying luge run that causes spinal injury, a hockey rink where the goalie's stick is a deadly scythe, and so forth.

In *The Running Man*, Schwarzenegger confronts sports training and performance – the apotheosis of heroic masculinity – as political torture put on for entertainment by a consumerist-totalitarian state. *The Running Man*, in effect, was Hollywood's unintentional way of stating the rather unpopular thesis that important forms of sport are a form of ritualized torture and that through their ethos of sacrifice and high performance, they culturally legitimate political torture and the rule of sadistic regimes. As Jean Marie Brohm writes,

Sport represents a veritable ideological apparatus of death. Physical torture, tolerated and put on as entertainment, is held up as politically neutral and culturally legitimate. Sport gets the masses used to wildly applauding the exploits of men and women submitting their bodies to a refined, superior form of internalized and accepted suffering. This sets up two kinds of beneficial effects for the defense of the established order. On the one hand, it legitimizes all the current forms of torture and ill-treatment by exorcising them on 'another stage' – on the sports field ... [On the other,] it conditions people to accept as 'natural' all the aggressions, injuries, mutilations and physical suffering so liberally dispensed by most contemporary governments.[53]

In the same light, in its role as an exemplar of biotechnology, high-performance sport has helped to validate and promote a masculinist and violent technologization of the body and of the biosphere, and is expected to continue performing this function. In his review of records and training techniques, Mark McDonald writes,

Sergei Bubka, who holds the world record in the pole vault, says the vaulter of the future will have world-class sprint speed, the upper-body strength of a weightlifter, the flexibility of an Olympic gymnast and the ability to long-jump 27 feet or more. These traits suggest a future of genetic tinkering and pharmaceutical hanky-panky, of sports biology taken to a new level, beyond the merely temporary effects of drugs and steroids.[54]

The attitudes of aggressive instrumentality and incursion typical of the technologies of this phase of capitalism, whether medical, industrial, or military, are seen by feminist critics of science as a masculinist thrust to control nature, driven by the need to rival women's and 'mother nature's' powers of birth. These imperatives, they argue, proceed under cover of therapeutic alibis, but are distinct from these.[55] If this is so (I think this is one important dynamic among several, of which commercialization is also fundamental), then the celebration of the technological modification of the human body through Olympic sport is masculinist at another very profound level.

All these factors explain why so much of the popular cultural production dealing with the future of the athleticized super-body has such a pessimistic and dystopian quality.[56] Few of its producers – particularly in film, television, and children's genres – take an explicitly critical stance in relation to the processes that promise to turn the body into a cyborg. Yet it is not possible to project the contemporary trends of global corporate domination, commercial sport, and masculinist biotechnological proliferation into the future and come up with a scenario in which science and sport are used benignly in the interests of the majority. The imaginary future depicted in these genres shows a foreboding and sinister appreciation of the 'higher-stronger-faster' cult that many also participate in celebrating.

Childhood and High-Performance Athletics

The IOC Olympic games are a powerful, mature corporate enterprise, dependent for raw material not on coal, or cotton, or microchips, but on kids. To mount the spectacle of elite high-performance sport, this enterprise needs a steady supply of disciplined young athletes who will pay any price to win gold, and a cadre of coaches and officials to run the organizations and events of local, regional, national, and international Olympic sport associations. From high-school gymnastics and community track clubs to the highest levels of the international sport federations and the IOC's Lausanne headquarters, this network produces the athletes who, at younger and younger ages, compete to break records and provide us with awesome performances. Its incentive structures move young people steadily in the direction of performance-enhancing regimes and drugs that are injurious to the athletes themselves. And its culture has given rise to a mentality among competitive athletes that is striking in its obedience and self-sacrifice. Here it is exemplified in Bob Goldman's famous 'two scenarios' survey, presented to 198 sprinters, swimmers, powerlifters, and other assorted athletes, most of them U.S. Olympians or aspiring Olympians.

[Scenario I:] You are offered a banned performance enhancing substance, with two guarantees. 1) You will not be caught. 2) You will win. Would you take the substance? One hundred and ninety-five athletes said yes; three said no. Scenario II: You are offered a banned performance enhancing substance that comes with two guarantees. 1) You will not be caught. 2) You will win every competition you enter for the next five years, and then you will die from the side effects of the substance. Would you take it? More than half the athletes said yes.[57]

Goldman conducted this survey first in 1982, and every two years thereafter. The response was similar each time.

Evaluating the social merit of professional sport for young athletes as well as for audiences raises a question concerning the positive value of this self-sacrificial mentality of high-performance sport. Answering that question requires that we understand how sport training shapes the psyches of young athletes and makes them obedient to the command to win, and hence vulnerable to the lure of steroids and other injurious practices. For where Olympic training once took place primarily among young adults (after high school), in the 1980s and 1990s the Olympic network has reached out to include children as young as five. Just as some parents attempt to prepare their children for a university education at Harvard while they are still in kindergarten, certain parents determine that their children will aim for the Olympics, and enter them into competition and rigorous training before they have learned to read. For coaches and other sport officials, this expansion from teen training into childhood has constituted an important employment opportunity. For the sponsoring and equipment corporations, it has created a larger market. But for many of the children and the families who have been caught up in this process – as sources of labour, as revenue generators, or as infrastructural support for the network – the results are not so uniformly positive. As with other difficulties in the sport world, 'problems' are less well known than 'benefits,' though they are no less ubiquitous.

Sport sociologist Peter Donnelly and his colleagues at McMaster University in Hamilton, Ontario, have studied a number of consequences of training child and adolescent athletes in the high-performance streams of children's sports in the 1980s and 1990s.[58] They have raised serious concerns about the expanding nature of children's involvement in elite sport. 'There is an obvious trend toward earlier and more intensive athletic involvement for younger and younger children,' they report, and that trend appears in sum, to be one of labour exploitation: under adult guidance and supervision 'large numbers of children are training and competing under highly worklike conditions for long hours and in many cases for immediate or potential remuneration.'[59] Other researchers have reached similar conclusions: 'If youngsters in a workplace were subjected to these physical, social, emotional and mental pressures, there would be a dramatic reaction on the part of the community,' Dr Andrew Pipe commented in 1996.[60] Dr Ian Toffler of the New Orleans Children's Hospital published an article in the *New England Journal of Medicine* warning that the overtraining, injuries, and psychological pressure characteristic of Olympic-level gymnastics are tantamount to child abuse.[61]

Because of the demands it places on children, sport reformers raise concerns that children are not allowed enough of the most important other developmental activities, social and intellectual, of childhood; that they may be victims of disrupted family life; exposed to excessive psychological stress; that they may as a result of all the above become detached from their larger society, and may face a type of abandonment on completion of their athletic careers. These are problems, they say, that mark in significant ways the careers of a majority of young elite athletes. Often, these problems take place within the framework of the athlete/coach relationship. This relationship frequently organizes and colours the child athlete's whole life, and much of his or her family's life as well. The coach becomes, in effect, part of the young athlete's extended family, and, not infrequently, the most important part. David Meggyesy has written that though he played time and again with injuries, he did so in order to 'get approval from the coaches ... We moved into Oedipal lockstep: the more approval they gave me, the more frantically I played.'[62] Alfie Kohn cites the work of Jennifer Levin who, in her interviews with young competitive swimmers, found that '"love," a "family" and the approval of a significant paternal figure ... came up time and again when women spoke of the early motivation to compete. The psychoanalytic equation runs something like this: winning = coach's approval = parent's acceptance = acceptance of self (self-esteem).'[63]

There are problematic dimensions to this coach-athlete-family constellation at the core of elite youth sport, for children of both sexes. For it places the child in a very vulnerable and dependent position – one in which pleasing parents can often mean having to please the coach whether his demands seem fair and appropriate or not. Hence a dynamic of obedience and submission often characterizes coach–athlete relationships. A great deal of emotional, physical, and sexual maltreatment takes place within the framework of this relationship. The issue that has received by far the lion's share of media attention is sexual abuse.

The 1990s witnessed an endless succession of disclosures about the sexual abuse of youth by adults in custodial positions in sport. Accounts of abuse of female athletes by male coaches were common, as gymnasts, swimmers, cyclists, runners brought charges against their coaches.[64] The press exploited these stories but defused the full scope of the problem by framing the acts primarily as problems in male–female relations, part of a 'larger culture' of sexism, and not as problems of the culture of sport. In 1996 and 1997, however, two scandals that rocked the hockey world cast a new light on the issue: a prominent junior hockey coach, Graham James, was convicted on charges of sexual abuse against NHL player Sheldon Kennedy when Kennedy had been a player on his minor team.[65] And charges of sexual abuse were laid against several Toronto men, former employees of Maple Leaf Gardens in Toronto, who were accused of using their positions at the arena to obtain sex with boys as young as thirteen. These stories, with their invocation of homosexual child abuse, received bigger headlines and provoked more intense scrutiny of youth sport than those of heterosexual activity, with their normative expectations of sexual coercion and exploitation. Anxiety about sport appearing as a homoerotic arena runs very deep. It remains to be seen whether this can motivate a constructive look at many of the abusive and authoritarian dimensions of normal, high-performance sport culture.

A good deal of verbal and emotional abuse is also standard practice in children's and youths' competitive sport culture, rationalized as necessary to toughen boys up. Lessons in values and comportment are conveyed not only in the words of coaches, but in their behaviour. Shouting and cursing, personal denigration, and humiliation are common coaching behaviours. These are often sexualized, even when there is no rape or molestation. Venerated track coach Bill Bowerman urinated on his high-school athlete's legs in a gesture that was homoerotic and dominating (see Chapter 7). Equating athletic failure with femininity is a constant theme of coaches' tirades. The coach is the social father, and he often employs means that are both authoritarian and sexualized to control 'his' athletes, whether male or female, and to derive a sense of personal power.

Hypermasculinity and masculinism are reproduced within this paternal culture of Olympic youth sport in part through the limitations on women's participation. The participation rates for girls are still much lower than those for boys, and the vast majority of Olympic sports are sex-segregated, with fewer resources going to women's sport. In equally significant part, however, they are also reproduced by the exclusion of women's concerns from the way such sports are coached and practised. Women athletes and coaches have not succeeded in changing the harmful standards of high-performance sport or their training norms. On the contrary, they have succeeded individually only by adopting the same training regimes, steroids and all, that men require to win. And mothers – the guardians and facilitators of the children and teenagers involved in the Olympic and other sport networks – have little power to affect the sport culture in which their children participate. In one study cited by Donnelly and Sergeant, none of the mothers interviewed

felt they had any say in the nature of their child's experience within the sport. Many talked about needing to be at their child's tournaments to 'protect' them from the ugliness they saw associated with that form of competition. They also spoke of the immense difficulty coping with dilemmas which arose when their child was unjustly disappointed or punished by the sport's bureaucratic decisions. They felt silenced by the spectre of the 'ugly parent' mythology, believing that if they ever complained it would be their child and her or his [sport] career which would suffer.[66]

The devoted mothers presented regularly in *Sports Illustrated* features on male athletes are claimed to be the major figures motivating their sons to participate in sport. In many families, the 'sport mom' is the primary supporter of her children's involvement; in others, mothers share with fathers the labour of organizing a child for training and competition. Yet many mothers find some of the authoritarian and violent conditions of their children's athletic participation more disturbing than fathers do, and at earlier stages in their children's athletic careers. Consequently, many are more ambivalent about their children's participation. In such cases, tension may develop between parents, consisting of implicit or explicit accusations from the father that the mother is overprotective, a wet blanket, a prude, or the potential cause of her son's homosexuality. Most mothers who have concerns about sport do not want to disrupt bonds between fathers, coaches, and their sons or to create conflict with their mates. Critical fathers do not want to be responsible for singling their sons out for special treatment by 'complaining.' And single mothers worry that without sport, their sons would have no male role models or companionship at all. This may be especially true when they can see some tangible benefits in skill acquisition and social mobility for their children, or when the alternative might be unemployment or crime.

Many male sport personnel see their role as 'hardening the boy' and 'making a man out of him' in the process of developing his specific, commercially lucrative athletic prowess (or, in some cases, breaking the girl, and making a 'woman' out of her). High-performance training for children and youth remains a realm in which the authority and ideals of the patriarch go largely unchallenged, in women's sport as well, despite the existence of many female athletes and coaches.

Elite Sport versus Popular Health

The problem of drug use and other harmful technologies to enhance performance in sport is often presented by Olympic and other officials as a fatal flaw in the testing system because detection methods will never keep up with pharmacological innovation and athletes' determination to take drugs. But the battle against harmful training aids will never be won by detection and repression, no matter how sophisticated its technology. The current system of sanctions against pharmacological abuse focuses on catching and punishing the individual athlete, yet leaves intact all the systemic incentives to use steroids. For many athletes these are, evidently, much more powerful than the fear of possible sanctions. Employers, whether corporations, schools, or governments, reward performances enhanced by banned practices, yet turn their backs when individual athletes are apprehended. The athletes take the rap for the system. If, by contrast, employers themselves were penalized for violations, they would likely provide incentives for athletes to avoid abusive practices. Testing would become a last resort for exceptional cases, not the sole weapon in a limited arsenal. To achieve this end, the upper strata of the sport nexus must be held accountable for the drug culture and other forms of athlete abuse that they have promoted. It is highly unlikely that these groups will initiate such measures on their own. Only pressure from the consuming and practising base of the sport nexus itself would be a powerful enough force to bring about such changes to the existing sport economy.

By the same token, proposals regarding the maltreatment of children and youth in sport, such as those suggested by Donnelly and Sargent, would be useful. In the spirit of child labour laws they recommend new procedures for training coaches, and athletic training legislation that governs both the ages of children athletes and the number of hours they may train. Such measures might help to rein in the worst forms of abuse, and set higher expectations of coaches and the sport experience. But in confronting the realities of sport's attitudes to the body and its many deleterious consequences, surely a larger question is posed: given that so many of the benefits of sport can be delivered in 'low-performance,' noncompetitive, and nonviolent ways, why should we continue to support elite and professional sport at all? What gains do we, as a society, derive from the attitudes to the body and to social performance promoted by the culture of the core men's sports, and what losses do we incur? David Meggyesy has commented that 'the individualized fine tuning and manipulation of every athlete's body raises the question of what kind of athletics we want to celebrate. Is our ideal a mechanically tuned killer cyborg coming down the track, or a vital, healthy, human being?'[67]

The counterposition of these ideals is not frivolous when we regard the record of physical activity and fitness for the people of North America who live in the current culture of sport. According to the 1997 report of the Surgeon-General, approximately 15 per cent of U.S. adults engage regularly in vigorous physical activity during leisure time. Approximately 22 per cent of adults engage regularly in moderate physical activity. Walking, yard work, and gardening, for example, are by far the most popular of any physical activities. Still, this leaves the majority of Americans – over 60 per cent – without much exercise, certainly much less than the amount recommended by bodies such as The President's Council on Fitness and Sport and the Centers for Disease Control and Prevention. Approximately 25 per cent of U.S. adults are not active at all. Among the most active sector of the population by age (young people age 12–21), only half are vigorously active on a regular basis. One-quarter report no vigorous or even moderate activity. The percentage of high-school students who were enrolled in physical education and who reported being physically active for at least twenty minutes in physical education classes in the United States, for example, declined from approximately 81 per cent to 70 per cent during the first half of this decade. Patterns of activity and inactivity follow the patterns of privilege and disadvantage: activity is more common among the affluent than the nonaffluent; more common among men than women; more common among whites than African-American and Hispanic adults; and more common among younger than older persons.[68]

Patterns for physical activity and inactivity in Canada show similar contours. According to the 1995 *Physical Activity Monitor*, only two in five Canadian adults are active enough to benefit their cardiovascular health.[69] Statistics Canada contends that only 17 per cent of Canadians exercise regularly in their leisure time.[70] Of active Canadians, the majority are only moderately active and favour nonsport activities such as walking (74 per cent), gardening, home exercise, social dancing, swimming, cycling, skating, baseball, bowling, jogging, weight training, and golf (in descending order of popularity). Gradual increases in population activity levels in the moderate-exercise category have been registered since 1981 in 'unstructured, low-cost activities that can often be done outside facilities,' reflecting a greater understanding of the importance of exercise in the population as a whole. But vigorous activity levels by about one-fifth of the population, overlapping with competitive sport participation, have not increased. The barriers to sport participation are, as in the United States, correlated to gender, socioeconomic status, and age: affluent Canadians exercise more often than nonaffluent Canadians; men exercise more than women; white persons exercise more than people of colour; young people exercise more than adults. Indeed, as the 1997 *Physical Activity Monitor* noted: The three resources or services that rank the highest in helping Canadians to be active are infrastructure supports: access to safe streets and public places, affordable facilities, services and programs, and paths, trails, and green spaces.'[71]

Advocates of high-performance sport often maintain that there should be a seamless continuum between popular recreation and Olympic sport. However, in practice, by supporting high-performance and professional sport, our public authorities have starved popular sport, and other popular physical activities that have nothing to do with sport. In Canada, where the federal government funds elite (Olympic) athletes directly and supports Olympic and team sports indirectly (through public university funding, business and tax concessions, and stadium subsidization), this trend can be plotted. As political scientist Jean Harvey notes, since 1961,

a much larger sum of money has been devoted to high performance sport than to recreational programs and fitness ... With regard to sport policy, those programs geared to mass participation faced cuts or freezes in their budgets if inflation is considered. This had a direct effect on the very programs devoted to equalization of opportunity. However, at the same time federal budgets for elite sport increased dramatically.[72]

In Canada, federal government subsidies to high-performance sport exceed those to community sport by a ratio of seven to one. Halting the decline in public recreational programs requires that public policy on sport, fitness, and recreation begin to reverse this ratio of spending at all levels of government, and extend support to the kind of activities – participatory and performative – that promote personal well-being and population health, not corporate profits.

From the perspective of personal well-being and public health, the culture of the core men's sports – team as well as Olympic sports – has not accompanied a general improvement in active physicality in society at large, even though it has participated in creating a social obsession with the ideal body and avid markets for products associated with obtaining it. This is because the primary obstacles to improving public health and levels of physical activity are the need for economic resources and social supports to make access to such activity a reality for the under-active majority of the population. But social supports for population fitness have gone the way of all 'soft' liberal expenditures while expenditures on professional and elite athletics have grown (as the next chapter discusses.)

Active physicality is important to good health. In the words of the U.S. Surgeon General's report,

The body responds to physical activity in ways that have important positive effects on musculoskeletal, cardiovascular, respiratory, and endocrine systems. [Physical activity is] consistent with a number of health benefits, including a reduced risk of premature mortality and reduced risks of coronary heart disease, hypertension, colon cancer, and diabetes mellitus. Regular participation in physical activity also appears to reduce depression and anxiety, improve mood, and enhance ability to perform daily tasks throughout the life span.[73]

Because of the health benefits of physical activity, increasing it among the majority of the population should be a central component of public preventive health policy. Consider the example of breast cancer, expected to kill one out of nine women in North America. According to studies published in the *Journal of the National Cancer Institute*, sufficient exercise alone – at least four hours per week – may reduce the incidence of this disease by more than 50 per cent.[74] One crucial aspect of a noninvasive solution to breast cancer, then, is exercise. Medical discourse and self-help magazines often frame the issue of getting exercise as a matter of individual lifestyle and 'choice.' But due to the hours of paid and unpaid work most women perform and their limited financial resources, inadequate exercise is a collective, indeed a class and gender, matter. Affluent women exercise much more than nonaffluent women. Likewise, affluent men exercise more often than poorer men.

For both sexes, lack of time and resources, not lack of access to an Olympic swimming pool or track or sport spectacle, are the leading causes of both inadequate exercise and ill health. These matters are in turn directly linked to wealth and poverty. The World Health Organization's report in 1995, for example, pointed out what many other organizations also reported: the gaps between the rich and poor are widening both within the industrialized countries and in the developing world. 'Inequities in health [are] growing between countries, between well-off and disadvantaged groups within countries and between the sexes.'[75] And these act as growing barriers to active physicality and good health. In the 1996 report *Physical Activity and Health*, the United States Surgeon General noted that 'many people report that they lack enough time to exercise, often need motivation and support to maintain the habit of regular activity, incorrectly make the association between fitness and thinness, and, in many communities, are concerned about the lack of safe and accessible places to exercise.'[76]

The results of a survey released by the health promotion group Shape Up America in 1995 also indicated that a lack of opportunity to exercise may be the reason why poorer people in the United States are more likely to be overweight than those of higher incomes. Both groups understood that burning calories through exercise was better for them than starving them off, but many of the poorer people considered their neighbourhoods too unsafe for them to exercise, including to walk or jog.[77]

The 'wealth–health' equation is best explained by the 'social determinants of health' theory, advanced in the late nineteenth and early twentieth centuries by social and medical reformers, who argued that sanitation, decent housing, and nutritious food for working people would do more to bring down the rates of infectious diseases than any pharmaceutical or medical intervention. The theory has enjoyed a renaissance and substantial development since the 1970s, when epidemiologists, medical sociologists, and health economists sought to understand why the vast expenditures on doctors and hospitals characteristic of many industrial countries in the postwar period were not bringing improved health status to their populations. In more recent years, as the findings of immunology, neurology, and psychology have been correlated with those of epidemiology, experts have been able to be more precise about the mechanisms that underlie the 'wealth–health' equation, and to refine our understanding of it.

Increasingly, the key factor identified as responsible for many different disease manifestations is an overload of stress on a weakened immune system. Stress may be physical or mental in origin, biochemical or social.[78] The ability to recover from stress is correlated not only to its severity but also to what is known as 'the span of control' – the ability of an individual to influence his or her surroundings in his or her own interests. Those at the bottom of the socioeconomic ladder have little span of control and less access to treatment and convalescence when they become ill. 'Our discussion has suggested that rank correlates inversely with stress, or with the ability to cope with stress,' write health economists Morris L. Barer, Robert G. Evans, and Theodore R. Marmor. Moreover, they found, 'the negative health effects of hierarchy operate not on some underprivileged minority of "them" over on the margin of society, to be spurned or cherished depending on one's ideological affiliation, but on all of us. And its effects are *large*.'[79] A steep hierarchy is dysfunctional for society as a whole, not only because a majority are at the bottom, but also because the health of those at the top is influenced by the larger indices of population health. Dramatic evidence of this comes from contrasting the health status of Sweden and Great Britain. 'Swedish males ... show an inverse gradient of age-adjusted mortality with socioeconomic class, just as the British do. But the Swedish gradient was much less pronounced. Moreover, mortality among the lowest social class of Swedes was lower than among the highest class of Britons.'[80] In other words, a society that shares wealth is a society that shares health. Since being physically active in healthful ways is correlated directly with privilege, the sharing of wealth through services and supports is also a condition of its democratization.

Understanding the wealth–health paradigm in these terms exposes some distinctly gendered dimensions of population health as well. Women are the poorest members of our society. By virtue of their relative poverty and longer hours of work, they are more disadvantaged with respect to self-care and recreation.[81] The deteriorating health of women under such conditions also impinges directly on the health and well-being of family members. In their role as guardians of children's and men's health, the health of women is also key to the health and well-being of the whole community. 'It is essential that the social status of women be improved,' says the World Health Organization. 'Women play a key role in health care, yet their own health is being jeopardized daily. The potential contributions of women to world development and improvement of the human condition are being wilfully squandered.'[82] These factors point once again to the negative social impact of a culture that values the heroic and hypermasculine and selectively funds its activities, facilities, and spectacles. As long as women are primary health providers, we need to devote extra attention to the health and active physicality of the majority of women, not obscure its importance. Public policy should target women's health by making active physicality an accessible reality through free memberships in widespread community centres for activities of women's choosing, and by providing the means for women to take time off from family and employment responsibilities to be active.

As this chapter has suggested, it is time for a major rethinking of our support of high-performance sport and the harmful culture of drug abuse it has spawned. Whatever the pleasure of spectacle it provides, the obsession with high performance is not good for children, for athletes, for communities, or for society. It is time to redirect energy and dollars into strategies that make pleasurable, health-promoting, recreational physical activity a reality for the majority of the population. This goal represents a real investment in population health, one that pays off both socially and economically. We do not need more steroids and betablockers, 'world-class' indoor tracks, or Olympic pools. We need green spaces to play in, relations of harmony and inclusion among participants, and the social wherewithal to re-create ourselves.

In the spirit of reclaiming our right to our own active physicality, the next, and concluding, chapter looks at issues for change in sport and its culture.

9

Re-creating Recreation:
Sport and Social Change

Family, fatherhood, nation, state, race, class, gender, sexuality, commerce, and communications – I have tried to show how the culture of sport co-evolved with, through, and because of these institutions in the nineteenth and twentieth centuries. I have argued that the hypermasculine heroic ideal that is the dominant social and gender ideal of capitalist culture has been modelled and moulded by sport culture. Sport culture is highly variegated in class, racial, ethnic, national, and civic terms. But it has also had a singular purpose and effect that has cut across these differences: the culture of sport has supported the greater power of men as a gender-class in the key economic, political, and military power apparatus of civil and state society. I have explored the evolution of our dominant myths of manhood and masculinity since the nineteenth century, and argued that the ideals they embody are best captured by the term hypermasculinity. I have used this term to refer to a style of masculinity that draws on ideals derived from those of the precapitalist warrior cult and ideals unique to capitalist technoindustrial culture. Whatever the positive attributes of this hypermasculinity (courage, strength, skill) may be, it is also characterized by many antisocial qualities: aggressive physicality, violent instrumentality, biotechnological rationalization, and homoerotic narcissism under a veneer of hyperheterosexuality. I have attempted to show how this ideal of manhood took shape in reaction to the key challenges and anxieties facing men and women through many periods of turbulent change on the one hand, and the media and publicity industries' intent to turn the feelings provoked by these changes into purchasing behaviour in a 'masculinity market' on the other. I have shown how both the training requirements of athletes and the influential aesthetics of the athleticized body carry injurious and antihuman, as well as sexist, values.

I have also attempted to demonstrate that, beyond the weighty impact that sport culture has on men and women in relations with one another, the evolution of hypermasculine culture has also had an impact on politics. The culture of hypermasculinity forged strong emotional beliefs in individualism, elite entitlement, physical force, and social stratification (hierarchy). These beliefs, when brought to bear on political decision-making, affect the course of finance, government, and state in ways easily mobilized by neoliberal economics and neoconservative politics. I have tried to show that games, leisure, and recreation (the activities that seem furthest away from work and politics), particularly as they are commercialized and commodified, are heavily laden with ideology and politics. In recreational activities, especially the ones involving ritual and ceremony such as organized sport, we both express and reconfirm, in Erving Goffman's words, 'ultimate doctrines about man and the world.'¹ In ways that are highly meaningful for the development of individual psyches and broader sociopolitical impulses. Recreation is re-creation − a powerful arena for the transmission of values and behaviours.

In recognition of this larger power of sport and recreation or in simple opposition to the evident harms, hypocrisies, and injustices of current sport institutions, many people today are working to change sport and its place in our culture. They include, among others, parents protesting the violence of children's hockey or the cruel hours of competitive swimming; parents who remove their kids from competitive sport altogether; creative educators and public officials who introduce physical activities such as performance rope-skipping, breakdancing, and yoga in class and as extracurricular activities; people fighting for equal resources for disadvantaged groups in their communities; and sport officials working with athletes on issues of violence and sexual responsibility. Though evident in many parts of the sport system, too often their efforts reflect individual dedication, not institutional policy and majority will. However dynamic and rewarding their efforts, without popular reinforcement, such individuals will not be able to move beyond minority reformer status to truly change the objectives and conventions of the larger hypermasculinist sport culture. Impulses toward change will be overpowered by the sheer magnitude of existing sport culture.

It would be ideal if professional athletes themselves were to lead the way in changing the current realities of sport by rejecting harmful performance standards, changing their games to validate the qualities and objectives now excluded, and sharing with their communities the resources amassed by their performances. But there is no sign that any of these possibilities is in the offing. With multimillion-dollar endorsements and playing contracts, star athletes are making enough money to join the owning class in sport. In 1995 Michael Jordan supported a move to have the NBA players association decertified, showing a clear identification with the owners rather than the players. Wayne Gretzky's 1993 disavowal of his previous opposition to fighting in hockey is another example of how a player's loyalty can shift when he is able to share in the huge profits to be made in professional sports.

With important individual exceptions, some of whom I have named in earlier chapters, athletes have proved to be largely an individualist and politically conformist lot. The baseball strike and hockey lockout of 1994 and 1995 showed that the top professional athletes have built strong guilds for master (professional) players, but care little for the poor conditions of the journeymen (minors), or for the apprentices (youths and children), or for their audiences. These events also demonstrated the lack of community awareness on the part of professional athletes. No player came forward to criticize the owners' demands for more profits or to suggest that they take less money themselves, send a decent portion of the profits back to the community, or contribute to making physical activity a reality for those without access to it.[2] Since the material rewards reaped by a small number of successful athletes are so great, and because success in sport is the most powerful social confirmation of masculinity that any male can attain in our culture, it is unlikely that those who succeed in it will challenge it. So far, no Spartacus has emerged among the gladiators to help those without the benefit of six-, seven- and eight-figure salaries, or to propose community ownership of sports franchises.

But this does not mean that change is impossible. It simply means that it must come from elsewhere – from those who understand the ways in which today's culture of sport does not benefit the majority of youths or adults, and are willing to act on their perceptions. By way of contributing to these efforts and concluding this work, I offer some thoughts on several issues that are highly political in their implications, and require political action to address. These are: the matter of public subsidy to commercial sport in the context of neoconservative politics and neoliberal economics; the need to change sport's place in physical education through public education and recreation systems; the monopoly of commercial sport on the means of mass communication; the contradictory nature of sport for women; parenting and violence in boys' and men's lives within the context of sport; and, finally, a brief program of broad principles and objectives to guide efforts toward change.

Sport and Public Spending in Neoconservative Times[3]

Until recently, public subsidies for privately owned sport enterprises went unquestioned. 'Amid all sport's sponsors, the largest and oldest barely speaks its name,' noted *The Economist* in 1992, under a subheading that read, 'Thanks for the subsidy.'[4] While public spending has been cut in many other areas since the late 1970s, a trend toward increasing public subsidy to professional sport is evident. In a 1995 article in *Financial World*, Andrew Osterland notes that in the 1980s, 'American cities spent about $750 million to renovate and construct new stadiums and arenas ... Since 1992, the figure is over $1 billion, and with about half of the 110 professional franchises clamoring for new or improved facilities, over $6 billion will probably be ponied up before the decade ends.'[5] *The Economist* suggested that the average cost to taxpayers for the construction of major new sport infrastructure in 1992 ran between US$100 to $200 million per facility.[6] Judging by more recent expenditures – $305 million by Missouri and St Louis and $540 million by Cleveland for new stadiums – the costs and the subsidies are still increasing.[7] Dennis R. Howard and John L. Crompton note that in 1950, nineteen per cent of stadiums and arenas facilities were publicly owned. In 1991, by contrast, seventy-seven per cent of stadiums and areas used by major league sports teams in North America were publicly owned; and since 1960, twenty-five of the twenty-nine new stadiums constructed have been publicly owned.[8] According to Robert Baade and Alan Sanderson, the incidence and proportion of public funding to such facilities has grown, despite cutbacks in direct funding to Olympic, educational, and recreational sport programs.[9] This form of public subsidy to a particular form of culture constitutes a massive affirmative-action program for masculinism.

In the 1990s, the pressure on the public purse to subsidize professional sport became intense, as more and more team owners threatened to leave their teams' home cities in search of greater revenue guarantees and/or new facilities. 'Stadium is now a synonym for blackmail,' Osterland observes. 'Fearful of losing their beloved teams, cities are sinking greater and greater amounts in renovating facilities or building new ones for "distressed" owners.'[10] Many cities have paid up rather than lose their teams.[11] Some, like St Petersburg and St Louis, even built stadiums before they had secured major-league franchises, though only St Louis succeeded in filling theirs. By threatening to move to the empty St Petersburg stadium, however, Chicago White Sox owner Jerry Reinsdorf got 'a brand new $185 million Comiskey Park across the street from where the old one stood, and a lease deal that helped make the White Sox the sixth most valuable franchise in major league baseball.'[12] In 1996, economist Carol M. Amidon noted that there was a 'nation-wide trend in which taxpayers are being asked to pay for projects benefiting a single corporation.' Attracting the former Cleveland Browns football franchise to Maryland, she calculated, 'will wind up costing $127,000 for every job created, vastly exceeding the $6,250 price of a job created by Maryland's economic development fund.'[13]

In recent years, as neoconservative governments seek to reduce services, including community-level sport and recreation programs, questions are finally being raised about the virtue of continuing public subsidies to professional sport and a few large corporations.[14] Some journalists are now beginning to argue what a number of academics and urban development experts have been telling us for some time: housing professional sport in huge stadiums does not make a strong economic contribution to communities, usually results in revenue-negativity for taxpayers, and should not be relied on as a strategy for municipal growth.[15] 'The gift that keeps on taking,' is how sports writer Stephen Brunt describes most franchises and stadiums and their relationship to their local economies. Initial construction provides good jobs when buildings and infrastructure are put into place, but it usually involves a large debt load for the government involved. After construction is complete, most of the jobs the stadiums provide are low-paid and low-skilled. Despite spill-offs for sport tourism, most of the huge revenues go directly into the private pockets of team and stadium owners and players, not back into the local economy or tax base to support the continuing public debt and operating infrastructure costs. As Brunt puts it: 'All kinds of talk about direct and indirect economic impact, about various trickle-down theories which suggest that dollars spent on baseball tickets somehow benefit the greater good, about mysterious multiplier effects ... all of that is pure voodoo.'[16] Franchise owners, however, continue to aggressively advance their sport megaprojects. For example, Seattle Seahawks owner Paul Allen has been widely praised as a philanthropist who, in an act of civic duty, agreed to save the Seahawks from extinction. He had one condition however: that the people of Seattle and Washington state finance a new stadium to house the team. He personally assumed the costs of a state referendum testing the citizens on their willingness to subsidize a new stadium that would cost $450 million. A vociferous debate ensued, and Allen and the Seahawks promoters won a narrow victory. *The Economist* noted that

Mr. Allen's financial backing of the statewide vote has drawn much criticism, some people suggest it seriously undermines the democratic process. After all, Washington state residents of more modest means must laboriously collect thousands of signatures to put initiatives on a ballot ... The more galling thought, from the taxpayers' point of view, is that Mr. Allen, whose net worth increased by $900 million in one recent day as Microsoft's stock price rose, could easily pay for a new stadium himself.[17]

The owners of sport teams and facilities and their counterparts in other sport-related industries present the public subsidy of sport infrastructure as a legitimate expense in the public interest. At the same time, through their support of neoconservative governments and neoliberal economic policies, they are complicit in withdrawing public subsidies from health, welfare, education, and publicly supported cultural enterprises such as PBS and the National Endowment for the Arts in the United States, and the CBC and the Canada Council for the Arts in Canada.)[18] In Cleveland, in 1995, for example, the city government managed to find $540 million for stadium construction after laying off 400 staff members (including 200 teachers) from its school system.[19] In effect, this city opted to subsidize the enterprises of masculinist culture rather than decent public education.[20] In that same year, the U.S. Congress voted to cut funding to health, education, and welfare by $9 billion and to give the Pentagon $7 billion more than it asked for. The hypermasculine inflection of neoconservative politics helps to frame the human services that were once part of a public economy as unnecessary, even bad and hence disposable, while it promotes major public expenditure on the state apparatus, the military, and crime-control industries, along with the kind of culture that is compatible with these.[21]

The right/left distinctions between neoliberal/neoconservative ideas of government (with their support to the masculine state apparatus) and liberal/social democratic ideas of government (with their support to redistributive measures that secure the well-being of society as a whole) are usually ascribed to identifications rooted in economic positions and interests – capitalist or petit bourgeois versus working class and socialist, for example. I am arguing that in addition to these identifications, others properly related to position and interests in the gender order are also at work. The ideas and the morality of neoliberals and neoconservatives have been informed by the relations of gender-class and the values of masculinism. Through political policy and state action, under macho neoconservatism (commonly known as monetarism), public dollars have been redirected from the poor to the rich, and from state departments charged with providing community (public) supports to armed forces and prisons. These policies have drastically exacerbated the very family breakdowns, small-business failures, and generalized violence in daily life against which the right typically rails. 'American violence is the result of our collective "moral choice" to maintain those social policies that in turn maintain our uniquely high level of violence,' writes James Gilligan. High levels of interpersonal violence and poverty-related crime have resulted in the fact that, for many years, the United States has had the highest per capita imprisonment rate in the world, substantially higher than the former Soviet Union and South Africa under apartheid.[22] This reality too is profoundly gendered, as the vast majority of those incarcerated are males.

Morality is a set of values transmitted through socialization of the young, rewards to the successful, codification in law, and celebration in collective ritual. American morality is characterized by a contradiction so deep that that it appears schizophrenic. On the one hand, much is made in political rhetoric of democracy, egalitarianism, peace, and national well-being. Every politician, regardless of affiliation, purports to speak in the name of these values. In sport discourse, these ideas are reflected in the ethos of good sportsmanship and inclusive participation. At the same time, in the elitist and coercive values endorsed and perpetuated by various institutions of hypermasculinist culture, especially sport, an alternative, indeed opposite, morality of coercive entitlement venerates behaviours that are antidemocratic, elitist, and bellicose. In sport discourses these values are reflected in the ethos of 'nice guys finish last' and 'winner takes all.' Because of its power in childhood and young adulthood, the culture of sport helps to establish the values of coercive entitlement in emotional impulses and core identifications. When the individual who feels them is confronted later in life with political choices, these impulses will often have a deeper influence than objective knowledge of the societal value of public services or impassioned appeals for socioeconomic equality. After a century of American sport culture, and the fusion of American patriotism with athletic hypermasculinity, many Americans conceive of democracy as a football game. Only the hero and his band of comrades-in-arms get to play. The biggest and strongest win at home and abroad. The word 'democracy' is still used constantly in American discourse. But for those who view life and society as the big game, its content and meaning have been entirely drained of their original political meaning. Basic and defining issues such as inclusivity, equality, representation, and accountability have no real purchase in this area of 'democracy.' Indeed, in this lexicon, the word and its traditional meaning are a contradiction in terms.

These are some of the broader political arguments against continuing sport's current privileged place in our society and in our children's lives. One strategic lever that can be exercised in numerous ways to diminish the magnitude and impact of the core men's sports is to end their public subsidy. Cities can withdraw tax breaks or infrastructural services, refuse to fund new megaprojects, and redirect funds toward the kind of services and facilities that make active physicality more accessible to ordinary people. It is heartening to note that, despite the lack of media coverage on the topic, in many North American cities citizens are beginning to organize in these directions and some city governments are beginning to hear their concerns. Considerable resistance to the public subsidization of sports megaprojects has developed in a number of cities on this continent and world-wide in the 1980s and 1990s. In Toronto, for example, a coalition of antipoverty activists, women's groups, urban planners, environmentalists, and labour leaders protested the city's bid for the 1996 Summer Olympics. The group, called 'Bread Not Circuses,' drew attention to the disruptive and destructive effects such a megaproject would have on the city's 'livability.' They challenged the claim that the Olympics would bring long-lasting productive jobs and raised questions about the kind of sport the Olympic games celebrate. As a result of the ensuing public debate about sport, the province of Ontario's social democratic government took a proactive stance against public subsidy of professional sport facilities by unloading the Toronto Skydome in 1993, selling it back to the private sector.[23] The Toronto campaign led to links among similar citizens' groups in Nagano, Japan, and Sydney, Australia. Prior to the Atlanta games, a number of groups organized a coalition to protect the city's poor from expropriation and to ensure that the poor downtown neighbourhoods derived improvements from the Olympic megaproject. They met with little success.[24]

Other forms of resistance against sport megaprojects, both professional team sport facilities and Olympic-related events, have ranged from tax revolts, to grass-roots campaigns focused on environmental and urban planning issues, to larger coalitions of social movements raising concerns about the process by which a city organizes to bid for a set of games or makes a deal involving a stadium with a professional franchise owner. Where they have been mounted, campaigns such as these have succeeded in addressing the problematic impacts of sport development. In some cases, they have even suggested alternative directions in physical culture. They also provide positive models of citizen action with respect to the apparently omnipotent alliances of sport, government, and big business. But because of the relative poverty of their supporters, compared with the power and wealth of the sport nexus, and because the mass media tend to minimize or ignore their activities and views, they have often remained marginal and ephemeral. Now that a more sceptical public climate exists in many cities, perhaps such campaigns will take larger strides.

Disestablishing Sport in Public Systems

In attempting to diminish the dominance of the core men's sports vis-à-vis other physical practices in society as a whole, the public education and recreation systems are strategically important. At least for the time being, they still exist in public, not commercial, space, and are therefore amenable to change by the direct action of parents, teachers, and students acting as citizens, not as consumers. Note, however, that incursions by the private sector, not least through sport, threaten the integrity and viability of this public sector.[25] The marketing campaigns of professional sport now reach into the heart of neighbourhood schools, which, strapped for funds, offer up our children as audiences for the corporate marketing machine. The 'public' nature of education is thus at risk and needs to be defended, even as its forms evolve. The public education and recreation systems are also important because they are key sites of sport and protosport socialization. These systems provide key functions of social parenting that shape children for life. We have learned from psychology that the early years are the most important. Changing the way physical culture is taught and practised in the public education and recreation systems is therefore one of the key priorities in effecting social change among children and subsequent generations of adults.

The very monolithism of sport is one of the central problems. Simply reducing the claim sport makes on society's attention and resources would open up space for other forms of physical culture to flourish and expand. At present, we are moving ever more rapidly to a professional sport monoculture. We need to encourage diversity in sports and other physical activities. As well, if we want our physical culture to encourage a more cooperative political culture, we should seek to restore elements of play, pleasure, and cooperation to the activities we include in our public systems for children and youth. By de-emphasizing sport in what are now publicly supported supply systems for professional sport (they supply both the athletes and the adult fans), we could begin to make effective changes to the popular base of the sport nexus, and therefore to its economic viability in its present form.

To effect such a change in the educational and socialization systems will require a change in the education of the educators – physical education teachers in the public school systems as well as sports and fitness instructors in community, sport, and fitness centres, both public and private. This requires parents and public officials to assert the importance of physical activity and physical education within public education. Schools across North America have lost huge numbers of physical educators because of cutbacks, and the results of inactivity for children and teens have been adverse. We need more, not less, physical activity for our children. At the same time, a general program of curriculum reform is necessary in the universities and colleges that train today's physical educators so that they can provide a less sport-centred and more inclusive experience of physical activity.

An important example of a curriculum of physical education that de-emphasizes high-performance sport and sport culture is the University of Toronto's Faculty of Physical Education and Health. The faculty, which offers both undergraduate and graduate degree programs and conducts university athletics, is one of five health sciences faculties at the university.[26] The school conceptualizes its graduates as health professionals whose mission is to increase participation in physical activity through pleasurable involvement. Population health paradigms as well as physiology and biomechanics inform the school's course offerings. Each student chooses one activity in four areas of physical skill specialization (individual, team, movement awareness, and cultural). In addition to basketball, field hockey, ice hockey, volleyball, cycling, diving, field events, gymnastics and tennis, students are also required to choose among ballet, modern, jazz, or world dance; karate-do; judo; cooperative games; and 'games of the world,' primarily the popular pastimes of non-European peoples. The curriculum seeks to validate both homosocial and heterosocial sport, with its emphasis on women's vigorous physicality and men's access to nonsport physical disciplines, better to balance the traditionally 'masculine' and 'feminine' repertoires. The curriculum also politicizes the study of attitudes toward the body, and makes their study a cultural as well as physical activity. Thus students learn about the social determinants of health, and how gender, class, race, ethnicity and sexuality are implicated in physical activity and well-being.[27]

The University of Toronto Faculty of Physical Education and Health curriculum represents a balanced, integrated approach to physical culture, which it hopes will be carried out into the public systems by its graduates as they become educators themselves or work in the health sector and public recreation. It is discouraging to note, however, that the majority of postsecondary schools of physical and health education do not share this orientation.[28] Even though sports studies have become an important field of scholarship, as a rule, universities are binding themselves more and more to high-performance sport and the purely biophysical aspect of physical activity.

Clearly sport is a major institution in the generation of normative gender ideals and accompanying sexual ideas. The instrumentalism, performance expectations, bodily aesthetics, sensual (or antisensual) expectations, narcissism, and violence modelled by hypermasculine sport and celebrated by the culture of sport affect broader ideals of masculinity and, hence, heterosocial life in many powerful ways. As well, however, sport incites homoeroticism while it punishes homosexuality. The incited and frustrated homoerotic sexual energy of the sporting experience is one important source for the violence of men's sport. If we want to reduce the sources of violence in sport, we should address the fear of the feminine that underlies its violent homophobia. By forging a physical culture in which the expressive and cooperative impulses are validated (as well as the assertive and instrumental), that fear could, at least in part, be attenuated, and its destructive consequences lessened.

Democratic, humanitarian, pro-health, and cultural perspectives all point toward norms that emphasize responsibility, equality, and mutual consent in sexual relationships.[29] These qualities imply cooperation, whereas their lack implies coercion – be it physical, economic, or cultural/psychological. Responsibility, equality, and consent are equal-opportunity qualities. They help girls and women to step out of the socially prescribed role of sexual victim, and teach boys and men to control their sexuality in responsible ways. They can be applied by anyone, regardless of their sexual orientation or even political ideology. If generalized, such qualities would cut down immensely not only on sexual crimes, but on the whole crime-control industry that now exists to apprehend and punish them. It would be socially beneficial if physical educators and athletes could teach and model paths to sexual connection and pleasure that stress these qualities. Northeastern University in Boston, for example, has a 'Mentors in Violence Prevention' program to encourage male student-athletes to get actively involved in stopping rape, battering, and sexual harassment. It has pioneered some new interactive programs for students; uses engaging, direct, and innovative methods; and provides training to other athletic departments and professional staff to help implement the program at other schools.[30] Programs like these help athletes understand the difference between an athletic and a sexual encounter, and help them see that there are different ways to be a sexual man.

The need for such major changes in sexual behaviour are urgent for well-known reasons. We are facing the havoc of AIDS and the need to prevent the spread of the disease. We want to minimize the transmission of other fertility and life-threatening diseases as well. We want to minimize unwanted pregnancies. We want, for our own and our children's sakes, to harmonize relations between the sexes and create better conditions for childrearing and parenting. All of this means we have to create the conditions that model responsibility for self and others in sexual relations. If we want to detach sexual pleasure from aggression and domination in the service of these goals, we need a physical culture that models and celebrates true consent between equals, not sado-masochistic rites of domination.

Sport and the Mass Media

I have sought to show how sport and its commercialized media culture have promoted hypermasculinity, and how this process has inhibited the cultural, practical, and political transformations necessary to achieve gender harmony and create adequate conditions for raising children and supporting families. As the great impresarios of the core men's sports, the mass media have created and used the myth of hypermasculinity to group huge and highly lucrative audiences of men – the masculinity market – whose relation to the sport spectacle is primarily one of consumption. The hypermasculine hero at the centre of the myth is in this sense widespread and dominant (we are all consumers) without being representative of the real variety of men and masculinities that exists in North American society today. The actions and body of this hero are as unattainable for most men as the lives and bodies of super-models are for most women. There is every reason for the majority of men – who are neither hypermasculine heroes themselves, nor want to be such heroes – to change the culture of sport. Yet many people find it difficult to imagine success in redirecting the funds allocated to professional sport to other forms of physical culture, or in changing the place of sport in the school and recreation system. The most important reason for this is the dominance of the commercial mass media in sport, and in men's culture more generally. For as long as the publicity machines relegate other forms of physical culture to the margins, it will be very difficult for emergent practices to gain the adherents that could make them popular mass alternatives.

That the freedom of the press belongs to those who own one, as the great sports writer A.J. Liebling used to say, has never been truer than it is today. In order to organize large audiences for sponsors – the raison d'être of commercial communications – vast amounts of capital are required.[31] The four major media-industry-sport constellations (General Electric-NBC, Time-Warner Turner, Disney-ABC, and Westinghouse-CBS) deploy billions of dollars throughout their holdings in radio and television, the movie industry, the daily and weekly press, and other publishing. They are supported by powerful political interests in Washington and Ottawa, who support in a variety of ways their existing monopolies. The result of such monopolies is that the world of communications is dominated by a small number of (mostly) male private citizens. Compared with this group, the vast majority of people, not simply the most disadvantaged, are simply too resource-poor to 'compete' with the communications power of the conglomerates.[32] This economic organization of communications, as writers such as Noam Chomsky, Ben Bagdikian, Herbert Schiller, Edward Herman, and Robert McChesney have shown, has produced one of the most effective systems of propaganda and institutional censorship ever devised – much more effective than command-economy ideology or fascist totalitarianism. For the popular tribunes of the mass media seductively 'manufacture consent' around the views, interests, and projects of their owners, rather than nakedly coercing compliance. If it is true, as I have argued, that a considerable part of the hypermasculinity of sport is due to its shaping by profit-driven, private interests, one key question that confronts us is how to unravel the communication of sport and physical culture from this imperative.

The neoliberal approach to culture assumes that the market and the public sphere are or should be one and the same. This guiding belief animates the commitment of neoliberal politicians and senior bureaucrats to privatize state services and, by withdrawing public subsidies from culture, make all cultural creation feel the unmediated force of the market.[33] This orientation presents no difficulties for the main corporate players in the sport nexus. For them, the opening up of new markets in previously protected public sectors such as public schools and universities via sport is most welcome.[34] On the other hand, liberal and social justice constituencies, who do not assume the ideal unity of public and commercial spheres, want to see more, not less, public support for all forms of culture and are faced with the crisis of a dissolving public sector and a shrinking public sphere. Neoliberals and neoconservatives have been highly successful in promoting antisocial state politics because they have been able to tap into a widespread sense of alienation from bureaucratized, indifferent, and sometimes dangerous 'big government.' Even when they are providing services, large governments and the bureaucracies they propagate are often not responsive, representative, or accountable — whether in a capitalist or a command economy – particularly to those without wealth. Thus a progressive answer to the crisis of the state, as political scientist Leo Panitch writes, 'must lie not in privatizing the public sector, but in democratizing it.'[35] The same approach must be adopted with respect to culture, including physical culture. In addition to protecting our embattled existing institutions of public culture from monetarist cuts, we need to develop some clear principles and practical vehicles for public support to physical culture – particularly to the activities that people currently enjoy that are not sport.

Media scholar James Curran argues that cultural funding to social organizations and the cultural producers associated with them is an important part of society's ability to include all its voices in public discourse and cultural production.[36] He suggests a number of ways in which government support can be public and pluralistic at the same time. Numerous models of arm's-length public subsidy to the arts exist and can be adapted and built upon in the area of physical culture. Britain's Channel 4 is a vibrant example of the innovation that results when public funding is made available to cultural producers associated with social movements and ethnic and arts communities. Until Margaret Thatcher disbanded it in 1986, the left-wing Greater London Council funded commercial cooperatives of minority and working-class cultural producers; members were able to learn a useful economic skill with which they could eventually support themselves.[37] Public funding for nonsport physical activities can create the conditions for new physical vocabularies and disciplines.

Sport in its current manifestation is a physical activity that is rationalized, bureaucratizied, intensified, and obsessed with records. Creating a nonmarket-dependent sector for physical culture could ensure a place for different ways of being physical. However creative and energetic such initiatives might be, it is clear that monopoly structures in the media exist nationally and internationally and have a major stake in maintaining that monopoly and in cultivating the rich masculinity market that has sustained it. It is highly unlikely that the present corporate players will voluntarily give way to, or finance, a noncorporate cultural sector. Hence, in the interests of democratizing communications and culture, including physical culture, it is appropriate to support initiatives that employ the tools of government to rewrite the criteria and objectives concerning the awarding of broadcasting licences, state subsidies (e.g., low postal rates, favourable tax status, antitrust legislation), and government regulatory bodies.[38]

To put such propositions forward in the United States today – when it has failed to create public health care or a tax-supported public broadcasting system – may seem utopian. To have to reaffirm such a proposition in Canada, as neoconservative politicians and bureaucrats dismantle the impressive network of public cultural institutions that were the pride of the country – is tragic. But without such a coherent and centralized approach, executed at the continental, federal, state, and provincial levels in such a way as to enable rather than strangle diverse expression, no emergent cultural development, including in the sphere of physical culture, can ever hope to challenge the dominance of corporate sport. Pluralism should be validated. At present, it is lauded in rhetoric, but absent in practice.

Where will the money come from for expanding the noncommercial cultural realm? To begin with, given the importance of physical activity to well-being, population health, and citizenship, governments should consecrate many more, not fewer, tax dollars to all initiatives and projects that encourage, support, and enable such activity for the majority of people. We know today that each dollar invested in preventive health programs such as Head Start saves American governments about $7.00 in funds that would be necessary for remedial education, social service, welfare and criminal agencies without the early intervention. We also know that a society in which the majority are exercising enough to maintain and strengthen their immunity – a society that *practises* preventive medicine – is a society in which the majority have the time and resources for such self-care. Spending on popular physical culture – from participation to performance – is a sound health investment. It is appropriate that financial support come in the form of increased taxes on corporate sport. These taxes would only seek to recover a part of the investment already made in that sport by the community.

Gender and the Culture of Sport on the Eve of the Twenty-First Century

This book is a study of gender with a focus on men and masculinity. Only secondarily and by direct specific comparison have I discussed women's relationships to sport. Nevertheless, having mentioned some of the key difficulties surrounding the rites of men, and having critiqued the exclusion of women by sport, and sport's participation in an oppressive culture of beauty, I would also like to address some of the issues raised by a greater engagement of women in sport, even the 'nontraditional' sports. There is no doubt that active physicality is important to physical and mental health and well-being. It is a powerful tool for learning about self and society. There is great value for girls and women in learning to be active and instrumental, in reclaiming the active, 'masculine' parts of themselves that their historical exclusion from sport was meant to suppress. Games such as hockey, volleyball, and basketball are good for developing physical mastery and group coordination for girls, just as they are for boys.

The importance of active physicality for girls and women is the basis on which feminist sport activists have sought to bring sport to girls and young women, and fought for resources and cultural change to achieve this.[39] Since Title IX was enacted in the United States, and women sport reformers in Canada began organizing in the mid-1970s, more resources have been allocated to women's sport at the college and national team levels, and several large cohorts of skilled young women athletes have been produced as a result.[40] A new cadre of female athletes, honed by the sport scholarship system, are ready to be commercially organized. So there are indications that the sport–media complex is responding to women athletes and women audiences as a potentially profitable market. This can be seen in the inauguration of two women's professional basketball leagues and the planned launch of a sport magazine for women to be published by *Sports Illustrated*. If such ventures succeed, we must ask to what extent does accepting the values and behaviours of hypermasculine men's culture, embodied in the core men's sports, strengthen or weaken women and society? There will be no social gain if, through learning the mind set and morality of hypermasculinity, women in effect lend their efforts to its broader perpetuation in the name of gender-neutrality or gender equality. As R. Goldman writes, 'Mass media advertising to women represents an aesthetically depoliticized version of a potentially oppositional feminism. It is feminism tailored to the demands of the commodity form.'[41] Given the profound relationship of sport to advertising and the role of advertising in shaping consciousness, discussed in Chapter 7, sport could act as a depoliticizing force among women as well as men. Feminist sport scholars and activists are well aware of the pitfalls in these, and other, dynamics involved in the commercialization of sport among women.

U.S. culture, influenced by men's culture, is marked by an intense denigration of the 'feminine' and its associated qualities of softness, receptivity, cooperation, and compassion. Today's erotic athletic flesh is hard, muscled, tense, and mean. The unquestioning emulation of hypermasculinity by women does not constitute 'androgyny' or 'gender neutrality,' but rather the triumph of hypermasculinism, its inherent sado-masochistic attitudes to the body and its affirmation of domination. It does not hold out the promise of producing an athlete, of either sex, in whom the feminine and masculine qualities are developed, balanced, and integrated. This so-called androgyny does not represent the 'feminization' of culture – that is, the restoration to their rightful place of principles and values long suppressed – even when women voluntarily seek it. While asserting their right to be physically active and strong and socially instrumental and influential, women should, nevertheless, be transforming physical culture into one that validates the expressive and cooperative dimensions of existence. Women need to continue to value those qualities in themselves and in cultural life, rather than abandon them to the hierarchism and violent instrumentality of the dominant sport culture. Perhaps women can contribute to a new definition of instrumentality, one not based on violence or coercion, but on give and take and mutual creation.[42]

Women as a group – and all parents – also need to actively resist the culture of physical 'smallness' – exemplified in thinness and delicacy – for women. Smallness is a symbol for youth, weakness, and subordination. To aspire to it requires extreme forms of bodily mortification: starvation, vomiting, deforming exercises and other biomechanical interventions, harmful cosmetic surgery, and – worst of all – an enervating self-loathing that drains women of the healthy energy both they and their society need. The aesthetic of youthful smallness is one of the most insidious and effective forms of mass internalized oppression among women. It literally cripples women physically, emotionally, and socially. Developing an aesthetic of diversity that values the strong, mature female body is thus an urgent cultural task, one that women sport reformers could well continue to work toward.[43]

With respect to men's engagement with the culture of sport, I want to cluster my concluding remarks around two themes: the problem of family and social fatherhood, and the matter of masculinity's cultural link with violence.

However unequal it was in terms of social power for the sexes, the family wage system did provide a framework that fulfilled the two great needs of daily life under capitalism: earning the means of general exchange (money – men's work) and sustaining the generations (childrearing, care of the elderly and infirm, feeding, health care, cleaning – 'women's work'). By the middle of the twentieth century, and as a result of great struggles on the part of working people, North American economic norms had assigned roughly forty paid hours per week in the male labour market to sustain the unpaid hours of women's work in a family of four or five people. In this context, sport provided the ideological support for a politically unequal but economically viable parenting and living arrangement.

Today, primary parenting remains a predominantly feminine occupation that most women must add on to the hours they work for pay outside the home. While men have not equalized their share of work done in the household, most are working longer hours outside the home, with a significant number topping the fifty-hour paid work week.[44] The great gender contradiction of the second half of the twentieth century is that the economic imperatives of capitalism – pushing women onto men's terrain in the paid labour market – have undermined the very territory of masculinity that capitalism's cultural industries have attempted to stake out, occupy, and defend. By forcing women to compete with men in the paid labour force (where women will inevitably seek out the male-dominated professions because remuneration and prestige are higher), the economic logic of capitalism has confronted men and women with a social phenomenon for which gender socialization has left them ill-prepared. The continuing remoteness of the father (in many cases, his total absence, as single mothers constitute almost one-fifth of the parenting population) continues to create males open to and needy of social and symbolic fatherhoods. 'Underfathered boys' (boys whose fathers spend fifty-five hours and more at the office each week), in the words of Australian family therapist Steve Biddulph, 'are the ones who think being masculine has to do with blood, killing and weapons. They are the boys who will not write a poem or take part in a play.'[45]

In discussing her findings with respect to time, family, and gender at a conference of the American Sociological Association in 1997, sociologist Arlie Hochschild, author of *The Time Bind*, commented on a Chicago study that indicated that fathers spend an average of five minutes a day talking one-on-one with their teenagers. She noted that most middle-school children are now home alone after school for at least part of the day and are more apt to experiment with drugs and alcohol. 'I fear we are adjusting to a lower level of emotional giving,' she said, 'and we may develop into less humane people.' She noted that many women preferred to work longer hours on the paid job because, in comparison with the work and stress at the home site, they found paid work easier to cope with and more rewarding.[46]

As the demands of paid work now begin to require women to spend as much time outside the home as male earners, and as many of the public services for children and young people are being cut or eroded, such services as parenting and elder care are being put in serious jeopardy. What additional damage is being done as women's hours of work outside the home increase while men's continue to grow? At the political level, fighting for the right of men, as well as of women, to parent means fighting for a shorter working week, a series of meaningful social and financial supports for parents, and more resources for truly popular physical recreation for people of all ages, so that women and men can equally sustain their own health, take care of their families, and participate in their communities. Such initiatives would help address the crisis in reproduction and gender that capitalism has created by eroding the traditional gendered division of labour. We need a systemic and radical answer to the gendered economic crisis of parenting and the disintegrated family-wage system, a policy of true family values that supports working parents of both sexes and all children within families. Also required is a policy that funnels social wealth and redistributes it through services and direct economic supports for the needs of families for shelter, sustenance, emotional/physical health, socialization, and education, and that redeploys the social surplus away from the military economy and culture toward an economy and culture of peace and well-being for the majority.[47]

This strategic direction is the only credible alternative to the program of patriarchal restoration that gender-based organizations such as Promise Keepers and the Nation of Islam are seeking to promote.[48] Although such groups espouse ideas of gender partnership, the key term in their gender discourse is 'family leadership,' which men must 'take back' and women must, with a sigh of relief, give over. In the final analysis, this model counterposes once again a father-headed family to one led by two equal partners. With the aim of developing men capable of seizing leadership, such movements are beginning to explicitly and aggressively address fatherhood by forging rituals of masculinity that draw on sport and war, as well as patriarchal religion, to animate the idea of religious manhood, reminding us of the men's religions of the late nineteenth century.

The remoteness or absence of fathers has long been an issue of contention in American politics, particularly with respect to the black community. Seen as especially 'fatherless,' the woman-led black 'non-family' has taken the blame for violence, crime, and drug addiction from the 1960s on. But in recent years the problem of absent fatherhood has been seized on as a key issue by and for a host of groups of many different political stripes, addressing difficulties in many different communities. David Blankenhorn, author of *Fatherless America*, calls absent fathers 'the most serious risk factor for children,' more than poverty, education, or any other socioeconomic indicator.[49] Blankenhorn calls for public policy changes to create a set of disincentives, especially for men, to divorce. Although he puts his case in the terms of a secular, social sciences discourse, his recommendations for jurisprudence and legislation resonate with ideas of the religious and right-wing men's movements.

The Promise Keepers is an evangelical Christian men's organization that combines proselytizing religious techniques with the language of athletics and combat. The group speaks to the need for masculine affirmation shared by hundreds of thousands of North American men in the 1990s.[50] Its founder, Bill McCartney, was a well-known evangelical opponent of equal rights for gays, and the head coach of the University of Colorado's football team who fused religion with his coaching style, and vice versa. By 1996, Promise Keepers was filling thirteen U.S. stadiums per year, and had an annual budget of $64 million.[51] The group emphasizes commitment and responsibility within a family that follows Dad's leadership. Similar themes have been used by Louis Farrakhan, head of the Nation of Islam, who organized a 1995 march on Washington by African-American men to 'atone' for their sins and to dedicate themselves to becoming good fathers and community members. Women were not welcome on the march, though some leading African-American women activists gave it their blessing. It is clear that Farrakhan and the Christian fundamentalists intend to build their base and their agenda on the mobilization of men's gender anxieties and issues of identity.

The messages of respect for women and commitment to children and community delivered in these men's religious organizations are important ones for men today, and clearly they are finding mass resonance. But the traditional patriarchal gender frameworks to which these messages are being attached – via the hypermasculinist metaphors of war and sport as part of the ritual invocation – will most likely organize men in a number of antisocial ways. In addition to being homophobic, these groups stress the reprivatization of parenting within the 'father-led' family and church community, the deconstruction of the family supports of the prosocial state, and the extension of supports to the traditional 'masculine' institutions of war and crime control – sport and the military. But this larger masculinist political orientation undermines the well-being of the very family to which the father is being urged to return. These phenomena, usually discussed in the language of class and religion, are profoundly gendered. They acutely reflect the need for changes in the way men relate to each other, across social divisions, and, crucially, across generations, within families, schools, communities, and within their own subcultures.

Finally, with respect to violence and what I have called the selective brutalization of males, human society has reached the stage at which a masculine gender identity built on violence and unthinking technological instrumentality is no longer compatible with species and environmental survival. Even if humans could survive the assault of industrial technology and the prosecution of wars like the one in the Persian Gulf, the environment cannot.[52] If we are to evolve as a species we will have to find ways to rethink masculinity as a central part of recasting our relationships to each other and our environment. To achieve such a recasting of masculinity, we will have to find ways to move our economies and our cultures away from war. While women have been complicit in supporting war cultures, men's special role in war gives them a tremendous responsibility, as a gender class, for removing its burden from human society. 'War truly has become a scourge,' writes military historian John Keegan, in concluding that humans must now find ways to eradicate war or face eradication themselves:

A world political economy which makes no room for war demands it must be recognized, a new culture of human relations. As most cultures of which we have knowledge were transfused by the warrior spirit, such a cultural transformation demands a break with the past for which there are no precedents. There is no precedent, however, for the menace with which future war now confronts the world.[53]

Women's inclusion in armed forces (armies and police forces) in recent decades has not changed the character of war or the masculinist nature of the forces that wage it. Indeed, though hard-fought, the right of women to participate in police and armed forces in many countries remains partial, grudging, and mined with hazards. The numerous sexual harassment cases in the U.S. military that have come to light in the 1990s drew attention to some of the profound problems women continue to encounter.[54] In Canada, photos of the brutal treatment of a woman officer-in-training by her peers, in the context of scandals over homoerotic and scatological initiation hazings at home, and the torture-murder of a Somali abroad, showed that the harsh, violent, masculinist warrior culture is still alive in the true North. Women's inclusion has not changed their generally subordinate position within military hierarchies, nor much of the sexist treatment of women by men. Most important, however, it has not changed the nature and purpose of the institutions themselves.

By the same token, despite women's attempts to reform sport and its culture, it is highly unlikely that their efforts, or their presence within sport, will effect the kind of changes that are needed to shift the core men's sports from coercive to cooperative cultures. We have yet to see qualitative transformations in men's sporting institutions, despite the extensive changes in family and kinship forms around them and the significant incursion of accomplished women into their structures and organizations. I believe this is because men as a gender have created a homosocial culture in which only their own judgment of each other really matters in issues of gender identity. If this is true, then however important women's claims may be as catalysts for men, ultimately only men in their changing interactions with each other can remake masculinity, its institutions, and its rites. If men do not collectively address the values of intermale ranking, competition, and violence that constitute idealized masculinity, and the selective brutalization of boys and men that inculcates these values, then the culture of sport will not change. Only men can fashion new ways to relate to each other that would be different from those of sport and war yet still be meaningful to them. Michael Messner and Donald Sabo have proposed an 'eleven-point strategy' for 'changing men through changing sports.' These points are: be a buddy to your body; stop excessive violence in athletics; recognize men's issues in sports; resist locker-room sexism; fight sexism in sport media; teach young athletes nonsexist values and practices; work for gender equity in athletics; confront homophobia and heterosexism in sport; become an advocate for minority-group athletes; get more women involved in sports; push the 'man question.'[55]

There is evidence that certain shifts in self-definition are taking place as 'men today must deal, on some level, with gender as a problematic construct, rather than as a natural, taken for granted reality,' Michael Messner writes. He suggests that 'men are changing, but not in any singular manner, and not necessarily in the directions that feminist women would like. Some of these changes support feminism, some express a backlash against feminism, and others (such as [Robert] Bly's retreat to an idealized tribal mythology of male homosociality) appear to be attempts to avoid feminist issues altogether.'[56] But insofar as these are changes of style and not major changes in behaviour at the structural level, they do not demonstrate a desire to cease 'being on top.' In that sense, these shifts can be seen as *renegotiations within masculinism* to fit late-twentieth-century needs, not the dissolution of masculinism.

At present, the most promising impulses for transformation may be found in organizations of men with a conscious profeminist stance, as Messner also suggests.[57] Groups geared to raise the consciousness of men about their own predicaments and losses in the current sex-gender order have appeared on a modest scale over the last twenty years. Pro-equality men have worked with women to effect changes in educational curricula that address important gender questions for boys and young men, as well as for girls and young women. In addition, mass-oriented campaigns against violence against women by men, such as the White Ribbon campaign, have been established to educate and engage men.[58]

These kinds of initiatives come none too soon, for there are also, as I just noted in speaking of Promise Keepers and the march sponsored by the Nation of Islam, very troubling signs among other – very broad – layers of men and their organizations. Explicitly anti-feminist groups have formed; and anti-abortion activists are prepared to use terrorist action to hurt women and the men who support them in making painful reproductive decisions. These armed attempts to defend the values of the previous gender order are atavistic responses to changing economic and social arrangements. Such attitudes seem to accompany, at the well-developed margins, the growth of a militant and fundamentalist right wing in the United States. Certainly they feed on the energy of men's gender anxiety and alienation, which is shared by men across many different boundaries of class, religion, race and ethnicity.

Can men, faced with the huge inequalities among them and the religious hypermasculinist ideology of mass media culture, find affirmation in a definition of masculinity that places cooperation and equality at its centre rather than domination and hierarchy? For the problems of male violence will only disappear if men face the issues of their own disparities – the fundamental breeding grounds for violence. In the autumn of 1997, the United Nations reported that gaps between developed and developing countries, as well as within the developing countries, were widening steadily; that the rich had gained everywhere and 'hollowing out' of the middle class had become a prominent feature of income distribution in many developing and developed countries; that the share of income accruing to capital had gained over that assigned to labour; that increased job and income insecurity was spreading; and that the growing gap between skilled and unskilled labour was becoming a global problem.[59] The U.S. census confirmed these trends for the United States as well. The inevitable conflicts such trends will provoke bode ill for the project of a peaceable masculinity, even as they illustrate its needs. The pessimism I feel as I regard this prospect is not because I believe that men are doomed to violence and war because of chromosomes or hormones. Rather it is caused by the hold that social mythologies of masculinity and domination have on human consciousness, their deployment by the corporate order via the mass media of communications, and the consequent obstacles they create to political imagination and political will toward equalization and environmental sustainability.

If men are to succeed in finding new heroic forms and myths of masculinity, then men's relationship to the tasks of generational reproduction, as well as to life in the public sphere, must change. Expecting these to change for the better in the context of a lengthening work week and scarcer dollars for the majority is wishful thinking. For this reason, facilitating better family and social fathering through social supports – including sport and its culture – is a necessary condition for diminishing the violent instrumentality that sustains the warrior as the dominant icon of heroic masculinity in our culture today.[60] And this in turn would be crucial in the larger process of social change that targets class, race, and other forms of inequality and social hierarchy. Changes in the gender conditioning of men are a precondition to lasting and meaningful changes toward equality in economics and politics.[61]

In assessing the relationship between organized athletics and other forms of organized violence, official and unofficial, we must also consider men's apparently persistent need for homosociality, that is, for forms of male-exclusive association. If such a need is natural and inevitable, should we seek ways to create masculine institutions that are not masculinist in their political thrust and effect? Or if men's proclivity to homosociality is socially constructed – that is, created fundamentally by the need to superimpose a secondary masculine identity on the primary feminine – does men's need for male-exclusive organizations need to be consciously and comprehensively deconstructed in its entirety throughout the institutions of society? The solution to this dilemma, I believe, is to find ways to support men and to permit their culture to evolve, diversify, and change according to their needs and through their existing organizations; men must be reference points for each other through change. Simultaneously, as a society, we must begin to work toward providing different answers to those needs by effecting other economic, social, cultural, and political reforms aimed at restructuring the gendered division of labour, bringing fathers and children closer together, deconstructing the military economy, and making the levers of social power as accessible to women as to men. To this end, however, as long as the male networks are strong, we must seek to create and give equal resources to female networks of association and to women's athletics. For men, sport serves the function of a men's club, a network of masculine associations that promote men's power. Ways must be sought to enable women to organize themselves homosocially and autonomously as well. As long as mixed culture is affected differentially by the genders due to the superior wealth, power, and organization of men's culture, masculinism will shape and dominate the body politic.

Active physicality and sport are not the same thing. Sport evolved as the dominant, indeed hegemonic, physical culture due to human choice and collective action. Games, physical activity, and ritual can evolve in other directions, provided we reinforce a public sphere that is distinct in meaningful ways from the market and that redirects public resources to different cultural forms. In addition, men must become increasingly active in transforming their own culture, which in turn affects the conditions under which they will parent and love, and in which their own children will have to make their way in the future. As men negotiate the demanding terrain of modern life, crises and changes are constantly provoking many to seriously question the ideals of masculinity they have incorporated into their own identities. Some have made connections between these often dysfunctional ideals and the culture of sport. But many others continue to deal with their gender anxieties by embracing, rather than questioning, the authoritarian and violent qualities associated with ideal manhood in that culture. They do so precisely because these are celebrated and legitimated. Such men are well represented in the ranks of organized sport and sport education. Men who think otherwise, though present and vocal, have been distinctly in the minority. To support them and the larger objective of bringing about a happier, healthier physical culture, I offer four basic principles that have many strategic and tactical applications.

1. *Diminish the selective brutalization of males inside and outside sport.* We need to bring an end to the physical and emotional brutalization of males that is crucial to maintaining the ideologies of hypermasculinity and coercive entitlement. Such brutalization, aimed at boys in the service of 'making men of them,' is often expressed in antisocial impulses and actions in adult social and political life. Reborn as political opinion, it supports war economies and violent cultures, as well as a masculinist gender order. This does not mean that physical culture should not include elements of risk or danger, rather, that such elements should be bound by and related to prosocial values and goals, and equalized between the genders.

2. *Change the 'sacrificial' nature of sport for both sexes.* Performance standards that involve harm to the physical, emotional, and mental well-being of athletes are sacrificial in nature and send at least three antisocial messages: first, that we value gladiator-like contests, whether of brutal intermale violence or the more refined self-administered violence of individual Olympic sports; second, that such violence, and hence other kinds of economic and social violence, is legitimated and rewarded; third, that self-harm in the service of conforming to physical and social standards is important for success in life. Sacrificial sport may be a good way to domesticate physicality for capitalism, but it is a bad way to encourage physical activity and social values.

3. *Shift the emphasis from aggressive and competitive to cooperative and expressive games and disciplines.* Values are instilled in young people through sport. If we instil a competitive and anti-empathetic ethic and sense of identification in young people through sport, we should not expect them to relate personally or politically in prosocial ways when they become adults. We need to develop a game culture of mutual benefit and personal realization through physical activity, not one of 'mutually exclusive goal attainment' or 'zero-sum' competition.

4. *Pursue lively physicality for the majority.* We need to shift resources and cultural initiatives away from masculinist sport culture toward the components of a prosocial physical culture that ensures that the majority of people, who today do not participate in physical activity, have access to

active physicality and to cultural performance. The governments of the United States and Canada have admirable goals and objectives for the fitness and health of their populations. But unless the resources are devoted to creating accessible services and facilities, and providing the social supports necessary to make access meaningful, all ideas of democratizing physical culture will remain just that – ideas without any hold in reality.

As we begin a new century, my hope is that more and more men with a partnership orientation to women in the world of sport will be encouraged by the support of parents, players, and audiences alike, and that the values and practices of the dominant sports and their culture will change accordingly. I hope these men will continue to build on the alliances they have made with their women counterparts to elaborate and enrich an emergent physical culture for both sexes and all ages. I hope that women will continue their difficult but steady march to reclaiming their bodies, with all their pleasures and strengths. I also hope that men and women will find ways to reject the ethic of competition and domination when it comes to their individual and family lives. I hope that dance and music will make a big comeback as family, community, and leisure activities. I hope that in reclaiming physical culture from corporate culture, we can balance 'masculine' with 'feminine' in our culture and within ourselves. And I hope that we can find ways to treat our bodies, our children, and our biosphere with respect and affirmation for our diverse and sensuous natures, and for the cooperative capacities that make us capable of helping, not just dominating, our fellow creatures.

Notes

Introduction

1 William Oscar Johnson, 'The fabulous games,' *Time* (April 29, 1996).
2 Norman Da Costa, reporting on a worldwide poll. *Toronto Star* (May 27, 1994).
3 William Nack, *Sports Illustrated*, 40th Anniversary Issue (September 19, 1994), 49–51.
4 *The World at Six*, CBC Radio News (July 8, 1997).
5 Writers such as Frank Deford, William Oscar Johnson, Rick Telander, John Underwood, Don Yaeger, and Steve Rushin are among the influential *Sports Illustrated* journalists in the United States. In Canada, Trent Frayne was always a pleasure to read. Michael Clarkson of the *Toronto Star*, Stephen Brunt of the *Globe and Mail*, Alison Gordon, former *Toronto Star* sports columnist, and Bruce Dowbiggin of CBC television always have something useful to say. The CBC Radio program *The Inside Track* has often offered intelligent coverage of sport.
6 Doug Sanders, 'And now, some words from their sponsors,' *Globe and Mail* (May 10, 1997).
7 Helen Lenskyj, *Women, Sport and Physical Activity: Research and Bibliography*, 3d ed. (Ottawa 1994). See also Ruth M. Sparhawk, Mary E. Leslie, Phyllis Y. Turbow, and Zina R. Rose, *American Women in Sport, 1887–1897: A 100-Year Chronology* (Metuchen, NJ, and London 1989).
8 See, for example, Cheryl Cole, 'Resisting the canon: Feminist cultural studies, sport and technologies of the body,' *Journal of Sport and Social Issues* 2 (August 1993), 77–105; Cheryl Cole and Susan Birrel, 'Double fault: Renee Richards and the construction and naturalization of difference,' *Sociology of Sport Journal* 7 (1990), 1–21; Melisse R. Lafrance, 'If you let me P.L.A.Y.,' paper presented to the University College Annual Conference, University of Torornto, February 1997; Alison Dewar, 'Incorporation or resistance? Towards an analysis of women's

responses to sexual oppression in sport,' *International Review for the Sociology of Sport* 26(1) (1991), 14–23; and M. Ann Hall, 'The discourse of gender and sport: From femininity to feminism,' *Sociology of Sport Journal* 5 (1988), 330–40.

9 With respect to men, masculinity, and sport, writers such as Robert Connell, Eric Dunning, John Hargreaves, Michael Kaufman, Bruce Kidd, Brian Pronger, Michael Kimmel, Michael Messner, and Donald Sabo have made many important contributions, some of which will be cited or discussed in subsequent chapters.

10 Brian Pronger, *The Arena of Masculinity: Sports, Homosexuality, and the Meaning of Sex* (Toronto 1990), 3.

11 Bruce Kidd, *The Struggle for Canadian Sport* (Toronto 1996); see also Bruce Kidd and John MacFarlane *The Death of Hockey* (Toronto 1972).

12 For a more extended explanation of my preferred terminology, including the way that power has moved from family fathers to larger aggregates and institutions with masculinist ideologies, see my 'Masculine dominance and the state,' in Ralph Milliband and John Saville, eds, *The Socialist Register* (London 1983), 45–89, 48–51.

13 Ibid.

14 Ralph Milliband, *Marxism and Politics* (Oxford 1977).

15 For this usage see *Concise Oxford English Dictionary*, 9th ed. (1995), 443.

Chapter 1. Societies, Bodies, and Ideologies: Terms and Approaches

1 William J. Baker, *Sports in the Western World* (Totawa 1982), vii–viii.

2 Michael Novack, *The Joy of Sport: Endzones, Bases, Baskets, Balls, and the Consecration of the American Spirit* (New York 1976).

3 For a discussion of the Mbuti tribe, see Gad Horowitz, *Repression: Basic and Surplus Repression in Psychoanalytic Theory: Freud, Reich, and Marcuse* (Toronto 1977), 118–19, 160–1.

4 Baker, *Sports in the Western World*, 68–71.

5 Ibid.

6 Allen Guttmann, *Games and Empires: Modern Sports and Cultural Imperialism* (New York 1994), 2–3; see also his earlier work *From Ritual to Record* (New York 1978). Eric Dunning has an even more differentiated template, in 'Industrialization and the incipient modernization of football,' *Stadion* 1(1) (1975), 110–11. See also J. Huizinga, *Homo Ludens, essai sur la fonction sociale du jeu* (Paris 1951); Novack, *The Joy of Sport*; Guttmann, *From Ritual to Record*; Jean-Marie Brohm, *Sport: A Prison of Measured Time* (London 1978); and Bruce Kidd, *The Political Economy of Sport*, Sociology of Sport Monograph Series, Canadian Association for Health, Physical Education and Recreation (Ottawa 1979).

7 Guttmann, *Games and Empires*, 2.

8 Novack, *The Joy of Sports*, 18–34.

9 Guttmann, *Games and Empires*, 2.

10 Sut Jhally, 'The spectacle of accumulation: Material and cultural factors in the evolution of the sports/media complex,' *The Insurgent Sociologist* 3(12) (1984), 41–57. For a more detailed assessment of the components of the contemporary sport nexus, see chapters 4, 5, 8, and 9 in this book. For discussions of the impact of broader media ownership structures and relations, see Ben Bagdikian, *The Media Monopoly*, 3d ed. (Boston 1983); Herbert I. Schiller, *Culture Inc.: The Corporate Takeover of Public Expression* (New York 1989); and Noam Chomsky, *Manufacturing Consent* (New York 1988) and *Media Control: The Spectacular Achievement of Propaganda*, Open Media Pamphlet Series (1997).

11 I am indebted to psychologist Adrienne Harris, and her excellent article on the tribal patriarchal elements of baseball. Adrienne Harris, 'Women, baseball, and words,' in Gary F. Waller, Kathleen McCormick, and Lois Fowlder, eds, *Lexington Introduction to Literature: Reading and Responding to Texts* (Lexington, MA, 1987).

12 John MacAloon, 'Olympic Games and the theory of spectacle in modern societies,' in John MacAloon, ed., *Rite, Drama, Festival, Spectacle* (Philadelphia 1984), 251.

13 Kirk Makin, 'The peanuts and beer on Canada's spectator sport,' *Globe and Mail* (May 21, 1994).

14 Ibid. See also Jim McKay, 'Sport and the social construction of gender,' in G. Lupton, T. Short, and P. Whip, *Society and Gender: An Introduction to Sociology* (Sydney 1992); on football hooliganism as a form of sacrificial violence within a sacred framework, see Michel Mafessoli, 'Hooligans,' *Quel Corps? Anthropophagie du sport*, no. 41 (April 1991), 66–9.

15 Isabel Vincent, 'Every four years "Copa" fever paralyzes a nation,' *Globe and Mail* (May 30, 1994). In historian Donald Mrozek's words sport has become 'the religious ritual of the machine age' in which he sees 'sacrifice without purpose, performance without magic, obsolescence without compensation, and values without meaning.' *Sport and American Mentality, 1880–1910* (Knoxville 1983), 11.

16 John Walters, 'School spirit,' Scorecard, *Sports Illustrated* (September 30, 1991).

17 Postmodern accounts of contemporary culture speak of a disintegration of the master narratives of modernism. In my view some of the master narratives they have identified are in various states of crisis and flux. But to speak of a disintegration of master gender narratives is to miss the historical and actual role that sport has played in modern and 'postmodern' definitions of masculinity.

18 Jean-Marie Brohm, *Sociologie politique du sport* (Nancy 1992). 126. For a contemporary paenization of the record and the significance of its hold, see Jack McCallum, 'The record company,' *Sports Illustrated* (January 8, 1990).

19 John MacAloon identifies spectacle, festival, ritual, and game as key in 'the roster of performance types found in an Olympic Games.' All these fit within the broader phenomenon of religion. J. MacAloon, 'Olympic games.'

20 This formulation may appear to turn the Marxist dialectic on its head – myth (culture) as the base for economy, rather than vice versa. In effect these are two moments of a perpetual process of interaction between physical existence and our ideas of it. It is however crucial to assert the effectivity, indeed agency of myth, and particularly as it is mobilized by specific economic interests. For the human need for paradigmatic stories and ideas is the basis of all the cultural industries, where myth becomes commodified. Chapter 4 addresses these points at length. For an interesting discussion of group and individual ritual by spectators and fans, see Susan Tyler Eastman and Karen E. Riggs, 'Televised sports and ritual: Fan experiences,' *Sociology of Sport Journal* 11 (1994), 249–74.

21 Erving Goffman, *Gender Advertisements* (New York 1979), 1.

22 Lucia Nixon, 'Rituals and power: The anthropology of homecoming at Queen's,' *Queen's Quarterly* 2 (Summer 1987), 312–13. This essay examines the anthropology of male rituals – centrally but not exclusively football – at an elite Canadian university. Nixon takes as significant and meaningful the fact that the terms of play and entitlement to participation are gender-determined. 'Bluntly put, Homecoming says that men define the world at Queen's, that they therefore have more power and prestige than women, that this is how things should be. It is a powerful ritual because it reinforces the asymmetrical female/male relationships described above for students, faculty and staff; Ibid., 326.

23 J. MacAloon, 'Olympic games,' 273.

24 Joseph Campbell, *The Hero with a Thousand Faces* (Princeton 1973), 4, 11.

25 McKay, 'Sport and the social construction of gender.' A similar approach to the 'veracity' of myths is taken by Sarah B. Pomeroy in her study of women in Greek and Roman civilizations. *Goddesses, Whores, Wives and Slaves: Women in Classical Antiquity* (New York 1975), 1.

26 McKay, 'Sport and the social construction of gender,' 247.

27 Jean-Marie Brohm's discussion of the physical and psychological conditioning of the athletic body into gestures and routines that support the social order is unparalleled. In *Sociologie politique du sport* and in his landmark *Sport: A Prison of Measured Time*, Brohm analyses how the repetitive and pain-related activities of sport act on the athlete's body and how these spectacles affect their audiences. He argues that the treatment of the human body as a machine should be considered constitutive of modern sport. *Sociologie politique du sport*, 80. I discuss some of these themes in chapters 5, 6, 7, and 8.

28 Gad Horowitz, *Repression*, 53–123 and 182–214.

29 Michael A. Messner, 'Sports and male domination: The female athlete as contested ideological terrain,' *Sociology of Sport Journal* 5 (1988), 206.

30 See Maria-Antonietta Macciocchi's treatment of fascist political mobilization of women's sexuality around patriarchal imagery and ideals in the 1920s and 1930s, and Jane Caplan's discussion of this topic. Maria-Antonietta Macciochi, ed.,

Éléments pour une analyse du fascisme, 2 vols, (Paris 1976) and 'Sexualité féminine dans l'idéologie fasciste,' *Tel Quel* 66 (Paris 1976). Jane Caplan, 'Introduction to female sexuality in fascist ideology,' *Feminist Review* 1 (1979), 56–68.

31 Michael Messner, 'Boyhood, organized sports, and the construction of masculinities,' *Journal of Contemporary Ethnography* 18(4) (January 1990), 416–44.

32 *Sunday Morning*, Centrepoint, CBC Radio transcript, (May 30, 1993) 1.

33 Ibid.

34 Ibid.

35 See discussion of fan anger in relation to the baseball strike in Tom Verducci, 'Anybody home?' *Sports Illustrated* (May 8, 1995), 20–3; Steve Wulf, 'An unwhole new ball game,' *Time*, (April 17, 1995), 48, and 'Hands of stone, hearts of gold,' *Time* (April 10, 1995), 94.

36 Brohm, *Sociologie politique du sport*, 26–8.

37 'Every culture has its own strategies of regeneration – beliefs, rituals and mechanisms for personal and social renewal ... The rationality and logic of regenerative behaviour depends essentially on the correspondence between a society's intent and the actual social result of the behaviour the society uses to attain it ... The constituent groups which favoured sport did so out of need. In different ways, each found in sport a strategy for regeneration and renewal.' Mrozek, *Sport and American Mentality*, 3–6.

38 Among the most influential early-twentieth-century anthropologists who argued what has come to be known as the social construction theory of gender and sexuality, was Margaret Mead. She argued that it was a society's gender template (its cultural patterns) that determined the dominant meanings of masculinity and femininity in any given society. 'Sometimes, one quality has been assigned to one sex, sometimes to the other ... Whether we deal with small matters, or with large, with the frivolities of ornament and cosmetics or the sanctities of man's place in the universe, we find this great variety of ways, even flatly contradictory, in which the roles of the two sexes have been patterned.' Margaret Mead, *Male and Female* (New York 1968), 38–9. In more recent years, Mead's empirical evidence, and hence her conclusions about the flexibility of human gender ascriptions, have been challenged, notably by Derek Freeman in *Margaret Mead and Samoa* (Cambridge, MA, 1983). See also Peggy Reeves Sanday, *Female Power and Male Dominance: On the Origins of Sexual Inequality* (Cambridge 1981), which argues for a variety of gender templates, and the primacy, if not exclusivity, of social, cultural, and ecological, rather than biological factors in the development of different gender templates.

39 In a paper presented to the International Olympic Academy in 1990, Dr Nikos Yalouris presented extensive evidence for women's athletics, and for the appearance of women within the primarily male spheres of philosophy, science, and the

arts in Ancient Greece. What his evidence shows is that, just as in other masculinist societies, the ideas of a prevailing gender order are not replicated in actual human life in any simple or monolothic sense. Nikos Yalouris, 'Women in Ancient Greece: Their contribution to letters, science, politics and sport,' *International Olympic Academy*, 30th International session (June–July, 1990).

40 Pomeroy, *Goddesses, Whores, Wives, and Slaves*, 79. 'While men spent most of their day in public areas such as the marketplace and the gymnasium, respectable women remained at home. In contrast to the admired public building, mostly frequented by men, the residential quarters of Classical Athens were dark, squalid and unsanitary.' Sparta was the exception to this general rule of female exclusion from athletics and politics.

41 For a good description and survey of the history of the ancient Olympic Games, see Baker, *Sports in the Western World*, 1–41.

42 I have adapted the term 'gender template' from anthropologist Peggy Reeves Sanday in *Female Power and Male Dominance*, 3. Her usage is based on the work of anthropologist Clifford Geertz.

43 Curry Jansen and Sabo, 'The sport/war metaphor,' 8.

44 Raymond Williams, *Problems in Materialism and Culture*, (London 1980), 38–42.

45 In Greenland, according to Allen Guttmann, the Innuit practice a 'culture of laughter' that seems to be even closer to the traditional pastimes. 'Typical of their "culture of laughter" is the drum-dance, a combination of sports, grotesque physical contortions, laughter, music, dance, poetry, shamanism, magic and collective ecstasy.' In the era of Danish colonization, this culture was threatened with extinction; it was revived by the Innuit Circumpolar Conference along with other indigenous folkways of Greenland, Alaska, Canada and Siberia. Guttmann, *Games and Empires*, 166–7.

46 See Barbara Ehrenreich, 'Whose gap is it, anyway?' *Time* (May 6, 1996), 43.

47 Mrozek, *Sport and American Mentality*, xx.

48 Foucault adds: 'This political investment of the body is bound up, in accordance with complex reciprocal relations, with its economic use; it is largely as a force of production that the body is invested with relations of power and domination; but, on the other hand, its constitution as labour power is possible only if it is caught up in a system of subjection (in which need is also a political instrument meticulously prepared, calculated and used); the body becomes a useful force only if it is both a productive body and a subjected body.' Michel Foucault, *Discipline and Punish: The Birth of the Prison* (New York 1979), 25–6.

49 For other discussions of similar themes, see Cheryl Cole, 'Resisting the canon: Feminist cultural studies, sport, and technologies of the body,' *Journal of Sport and Social Issues* 2 (August 1993), 77–97; John Hargreaves, 'The body, sport and power relations,' in *Sport, Power and Culture* (Cambridge 1986); R.W. Connell,

'Men's bodies,' in *Which Way Is Up? Essays on Sex, Class and Culture* (Sydney 1983).

50 Pronger, *The Arena of Masculinity: Sports, Homosexuality, and the Meaning of Sex* (Toronto 1990), 42.

51 Sigmund Freud, *Group Psychology and the Analysis of the Ego* (New York 1959); see also essays collected in Philip Rieff, ed., *General Psychological Theory: Papers on Metapsychology* (New York 1963).

52 For example, see Andrea Dworkin, *Pornography: Men Possessing Women* (New York 1979) and Catharine MacKinnon and Andrea Dworkin, 'Pornography and civil rights: A new day for women's equality,' in *Organizing against Pornography* (Minneapolis 1988).

53 This summary is from Michael Kimmel, 'Clarence, William, Iron Mike, Magic – and us,' *Changing Men* (Winter/Spring 1993), 9–10. This is Kimmel's adaptation of Brannon's typology.

54 For a fascinating discussion of the sociopolitical dimensions of the mystery genre, see Ernest Mandel, *Delightful Murder: A Social History of the Crime Story* (London 1984).

55 One former athlete suggested that men crave the pain of athletic activity because they crave the rush of endorphins that comes from breaking through the wall of pain; that they are encouraged into activities where this happens and they 'get hooked on the rush.' Pain is the precondition to pleasure in this sequence, because of the endorphin addiction it creates. Therefore, he reasoned, they will be more likely to seek or initiate it in (official) erotic life; and in other spheres of life as well. Keep in mind that endorphins can also be provoked by music, dance, yoga and making love, among other things.

56 Gad Horowitz, *Repression*, Chapter 4, 'The renunciation of bisexuality,' 81–123.

57 James Gilligan, *Violence: Our Deadly Epidemic and Its Causes* (New York 1996), 16–17, 232–3.

58 John Keegan, *A History of Warfare* (Toronto 1993), 75–6.

59 Burial sites, myths, and historical reports (e.g., Tacitus) of central European and Celtic tribes that existed coterminously with Roman civilization indicate that at least some women were warriors. There are accounts of African warrior women as well. Some archaeologists argue that there is evidence for military training – or at least rigorous physical training – for women in the Minoan civilization on Crete. The women of classical Sparta are known to have trained in athletic and martial arts. The 'Amazons' – the women warriors described by Herodotus in Asia Minor – are well known if still controversial. Iroquoian women controlled the wealth of their society, held their own councils, and had a say in the prosecution of war. Elizabeth Fisher, *Woman's Creation: Sexual Evolution and the Shaping of Society* (New York 1979), 368–72.

60 Camille Paglia, *Sexual Personae: Art and Decadence from Nefertiti to Emily Dickinson* (New York 1991), 8.
61 See, for example, E.O. Wilson, *Sociobiology* (Cambridge, MA 1980). See also J. Arthur Caplan, ed., *The Sociobiology Debate* (New York, 1978) and Robert Wright, *The Moral Animal – Why We Are the Way We Are: The New Science of Evolutionary Psychology* (New York 1994).
62 Robert Sapolsky, 'The graying of the troops,' *Discover* (March 1996), 46–52. See also Frans De Waal, *Bonobo: The Forgotten Ape* (Berkeley 1997).
63 Robert Evans, Morris Barer, and Theodore Marmor, *Why Are Some People Healthy and Others Not? The Determinants of the Health of the Population* (New York 1994), 19.
64 For a journalistic account of the apparent increasing violence among women, see Alanna Mitchell, 'Are women becoming as violent as men?' *Globe and Mail* (July 15, 1995).
65 'Nature creates by violence and destruction ... Lust and aggression are fused in male hormones ... The more testosterone, the more elevated the libido. The more dominant the male, the more frequent his contributions to the gene pool.' Paglia, *Sexual Personae*, 24, 26–7.
66 See Mary O'Brien, *The Politics of Reproduction* (Toronto 1981).
67 Alfie Kohn, *No Contest: The Case against Competition* (Boston 1996), 116.
68 The child does not know the reasons for this pressure to outdo his friends in this way. He just knows that, as Kohn notes, '"doing his best" is a code that means beating his peers.' Ibid., 28.
69 Kohn reports that in the mid-1970s, educational psychologist Carole Ames conducted studies to explore how children act under competitive conditions. She found that 'competition (and its associated feelings of pain and insufficiency) can cause people to believe that they are not the source of – or in control of – what happens to them.' Ibid., 107.
70 Ibid., 143.
71 Ibid., 115.
72 Ogilvie and Tutko, cited in Kohn, *No Contest*, 134. Also discussed are the views of sport psychologist Terry Orlik. As a result of his cross-cultural work with children, he concluded that competition is generally bad for psychological health; rather, 'experiences in human cooperation are the most essential ingredients for the development of psychological health.' Ibid., 108.
73 Gilligan, *Violence*, 231.
74 I made this argument at length in 'Economy, sexuality, politics: Engels and the sexual division of labour,' *Socialist Studies*, University of Manitoba Press (1983).
75 'Tomorrow's second sex,' *The Economist* (September 28, 1996).

Chapter 2. 'To Raise the Wolf in a Man's Heart': Sport and Men's Culture in the Nineteenth Century

1 Allen Guttmann's *Games and Empires: Modern Sports and Cultural Imperialism* (New York 1994) provides rich accounts of the growth of cricket, soccer, baseball, basketball, American football, and the Olympic games, including their nineteenth-century roots, as does William J. Baker's cross-epochal account of sport, *Sports in the Western World* (Totawa 1982). Bruce Kidd's *The Struggle for Canadian Sport* (Toronto 1996) provides a good account of how sport associations developed as enterprises of the influential classes and dominant gender in late-nineteenth-century Canada as well.

2 This view of the origins of modern sport is shared by a number of scholars. See Baker, *Sports in the Western World*, 115–88.

3 Ibid., 193.

4 Eric Dunning, 'Industrialization and the incipient modernization of football,' *Stadion* 1(1) (1975) 103–39, and 'Sociological reflections on sport, violence and civilization,' *Review for International Sociology of Sport* 25 (1990), 65–81.

5 Baker, *Sports in the Western World*, 57–114.

6 Ibid., 103–7.

7 Ibid., 165–6. See also Dunning, 'Industrialization and the incipient modernisation of football,' 111–14.

8 Kidd, *The Struggle for Canadian Sport*, 22–3.

9 'Beginning in 1842, a group of affluent merchants, professional men, and white-collar clerks began playing the New York game regularly on a vacant lot at 27th Street and Fourth Avenue in Manhattan ... They were an elite social clique as well as a sports club. Common labourers, poor immigrants, or black Americans need not have applied for membership. America's first organized baseball team, the Knickerbockers, prided themselves on being exclusively "gentlemen."' But the game turned out to be so popular that by the 1860s, it was being played by men of all social classes, in cities, towns, villages, and the countryside. Baker, *Sports in the Western World*, 139–41.

10 *Metropolitan Magazine* (June 27, 1883), cited in Stephen Gelber, 'Working at playing: The culture of the workplace and the rise of baseball,' *Journal of Social History*, 16 (Summer 1983), 8.

11 Stephen Gelber, 'Working at playing,' 9–10.

12 See, for example, Helen Lenskyj, *Out of Bounds: Women, Sport and Sexuality* (Toronto 1986).

13 Mark C. Carnes, *Secret Ritual and Manhood in Victorian America* (New Haven 1989), 107–10.

14 Ibid., 107–8.
15 'If sons were to be apprenticed, fathers advised and often dictated the choice of occupations and masters. Although boys imagined that apprenticeship would lead to a loosening of paternal authority, the domination of surrogate fathers often proved even more extreme.' Ibid., 108.
16 'For the emerging middle classes of the early nineteenth century, work no longer consisted in completing specific seasonal chores but instead entailed a continuous commitment to enterprise of an unbounded character. Perhaps even more important, in an age when most middle-class men were self-employed and business was subject to the vagaries of volatile financial markets and competitive pressures, the precariousness of their livelihood absorbed men's emotional energies in a way that further distanced them from the home.' Ibid., 110.
17 Anne McClintock, *Imperial Leather: Race, Gender, and Sexuality in the Colonial Contest* (New York 1995), 5–6.
18 Ibid., 34–6.
19 'Mothers could exert a more profound influence upon their children in part because they had far fewer of them: the average number of children born of a white woman of childbearing age declined from 7.04 to 3.56 during the nineteenth century.' Carnes, *Secret Ritual*, 112.
20 Ibid.
21 E. Anthony Rotundo, 'Body and soul: Changing ideals of American middle-class manhood, 1770–1920,' *Journal of Social History* 16 (1983), 30–2.
22 McClintock, *Imperial Leather*, 85.
23 See Sigmund Freud, *Civilization and Its Discontents* (New York 1989) and *The Ego and the Id* (New York 1962).
24 See Anthony Rotundo, 'Patriarchs and participants: A historical perspective on fatherhood in the United States,' in Michael Kaufman, ed., *Beyond Patriarchy: Essays by Men on Pleasure, Power, and Change* (Toronto 1987), 64–78. See also Carnes, *Secret Ritual*, esp. 113–15.
25 See Dorothy Dinnerstein, *The Mermaid and the Minotaur: Sexual Arrangements and Human Malaise* (London 1976); and Michael Kaufman, *Cracking the Armour: Power, Pain, and the Life of Man* (Toronto 1993).
26 As McClintock has noted, keeping servants was the criterion for membership in the middle class. *Imperial Leather*, 85.
27 In the last quarter of the nineteenth century, despite strenuous objections by women to the systemic discrimination against them, many male-dominated unions in Britain, the United States, and Canada jealously banded together to guard the more skilled working-class occupations from women. These unions were actively complicit with employers and governments in maintaining lower wages for women where the sexes worked at the same industrial jobs. In this way male employers,

politicians, and unions closed ranks *as men* against women. Varda Burstyn, 'Masculine dominance and the state,' in Ralph Milliband and John Savile, eds, *The Socialist Register* (1983), 45–89.

28 Judith Walkowitz, *Prostitution and Victorian Society: Women, Class, and the State* (Cambridge 1980); see especially Chapter 1, 'The common prostitute in Victorian Britain,' 13–31.

29 Friedrich Engels, 'The condition of the working class in England in 1844,' in Robert Tucker, ed., *The Marx–Engels Reader* (London 1978), 429–35.

30 For a discussion of men who supported the early feminists, see Michael S. Kimmel and Thomas E. Mosmiller, eds, *Against the Tide: Pro-Feminist Men in the United States, 1776–1990* (Boston 1992).

31 Baker, *Sports in the Western World*, 113.

32 Ibid.

33 Cited in Jean Harvey, 'Sport policy and the welfare state,' *Sociology of Sport Journal* 5 (1988), 320.

34 See Stephen Hardy and Alan G. Ingham, 'Games, structures and agency: Historians on the American play movement,' *Journal of Social History* (Winter, 1983), 285–301.

35 Guttmann, *Games and Empires*, 66.

36 See McClintock, *Imperial Leather*, esp. Chapter 3, 'Imperial leather,' 132–80.

37 William J. Baker, 'The making of a working-class football culture in Victorian England,' *Journal of Social History* 2 (1979), 245.

38 Bill Buford, *Among the Thugs* (London 1990), 24.

39 Lesley Hall, *Hidden Anxieties: Male Sexuality 1900–1950* (Cambridge 1991), 20.

40 Cited in Ann Crittenden Scott, 'Closing the muscle gap,' *Ms.* (September 1974), 63. Women athletes have proved with their performances that the female body is as athletically gifted and tough as the male's, in some identical and some different ways. In fact, the experience of women athletes has shown that bearing a child actually increases circulatory and cardiac strength, in direct contradiction to the paradigm employed by Dr Gilman. Scholars such as Ann Hall, Helen Lenskyj, Lucinda San Giovanni, and Mary Boutilier have traced the masculinist ideology – the clearly dominant ideology – that accompanied the growth of the vast networks of modern sport and demonstrated the way in which the values of the gender order were mobilized in these apparently objective fields for the purpose of maintaining gender exclusivity.

41 For a discussion of Charlotte Perkins Gilman and those U.S. feminists who believed in the importance of a vigorous physicality to the mental and physical health of women, see Patricia Vertinsky, 'Feminist Charlotte Perkins Gilman's "Pursuit of health and physical fitness" as a strategy for emancipation,' *Journal of Sport History* 16(1) (Spring 1989) 5–26.

42 See Carnes, *Secret Ritual*; Donald Mrozek, *Sport and American Mentality 1880–1910* (Knoxville 1983); and E. Anthony Rotundo, 'Body and soul.'

43 Carnes, *Secret Ritual*, 116.

44 Ibid., 114.

45 Ibid., 1.

46 Ibid., 115.

47 Ibid., 79.

48 Ibid., 106.

49 See McClintock, *Imperial Leather*, 232–57, on the development of the trope of the Family of Man as signifying the superiority and rule of white, middle-class Victorian men.

50 Mrozek, *Sport and American Mentality*, 233.

51 Canadian statistics from 'Health renewal and women's health,' Women's Health Bureau, Health Canada (1995).

52 John Keegan, *A History of Warfare* (Toronto 1993), 20–1.

53 Ibid., 21.

54 Ibid., 22.

55 Mrozek, *Sport and American Mentality*, 28–30.

56 Ibid., 30, 22, 61.

57 Ibid., 51–9.

58 Rotundo, 'Body and soul,' 26–7.

59 Baker, *Sports in the Western World*; Guttmann, *Games and Empires*.

60 David Riesman and Reuel Denney, 'Football in America: A study in cultural diffusion,' in Eric Dunning, ed., *The Sociology of Sport: A Selection of Readings* (London 1971), 154.

61 'One example of scores of similar games played with feet and a ball that flourished in the British Isles, Europe, and the Americas for hundreds of years before the Industrial Revolution is still traditionally played on New Year's Day in the Orkney town of Kirkwall. This game, which is known as kirkball, begins at dawn, when a rowdy torrent of men and boys dressed in working-men's clothes, pours through the city's streets and enters the town square. At first the crowd resembles the beginnings of a militant demonstration, or even a riot: gestures, shouts, pacing are all rough. But it quickly becomes apparent that somewhere in the centre of the mêlée the men are kicking a ball and playing a game. Heading through the town, the crowd makes for the surrounding countryside. It scrambles over meadows and woods, through streams and fields, comes back again through town, even through private houses and gardens, before the game draws to an end at sunset. The women, who have been looking on throughout the day, provide festive food and drink for the players, all the boys and men of the town fit enough to keep up the

punishing pace.' Background interview with Bruce Kidd for Varda Burstyn, 'Play, performance and power,' *Ideas*, CBC Radio (1986).

62 Eric Dunning, 'Industrialization and the incipient modernization of football,' 115.

63 Ibid. 114.

64 See James A. Managan, *Athleticism in the Victorian and Edwardian Public Schools: The Emergence and Consolidation of an Educational Ideology* (Cambridge 1981) and 'Social Darwinism, sport and English upper class education,' *Stadion* 7 (1982), 93–110.

65 Dunning, 'Industrialization and the incipient modernization of football,' 112–19.

66 Alan Tomlinson, in Burstyn, 'Play, performance and power,' transcript 2.

67 Mrozek, *Sport and American Mentality*, 30.

68 Riesman and Denney, 'Football in America'; see also Baker, *Sports in the Western World*, 119–22, and Dunning, 'Industrialization and the incipient modernization of football.'

69 Rogan Taylor, *Sunday Morning*, Centrepoint, CBC Radio (May 30, 1993), 2.

70 Riesman and Denney, 'Football in America.'

71 See Allen L. Sack, 'When Yale spirit vanquished Harvard indifference,' *Harvard Magazine* (November 1975), 27–8.

72 Ibid.

73 Ibid., 29–50.

74 Ibid., 50; see also Baker, *Sports in the Western World*, 129–33.

75 Sack, 'When Yale spirit vanquished Harvard indifference,' 29.

76 Baker, *Sports in the Western World*, 130.

77 David Meggyesy, in Burstyn, 'Play, performance and power,' 5.

78 Raymond G. Gettell, cited in Mrozek, *Sport and the American Mentality*, 66.

Chapter 3. 'Taming the Beast': Sport, Masculinity, and Sexuality in the Late Nineteenth and Early Twentieth Centuries

1 Allen Guttmann, *Games and Empires: Modern Sports and Cultural Imperialism* (New York 1994), 18.

2 Nicholas Fishwick, *English Football and Society, 1910–1950* (Manchester 1989), cited in ibid., 43.

3 Donald Mrozek, *Sport and American Mentality, 1880–1910* (Knoxville 1983), 27.

4 Of the spiritual-ideological wellsprings of mid- and late-nineteenth century American society, Mrozek writes 'The search for renewal came largely in reaction to the fear of exhaustion, and it became an open concern in society. The obvious activity of society as a whole suggested the need for some means of replenishing the reserves ... Seeing power in material and even physical terms, Americans

readily opted for material and physical remedies for deficiencies observed, imagined or predicted.' Ibid., 19–20.

5 Steven Marcus, *The Other Victorians: A Study of Sexuality and Pornography in Mid-Nineteenth-Century England* (New York 1985). See also Anne McClintock, *Imperial Leather* (New York/London 1995), esp. 1–17.

6 Mrozek, *Sport and American Mentality*, 20–6; 148.

7 Ibid., 20.

8 Michel Foucault, *The History of Sexuality* (New York 1980), 105.

9 Kevin White, *The First Sexual Revolution* (New York 1993), 11.

10 It was the job first of medical doctors and psychologists, then of politicians and the law, to provide the correct guidance on sexual matters as an alternative to the 'nefarious,' 'deviant,' and 'sinful' ideas of the 'unofficial' discourse. In 1857, the *Lancet* reviewed a work of Lord Acton – one of the most influential writers on sex during the last half of the nineteenth century. In approving his professional discussion of sexual subjects it noted that 'the only way by which some of the most important functional ailments affecting humanity can be rescued from the grasp of the most disgusting and villainous quackery, and treated with benefit to the patient, is by the scientific and conscientious practitioner openly taking them under his own charge.' Hall, *Hidden Anxieties*, 55.

11 Mrozek, *Sport and the American Mentality*, esp. 147–8, 227, 240, 243, 255.

12 Hall, *Hidden Anxieties*, 17.

13 Acton was singled out by the later sexologist Havelock Ellis as the epitome of what was both typical of and wrong with Victorian attitudes to sex. Ibid., 16, 3.

14 Havelock Ellis, *Studies in the Psychology of Sex*, vol. 3: *Analysis of the Sexual Impulse; Love and Pain; The Sexual Impulse in Women*, cited in Hall, *Hidden Anxieties*, 3.

15 Ibid., 16. See also Marie Stopes and Ruth Hall, eds, *Dear Dr Stopes* (Markham, ON, 1981); Wally Seccombe, *Weathering the Storm: Working Class Families from the Industrial Revolution to the Fertility Decline* (London and New York 1993), Chapter 5, 'Starting to stop: The proletarian fertility decline,' 157–93; Jeffrey Weeks and Sheila Rowbotham, *Socialism and the New Life: The Personal and Sexual Politics of Edward Carpenter and Havelock Ellis* (London 1977).

16 Ibid., 57.

17 Mark C. Carnes, *Secret Ritual and Manhoood in Victorian America* (New Haven 1989); Karen Dubinsky, *Improper Advances: Rape and Heterosexual Conflict in Ontario, 1880–1929* (Chicago 1993); Hall, *Hidden Anxieties*; Mrozek, *Sport and American Mentality*; Anthony Rotundo, *American Manhood: Transformations in Masculinity from the Revolution to the Modern Era* (New York 1993); Wally Seccombe, *A Millennium of Family Change* (London 1992); Kevin White, *The*

First Sexual Revolution: The Emergence of Male Heterosexuality in Modern America (New York 1993).

18 The evidence of castration anxiety in men who had been raised in late-nineteenth and early-twentieth-century European and Anglo-American societies was so profound that Freud read it as constitutive of culture itself, as demonstrated by his theorization of its critical role in the Oedipus complex. Sigmund Freud, *Civilization and Its Discontents*, James Strachey trans. (New York 1962); *Ego and the Id*, (New York 1960), 47–51; *Group Psychology*, (New York 1959), 39–40; *Moses and Monotheism* (New York 1967), 99, 107, 116, 127, 156. In his most radical theoretical move, Freud denaturalized and problematized, rather than accepting as pregiven, men's normative heterosexuality. Freud demonstrated in ways that were ultimately subversive to his own personal value system (patriarchal) how the socialization that attends 'anatomy' creates 'destiny,' though with more success for men than for women.

19 'Such assaults and abuse were not unique to the male child. Sons of the privileged classes, however, sent away to school at a very early age, faced perils to which their sisters were not exposed. Much of the rhetoric of the sex-education movement was predicated on the assumption that public and boarding schools could be hotbeds of vice.' Hall, *Hidden Anxieties*, 42.

20 The term 'intermale pecking order' is from Mike Messner, 'When bodies are weapons,' in Michael A. Messner and Donald F. Sabo, eds, *Sex, Violence, and Power in Sports* (Freedom, CA, 1994), 89–98.

21 Within this perspective, Freud's views – and those of his important colleagues and students – are still of vital interest. Far from losing its relevance, the idea of castration anxiety has been retained by a number of modern psychoanalytic thinkers. See Joel Kovel, 'The castration complex reconsidered,' in J. Strouse, ed., *Women and Analysis* (New York 1974); Gad Horowitz, *Repression: Basic and Surplus Repression in Freud, Reich and Marcuse* (Toronto 1978); Gad Horowitz and Michael Kaufman, 'Male sexuality: Toward a theory of liberation,' in Michael Kaufman, ed., *Beyond Patriarchy: Essays by Men on Pleasure, Power and Change* (Toronto 1987), 81–102.

22 See discussions of fear of men in Michael Kaufman, ed., *Beyond Patriarchy*; and Paul Kivel, 'The fear of men,' *Changing Men* 17 (Winter 1986).

23 McClintock, *Imperial Leather*, 23–4.

24 For example, see Joseph Conrad, *Heart of Darkness* (New York 1969).

25 McClintock, *Imperial Leather*, 22.

26 Ibid., 31.

27 'Sir Thomas Herbert observed of Africans "the resemblance they bear with Baboons, which I could observe kept frequent company with the Women." Long

saw a lesson closer to home in the African spectacle of female sexual excess, for
he identified British working-class women as inhabiting more naturally than men
the dangerous borders of racial and sexual transgression: "The lower class of
women in England," he wrote ominously, "are remarkably fond of the blacks."
The traveler William Smith likewise warned his readers of the perils of traveling as
a white man in Africa, for, on that disorderly continent, women, "if they meet a
Man they immediately strip his lower Parts and throw themselves upon him."'
Ibid., 22–3.

28 Ibid., 86–7.

29 Hall, *Hidden Anxieties*, 46–7.

30 See Judith Walkowitz, *Prostitution and Victorian Society: Women, Class and the
State* (Cambridge 1980), 248–52. See also Hall on prostitution, *Hidden Anxieties*,
46–54.

31 Thus in the 1890s in England, after thirty years of social struggle around prostitution, 'The prostitute conducting her trade with discretion was far more likely to be
arrested than a man blatantly making himself offensive to female passers-by.
Scarcely more than a hundred or so men were charged with accosting women to
their annoyance in the course of two or three years, but "6000 unfortunate women
were arrested every year for alleged annoyance of men."' Hall, *Hidden Anxieties*, 47.

32 For discussion of the politics of the prostitution campaigns, see Walkowitz,
Prostitution and Victorian Society; Carol Lee Bacchi, *Liberation Deferred? The
Ideas of the English-Canadian Suffragists, 1877–1918* (Toronto 1983); Barbara
Epstein 'Family, sexual morality, and popular movements,' in Ann Snitow,
Christine Stansell, and Sharon Thompson, eds, *Powers of Desire: The Politics of
Sexuality*, (New York 1983); and Varda Burstyn, 'Political precedents and moral
crusades,' in V. Burstyn, ed., *Women against Censorship* (Toronto 1985).

33 Patrick Geddes and J. Arthur Thomson, *The Evolution of Sex*, 2d ed., (1901), cited
in Hall, *Hidden Anxieties*, 20.

34 'In keeping with the discourse on degeneration, the more menial, paid work a
woman did, the more she was manly and unsexed; the more she was a race apart.'
McClintock, *Imperial Leather*, 103.

35 Mrozek, *Sport and American Mentality*, 148–9.

36 Paul Hoch, *White Hero Black Beast: Racism, Sexism and the Mask of Masculinity*
(London 1979), 44.

37 White, *The First Sexual Revolution* (1993), 8.

38 Paul Hoch, *White Hero Black Beast*; Anne McClintock, *Imperial Leather*.

39 'There was a certain class dimension to this question of control over male desire.
Mastery over baser lusts was seen as appropriate and desirable behaviour (a form
of internalized moral policing) for the middle classes or would-be respectable, but
hardly to be expected of the lowest classes.' Hall, *Hidden Anxieties*, 3–4.

40 See Hoch, *White Hero Black Beast*, chaps 2 and 3.

41 In addressing directly the homoeroticism of sport, let me make the following points on terminology. *Homosociality* is the term I use to refer to the desire and custom of men to be in male company exclusively. *Homoeroticism* I use to denote the physical desire of men for other men. In this sense, many of the men's cultural genres are very homoerotic – the celebration of limbs, muscles, bodies, and their interactions. However, I do not use the term homoerotic as a synonym for homosexual. Rather *homosexual* is meant to denote a conscious awareness of a clear genital/affectional orientation toward persons of the same sex. As Pronger does, I use the term *gay* to denote a conscious and positive attitude toward homosexuality. And I use the term *homophobia* to denote a visceral fear, often accompanied by hatred, of homosexuality and gayness, though not necessarily of homosociality and homoeroticism.

42 Kevin White addresses how ideas of black masculinity spread in the United States in the early twentieth century. Black men were described in unusually physical and erotic terms in the literature of the day, and 'stereotypical descriptions of black male attitudes toward women predominated. Violence toward women was the norm. This ... indicated one direction in which the glorification of perceived working-class models of manliness were headed by the late 1920s: towards an imagined more virile, spontaneous, sexual yet violent model that derived from perceptions of black manliness.' White, *The First Sexual Revolution*, 50.

43 Baker, *Sports in the Western World*, 205.

44 Ibid., 205.

45 White, *The First Sexual Revolution*.

46 Also see my discussion of hypermasculinity and homoeroticism in chapters 6 and 7.

47 E. Anthony Rotundo, 'Body and soul: Changing ideals of American middle-class manhood, 1770–1920,' *Journal of Social History* 16 (1986), 27.

48 Ibid., 27.

49 Cited in Mrozek, *Sport and American Mentality*, 25–6.

50 Ibid., 24.

51 Ibid., 229.

52 Ibid., 23.

53 Ibid., 22–4, and passim.

54 White, *The First Sexual Revolution*, 7–12.

55 Ibid., 7.

56 Valerie Steele, *Fashion and Eroticism: Ideals of Feminine Beauty from the Victorian Era to the Jazz Age* (New York 1985), 52–3.

57 Ibid., 53.

58 Ibid., 57.

59 Ibid., 92.

60 White, *The First Sexual Revolution*, 16. See also Stuart and Elizabeth Ewen, *Channels of Desire: Mass Images and the Shaping of American Consciousness*, 2d ed. (Minneapolis 1992).

61 Cited in Steele, *Fashion and Eroticism*, 119.

62 These terms are mine. For an excellent sociopolitical reading of fashion and gender, see also Stuart and Elizabeth Ewen, *Channels of Desire*.

63 Thomas Waugh, *Hard to Imagine: Gay Male Eroticism in Photography and Film from Their Beginnings to Stonewall* (New York 1996), 183–4, describes the extent to which the athletic spectacle was consumed by male-exclusive publics.

64 Ibid., 177–91.

65 Ibid., 182–4.

66 White, *The First Sexual Revolution*, 8.

67 For a discussion of the relation between imperialism, sexuality, gender, and cleanliness see McClintock, *Imperial Leather*, chap. 3.

68 Mrozek, *Sport and American Mentality*, 42.

69 Waugh, *Hard to Imagine*, 178.

70 Ibid., esp. 177–91, where Waugh discusses the role of athletic images in forging gay male eroticism.

71 Mrozek, *Sport and American Mentality*, 41–2.

72 Early in the twentieth century, according to Lesley Hall, 'an enquiry into *The Army and Religion* ... mentioned the "constant flow of filthy language, the drunkenness, and, more specially, the immorality" ... The extreme and habitual crudity of male speech in the forces was such that works such as T.E Lawrence's *The Mint* and Frederic Manning's *Her Privates We*, which aimed at a realistic depiction of forces life during and just after the First World War, were not published until well after the Second World War, having previously been regarded as unacceptable.' *Hidden Anxieties*, 43.

73 Waugh, *Hard to Imagine*.

74 Xavier Mayne, *The Intersexes* (Private printing 1908), cited in Waugh, *Hard to Imagine*, 187–8.

75 One important theory of homosexuality to gain credibility during this period was the 'third-sex' theory. Developed by German sexologist Magnus Hirschfield, the 'third-sex' theory defined homosexuals as *Zwischenstufen*, or sexual intermediates.' His model of homosexuality as biological destiny presented the idea of three types of gendered bodies: male, female and 'unity' (androgynous or hermaphroditic). Waugh, *Hard to Imagine*, 378–81. In general, many theories addressed the apparent gender-bending that went with same-sex sexual engagement.

76 Foucault, *The History of Sexuality*, vol. 1: *An Introduction*, trans. Robert Hurley (New York 1980), 43.

77 Pronger, *Arena of Masculinity*, 138–9.

78 In an essay on gay culture in Nicaragua, Barry Adams indicates that men who have sex with other men define themselves alternatively as 'activos' or 'pasivos,' and that only the 'pasivos' are considered and consider themselves to be homosexual. Barry Adams, 'Pasivos y activos: Homosexuality without a gay world,' *Outlook* (Winter 1989), 74–82.

79 Allen Dundes, 'Into the endzone for a touchdown: A psychoanalytic consideration of American football,' *Western Folklore* 37 (1978), 87.

80 'A phobia is one means by which the ego tries to cope with anxiety,' writes Michael Kaufman in *Beyond Patriarchy*. 'Homophobia is a means of trying to cope, not simply with our unsuccessfully repressed, eroticized attraction to other men, but with our whole anxiety over the unsuccessfully repressed passive sexual aims, whether directed toward males or females ... A key expression of homophobia is the obsessive denial of homosexual attraction; this denial is expressed as violence against other men.' Kaufman, *Beyond Patriarchy*, 21. For a brilliant psychoanalytic explication of the repression of femininity in males under compulsory heterosexuality, see Gad Horowitz, *Repression: Basic and Surplus Repression in Psychoanalytic Theory: Freud, Reich, and Marcuse* (Toronto 1977). See also Michael Kaufman, *Cracking the Armour: Power, Pain and the Lives of Men* (Toronto 1993).

81 Pronger, *Arena of Masculinity*, 138.

82 White, *The First Sexual Revolution*, 65.

83 Walter L. Williams, in review of 'Ritualized homosexuality in Melanesia,' by Gilbert H. Herdt, in *Changing Men* 15 (Fall 1985), 37.

84 Kaufman, *Beyond Patriarchy*, 21.

85 McClintock notes that 'it is no accident that the historical subculture of S/M emerged in Europe toward the end of the eighteenth century with the emergence of imperialism in its modern industrial form.' McClintock, *Imperial Leather*, 142–3.

86 White, *The First Sexual Revolution*, 11.

87 Rotundo, 'Body and soul,' 26.

88 Dundes suggests that men may be biologically programmed to enact ranking through actions of sexual domination and submission, a legacy from the primate past. He further suggests that war is a form of homosexual engagement, like sport, driven by men's desire (need?) to assert sexual dominance over one another. Alan Dundes, 'The American game of "smear the queer" and the homosexual component of male competitive sport and warfare,' *Passing Through Illusions: Essays by a Freudian Folklorist* (Madison 1987), 192.

Chapter 4. Delivering the Male: Sport Culture, the Mass Media, and the Masculinity Market

1 Football: Jim Brown, Pete Rozzell, Joe Namath, Joe Montana, Bear Bryant, and Pele (soccer); baseball: Pete Rose, Hank Aaron, Roberto Clemente, Nolan Ryan;

basketball: Michael Jordan, Larry Bird, Magic Johnson, John Wooden, Bill Russell; hockey: Wayne Gretzky, Bobby Orr; boxing: Muhammad Ali, Sugar Ray Leonard, Don King; track and field: Carl Lewis, Jim Fixx; golf: Arnold Palmer, Jack Nicklaus; tennis: Arthur Ashe; auto racing: Richard Petty; cycling: Greg LeMond. Gary Smith 'Forty for the ages,' *Sports Illustrated* (September 19, 1994). All the other 'most influential people' within the world of sport included in the survey were also men: Roone Arledge (ABC Sports), Marvin Miller (Major League Baseball Players Association), Mark McCormack (sports agent), Harold Gores (inventor, astro-turf), Dr Robert Jackson (pioneer, sports medicine), Bill Rassmussen, founder of ESPN.

2 For a detailed analysis of the gender culture and sexual dimensions of this widespread youth culture, and the role of advertising and consumerism within it, see Kevin White, *The First Sexual Revolution: The Emergence of Male Hetero-sexuality in Modern America* (New York 1993). These subjects are discussed throughout the whole work, but see especially chaps 2 and 3.

3 Sut Jhally, 'The spectacle of accumulation: Material and cultural factors in the evolution of the sports/media complex,' *The Insurgent Sociologist* 3(12) (1984), 43.

4 Ibid.

5 John Rickards Betts, *America's Sporting Heritage, 1850–1910*, (Don Mills, ON, 1974), cited in Jhally, 'The spectacle of accumulation,' 44.

6 See Steven Riess, *City Games: The Evolution of American Urban Society and the Rise of Sports* (Urbana 1991), 194–200, and Bruce Kidd, *The Struggle for Canadian Sport* (Toronto 1996), 12–37.

7 Ibid. See my discussion of current government/stadium issues in Chapter 9.

8 William J. Baker, *Sports in the Western World* (Totawa 1982), 189–228. Baker emphasizes how much sport was affected by and implicated in major civic, national, and international political events of the time.

9 Alan Tomlinson, 'Good times, bad times and the politics of leisure: Working class culture in the 1930s in a small northern English working class community,' in Hart Cantelon, Robert Hollands, Alan Metcalfe, and Alan Tomlinson, *Leisure, Sport, and Working Class Cultures* (Toronto 1988).

10 'During the autumn of 1905, no less than eighteen fatalities resulted from intercollegiate [football] games [in the United States] ... Some leading universities ... called a momentary halt to football ... [until 1906, when new rules] overhauled the tactics of the game and [reduced its lethality ... Still] in 1909 six tackles died of injuries.' Baker, *Sports in the Western World*, 201–2.

11 Ibid., 215.

12 One significant exception to this rule were the Green Bay Packers of the National Football League, who for financial reasons sold shares to the people of the town in

the 1930s, and have been publicly owned ever since. The most important twentieth-century coach in American football, Vince ('winning isn't everything, it's the
only thing') Lombardi made his reputation in Green Bay. In a pre-Superbowl
profile of the team in January 1997, its manager and coach and a number of its
leading athletes discussed the superiority of working for a public corporation rather
than for individual, private owners. TSN, Superbowl coverage, Jan. 24, 1997.

13 Baker, *Sports in the Western World*, 217.
14 Ibid., 220.
15 Jeremy Rifkin, *The End of Work: The Decline of the Global Labor Force and the
    Dawn of the Post-Market Era* (New York 1995), 19.
16 For an analysis of the impact of advertising culture on styles of masculinity in the
    United States between 1900 and 1930, see White, *The First Sexual Revolution*,
    1–5, 180–9.
17 Rifkin, *The End of Work* 19–20.
18 Ibid., 20.
19 Ibid., 21.
20 White, *The First Sexual Revolution*, 27.
21 Baker, *Sports in the Western World*, 237.
22 Ibid., 235.
23 As early as 1881, Chris Van Der Ahe of St Louis, a beer baron and baseball fan,
    had purchased a piece of the St Louis Brown Stockings. In 1915, Jacob Ruppert of
    New York's Ruppert Brewery purchased the New York Yankees, and August A.
    Busch Jr., of what was to become Annheuser Busch, continued the trend by pur-
    chasing the St Louis Cardinals, The Brown Stockings' descendants, as late as
    1953. William Oscar Johnson, 'Sport and suds,' *Sports Illustrated*, (August 8,
    1988).
24 Kidd, *The Struggle for Canadian Sport*, 18.
25 Jhally, 'The spectacle of accumulation,' 44.
26 Cited in ibid., 45.
27 For example, in the 1960s CBS bought the New York Yankees, Molson's Brewer-
    ies bought the Montreal Canadiens, and Annheuser Busch bought the St Louis
    Cardinals. In the 1970s, Labatt's Breweries bought both The Sports Network
    (TSN) and the Toronto Blue Jays.
28 Jhally, 'The spectacle of accumulation,' 49–50. For a discussion of the bill, see Ira
    Horowitz, 'Sports telecasts: Rights and regulation,' *Journal of Communications*
    27(3) (1977).
29 See William Taafe, 'TV to sports: The bucks stop here,' *Sports Illustrated*
    (February 24, 1986), and Vance Packard, *The Hidden Persuaders* (New York
    1957). For an excellent discussion of advertising and television see Joyce Nelson,
    The Perfect Machine: TV in the Nuclear Age (Toronto 1987).

30 Barbara Ehrenreich, *The Hearts of Men: American Dreams and the Flight from Commitment* (Garden City/New York 1983), 119–21.

31 Susan Faludi, 'Statistically challenged,' *The Nation* 262(15) (April 15, 1996).

32 Cited in Jhally, 'The spectacle of accumulation,' 48–9.

33 William Oscar Johnson and John Walter, 'Every day is game day,' *Sports Illustrated* (December 2, 1992). ESPN, a U.S. all-sports cable network, began broadcasting in 1979. By 1994, it had become a billion-dollar company that reached 60 million viewers.

34 For a case study of the power of a star to sell a sport, see Stehen Brunt's assessment of Wayne Gretzky's impact on hockey in Los Angeles, 'The Gretzky effect,' *Report on Business Magazine* (April 1990).

35 'Jordan again tops Forbes list with record $78 million,' ESPN SportsZone (November 30, 1997).

36 Naomi Klein, 'What's up, doc? Just ask the marketers,' *Toronto Star* (November 18, 1996).

37 Taafe, 'TV to Sports.'

38 Dan Turner, 'Super Bowl advertisers spending huge sums to reach far fewer viewers,' *Los Angeles Business Journal* (January 20, 1997).

39 Jeff Jensen, 'After Olympics, Coke heads for "Red Zone," ' *Advertising Age* (July 15, 1996).

40 Cited in James U. McNeal, 'From savers to spenders: How children became a consumer market,' *Media and Values* 52–53 (Fall/Winter 1991), 5. *Sports Illustrated* even supplies rental heroes for a price. 'Nothing brightens up an audience like a star from the world of sport,' runs the text for an ad for the *SI* Speakers Bureau. 'And the *Sports Illustrated* Speakers Bureau has 2000 of them ready to sparkle at sales meetings, award dinners, conventions, store openings or wherever else the color and excitement of sports can help you shine.' *Sports Illustrated* (July 15, 1985).

41 Steve Rushin, 'How we got here,' *Sports Illustrated* (August 16, 1994).

42 For some idea of the reach and extent of the sport nexus in 1992, see the survey by Stephen Hugh-Jones, 'The sports business: Faster, higher, richer,' *The Economist* (July 25, 1992).

43 Tom Fennell, Ann Walmsley, D'Arcy Jenish, et al., 'The riches of sport' *Maclean's* (April 9, 1990).

44 *National News*, CBC television, November 7, 1995.

45 Hugh-Jones, 'The sports business.'

46 White, *The First Sexual Revolution*, 16–56.

47 See Allan Bérubé, 'Marching to a different drummer: Lesbian and gay GIs in World War II,' and John D'Emilio, 'Capitalism and gay identity,' in Ann Snitow,

Christine Stansell, and Sharon Thompson, eds, *Powers of Desire: The Politics of Sexuality* (New York 1983), 88–99, 106–7; and Allan Bérubé, *Coming Out under Fire: The History of Gay Men and Women in World War II* (New York 1990).

48 Geoffrey S. Smith, 'Commentary: Symposium on culture, gender and foreign policy,' *Diplomatic History* 18(1) (Winter 1994), 85–6; see also Rosenberg, '"Foreign affairs" after World War II,' 59–70, and Allan Bérubé, 'Marching to a different drummer,' 88–99.

49 Smith, 'Commentary,' 86.

50 See Marty Jezer, *The Dark Ages: Life in the United States, 1945–1960* (Boston 1982), esp. chaps 12–14. Jezer dubs the 1950s 'the horny fifties,' and reminds us of just how large and substantial were the parts of American society (people of colour, women, workers, writers and artists, for example) experiencing multiple tensions with mainstream corporate cultural expectations of them, as well as how powerfully those expectations were diffused through the mass media, especially television.

51 Emily S. Rosenberg's '"Foreign affairs" after World War II,' deconstructs films that linked themes of threatened domesticity at home and America's missions abroad. *Diplomatic History* 18(1) (Winter 1994), 59–70. A similar connection between domesticity at home and imperial interests abroad in the nineteenth century was noted by McClintock in *Imperial Leather*.

52 Geoffrey S. Smith, 'National security and personal isolation: Sex, gender and disease in the cold-war United States,' *The International History Review* 14(2) (May 1992), 332, and 'Commentary: Symposium on culture, gender and foreign policy,' 85–90.

53 For a discussion of gender and politics in film and film noir, see E. Ann Kaplan, *Women and Film: Both Sides of the Camera* (New York 1983), 60–72; see also E. Ann Kaplan, 'Introduction,' Christine Gledhill, '*Klute*: A contemporary film noir and feminist criticism,' Sylvia Harvey, 'Woman's place: The absent family in film noir,' and Janey Place, 'Women in film noir,' in E. Ann Kaplan, *Women and Film Noir* (London 1978). On gender and issues of national security, see Geoffrey Smith, 'National security and personal isolation,' 331–2.

54 Smith, 'Commentary,' 85.

55 Ibid., 85–6.

56 On the evils of wives and families in the *Playboy* world-view, see Ehrenreich, *The Hearts of Men*, 42–51.

57 On the emergence of liberal masculinism around themes of sexuality, see my 'Political precedents and moral crusades,' in V. Burstyn, ed., *Women against Censorship* (Toronto 1985); see also V. Burstyn, 'Masculine dominance and the

state,' in Ralph Milliband and John Saville, eds, *The Socialist Register* (London 1983), 45–89.

58 For insightful discussions of how these processes unfolded, the place of homosexual identity and culture within them, and the impact of homosexual identity and subcultures on straight and mainstream commercial culture, see Dennis Altman, *The Homosexualization of America, the Americanization of the Homosexual* (New York 1982), esp. chap. 3, 'Sex and the triumph of consumer capitalism,' 79–107. On the interaction of gender, sex, and commerce in mainstream film in the 1970s, see my 'The seductive illusion: Women, sex and class in the Hollywood Cinema, I and II,' *Canadian Woman Studies* 3(2) (1981), 22–8. For a broad analysis of the postwar disintegration of the traditional family under the impact of consumer capitalism, see Eric Hobsbawm, *Age of Extremes* (London 1995), 320–43

59 See Ethel Spector Person, 'Sexuality as the mainstay of sexual identity: Psychoanalytic perspectives,' in Catharine R. Stimpson and Ethel Spector Person, eds, *Women: Sex and Sexuality* (Chicago 1980).

60 Hendrick M. Ruitenbeek, in Hendrick M. Ruitenbeek, ed., *Sexuality and Identity* (New York 1970), 6–7.

61 Chip Kidd, *Batman Collected* (New York 1996).

62 Michael Messner, 'The changing meaning of male identity in the lifecourse of the athlete,' *Arena Review* 9(2), 33.

63 Joan Mellen, *Big Bad Wolves: Masculinity in the American Film* (New York 1977), 249–50.

64 'The interest in soccer of working-class men would determine that Friday evening would be spent in the pub discussing the likely outcome of the following day's game, Saturday lunchtime would be spent watching preview programs on BBC ... or commercial television prior to going to the game itself ... Saturday evening would be spent in post-mortems, usually again in the local pub ... And there might even then be on the Sunday a viewing ... of a weekend game ... So the entire weekend ... would be organized around the interest of either the patriarch or the male offspring.' Sociologist and criminologist Ian Taylor, cited in Varda Burstyn, 'Play, performance and power,' *Ideas*, CBC Radio (October 1986), transcript 2–3.

65 Varda Burstyn, 'Economy, sexuality, politics: Engels and the sexual division of labour,' *Socialist Studies/Études Socialistes: A Canadian Annual* (1983), 19–39. For a discussion of the contemporary implications of differences in leisure for women and men, see 'The sociology of women's leisure and physical recreation: constraints and opportunities,' Diana Woodward, Eileen Green, and Sandra Hebron, *International Review for the Sociology of Sport* 24 (1989), 121–133.

66 *Advertising Age* (May 25, 1992).

67 Ibid.

Chapter 5. Spectacle, Commerce, and Bodies: Three Facets of Hypergender in the Sport Nexus

1 Michael Novak, *The Joy of Sports: Endzones, Bases, Baskets, Balls, and the Consecration of the American Spirit* (New York 1976), xii.
2 For an example of this perspective in academic writing, see John J. Sewart, 'The commodification of sport,' *International Review for the Sociology of Sport* 22(3) (1987), 171–90. For an example of this perspective in mainstream sports journalism, see Frank Deford, 'No longer a cozy corner,' *Sports Illustrated* (December 1985).
3 Sewart's, 'The commodification of sport' is only one example of scholarly and popular literature on this subject. Bruce Kidd and John MacFarlane, *The Death of Hockey* (Toronto 1972); Bruce Kidd, *The Struggle for Canadian Sport* (Toronto 1996); Frederic Baillette et al., 'La barbarie olympique,' *Quel corps?* 36 (Septembre 1988); Vyv Simson and Andrew Jennings, *The Lords of the Rings: Power, Money and Drugs in the Modern Olympics* (Toronto 1992) all address the corrosive impact of the media and major sponsoring industries on sport and physical culture. See also 'Monday night football,' special advertising section, *Sports Illustrated* (Sept. 4, 1989), n.p., in which Howard Cosell is quoted as saying: '*Monday Night Football* made the NFL the dominant professional sports league in America.'
4 Sewart, 'The commodification of modern sport,' 186, and 'The rationalization of modern sport: The case of professional football,' *Arena* 5(2) (1981), 49. See also Richard Gruneau, 'Commercialism and the modern Olympics,' in Alan Tomlinson and Gary Whannel, eds, *Five Ring Circus* (London 1983).
5 'The rationalization of modern sport,' 45–53.
6 For a discussion of these phenomena in the 1990s, see Charles McGrath, 'Rocking the pond,' *New Yorker* (January 24, 1994).
7 Cited in Varda Burstyn, 'The sporting life,' *Saturday Night* (March 1990).
8 V. Burstyn, 'Play, performance and power,' *Ideas*, CBC Radio (1986).
9 David Meggyesy, in Burstyn, 'Play, performance and power,' transcript 7.
10 Jill Lieber, 'Maximum exposure,' *Sports Illustrated* (May 1, 1989).
11 Ibid.
12 Alan Sack in Burstyn, 'Play, performance and power,' transcript 7–8.
13 See David Seglins, 'Violence, hockey and masculinity in Central Canada, 1890–1910' (unpublished Master's thesis, Queen's University, 1995).
14 Jay Greenberg, 'A real spiritual game,' *Sports Illustrated* (March 12, 1990).
15 William Houston, 'Decline in skills evident at all levels,' *Globe and Mail* (May 12, 1997). Other articles in the series are 'Young hockey talent failed by the system' (May 10); 'System's culture of silence hides flaws' (May 13).

16 Jay Greenberg, 'A real spiritual game.'
17 Al Strachan, 'Gretzky no longer fighting against fighting,' *Globe and Mail* (February 23, 1994).
18 David Meggyesy in Burstyn, 'Play, performance and power,' transcript 8.
19 Ibid.
20 Rick Telander, *The Hundred Yard Lie: The Corruption of College Football and What We Can Do to Stop It* (New York 1990) and 'Something must be done,' *Sports Illustrated* (October 2, 1989); John Underwood, 'The writing is on the wall,' *Sports Illustrated* (May 19, 1980), 36–72. Athletes who practise Olympic sports face similar traumas when they exit full-time competition, especially in recessionary times. For a report on the status of Canadian former Olympic champions in 1994, see Al Sokol, 'After the gold rush,' *Toronto Star* (October 1, 1994).
21 Mickey Mantle, 'My life as an alcoholic,' *Sports Illustrated* (April 18, 1994).
22 Dean A. Purdy, D. Stanley Eitzen, and Rick Hufnagel, 'Are athletes also students? The educational attainment of college athletes,' *Social Problems* 29(4) (April 1982); Telander, *Hundred Yard Lie*; Ted Gup, 'Foul,' *Time* (April 3, 1989); Murray Sperber, 'Flagrant foul,' *Lingua Franca* (November/December 1993), 26–31; see also the award-winning American documentary about young, black, inner-city basketball players, *Hoop Dreams* (1994).
23 See Harry Edwards, 'Are we putting too much emphasis on sports?' *Ebony* (August 1992), and his book *Sociology of Sport* (Homewood, IL, 1973).
24 See Jay Coakley, *Sport in Society: Issues and Controversies*, 6th ed. (St Louis/Toronto 1998).
25 See Joan Chandler, *Television and National Sport: The United States and Britain*, (Urbana, IL, 1988). 'British soccer matches are serious affairs, while football games are structured to provide spectacle ... The British do not demand concessions, bands, a half-time show, mascots, cheerleaders, information from an announcer, referee or voluminous electronic scoreboards which do everything but play the game, or even seating in the stadium. A British soccer crowd creates its own entertainment; all supporters quickly learn the drawn-out chants peculiar to each team' (22).
26 Sue Curry Jansen and Don Sabo, 'The sport/war metaphor: Hegemonic masculinity, the Persian Gulf War and the new world order,' *Sociology of Sport Journal* 11(1) (March 1994), 6.
27 Joyce Nelson, *The Perfect Machine: TV in the Nuclear Age* (Toronto 1987), 74.
28 Cited in Donald Katz, 'The triumph of swoosh,' *Sports Illustrated* (August 16, 1993).
29 John Berger, *Ways of Seeing* (London 1972).
30 Cited in Katz, 'The triumph of swoosh.'

31 According to Malcolm Gladwell, men and women read advertising text (print and electronic) differently. Women respond to complex texts and messages; men to simple ones. Advertisers hence honed the craft of gender appeal even more differentially on the basis of this information. Malcom Gladwell, 'Listening to khakis,' *New Yorker* (July 28, 1997).

32 Steve Rushin, 'How we got here,' *Sports Illustrated* (August 16, 1994). 'Atlanta Brave Chiper Jones, who is under an $8.25 million contract, refused to sign an autograph at a charity function, citing a "conflict of interest" because he receives $200,000 a year to sign for a memorabilia firm.' 'Scorecard,' *Sports Illustrated* (August 19, 1996).

33 Katz, 'The triumph of the swoosh.'

34 Rick Telander, 'Senseless,' *Sports Illustrated* (May 14, 1990); William Leith, 'Pump it up,' *The Independent* (July 8, 1990).

35 Leigh Montville, 'Listen up!' *Sports Illustrated* (November 4, 1996).

36 Rushin, 'How we got here.'

37 Richard J. Barnet and John Cavanagh, *Global Dreams: Imperial Corporations and the New World Order* (New York/Toronto 1994). For other interesting assessments of the Nike corporation, see J.B. Strasser and Laurie Becklund, *Swoosh: The Unauthorized Story of Nike and the Men Who Played There* (New York 1993); Katz, 'The triumph of swoosh'; Frank Deford, 'Running man,' *Vanity Fair* (August 1993). For an overview of corporate-sport-government relationships in the Olympic sector, see Simson and Jennings, *The Lords of the Rings*. Total sales for Nike in 1994 were $4.73 billion. Christopher Hume, 'Nike selling the swoosh along with the shoes,' *Toronto Star* (October 28, 1994).

38 Barnet and Cavanagh, *Global Dreams*, 325–6. See also, Nat Hentoff, 'Michael Jordan: Capitalist tool,' *Village Voice* (December 16, 1997).

39 Anne McClintock, *Imperial Leather: Race, Gender and Sexuality in the Colonial Contest* (New York 1995), 213.

40 Katz, ' The triumph of swoosh.'

41 Ibid. See also Robert Lipsyte, 'Knight: Can a logo conquer all?' *New York Times* (February 7, 1996).

42 Ibid.

43 Cited in Nelson, *The Perfect Machine*, 77. See also Marion Woodman, *Addiction to Perfection: The Still Unravished Bride* (Toronto, 1982) for a discussion of contemporary womanhood from a Jungian and feminist perspective.

44 American Automobile Association's Foundation for Traffic Safety in William Oscar Johnson, 'Sports and suds,' *Sports Illustrated* (August 8, 1988).

45 Karen Shanor, *The Shanor Study: The Sexual Sensitivity of the American Male* (New York 1978), 122–4.

46 I have discussed numerous aspects of this process at length elsewhere, including 'Public sex,' CBC Radio *Ideas* four-hour documentary series (1983); 'Art and censorship,' *Fuse* (September/October 1983); 'Anatomy of a moral panic,' *Fuse* (Summer 1984); and 'Porn again,' *Fuse* (Spring 1987). See also my 'The left and the porn wars,' in H. Buchbinder, V. Burstyn, D. Forbes, and M. Steadman, eds, *Who's on Top? The Politics of Heterosexuality* (Toronto 1987), 'Fantasy and desire, patriarchy and progressive people,' *Canadian Dimension* (March 1989); 'The seductive illusion: sex and class in the Hollywood cinema 1 & 2,' *Canadian Woman Studies* 3(2) 1981; and 'The heat is on: Women, art and sex,' *Canadian Art* (Spring 1986).

47 Joan Mellen, *Big Bad Wolves: Masculinity in the American Film* (New York 1977).

48 Susan Jeffords, *The Remasculinization of America: Gender and the Vietnam War* (Bloomington 1989); James William Gibson, *Warrior Dreams: Violence and Manhood in Post-Vietnam America* (New York 1994).

49 A. Schwarzenegger, *Muscle & Flex: Special Issue* (Spring 1994).

50 Samuel Wilson Fussell, *Muscle: Confessions of an Unlikely Bodybuilder* (New York 1991), 62–4.

51 People with a variety of erotic preferences are sought through advertising in muscle magazines. Some ads appeal to a straight sensibility that appreciates the eroticized athletic female body ('New bodybuilding sensation in the buff! Tanned, blonde beauty totally revealed!'). The women in these ads look like *Playboy* models. Some advertisements emphasize the muscularity and hardness of women bodybuilders ('Muscular amazons clash on the mat in brutal competition!'), celebrating butch qualities and lesbian desire. Yet others are pitched to men with submissive sexualities ('Exciting mixed wrestling action – Female bodybuilders versus men! Experience the intense power and beauty of female muscle!') Even taken together, these advertisements don't come close to matching ads for tapes featuring pure beefcake.

52 Richard Dyer, 'Don't look now – Richard Dyer examines the instabilities of the male pinup,' *Screen* 23 (3–4) (September–October 1982), 61–73. For a thoughtful discussion of the meanings of masculinity found in body-building magazines, with special attention to the advertising discourses, see Philip G. White and James Gillett, 'Reading the muscular body: A critical decoding of advertisements in *Flex* magazine,' *Sociology of Sport Journal* 11(1) (March 1994), 18–39.

53 Alexander Wolff, 'The slow track,' *Sports Illustrated* (September 28, 1992).

54 Sheila Robertson, 'The life and times of CAAWS,' *Canadian Woman Studies* 15(4) (1995), 16–21. See also David Whitson and Donald MacIntosh, 'Gender and power: Explanation of gender inequalities in Canadian national sport organisations,' *International Review for the Sociology of Sport* 24(2) (1989), 137–

50. Whitson and MacIntosh found severe marginalization of women in Canadian national coaching, managing and governance structures in professional and elite sport. 'Women still make up only seven per cent of the ranks of Canada's head coaches, 17 percent of the technical directors, 24 percent of the executive directors, and 21 per cent of the membership of the boards of directors of these organizations.' The literature on women's marginalization in the world of sport is very extensive. See Helen Lenskyj, *Women, Sport and Physical Activity: A Comprehensive Resource Guide to Work Done on Women and Sport* (Ottawa 1991).

55 'Jordan again tops Forbes list,' *ESPN* SportsZone; 'Forbes highest paid athletes list,' *Washington Post* (December 1, 1997).

56 Mary A. Boutilier and Lucinda San Giovanni, *The Sporting Woman* (Champaign, IL, 1983), 185–6.

57 Jane Crossman, Paula Hyslop, and Bart Guthrie, 'A content analysis of the sports section of Canada's national newspaper with respect to gender and professional/amateur status,' *International Review for the Sociology of Sport* 29(2) (1994), 124.

58 Gina Dadario, 'Chilly scenes of the 1992 Winter games: The mass media and the marginalization of the female athlete,' *Sociology of Sport Journal* 11(3) (September 1994), 286–6. See also Margaret Carlise Duncan, 'Sports photographs and sexual difference: Images of women and men in the 1984 and 1988 Olympic Games,' *Sociology of Sport Journal* 7 (1990), 22–43.

59 Boutilier and San Giovanni, *The Sporting Woman*; Helen Lenskyj, *Out of Bounds: Women, Sport and Sexuality* (Toronto 1986). See also Laura Robinson, 'Beating the pink ribbon syndrome,' *Globe and Mail* (August 23, 1990).

60 For a recent discussion of this phenomenon, see Don Gillmor, 'The third sex,' *Toronto Life* (January 1997), 60–5.

61 For a consideration of this problem, as well as a larger discussion of thinness, see Jane Caputi, 'One size does not fit all: Being beautiful, thin and female in America,' in Christopher Geist and Jack Nachbar, eds, *Popular Culture Reader* (Bowling Green, KY, 1983).

62 The heroization of women by the Hollywood cinema is similar ideologically to its other conventions – progressive in certain respects, reactionary in others. Highly problematic is the fact that heroization itself is figured, as the ability to wield physical violence, and the options women characters are presented with by these fictive narratives are limited to the choice of kill or be killed. This heroic paradigm is a primarily masculinist operation, key to the development of genre and myth.

63 I am indebted to Michael Kaufman, who emphasized the importance of sport in teaching the abstract principles of patriarchy to women as well. Women who 'learn masculinity' through sport and who behave like men in the work, political, and physical spheres maintain a system of gender oppression even if their very presence in these spheres seems evidence of the passing away of the old order. I

discussed this point in terms of the masculinist constitution of the modern industrial state in 'Masculine dominance and the state,' *The Socialist Register* (1983), 45–89, and I return to it in Chapter 9.

64 Ann Hall, in Varda Burstyn, 'Play, performance and power.' See also Caputi, 'One size does not fit all'; Susie Orbach, *Fat Is a Feminist Issue: The Anti-Diet Guide to Permanent Weight Loss* (New York 1979); Nicky Diamond, 'Thin is the feminist issue,' *Feminist Review* (Spring 1985), 45–64; Kim Chernin, *The Obsession: Reflections on the Tyranny of Slenderness* (New York, 1981); and Susan Bordo, 'Reading the slender body,' in M. Jacobus, M.E. Fox Keller, and S. Shuttleworth, eds, *Body Politics: Women and the Discoveries of Science* (New York 1990).

65 Clare Wiseman, 'Social studies,' *Globe and Mail* (December 7, 1995).

66 Maggie Fox, 'Friendless and fat equals diet in girls – Study,' *Mercury Mail* Internet news service (April 15, 1997).

67 See Liz Nickson, 'She's not heavy, she's my sister,' *Globe and Mail* (April 13, 1996).

68 When, for example, U.S. gymnast Kerri Strug competed at the 1996 Atlanta games in the Olympic gold medal final on a sprained ankle (even though her second vault was not necessary to win the gold medal) and collapsed after the vault, she was celebrated for extraordinary heroism, not pitied for deploying courage in the service of mindless and destructive obedience, of which starvation is usually a part. Nor was her coach upbraided in the national press for encouraging her to compete when she was so badly injured. Instead, accolades and rewards followed. See Stephen Brunt, 'Teeny-tiny heroine looking at giant profit from one vault,' *Globe and Mail* (August 3, 1996).

69 'Women's gymnastics before had been more like an athletic ballet, and its champions were adults. Larissa Latynina of the Soviet Union had been 29 and a mother when she won six gold meals eight years earlier in Tokyo. Now, here was this waif throwing herself around the uneven bars and backward off the balance beam in a series of moves that seemed almost death-defying. What mature woman could do what she did? Or would even try?' Leigh Montville, 'Olga Korbut,' *Sports Illustrated* (September 19, 1994).

70 Ibid.

71 Frank Deford, 'A special child,' quoted in *Newsweek* (August 10, 1992).

72 Trish Wilson, 'What price glory? Effects of gymnastics on physical and emotional health,' *Sojourner* 22(8) (April 30, 1997).

73 Jim Proudfoot, '4-foot-8 Texas moppet makes ice history,' *Toronto Star* (March 23, 1997).

74 'Gymnastics: Strug's teammates key to decision to give up scholarship,' *Associated Press* (August 2, 1996).

75 A study by Farid F. Chebab et al., 'Early onset of reproductive function in normal female mice treated with leptin,' *Science* (January 3, 1997), shows how the presence of certain levels of body fat appear to trigger the brain into releasing the hormones necessary to bring about sexual maturation. While such a mechanism is hypothesized for males by Chebab and his colleagues at the University of California at San Francisco, it has not yet been demonstrated experimentally. Chebab et al. have studied females, and their study led them to develop the 'critical-fat' hypothesis, summed up as follows by Natalie Angier: 'a girl must reach a certain weight, or level of body fat, signaled to the brain by leptin, before her brain feels comfortable that she is capable of sustaining a pregnancy. Only with that level of body fat, will the brain provide the hormonal green light to puberty. Starvation prevents the attainment of such body fat, and thus directly hormonally retards puberty.' Natalie Angier, 'The perpetrator of puberty,' *Globe and Mail* (January 18, 1996). See also Kalyani Vittala, 'Study links chemical changes, anorexia,' *Globe and Mail* (August 25, 1994); see also 'Hunger to win,' 1994.

76 Wilson, 'What price glory.'

77 LeBrun told *Inside Track* in 1994: 'It is like building up your bone in a bone bank. If you don't lay down enough bone during this critical time, or if you lose more bone than you should during that time, then you will be at risk for the rest of your life.' 'Hunger to win,' *Inside Track*, CBC Radio (April 16, 1994). See also Kalyani Vittala, 'Study links chemical changes, anorexia,' *Globe and Mail* (August 25, 1994), and interviews with Merrie-Ellen Wilcox and Margaret MacNeill, in Burstyn, 'Play, performance and power,' transcript 11.

78 Rod Mickleburgh, 'Young gymnasts suffering in gold quest, doctors told,' *Globe and Mail* (August 18, 1992). For a fascinating account of the complex pressures and experiences faced by a young Olympic-level gymnast, see Merrie-Ellen Wilcox, 'The power to move,' *The Idler* (May–June 1989).

79 'Hunger to win.' According to Trish Wilson, 'the prevalence of eating disorders among female athletes is reported to be somewhere between 15 and 62 percent. Even at the lower estimate, this is much higher than the 1 to 3 percent in the general population.' 'What price glory?' And, reporting on the results of a three-year clinical study presented at the 1994 Seventh International Congress on Obesity, Kalyani Vittala notes that 'among the 45 patients in the study who were admitted to hospital for anorexia, more than half – 27 – were competitive athletes.' 'Study links chemical changes, anorexia.'

80 'Hunger to win.' Cathy Rigby, 'America's Sweetheart,' a competitor at the 1968 and 1972 Olympic games, has painted a grim picture of weight control: 'I really believe that it was important that I was thin, that's what was drilled into your head ... This is how we started the diet phase of our careers. We would starve ourselves

... We were working out six hours a day.' See also 'Play, performance, and power,' Hour 2; and 'A hidden epidemic,' Scorecard, *Sports Illustrated* (August 14, 1989). 'By all indications, eating disorders have become alarmingly prevalent among top athletes in swimming, distance running, gymnastics, and other sports that require weight control. Eating disorders may be unpleasant to discuss, but they are as serious a threat to the health of athletes as anabolic steroids.'

81 Margaret MacNeill, 'Self-abuse stupid, not courageous,' 'Letter of the week,' *Toronto Star* (August 3, 1996).

82 Molly Haskell, *From Reverence to Rape: The Treatment of Women in Movies* (New York 1974).

83 Robin Wood and Richard Lippe, eds, *American Nightmare: Essays on the Horror Film* (Toronto 1979).

84 See Frigga Haugg et al., eds, 'Notes on women's gymnastics,' *Female Sexualization: A Collective Work of Memory* (London 1987), 176; for a hair-raising story of these same dynamics in classical ballet, see Gelsey Kirkland, with Greg Lawrence, *Dancing on My Grave* (New York 1986).

85 Margaret MacNeill, in Burstyn, 'Play, performance and power,' Hour 2: 'The Women,' *Ideas*, CBC Radio, transcript 11.

Chapter 6. 'Hit, Crunch, and Burn': Organized Violence and Men's Sport

1 Rupert Cornwell of the *Independent* (London) cited in 'The O.J. case: Further words of testimony' (compilation of excerpts for the press), *Globe and Mail* (October 7, 1995); see also Josh Freed, 'Merchandising murder,' *Witness* CBC TV (November 15, 1994).

2 According to Peter Heller, Tyson was a small, victimized child, abandoned by his father to survive as best he could with a poor, struggling mother in the poorest reaches of Brooklyn. Tyson has said his parents were 'a pimp and an alcoholic.' The streets he had to walk were gang battle zones. When his body matured, he struck back. He ended up in the correctional system, and was discovered there by Cus D'amato, who harnessed Tyson's power, intelligence, and fury. The O.J. Simpson story is a cautionary tale of the same order. Peter Heller, *Bad Intentions: The Mike Tyson Story* (Toronto 1990); Don Davis, *Fallen Hero* (New York 1994); and David Remnick, 'Kid Dynamite blows up.' *New Yorker* (July 4, 1997).

3 Cited in William Nack and Lester Munson, 'Sport's dirty secret,' *Sports Illustrated* (July 31, 1995). See also Mariah Burton Nelson, 'Jock violence hits home,' *Globe and Mail* (June 23, 1994); Timothy Jon Curry, 'Fraternal bonding in the locker room: A profeminist analysis of talk about competition and women,' *Sociology of Sport Journal* 8 (1991), 119–35; and Mary Jollimore, 'Abuse of women bred in macho sport world's attitudes,' *Globe and Mail* (June 27, 1994).

4 For an insightful look at the pressures on Tyson in 1997, see David Remnick, 'Kid Dynamite blows up.'

5 Tyson made $25 million on a pay-per-view fight after he was released from prison in 1995. Howard Witt, 'Churches and comics,' *Montreal Gazette* (Chicago Tribune Service) (October 2, 1995).

6 Michael Messner discusses how athletes themselves make sense of the violence of their activity. He makes this point in specific relation to Jack Tatum's paralysing hit on Daryl Stingley (see previous chapter) and Pete Rose's collision with Ray Fosse which hurt Fosse and undermined his own baseball career. Messner observes that there is 'a contextual morality in Tatum's and Fosse's constructions of meaning surrounding these two violent collisions. The rules of the game provide a context that frees the participants from the responsibility for moral choices ... [They] also understand that they are entitled to "respect" – that form of emotionally distant connection with others that is so important to traditional masculine identity ... Both Tatum and Fosse appear mystified by the public perspective on events in terms of individual choice or morality. They just play by the rules.' Michael Messner, 'When bodies are weapons,' in Michael A. Messner and Donald F. Sabo, eds, *Sex, Violence and Power in Sports: Rethinking Masculinity* (Freedom, CA, 1994), 94–5.

7 Cited in Jean-Marie Brohm 'Figures sportives de la mort,' *Sociologie du Sport: Quels corps?* 30/31 (June 1986), 65.

8 James Gilligan, *Violence* (New York 1996), 32.

9 For an excellent discussion of how masculinism and capitalism shape the conceptualization of crime and the application of punishment, see James W. Messerschmidt, *Capitalism, Patriarchy, and Crime: Toward a Socialist-Feminist Criminology* (Totowa, NJ, 1986).

10 'Sport is a war of a new type ... The system of sport competition ... is presented in the practice of spectacle as an immense affirmation of aggressivity and of hatred for the adversary, time and the self.' Jean-Marie Brohm, 'Figures sportives de la mort,' *Sociologies du sport*. Special issue of *Quel corps?* nos. 30/31 (June 1986), 66. This article explores sport and war through the lens of the Freudian idea of the death instinct, and has important insights into athletic sado-masochism.

11 'On the ropes,' *Sunday Morning*, CBC Radio (January 23, 1994).

12 Vince Bagnato, ibid.

13 Bob Richardson, 'Hockey violence: Street gangs on skates,' *Toronto Star* (January 26, 1990).

14 Writing in 1997, William Houston lamented the continued degradation of hockey skills due to the emphasis on violence. William Houston, 'Young hockey talent failed by the system,' *Globe and Mail* (May 10, 1997). See also Randy Starkman, 'Gut reaction,' *Toronto Star* (November 10, 1966) on the prominence of painful abdominal and groin injuries in the NHL.

15 Underwood. 'Brutality: The crisis in football,' *Sports Illustrated* (August 14, 1978). In football, as well as in the other core men's sports, many technological innovations have been introduced over the twentieth century, geared to either improving the entertainment value of sports or 'protecting' the athlete. Edward Tenner reviews the numerous 'revenge effects' of technological change in boxing, football, running, skiing, and climbing, and notes the new types of injuries and disabilities they have ushered in. He notes that 'by prescribing and proscribing equipment, association executives and professional athletes shape the future of their sports,' exemplifying Langdon Winner's notion of the 'politics of artifacts.' 'A livelier ball, a faster surface, or a new refueling system may either stimulate or reduce revenues of professional players, entrepreneurs and manufacturers. Decisions about technology are political ones determining the balance of power among competitors.' E. Tenner, *Why Things Bite Back, Technology and the Revenge of Unintended Consequences* (New York, 1997), 273.

16 National Football League Players' Association, Study, (1986), Washington, D.C. Emphasis in original.

17 Underwood, 'Brutality: The crisis in football.'

18 Tony 'The Kid' Pep, 'On the ropes,' *Sunday Morning*, CBC Radio (January 24, 1994).

19 Dr Michael Schwartz, ibid.

20 Stephen Brunt, ibid.

21 'Researchers estimate there are 300,000 sports-related brain concussions every year. At least 17 cases of second impact syndrome have occurred since 1992, while only four cases were reported between 1984 and 1991, to the Centres for Disease Control.' Mike Cooper, 'U.S. sees more sports-related brain injuries,' *Mercury Mail* Internet News Service (March 13, 1997). Both recent deaths cited in the study were in football, but brain injuries also occur frequently in 'hockey, soccer, baseball, basketball, and boxing.'

22 Michael Clarkson, 'Jordan talkin' trash,' *Toronto Star* (March 9, 1997).

23 Ibid.

24 Ibid. Clarkson has written with insight about the psychology of athletes and drawn attention to the number of top athletes who come from either fatherless families (the majority) or families with obsessive fathers.

25 Ibid.

26 Nack and Munson, 'Sport's dirty secret'; David Holmstrom, 'Do aggressive sports produce violent men?' *Christian Science Monitor* (October 16, 1995); Robin Warshaw, *I Never Called It Rape: The Ms. Report on Recognizing, Fighting and Surviving Date and Acquaintance Rape* (New York 1988).

27 Nack and Munson, 'Sport's dirty secret.'

28 Rick Hoffman, 'Rape and the college athlete,' *Philadelphia Daily News*, cited in Warshaw, *I Never Called It Rape*, 113–14.
29 M.A. Messner, 'Women in the men's locker room?' in Messner and Sabo, eds, *Sex, Violence and Power in Sports*, 50. See also Mariah Burton Nelson, 'Jock violence hits home,' *Globe and Mail* (June 23, 1994); Curry, 'Fraternal bonding in the locker room'; John L. Gray, 'Women losers in Super Bowl,' *Globe and Mail* (January 27, 1992); and Alexander Wolff, 'Out of control,' *Sports Illustrated* (May 15, 1995).
30 Nack and Munson, 'Sport's dirty secret.'
31 Cited in Varda Burstyn, 'Play, performance and power,' *Ideas*, CBC Radio (October 1986).
32 Nack and Munson, 'Sport's dirty secret.'
33 Jeffrey O. Segrave, 'The perfect 10: "Sportspeak" in the language of sexual relations,' *Sociology of Sport Journal* 11(2) (1994), 102.
34 For an excellent discussion of metaphors, masculinity, war and sport, see Greg Malszecki, 'Fight like a man: Metaphors of war in sport and the political linguistics of virility,' unpublished research paper, York University, Toronto, 1994.
35 Robin Warshaw, *I Never Called It Rape*, 112.
36 Alisa DelTufo is a research fellow at the Institute for Child, Adolescent and Family Studies in Manhattan. Quoted in Nack and Munson, 'Sport's dirty secret.'
37 Nack and Munson, 'Sport's dirty secret,' 70.
38 Warshaw, *I Never Called It Rape*, 112.
39 See Michele Landsberg, 'Films expose horrors of Bosnian "rape camps,"' *Toronto Star* (March 16, 1997).
40 Todd Crosset, cited in Nack and Munson, 'Sport's dirty secret.' 'It was this attitude that moved a high school football coach in Los Angeles to paint the picture of a vagina on the tackling dummies. And it was surely what inspired Indiana Basketball coach Bobby Knight – "I think if rape is inevitable, relax and enjoy it" – to put a sanitary napkin in the locker of an athlete whose maleness he was challenging.' Nack and Munson, 'Sport's dirty secret.'
41 Loren Baritz, *Backfire: A History of How American Culture Led Us into Vietnam and Made Us Fight the Way We Did* (New York 1985), 22–3.
42 Linda Bird Francke, *Ground Zero: The Gender Wars in the Military*, cited in 'In the company of wolves,' *Time* (June 2, 1997).
43 Donald F. Sabo, 'Doing time doing masculinity: Sports and prison,' in M. Messner and D.F. Sabo, eds, *Sex, Violence, and Power in Sports* (Freedom, CA, 1994), 168.
44 Gilligan, *Violence*, 47.
45 Ibid.
46 Ibid., 16–17.

47 'In common with most Asians, the Vietnamese had one custom that American soldiers could not tolerate. The people of Vietnam hold hands with their friends. Two Vietnamese soldiers would walk down the street holding hands. An American marine from South Boston noticed this custom: "They all hold hands, see. I fucking hated that." The intensity of this marine's reaction was characteristic of America's fighting men. The custom proved to the GIs that South Vietnamese men were homosexuals, and this diagnosis explained why the Vietnamese were incompetent warriors, raising the question about why Americans had to die in defense of perverts.' Baritz, *Backfire*, 22.
48 Susan Jeffords, *The Remasculinization of America: Gender and the Vietnam War* (Bloomington and Indianapolis 1989), 1.
49 Ibid.
50 Ibid.
51 William Broyles Jr, 'Why men love war,' *Esquire Magazine* (November 1984).
52 See Sue Curry Jansen and Donald F. Sabo, 'The sport/war metaphor: Hegemonic masculinity, the Persian Gulf War, and the new world order,' *Sociology of Sport Journal* 11(1) (March 1994), 1–17; Paul N. Edwards, 'The army and the micro world: Computers and the politics of gender identity,' *Signs* 16(1) (Autumn 1990), 118.
53 Cited in Michael Messner, 'When bodies are weapons,' 90. See also Susan Jeffords's discussion of Norman Mailer's characterization of 'America as giving birth,' in *The Armies of the Night* in *The Remasculinization of America*, 45–8.
54 Donald F. Sabo, 'Pigskin, patriarchy and pain,' in Messner and Sabo, eds, *Sex, Violence and Power in Sports*, 84.
55 Broyles, 'Why men love war.'
56 Ibid.
57 David Meggysey, in Burstyn, 'Play, performance and power.'
58 Ibid., 62. French anthropologist and thanatologist Louis-Vincent Thomas observes that 'the closer the game, the more exciting it is, even more so if the risk of death really exists. This is what happens in bullfighting where the triumph of life is all the more savoured: this is Eros confronting Thanatos, the desire to live under assault from the fear of death; one understands that in this exacerbated sense of desire and fear voluptuous pleasure insinuates itself, that of sexual pleasure. For games of death are, in fact, erotic games.' Louis-Vincent Thomas, *Mort et pouvoir* (Paris 1978), 139. Many insights into the fusion of sexuality and lethality in late-twentieth-century men's culture can be found in the work of French sport scholar Patrick Baudry. See his *Le corps extrême: Approche sociologique des conduites à risque* (Paris 1991), and 'La brutalité érotique,' in *Une galaxie anthropologique.* Special issue of *Quel corps?* nos 38/39 (1989).

59 Don Pendleton, *The Executioner*, cited in Sandra Rabinovitch, 'The new warriors,' *Ideas*, CBC Radio, November 7, 14, 1986, transcript 4–5. This documentary is a rich source of information on and analysis of the genre. Pendleton was the original author of the series entitled, after its first novel, *The Executioner*. Pendleton first wrote in 1969 at the height of polarization over the Vietnam war, in an attempt to redeem the American fighting man. Written for and aimed at the Vietnam veteran, *The Executioner* became an overnight bestseller with much wider audiences, and his successor novels continue to sell millions of copies. Series clones have included *The Destroyer, The Penetrator, The Butcher, Death Merchant, The Survivalist*, and *Doomsday Warrior*. Clearly, their themes resonate with the fantasies of North American men at large. Market research has indicated that men of all classes, professions, and ages read the books. These books are to men what Harlequin romances are to women – drams of existential resolution through success in gendered myth, the fantasy fulfilment of deep wishes for a special place in the gendered order – repeated in almost infinite variation in the words of pulp fiction. In 1997, there were 226 titles in *The Executioner* series alone.

60 Jeffords, *The Remasculinization of America*, 13. See also Steve Neale, 'Masculinity as spectacle: Reflections on men and mainstream cinema,' *Screen* 25(4–5) (July–October 1984), 2–16, for an excellent discussion of this proposition, and the way in which it leads to, among other things, the accentuation of sado-masochistic elements in dramatic action and narrative. Neale also makes a number of interesting points about processes of identification with fictive heroes that are valuable in thinking about sport.

61 Jeffords, *The Remasculinization of America*, 13. In speaking of the way sexuality and violence were associated in the pages of the men's magazine *Newlook* as a case study in the sexuality of the extreme body of today's sport, particularly of the so-called 'extreme sports,' Patrick Beaudry observes: 'Eroticism is present in deadly sequences and, inversely, Thanatos is present in the erotic sequences ... Horror can be exciting, exploits ecstatic. And the ecstasy of the erotic sequences can be associated with torture, war, madness, delerium.' Beaudry, *Le corps extrême*, 140.

62 Ibid.

63 Lisa Grayson, 'The nuclear Kama Sutra,' *Mother Jones* (January 1986), offered several quotations from the U.S. Office of Technology Assessment (OTA) on matters of weaponry. One air force general said that the MX missile 'looked like a giant erection' emerging from its trench – a 'Zipperditch.' The OTA noted that the MX can be deployed vertically or horizontally, depending on 'hardness' and 'insertion and removal times.' However 'performance ... might be degraded by shortcomings in hardening ... Dormancy increases response time since guidance

systems require warm-up time to attain their design accuracy.' Fortunately, the MX can all upon 'escort jamming for deep strike missions' and 'active and passive penetration aids' such as 'aerosols, jammers and balloons.' By way of reassurance to missiles with performance anxiety, the OTA says that 'once the limited single-shot goal is accepted, a relatively poor system is as good as a perfect one.' The MX is invaluable for its 'ability to place at risk a portion of the most valued Soviet super-hardened force structure.'

64 For discussions of the relationship between Eros and Thanatos, see Louis-Vincent Thomas, *Mort et pouvoir*, 16–22 and Patrick Beaudry, *Le corps extreme*, 123, 132.

65 See, for example, Pat H. Broeske, 'Real men don't need kisses,' *Calender/Los Angeles Times* (June 22, 1986). For a discussion of the underlying misogyny found in James Cameron's film *True Lies*, starring Arnold Schwarzenegger, see Laura Miller, 'The humiliator,' *San Francisco Examiner* (August 4, 1994).

66 Broyles, Jr, 'Why men love war'; see also Katherine Dunn, 'In this ring,' *Mother Jones* (September/October 1993), for a discussion of how love, comradeship, and brotherhood are forged in the boxing gym.

67 Lewis H. Lapham, *Money and Class in America* (New York 1988), 6–7.

68 Broyles, 'Why men love war.'

69 'Hit men,' *Sports Illustrated* (September 4, 1989).

70 Frank Lidz, 'Wise guy,' *Sports Illustrated* (October 30, 1989).

71 Ibid.

72 Ibid.

73 See Susan Faludi, 'The naked citadel,' *New Yorker* (September 5, 1994).

74 Jay Coakley, *Sport in Society: Issues and Controversies* (St Louis/Toronto, Santa Clara, 1986) 180.

75 Ibid.

76 Curry Jansen and Sabo, 'The sport/war metaphor,' 3. For one example of how sport and war tropes were woven together, see Leigh Montville's account of U.S. forces preparing for and watching the 1991 Superbowl. 'Super ... and surreal,' *Sports Illustrated* (February 4, 1991). *Sports Illustrated*'s editors linked sport, patriotism, and support for the war in the Persian Gulf in 'Scorecard,' (February 25, 1991). For a critical voice, see David Meggyesy, 'Commentary: Football and war,' *Los Angeles Times* (February 8, 1991).

77 Excerpts from Geoffrey S. Smith, 'Security, gender and the historical process,' *Diplomatic History* 18(1) (1994), 87. See also Smith, 'National security and personal isolation: Sex, gender and disease in Cold-War United States,' *International History Review* 14(2) (May 1992), 307–37.

78 Smith, 'Security, gender and the historical process,' 87.

79 Curry-Jansen and Sabo, 'The sport/war metaphor,' 3.

80 Jeffords, *The Remasculinization of America*, 45.
81 Jeffords makes a similar point. 'The final step in this process [of remasculinization] was to transfer the accumulated negative features of the feminine to the government itself, the primary vehicle for legislated and enforced changes in civil rights.' *The Remasculinization of America*, 169. See also Judith Williamson, 'Woman is an island: Femininity and colonization,' in T. Modleski, *Studies in Entertainment* (Bloomington 1986) for a discussion of the psychological operations that take place in the 'feminization' of certain spheres of life in the dominant ideology generally, and through advertising specifically.
82 Tara-Jen Ambrosio and Vincent Schiraldi, *From Classrooms to Cell Blocks: A National Perspective*, Report of the Justice Policy Institute (Washington, D.C., 1977).
83 Jeffords, *The Remasculinization of America*, 5.
84 Julian Schmidt, 'Arnold,' *Muscle and Fitness and Flex: Special Issue* (June 15, 1994). More recently, Bill Clinton confessed to the press that in the week before the Arkansas Razorbacks played in the NCAA Final Four in March 1994, he had a hard time keeping his mind on matters of state. Alexander Wolff, 'The first fan,' *Sports Illustrated* (March 21, 1994).
85 Suren Lalvani, 'Carrying the ideological ball: Text, discourse, and pleasure,' *Sociology of Sport Journal* 11(2) (1994), 155.
86 Curry-Jansen and Sabo, 'The sport/war metaphor,' 3.
87 Ibid., 5.
88 Richard Grey Sipes, 'War, sports and aggression: An empirical test of two rival theories,' *American Anthropologist* 75 (1973), 64–86.
89 Tom 'The Bomb' Glesby, cited in 'On the ropes.'
90 Eric Dunning, 'Sociological reflections on sport, violence, and civilization,' *Review for International Sociology of Sport* 25(1) (1990), 66.
91 Sipes, 'War, sports and aggression,' 80. See also Joseph X. Lennon and Frederick C. Hatfield, 'The effects of crowding and observation of athletic events on spectator tendency toward aggressive behaviour,' *Journal of Sport Behaviour* 3(2) (August 1980), 61–8.
92 Alfie Kohn, *No Contest: The Case against Competition* (Boston 1992), 144.
93 Ibid., 144–5.
94 Kenny Hill cited in ibid., 238.
95 'A report commissioned by the National Cable Television Association found that cartoons and other children's TV programs rarely depict the real consequences of violence and often glorify the attacker. Of all genres, children's programs contain the greatest number of these high risk-portrayals.' Associated Press, 'Cartoons glorify violence, cable TV study finds,' *Toronto Star* (March 27, 1997).
96 Gilligan, *Violence*, 212, 6.

97 Ibid., 232–3.

98 For a fascinating discussion of how an extreme form of masculine dominance such as mid-European fascism functioned with the complicity of women, as well as of junior and nonprivileged men, see Jane Caplan, 'Introduction to female sexuality in fascist ideology,' *Feminist Review* I (1979), 59–68, discussing the work of Maria-Antonietta Macciochi; and Maria-Antonietta Macciochi, ed., *Éléments pour une analyse du fascisme*, 2 vols (Paris 1976) and 'Sexualité féminine dans l'idéologie fasciste,' *Tel Quel* 66 (Paris 1976). From a Reichian perspective, Macchiochi argued that the idea of the fascist leader resonated deeply with other patriarchal ideals of masculine potency, and thus drew, for important social support, on the ways Italian women's sexuality had been shaped by the ideals and discourses of the church. 'Macciochi interprets th[e] role of the fascist Leader as sexually exploitative of both women and men,' Caplan comments. 'The Leader symbolically castrates all men in the act of expropriating the sexual capacity of women ... Macciochi examines the homosexual imagery of fascist society, condensed in the striking phrase "The Nazi community is made by homosexual brothers who exclude the woman and valorize the Mother."' In practice, however, this translates into sexual access for an 'oligarchy' of men, with sexual domination of the majority.

99 Gilligan, *Violence*, 230.

Chapter 7. 'Hooligans, Studs, and Queers': Three Studies in the Reproduction of Hypermasculinity

1 James Christie, 'The Bulls steal one, and the fans go wild,' *Globe and Mail* (June 23, 1993).

2 Buford, *Among the Thugs* (London 1992), 278.

3 'A police escort is an exhilarating thing ... I was sharing something of the experience of those around me, who ... now felt themselves to be special people.' Ibid., 42.

4 Ibid., 88.

5 Ibid., 207.

6 William Broyles, Jr, 'Why men love war,' *Esquire Magazine* (November 1984).

7 See Ian Taylor, 'Putting the boot into a working class sport: British soccer after Bradford and Brussels,' paper delivered to the Annual Conference for the Sociology of Sport (Boston, November 1985). Speaking in a 1986 radio documentary about the Heyschel incident, Taylor said: 'The violence at Brussels was not committed just by, or indeed predominantly by, young poor, white male supporters of the Liverpool football club. Instead, what one is seeing there is the desperation or the nihilism of a more affluent section of the upper working class in Britain; a

fraction of the class that has always existed in that society; a fraction of the class that has always been rather more individualistic, self-interested, proprietorial than the working class as a whole.' In Varda Burstyn, 'Play, performance and power,' *Ideas*, CBC Radio (1986).

8 Buford, *Among the Thugs*, 265.
9 Ibid., 125.
10 Ibid., 38.
11 Ibid., 43, 304.
12 Klaus Theweleit, *Male Fantasies*, vol. 1: *Women Floods Bodies History* (Minneapolis 1987).
13 James Gilligan, *Violence* (New York 1996), 76.
14 James Gilligan accounts for the appearance of the fascist thug in Nazi Germany as well. He notes that 'by the time of the Depression, on the crest of which Hitler rose to power in 1933, the group who supported him most strongly at the polls were the lower middle classes. The members of this group felt in danger of losing their capital and suffering a loss of social and economic status, a degradation, by becoming part of the humiliated, inferior, poverty-stricken lower class, or felt they had already suffered that humiliating sea-change into something poor and strange, and were eager for revenge – for a way of re-establishing their status or sense of power – which Hitler and his Nazi party promised them in abundance. Downward social mobility, unemployment, and homelessness are among the most potent stimuli of shame, are a key to the politics of violence ... Nazis felt both intense shame and envy, and especially envy of the Jews.' Ibid., 66, 69. For another treatment of the centrality of violence to manhood and its expression in political and personal behaviour, see Joseph D. Kuypers, *Man's Will to Hurt: Investigating the Causes, Supports, and Varieties of His Violence* (Halifax 1993), and Michael Malzecki, 'Fight like a man: Metaphors of war in sport and the political linguistics of virility,' unpublished research paper, York University (1994).
15 Buford, *Among the Thugs*, 155.
16 'Scorecard,' *Sports Illustrated* (March 10, 1997).
17 See Rick Reilly, 'Strokes of genius,' *Sports Illustrated* (April 21, 1997); Randy Starkman, 'Tiger Woods: A man on a mission,' *The Toronto Star's Golf '97 Preview* (April 13, 1997); James Christie, 'Woods out to change world if proud father has his way,' *Globe and Mail* (April 15, 1997).
18 Chris Young, 'Thomas takes place as true pioneer,' *Toronto Star* (April 22, 1997).
19 Paul Kooistra, John S. Mahoney, Lisha Bridges, 'The unequal opportunity for equal ability hypothesis: Racism in the National Football League?' *Sociology of Sport Journal* 10 (1993), 243. See also William Oscar Johnson, 'A matter of black and white,' *Sports Illustrated* (August 5, 1991), and John Schneider and D. Stanley Eitzen, 'Racial segregation by professional football positions, 1960–1985,'

Sociology and Social Research 70 (July 1986), 259–62. As well, the entire sport scholarship system – in which many black athletes are exploited for a few years, then discarded – is a product of systemic racism. See Juan R. Palom, 'Affirmative action takes on athletic twist,' *USA Today* (April 10, 1997). See also John Schneider and D. Stanley Eitzen, 'Racial discrimination in American sport: Continuity or change,' *Journal of Sport Behavior* 2(3), (August 1979) 136–42; and 'The black athlete,' *Sports Illustrated* Special Issue (August 5, 1991).

20 For a description of a football game that demonstrated both racism and a community contestation of it, see Colin Soloway, 'More than a football game,' *The Nation* (January 22, 1990). His subject is a football confrontation that took place in Charleston on New Year's Day, 1990, between the white, confederate-identified Citadel Military College of South Carolina and the predominantly black South Carolina State College.

21 It is interesting to note how *Sports Illustrated* framed Jackie Robinson's achievement within the conventions of the celebrity culture. The May 5, 1997, edition featured the headline: '14 days in May: When Jackie Robinson proved he was not just a pioneer but a star.'

22 Henry Louis Gates, Jr, 'The black man's burden,' in Michelle Wallace and Gina Dent, eds, *Black Popular Culture* (Seattle 1992), 79. See also Ellis Cose, *The Rage of a Privileged Class* (New York 1993) and *A Man's World: How Real Is Male Privilege – and How High Is Its Price?* (New York 1995). For discussion of issues of black sexuality, and of sexuality as a site of power in relations between colonized and colonizer, see Franz Fanon, *Black Skin, White Masks* (New York 1967), and Eldridge Cleaver, *Soul on Ice* (New York 1970).

23 Peter Heller, *Bad Intentions: The Mike Tyson Story* (Toronto 1989), 6–54.

24 '[B]lack existential angst derives from the lived experience of ontological wounds and emotional scars inflicted by white supremacist beliefs and images permeating US society and culture. These wounds and scars attack black intelligence, black ability, black beauty and black character daily in subtle and not-so-subtle ways.' Cornell West, 'Nihilism in black America,' in Wallace and Dent, *Black Popular Culture*, 42. For a discussion of issues and patterns in sexuality for black males, see Robert Staples, 'Black male sexuality,' *Changing Men* (Winter 1986) 3–4, 46–47. For a discussion of the development of 'cool pose' as 'an expressive lifestyle of resistance' with both liberating and limiting dimensions, and the role of sport in this, see Richard Majors, 'Cool pose: Black masculinity and sports' in M.A. Messner and D.F. Sabo, eds, *Sport, Men, and the Gender Order* (Champaign, IL, 1990) and 'Cool pose: The proud signature of black survival,' *Changing Men* (Winter 1986), 3–6.

25 See the discussion of black gender politics of the 1960s in Wallace, *Black Macho and the Myth of the Superwoman* (New York 1979), 3–33, and a critical review of

it by Linda C. Powell, 'Review,' in Lorraine Bethel and Barbara Smith, eds, *Conditions Five: The Black Women's Issue* (1979), 165–72.

26 Steve Rushin, 'How we got here,' *Sports Illustrated* (August 16, 1994).

27 bell hooks, in bell hooks and Cornel West, *Breaking Bread: Insurgent Black Intellectual Life* (Toronto 1991), 41.

28 Television has played an important role in this process of cultural mentoring. The 1992 Nielsen ratings showed that the average black household watched eleven hours of television every day – about two-thirds of their waking hours. Jacquie Jones, 'The accusatory space,' in Wallace and Dent, *Black Popular Culture*, 97. With sport as surrogate father, many black single mothers have raised successful athlete-sons, finding in sport one of the least destructive options open to their children. See Michael Clarkson, 'In praise of single mothers,' *Toronto Star* (August 25, 1995). According to Clarkson, twenty-three of the top thirty NBA players had grown up without their natural fathers. On the basis of interviews with the players, Clarkson also comments on how strongly the absence of a father made them want to succeed in sport.

29 Jim Brown quoted in Rushin, 'How we got here.'

30 West, 'Nihilism in black America,' 40–1. For a powerful summary of key issues in black life in the 1990s, see Andrew Hacker, 'The crackdown on African-Americans,' *The Nation* (July 10, 1995), 45–9. See also Editorial, 'Elucidating the relationships between race, socioeconomic status and health,' and Annotation, 'Analyzing socioeconomic and racial/ethnic patterns in health and health care,' *American Journal of Public Health* 84(6) (1994), 892–3 and 1086–7.

31 Jim Brown, cited in Rushin, 'How we got here.'

32 Cornel West, in hooks and West, *Breaking Bread*, 8.

33 Cornel West, 'Nihilism in black America,' 41.

34 bell hooks, in hooks and West, *Breaking Bread*, 39.

35 Phil Taylor, 'Bad actors,' *Sports Illustrated* (January 30, 1995). The magazine's cover and five out of six of the photos in the article depicted black athletes.

36 West in hooks and West, *Breaking Bread*, 95. I use the term narcissism to refer not to a healthy sense of self-regard, important both to individual and community strength and well-being, but rather, to an obsession with the self combined with the belief that appearance, status, and possessions are the forms of self-cultivation that will bring happiness. This form of narcissism is individualistic in political valence, cultivated, in Eric Hobsbawm's words 'in the name of the unlimited autonomy of individual desire. It assume[s] a world of self-regarding individualism pushed to its limits.' *Age of Extremes* (London 1995), 334.

37 Michael Messner, 'When bodies are weapons,' in Michael A. Messner and Donald F. Sabo, eds, *Sex, Violence, and Power in Sport: Rethinking Masculinity* (Freedom, CA, 1994), 98.

38 'When Jim Brown tried to establish himself as an actor,' Steve Rushin writes, 'Brown said that he "always played the same character ... even the names didn't change much: Fireball, Slaughter, Gunn, Hammer, Pike. I began to wonder," Brown said. "Do I have to be called nigger in *every* script?"' Steve Rushin, 'How we got here.'

39 Paul Hoch, *White Hero Black Beast* (London 1979), 44–5. Emphasis in original.

40 When asked about the charges, Brown denied them, adding 'I like sex ... I mess with young women. I know it's bad, but I'm bad.' Steve Rushin, 'How we got here.'

41 William Nack and Lester Munson, 'Sport's dirty secret,' *Sports Illustrated* (July 31, 1995).

42 Hoch provides one example of this kind of consciousness in the pornographic discourse of the early 1970s that illustrates this point. These are the words of a white film producer in Terry Southern's pornographic novel *Blue Movie:* 'He's waiting to fuck her – the *incredible* stud, *with his monstrous black, throbbing, animal cock! Full of fantastic pent-up black lust for the beautiful blonde, and a gallon of black jissem!* ... You know how I'd like to fuck her now? I just realized – if I could get into a *spade bag* ... like if I could pretend to be a spade ... yeah, that's it, a *spade-rape* bag' (emphasis in original). Hoch, *White Hero Black Beast*, 55.

43 *Sports Illustrated* (August 8, 1994), cover.

44 *Vanity Fair* (November 1994), cover.

45 Kenny Moore, 'The eternal example,' *Sports Illustrated* (December 21, 1992). For Arthur Ashe's own thoughts on some of these matters, see his *Days of Grace* (New York 1993).

46 Messner, 'When bodies are weapons,' in Messner and Sabo, eds, *Sex, Violence, and Power in Sport*, 98.

47 Jim Brown, quoted in Rushin, 'How we got here.'

48 Ernest Cashmore, 'The champions of failure: Black sportsmen,' *Ethnic and Racial Studies* 6(1) (January 1983), 99.

49 Ibid., 101.

50 For some examples of the evolution of black women's assessment of gender and sexual relations in the black community and with whites, see Toni Cade, ed., *The Black Woman*, (Toronto 1970); Wallace, *Black Macho and the Myth of the Superwoman*, and a critical review of it by Powell, in Bethel and Smith, eds, *Conditions Five*; Barbara Smith, ed., *Home Girls* (New York 1983); bell hooks, *Yearning: Race, Gender, and Cultural Politics*, (Toronto 1990), and with Cornel West, *Breaking Bread*, Pearl Cleage, *Deals with the Devil* (New York 1993); and Wallace and Dent, *Black Popular Culture*.

51 Cornel West: 'Sadly, the combination of the market way of life, poverty-ridden conditions, black existential angst, and the lessening of fear toward white authori-

ties has directed most of the anger, rage and despair towards fellow black citizens, especially black women. Only recently has this nihilistic threat – with its ugly inhuman action and outlook – surfaced in the larger American society. And it surely reveals one of the many instances of cultural decay in a declining empire.' 'Nihilism in Black America,' in Wallace/Dent, *Black Popular Culture*, 43.

52 '[It is] a forum,' writes Houston A. Baker, Jr, 'that has raps dedicated to the education of black children and white children; that says, "be a father to your child"; that strongly advocates the rights of women; that is perhaps one of the only sites available to young people in this society that says "this is what policing and surveillance are about. These are your rights in a free society."' 'You cain't trus it: Experts witnessing in the case of rap,' in Wallace and Dent *Black Popular Culture*, 136–7. See also Farai Chideya, 'All eyez on us,' *Time* (March 24, 1997). Shirley Ann Williams, 'Two words on music: Black community' and Jacqui Jones, 'The Accusatory Space' in the same collection, Wallace and Dent, *Black Popular Culture*.

53 Baker, 'You cain't trus it,' 136.

54 For a highly unusual story about a gay athlete, see E.M. Swift, 'On a roll,' *Sports Illustrated* (March 11, 1996). It discusses the career of Rudy Galindo, 'U.S. figure skating's first openly gay champion.'

55 Brian Pronger, *The Arena of Masculinity: Sports, Homosexuality, and the Meaning of Sex* (Toronto 1990), 10–11.

56 'The last closet,' *Inside Track*, CBC Radio (October 16, 1993).

57 Geoffrey S. Smith, 'National security and personal isolation: Sex, gender and disease in Cold-War United States,' *International History Review*, 14(2) (May 1992), 307–37; Kim Tomzack and Lisa Steele, *Legal Memory*, videotape, V-Tape, Toronto. Steele and Tomzcak's videotape 'Legal memory' is a brilliant study of the 1950s culture of homophobia and the crass political use that was made of it in Canada. Available from V-Tape, Toronto.

58 David Kopay and Perry Deane Young, *The David Kopay Story* (New York 1977), 56.

59 See Alan Dundes, 'Into the endzone for a touchdown: A psychoanalytic consideration of American football, *Western Folklore* 37 (1978), 75–88, and 'The American games of "smear the queer" and the homosexual component of male competitive sport and warfare' in *Passing through Customs: Essays by a Freudian Folklorist* (Madison 1987), for an astute elaboration of the psychodynamics of male competitive and rank-obsessed homoeroticism as driving forces in sport and in war.

60 See Walter L. Williams's review of Gilbert H. Herdt, ed., *Ritualized Homosexuality in Melanesia, Changing Men* 15 (Fall 1985), 37.

61 William Arens, 'The great American football ritual,' quoted in Dundes, 'Into the endzone,' 76–7.

62 J.B. Strasser and Laurie Becklund, *Swoosh: The Unauthorized Story of Nike and the Men Who Played There* (New York 1993), 23.

63 For a consideration of homoeroticism, violence, and boxing, see Robin Wood, 'Raging bull: The homosexual subtext in film,' in Michael Kaufman, ed., *Beyond Patriarchy, Essays by men on Pleasure, Power, and Change* (Toronto 1987), 266–76. See also Katherine Dunn, 'In this ring,' *Mother Jones*, 30–5.

64 Pronger, *The Arena of Masculinity*, 9.

65 Ibid.

66 Messner, 'When bodies are weapons,' in Messner and Sabo, *Sex, Violence, and Power in Sport*, 96–8.

67 Gilligan, *Violence*, 47.

68 Dennis Altman, *The Homosexualization of America, the Americanization of the Homosexual* (New York, 1982), 96–7.

69 Michelangelo Signorile, 'The incredible bulk,' *Out* (May 1997).

70 Ibid. This phenomenon is, of course, by no means restricted to gay men. For a review of steroid use by young men in general, see 'Doping in sport and athletic training: Literature review,' *Price Waterhouse* (July 3, 1992).

71 Andrew Sullivan, 'Flogging underwear,' *New Republic* (January 18, 1988). See also Jennifer Nicholson, 'The advertiser's man,' *Adbusters* (Summer/Fall 1992).

72 A number of cultural scholars have argued that men have been 'feminized' in advertising. One of the most interesting treatments of men in advertising from the mid-1960s to the late 1980s is Andrew Wernick, 'From voyeur to narcissist: Imaging men in contemporary advertising,' in Michael Kaufman, ed., *Beyond Patriarchy*, 277–97. See also Andrew Sullivan, 'Flogging underwear.'

73 Sullivan, 'Flogging underwear,' 20–4.

74 Lee Quint, 'Spectacular men: Power, masculinity, and self-surveillance in the age of the image,' paper presented to the Popular Culture Association National Meeting, Montreal, March 1987, 7.

75 Ibid, 4.

76 Ibid.

77 Note that the organizers of the Gay Games were refused the right to use the term 'Olympics' by the IOC.

Chapter 8. High Performance: Drugs, Politics, and Profit in Sport

1 For an intelligent dissenting view of the Ben Johnson steroid case, see Trent Frayne, 'Who banned these drugs, anyway?' *Globe and Mail* (March 3, 1989). For a study of similar themes in an academic context, see Jim McKay, 'The "moral panic" of drugs in sport,' paper presented to the Australian Sociology Association Annual Conference (December 1990).

2 At least two books by key members of the inquiry resulted. See Angela Issajenko (as told to Martin O'Malley and Karen O'Reilly), *Running Risks* (Toronto 1990), and Charlie Francis with Jeff Coplon, *Speed Trap: Inside the Biggest Scandal in Olympic History* (Toronto 1990).

3 Canada Commission of Inquiry into the Use of Drugs and Banned Practices Intended to Increase Athletic Performance/Charles L. Dubin, *Commission of Inquiry into the Use of Drugs and Banned Practices Intended to Increase Athletic Performance* (Ottawa 1990).

4 For an excellent historical review of pharmaceutical testosterone, the therapeutic uses, benefits, and drawbacks of androgenic hormones for both men and women, and the use of these hormones in high-performance sport, see John M. Hoberman and Charles E. Yesalis, 'The history of synthetic testosterone,' *Scientific American* (February 1995), 76–81.

5 There are numerous accounts of the effects of different performance-enhancing drugs on the body. See Bob Goldman with Patricia Bush and Ronald Klatz, *Death in the Locker Room: Steroids, Cocaine, and Sports* (Tuscon 1984). See also Terry Todd, 'The steroid predicament,' *Sports Illustrated* (August 1, 1983); and Jean-Pierre de Mondenard, *Drogues et dopages: Sport et santé* (Paris 1987). For a list of banned substances, see 'Guide to banned medications,' *United States Olympic Committee Drug Education and Doping Control Program* (May 27, 1993). One tragic story of the abuse of steroids is that of body-builder Steve Michalik, told by Paul Solotaroff in 'The power and the gory,' Thomas McGuane, ed., *The Best American Sports Writing, 1992* (Boston 1992). See also John Scher, 'Death of a goon,' *Sports Illustrated* (August 24, 1992), and Harrison G. Pope and David L. Katz, 'Affective and psychotic symptoms associated with anabolic steroid use,' *American Journal of Psychiatry* 145(4) (April 1988), 487–90.

6 For a discussion of how the use of steroids disrupts assumptions that 'bodies naturally fit into unambiguous bi-polar categories of gender,' see Laurel R. Davis and Linda C. Delano, 'Fixing the boundaries of physical gender: Side effects of anti-drug campaigns in Athletics,' *Society of Sport Journal* 9 (1992), 1–19. For a feminist critique of Olympic sport, see Mary A. Boutilier and Lucinda F. San Giovanni, 'Individual and team sports in the Olympics: A question of balance,' *International Review for the Sociology of Sport* 27(2) (1992), 177–89.

7 For a discussion of how Olympic ritual carries specific multiple meanings yet 'forms a single performance system,' and an assessment of de Coubertin's views about sport, see John J. MacAloon, 'Olympic games and the theory of spectacle in modern societies,' in John J. MacAloon, ed., *Rite, Drama, Festival, Spectacle* (Philadelphia 1984), 241–80.

8 I use the term 'amateur' to mean that the athlete achieved no economic gain by his pursuits, not that he was unskilled. For a discussion of the meaning of the ideal of

amateurism, its evolution, its ideological valences, and its vicissitudes in the era of corporate sport, see D. Stanley Eitzen, 'The sociology of amateur sport: An overview,' *International Review for the Sociology of Sport* 24(2) (1989), 95–105.

9 For brief histories of the place of women with respect to the IOC and the Olympic games, see Paula Welch and D. Margaret Costa, 'A century of Olympic competition,' in D. Margaret Costa and Sharon R. Guthrie, *Women and Sport: Interdisciplinary Perspectives* (Urbana–Champaign 1994), 123–13; Joanna Davenport, 'The role of women in the IOC and IOA,' *Journal of the American Association of Physical Education, Recreation and Dance (JOPERD)* (March 1988), 42–45, and Lynne Emery, 'Women's participation in the Olympic games: A historical perspective,' *JOPERD* (May/June 1984) 62–72.

10 Bruce Kidd, *The Struggle for Canadian Sport* (Toronto 1996), 150–6.

11 See Xavier Pujadas and Carles Santacana, 'The popular Olympic games, Barcelona 1936: Olympians and antifascists,' *International Review for the Sociology of Sport*, 27(2) (1992), 139–49.

12 Richard D. Mandell, *The Nazi Olympics* (New York 1971), cover.

13 Diefenbaker recalled those games in a conversation with Bruce Kidd, who recounts it like this: 'Eight rows behind Hitler, taking in every moment of the games and the behaviour of the Fuhrer, sat the young John Diefenbaker, future prime minister of Canada. Diefenbaker was in Europe at that time to attend the unveiling of the Vimy memorial. Because he had always wanted to see the Olympics, he went on to Berlin ... Throughout the entire track and field competition, Diefenbaker watched the athletes with one eye and Hitler with the other. When Son Ki-Chong won the marathon, which the Germans had been favoured to win, he said Hitler stormed out of the stadium, never to return again.' Cited in Varda Burstyn, 'The sporting life,' *Saturday Night* (March 1990).

14 In 1961, as architect of the Sport Fitness Act, Canada's policy for sport, Diefenbaker declared to the House of Commons that there were 'tremendous dividends in national pride from success in athletics. The uncommitted countries of the world are using athletic contests as measurements of evidence of the strength and power of the nations participating.' Kidd, cited in Burstyn, 'Sporting life.'

15 For a broader discussion of national and Olympic projects, see John Hargreaves, 'Olympism and nationalism: Some preliminary consideration, *International Review for the Sociology of Sport* 27(1) (1992), 119–35.

16 See Hart Cantelon, 'Stakhanovism and sport in the Soviet Union,' *Proceedings of the 4th Canadian Symposium on the History of Sport and Physical Education* (1979); see also Hart Cantelon, 'The Leninist/proletkultist cultural debates: The implications for sport among the Soviet working class,' in Hart Cantelon et al., *Leisure, Sport and Working Class Cultures: Theory and History* (Toronto 1984), 77–99.

17 See my discussion of the gendered nature of the Soviet state in 'Masculine dominance and the state,' in Ralph Milliband and John Saville, eds, *The Socialist Register* (London 1983), 45–89.
18 When the state infrastructure collapsed, so did the huge sport infrastructures. The affiliation of sport with state, commercial, and religious forces is now undergoing a major transition in these countries and is slowly being colonized by the transnational corporate sector. The old Red Army hockey team, for example, once the global standard-bearer for excellence in hockey, has been renamed the Moscow Penguins, after the Pittsburgh team whose owners have a large share in the Russian team.
19 John Ziegler, 'Introduction' to Bob Goldman's *Death in the Locker Room*, 1–3.
20 'Drugs in the locker room,' *Sports Illustrated* (August 1, 1983); see also Ziegler in Goldman, *Death in the Locker Room*.
21 Ziegler in Goldman, *Death in the Locker Room*.
22 Steve Rushin, 'Jock schools USA,' *Sports Illustrated* (April 28, 1997).
23 The basic structure of the 1970s carding system remains in place today. 'A' cards are awarded to athletes with records equal to those of the top eight in the world. For this extraordinary achievement, in 1997, A card athletes received an income of Can$9,720, an income below the poverty line. 'B' card athletes, who must rank on a par with the top nine to sixteen worldwide, received $8,220; 'C' cards, which go to athletes who show good international potential, were worth $6,720 and $5,220 per year.
24 Rob Beamish and Jan Borowy, *Q. What Do You Do for a Living? A: I'm an Athlete*, (Kingston, ON, 1988).
25 'The sports business,' *The Economist* (July 25, 1992).
26 Richard Gruneau, quoted in 'The sporting life.'
27 Men get many more endorsements than women. Male athletes with a 'bad' image (e.g., NBA star Charles Barkley) get lots of endorsements, but only 'good' women like Nancy Kerrigan and Mary Lou Retton have any real chance at scoring the pot of Olympic gold. Black women athletes get almost no endorsements at all. Debi Thomas, a brilliant African-American skater who competed in Calgary and Albertville, told PBS news ('MacNeil-Lehrer Hour,' February 1994) that she had received virtually no offers. Even Jackie Joyner Kersee, arguably the finest woman athlete in the world at the time, received no major offers.
28 Vyv Simson and Andrew Jennings, *The Lords of the Rings: Power, Money, and Drugs in the Modern Olympics* (Toronto 1992).
29 William Oscar Johnson and Anita Verschoth, 'Olympic circus maximus,' *Sports Illustrated* (October 26, 1986). See also Andrew Jennings, 'Ring toss: How Olympic insiders betray the public trust,' *The Nation* (July 29/August 5, 1996).

30 'Getting the results of 61 events to 7,000 journalists, 2000 athletes, 1,400,000
spectators, 2,000,000,000 fans in 75 countries from a tiny town in Norway is just
another day at the office,' exclaimed Xerox's television advertisement about their
'donation' of services to the Lillehammer winter games.

31 For a discussion of the scope and impact of U.S. television revenue on the
Olympics from 1960 to 1986, see Richard K. Alaszkiewicz and Thomas L.
McPhail, 'Olympic television rights,' *International Review for the Sociology of
Sport* 21(2/3) (1986). See also William Oscar Johnson, 'The fabulous games,' *Time*
(April 29, 1996).

32 See Sally Jenkins, 'Peacock power,' *Sports Illustrated* (December 25, 1995).

33 Frank Deford, 'Cheer, cheer, cheer for the home team,' *Sports Illustrated* (August
20, 1984).

34 For a lament on the corporatization of the Barcelona games, see Frank Deford,
'Bring back the communists!' *Newsweek* (August 10, 1992). For a commentary on
the particular ironies of the Barcelona games, and how Barcelona was able to use
the games to improve rather than destroy poor and working-class neighbourhoods,
see Vincente Navarro, 'The Olympics' untold stories,' *In These Times* (September
2–15, 1992). For reflections on the use of the Nancy Kerrigan–Tonya Harding
story to market the 1994 Lillehammer Winter Olympics, see Lewis Cole, 'Going
for the green,' *The Nation* (March 28, 1994).

35 The ads were echoed by the athletes as well. 'Before, we had to win for the
government, for politics, for communism. The freedom we now have can lead us to
making very good money for ourselves. Now we can reap what we sow. Now, if I
win, I become a famous person, I become a rich person. All athletes respond to this
motivation.' Russian swimmer Yevgeny Sadovyi, quoted in William Oscar
Johnson and Jeff Lilley, 'Swimmers for sale,' *Sports Illustrated* (August 10, 1992).

36 Deford, 'Running man,' *Vanity Fair* (August 1993).

37 Gruneau, quoted in Burstyn, 'The sporting life.'

38 Quoted in ibid.

39 For a summary review of records in key Olympic events, and of the development
of high-performance training, see Mark McDonald, 'Pushing the envelope,'
Civilization (May/June 1996), 40–7; Jay. T. Kearney, 'Training the Olympic
athlete,' *Scientific American* (June 1996), 52–63; and David Bjerklie, 'High-tech
Olympians,' *Technology Review* (January 1993), 24–30. For a comment on the
'flattening out' of women's records, see Kenny Moore, 'Missing the mark,' *Sports
Illustrated* (January 20, 1992). For a discussion of women's records and the limits
of the human body, see Jean-Jacques Bozonnet, 'Trajectoires de femmes,' *Le
Monde* (January 8, 1992).

40 The sensational performances of a group of young Chinese women middle-distance
runners in the fall of 1993 and swimmers in the summer of 1994, show that women

can still make relatively large gains. The Chinese coaches have said that they employ traditional Chinese medicine (herbs, acupuncture, tai chi) along with Western training techniques. Although some of these techniques may have given the Chinese women an edge over their Western competitors, there has also been evidence that steroids have been implicated in their extraordinary performances. See Mark Bloom, 'What is limit for Chinese women?' *New York Times* (September 28, 1993).

41 Michael Bamberger and Don Yaeger, 'Over the edge,' *Sports Illustrated* (April 14, 1997). The cover caption read 'Bigger, stronger, faster,' superimposed on a full-frame image of a massive bicep being penetrated by a needle.

42 Ibid.

43 David Meggyesy, cited in Burstyn 'The sporting life.'

44 'The sports business.'

45 Bamberger and Yaeger, 'Over the edge.'

46 Ibid.

47 John Hoberman, *Mortal Engines: The Science of Performance and the Dehumanization of Sport* (New York, 1992), 260–1.

48 For two contemporary feminist readings of Shelley that raise key issues of human rights, see Monette Vacquin, *Frankenstein ou les délires de la raison* (Paris 1989), and Gwynne Basen, 'Following Frankenstein: Women, technology and the future of procreation,' in Gwynne Basen, Margrit Eichler, and Abby Lippman, eds, *Misconceptions: The Social Construction of Choice and the New Reproductive and Genetic Technologies*, vol. I, (Hull, PQ, 1993).

49 For discussions of many of the controversial issues in genetic science, including feminist critiques, see Daniel J. Kevles and Leroy Hood, 'The code of codes: Scientific and social issues in the Human Genome Project,' Hastings Center Report 24(2) (March/April 1994), 42–3, and Abby Lippman, 'Prenatal diagnosis: Reproductive choice? Reproductive control?' in Christine Overall, ed., *The Future of Human Reproduction* (Toronto 1989).

50 See Peter Nicholls and John Clute, *The Multimedia Encyclopedia of Science Fiction* (Danbury, CT, 1995). See entries under androids, automation, communication, computers, cyborgs, intelligence, and robots for histories and discussions of these terms in science fiction. For feminist approaches to cyberculture, see also Vivian Sobachak, 'New age mutant ninja hackers: Reading mondo 2000,' and Anne Balsamo, 'Feminism for the incurably informed,' in Mark Dery, ed., *Flame Wars: The Discourse of Cyberculture, The South Atlantic Quarterly* 92(4) (Fall 1993), 569–84, 680–712. See also Mark Dery, *Escape Velocity: Cyberculture at the End of the Century* (New York 1996).

51 Balsamo suggests that most cyberpunk science fiction 'remains stuck in a masculinist frame,' in that cyberpunk dramas, like most video game narratives, are 'focused on the struggle of the male protagonist ... to wend his lonely way through

the worlds.' Balsamo, 'Feminism for the incurably informed,' 683. Andrew Ross, quoted in ibid., 692, states: 'One barely needs to scratch the surface of the cyberpunk culture, no matter how maturely sketched out, to expose a baroque edifice of adolescent male fantasies.' See also Claudia Springer, 'Sex, memories, and angry women,' in Dery, ed., *Flame Wars*, 713–33.

52 James Wolcott, 'A man's life,' *Vanity Fair* (June 1997).
53 Jean-Marie Brohm, *Sport: A Prison of Measured Time* (London 1978), 27–8.
54 Mark McDonald, 'Pushing the envelope,' 46.
55 See Carolyn Merchant, *The Death of Nature: Women, Ecology, and the Scientific Revolution* (San Francisco 1982), Patricia Hynes, ed., *Reconstructing Babylon: Essays on Women and Technology*, (Bloomington 1990). See also various works of Ursula Franklin, Ruth Hubbard, and Evelyn Fox Keller.
56 The literary production of science fiction involves myriad investigations of the possibilities and implications of developments in science, technology, politics, gender, and sex. While the utopian strain is a thin one, it can be found in books (for example, Ursula LeGuinn's *Dispossessed*, Kim Stanley Robinson's *Red, Blue and Green Mars*). The literary genre is still capable of communicating the complex, imaginative, and oppositional ideas of its producers – in this case writers – directly to their consumers. By contrast, film, television, and video game sci-fi production are generally dystopic, and offer little in scientific or socio-political exploration. In the vast majority of 'sci-fi' films, for example, science is used to set up a dramatic situation involving some form of phallic high-tech weaponry employed by both the bad guys and the good guys who fight it out. For the most part the gender order is still masculinist. The heroes are one-dimensional, the dramatic tensions similar to those of the standard men's action flick, discussed in chapters 5 and 6. The communication of collective fantasy in commercial film is shaped by intentionally commercial considerations, and by a variety of commercial gatekeepers, notably directors, producers, owners, and distributors.
57 Bamberger and Yaeger, 'Over the edge.'
58 See Peter Donnelly and Laura Sergeant, 'Adolescents and athletic labour: A preliminary study of elite Canadian athletes,' Paper presented at the Seventh Annual Conference of the North American Society for the Sociology of Sport, (Las Vegas 1986); and Peter Donnelly (with the assistance of Erika Casperson, Laura Sergeant, and Brenda Steenhof), 'Problems associated with youth involvement in high performance sport,' in B.R. Cahill and A.J. Pearl, eds, *Intensive Participation in Children's Sports* (Champaign, IL, 1993), 95–126.
59 Donnelly and Sergeant, 'Adolescents and athletic labour,' 2.
60 Leslie Papp, 'Child abuse issue in gym,' *Toronto Star* (July 27, 1996).
61 See 'Coach jailed for death,' *Toronto Star* (February 1, 1995) and Rod Mickleburgh, 'Young gymnasts suffering in gold quest, doctors told,' *Globe and Mail* (August 18, 1992).

62 Meggyesy, *Out of Their League* (New York 1971), 12, 79.

63 Alfie Kohn, *No Contest: The Case against Competition* (Boston 1992), 106.

64 'Crossing the line,' *The 5th Estate,* CBC Television, November 2, 1993.

65 Alan Adams, 'Top hockey coach jailed in sex case,' *Toronto Star* (January 3, 1997). See also, Alanna Mitchell, 'Hockey coach pleads guilty to sexual assault charges,' *Globe and Mail* (January 3, 1997).

66 Cited in Donnelly et al., 'Problems associated with youth involvement in high performance sport,' 102.

67 Meggyesy, cited in Burstyn 'The sporting life,' 49.

68 *Physical Activity and Health: A Report of the Surgeon General,* U.S. Department of Health and Human Services, Washington D.C., July 1996.

69 *1995 Physical Activity Monitor,* The Canadian Fitness and Lifestyle Research Institute, Ottawa, 1995.

70 *National Population Health Survey Overview, 1994–95* (Ottawa: Statistics Canada, 1997), 12.

71 *1997 Physical Activity Monitor* (Ottawa: The Canadian Fitness and Lifestyle Research Institute, 1997).

72 Jean Harvey, 'Sports policy and the welfare state,' *Sociology of Sport Journal 5* (1998), 324–6. See also Bruce Kidd, 'The philosophy of excellence: Olympic performances, class power, and the Canadian state,' in Pasquale Galasso, ed., *The Philosophy of Sport and Physical Activity* (Toronto 1998), 11–31.

73 *Physical Activity and Health.*

74 For discussions of the relationship between the reduced risk of breast cancer and exercise, see Leslie Bernstein et al., 'Physical exercise and reduced risk of breast cancer in young women,' and Louise A. Brinton, 'Ways that women may possibly reduce their risk of breast cancer,' in *Journal of the National Cancer Institute* 86 (18) (September 21, 1994), 1403–8, 1371–2.

75 See Chris Mulhill, 'Poverty is the world's greatest killer,' *Guardian Weekly* (May 7, 1995); see also Gregory Papas, 'Elucidating the relationships between race, socioeconomic status and health,' *American Journal of Public Health* 84(6) (June 1994), 892–3.

76 *Physical Activity and Health.*

77 Associated Press, 'Poor and overweight,' *Globe and Mail* (December 5, 1995).

78 See Robert Evans, Morris Barer and Theodore Marmor, *Why Are Some People Healthy and Others Not? The Determinants of the Health of the Population* (New York 1994), 6–7.

79 Ibid., 15.

80 Ibid., 22.

81 'Women's double or triple workdays constitute one of the primary barriers to taking up a sport or physical activity as a leisure pursuit,' writes feminist sport scholar Helen Jefferson Lenskyj. 'For example, for women whose workdays

330 Notes to pages 250–5

include paid employment, childcare and domestic work, part-time study and volunteer work ... the idea of entitlement to leisure may seem laughable.' 'What's sport got to do with it?' *Canadian Woman Studies* 15(4) (Fall 1995), 8.

82 World Health Organization, *Bridging the Gaps*, cited in Mulhill, 'Poverty is world's greatest killer.'

Chapter 9. Re-creating Recreation: Sport and Social Change

1 Erving Goffman, *Gender Advertisements* (New York 1976), 1.

2 David Meggysey has proposed such a scheme. See Matthew Goodman, 'Sports today: David Meggyesy interview,' *Z Magazine* (June 1990), 89.

3 I use the term 'neoconservative politics' to refer to the mélange of social and economic policies that have guided the machinery of state in the United States since the election of Ronald Reagan in 1980. Typically, neoconservative social policies are characterized by a heavy-handed appeal to so-called traditional values, including the father-headed family, compulsory heterosexuality, and a general disdain for either the systemic manifestations of racism or the claims of environmentalism. The typical economic policies of this approach, though they tend to be advanced by politicians who support neoconservative policies, are more accurately called neoliberal because of their 'laissez-faire' nature (i.e., removal of government interference in the flow of trade and capital) and are reminiscent of Ricardian economics. In the United States, neoconservative politics and neoliberal economics have marched in lock-step, though certain key neoliberal economic beliefs have also been embraced by some who do not subscribe to neoconservative social policies. In Canada, neoliberal economics have been taken up by all the parties of the political centre and right, while neoconservative social policies tend to be popular with a smaller proportion of the population on the right. Hence, the two sets of policies – social and economic – may be independent of each other; in practice, especially in the United States, they often go together.

4 'Greek cities supported the ancient Olympics, modern governments put billions into the infrastructure of sport, in schools, local playing fields and leisure centres. Less publicly, they also hand out taxpayer's millions to professional sport.' 'The sports business,' *The Economist* (July 25, 1992).

5 Andrew Osterland, 'Field of nightmares,' *Financial World* (February 14, 1995). See also Dennis R. Howard and John L. Crompton, *Financing Sport* (Morgantown, WV, 1995), 35–7. Sougata Mukherjee, ' "Sports welfare" growing with more subsidies to U.S. stadiums,' *Houston Business Journal* (September 16, 1996); and Bruce Kidd, 'Toronto's Skydome: The world's greatest entertainment centre,' in John Bale and Olaf Moen, eds, *The Stadium and the City* (Keele, England, 1993).

6 'The sports business.'

7 'Footloose football,' *The Economist* (September 9, 1995).

8 Howard and Crompton, *Financing Sport*, 35.

9 Robert Baade and Alan Sanderson, 'Field of fantasies,' *Intellectual Ammunition* (March/April 1996).

10 Osterland, 'Field of nightmares.' See also 'Football and the reluctant voter,' *The Economist* (June 14, 1997).

11 See 'Marcia Beress, 'Big league blackmail,' *Forbes* (May 11, 1992), 45, and Tim Crothers, 'The shakedown,' *Sports Illustrated* (June 19, 1995).

12 Osterland, 'Field of nightmares'; see also Marty York, 'New stadium for Expos – Or else,' *Globe and Mail* (June 18, 1997).

13 Carol M. Amidon, 'Sports stadiums bring no economic boom,' *USA Today Newsview* (December 1996), 10. See also Sougata Mukherjee, 'Sports welfare,' and Baade and Sanderson, 'Field of fantasies.'

14 See David Whitson and Don McIntosh, 'Becoming a world-class city: Hallmark events and sports franchises in the growth strategies of western Canadian cities,' *Sociology of Sport Journal* 10(3) (1993), 221–40.

15 Note this is not true of the cultural sector as a whole, at least in Canada, where every dollar given in public subsidies to arts organizations yields $8 in job creation and new revenues.

16 Stephen Brunt, 'Expos ready to deliver last pitch,' *Globe and Mail* (June 19, 1997).

17 'Football and the reluctant voter.'

18 Regarding the politics of the National Endowment for the Arts and broader left/right cultural conflicts, see William Martin, *With God on Our Side: The Rise of the Religious Right in America* (New York 1997); Richard Bolton, ed., *Culture Wars* (New York 1992); and Robert Hughes, *Culture of Complaint: The Fraying of America* (New York 1993). On the politics of public broadcasting, see James Ledbetter, *Made Possible by ... The Death of Public Broadcasting in the United States* (London 1997); Willard D. Rowland, Jr, and Michael Tracey, 'Worldwide challenges to public broadcasting,' *Journal of Communication* 40(2) (Spring 1990) 8–27; Edward S. Herman and Robert W. McChesney, *The Global Media: The New Missionaries of Corporate Capitalism* (London 1997). Regarding the crisis of public broadcasting in Canada, see Wayne Skene, *Fade to Black: A Requiem for the CBC* (Vancouver/Toronto 1997).

19 'Footloose football.'

20 'Budget scandal,' *The Nation* (August 28/September 4, 1995).

21 Tara-Jen Ambrosio and Vincent Schiraldi, *From Classrooms to Cellblocks: A National Perspective* (Washington, DC: Justice Policy Institute, February 1997). See also Mike Davis, 'Hell factories in the field,' and 'The prison boom,' *The Nation* (February 20, 1995). Affirmative action was killed in all California state universities, with the exception of one small group of students: athletes. See Tom

Hayden and Connie Rice, 'California cracks its mortarboards,' *The Nation* (September 18, 1995).

22 Gilligan, *Violence*, 23.

23 This sale succeeded in recovering only $150 million of the much larger public contribution. For a full discussion of the Skydome experience within the context of public subsidy for professional sport, see Kidd, 'Toronto's SkyDome.'

24 'Impact of Olympic redevelopment on Atlanta's homeless people,' press release, Atlanta Olympic Conscience Coalition, 1996. See also Caleb Hellerman, 'Athletic development,' *The Nation* (July 29/August 5, 1996).

25 See Alex Molnar, *Giving Kids the Business* (Boulder, CO, 1996).

26 In a recent statement of principles, the faculty proposed that athletics should provide an 'opportunity for self-discovery, social interaction, pleasure, health and physical, mental and spiritual development, in the context of striving for physical and mental self-mastery.' *Final Report of the Task Force on Intercollegiate Athletics*, DAR Council, University of Toronto (April 2, 1997).

27 At the same time, the school is seeking ways to make the university's own athletic programs, previously oriented to high-performance sport, express these perspec-
·   tives. A task force reporting on strategic directions for reorganizing collegiate athletics in 1997, for example, recommended that the eligibility for such athletics be extended and democratized, that funds go to subsidize all activities for which there is interest, not only the high-performance teams in competition; and that professional leadership (i.e., coaching) put a 'premium on the "whole person" development of the students ... which involves the student directly in the planning and evaluation of that experience.' *Final Report of the Task Force on Intercollegiate Athletics*.

28 See Steve Rushin, 'Jock schools USA,' *Sports Illustrated* (April 28, 1997).

29 'Sexual democracy, just like political democracy, relies on a balance between rights and responsibilities, between the claims of the individual and the claims of the community,' writes Michael Kimmel in a discussion of the idea of a sexual bill of rights. 'Sexual democracy [is about] treating your partner as someone whose lust is equal to yours and also as someone whose life is equally valuable.' Michael S. Kimmel 'Clarence, William, Iron Mike, Magic – and Us,' *Changing Men* 25 (Winter/Spring 1993), 13.

30 For a discussion of this program, see David Holmstrom, 'Do aggressive sports produce violent men?' *Christian Science Monitor* (October 16, 1995).

31 In the U.K. it costs 'over 10 million pounds to establish a national cable TV channel, some £20 million to establish a new national newspaper, and many times this to start up a new, transnational satellite TV service,' notes James Curran, 'Media soundings,' *Soundings* 5 (Spring 1997), 135.

32 Curran, 'Media soundings,' 127–36. For an extended analysis of the transnational corporate order in global media, see also Herman and McChesney, *The Global Media.*

33 Jonathan Burston, 'Fear and loathing among the kulturcrats: Brian Mulroney, Canadian cultural bureaucracy, and the neoconservative revolution,' unpublished paper, University of Toronto, 1994.

34 See 'The national entertainment state,' *The Nation* (June 3, 1996), and my discussion of this topic in Chapter 4.

35 Leo Panitch, 'A different kind of state?' in Gregory Albo, David Langille, and Leo Panitch, eds, *A Different Kind of State? Popular Power and Democratic Administration* (Toronto 1993), 5.

36 Curran, 'Media soundings.' See also Herman and McChesney, *The Global Media.* For their discussion of alternatives, see 189–54.

37 On GLC Cultural policy and initiatives, see Geoff Mulgan and Ken Worpole, *Saturday Night or Sunday Morning? From Arts to Industry – New Forms of Cultural Policy* (London 1986).

38 See Monroe E. Price, 'Making antitrust work,' *The Nation* (June 3, 1996), for a discussion of strategies and tactics that can be employed in working toward a more democratic field of communications in the United States. For many interesting strategies and tactics for a democratic media, see Jeffrey A. Chester and Anthony Wright, 'A twelve-step program for media democracy,' *The Nation* (June 3, 1996), insert. For a discussion of the problems of commercial concentration, see Mark Crispin Miller, 'Free the media,' *The Nation* (June 3, 1996). For further proposals, and a discussion of issues of pluralism, cultural independence from both state and commerce, support to the civic communications sector, and a consideration of television and publishing, see Curran, 'Media soundings.'

39 See Jennifer A. Hargreaves, 'Gender on the sports agenda,' *International Review for the Sociology of Sport* 25(4) (1990), 287–305; David Whitson, 'The embodyment of Gender: Discipline, Domination and Empowerment,' in Susan Birrell and Cheryl L. Cole, eds, *Women, Sport and Culture* (Urbana–Champaign, IL, 1994), 353–71; Sarah Gilroy, 'The emBody-ment of power: Gender and physical activity,' *Leisure Studies* 8 (1989); Helen Jefferson Lenskyj, 'What's sport got to do with it?' *Canadian Woman Studies*, 5(4) (Fall 1995), 6–10.

40 Sheila Robertson, 'The life and times of CAAWS,' *Canadian Woman Studies* 15(4) (Fall 1995), 16–21.

41 R. Goldman, cited in Mélisse Lafrance, 'If you let me P.L.A.Y.,' paper presented at the University College Annual Conference, University of Toronto, February 1997. For an earlier discussion of the pitfalls of corporate commercialization in women's sport, see Michael A. Messner, 'Sports and male domination: The female athlete as contested ideological terrain,' *Sociology of Sport Journal* 5 (1988),

197–211. See also Lewis Cole, 'Going for the green,' *The Nation* (March 28, 1994); Alison Dewar, 'Incorporation of resistance? Towards an analysis of women's responses to sexual oppression in sport,' *International Review for the Sociology of Sport* 26(1) (1991), 15–22; M. Ann Hall, 'The discourse of gender and sport: From femininity to feminism,' *Sociology of Sport Journal* 5 (1988), 330–40.

42 Jennifer Hargreaves argues that 'by stressing recreation, health, a full range of physical skills and sensuous pleasure in movement, a practical and ideological shift away from an aggressive, male-dominated competitive model of sport would result.' Hargreaves, 'Gender on the sports agenda,' 302.

43 We now know much about how women and men are differentiated through the institutions of sport. However, a number of other areas of research need to be explored with respect to women and sport culture – for example, How do women relate to sport in the raising of their male and female children? Why are so many women critical of sport yet still support it for their boys? Which mothers are pursuing sport for their girls? As well, it would be useful to learn much more about the meaning of sport in courtship, sexuality and mating. How does men's sport speak to the eroticism of different women? How do women derive personal gratification from sport when their identifications with athletes and teams are not gender based? What value, if any, do wives get out of institutions such as the 'the soccer weekend' or 'Monday night football,' or 'Saturday night hockey?' It would also be useful to understand the nature of the bond women make through sport with male lovers and mates around shared or conflicting meanings of masculinity, femininity, eroticism, parenting, and community.

44 In Canada, Statistics Canada reports that in the first quarter of 1997, about 1.1 million adult men worked overtime (compared with 686,000 adult women). 'Those who worked overtime put in fairly long hours over and above their regular work week – an average of just over 9 overtime hours. Statistics Canada, 'Labour force update: Hours of work, first quarter 1997,' Ottawa, July 14, 1997. In the United States, according to the Economic Policy Institute, 'the demands on U.S. workers for more hours are increasing. As hours per week fall among our major industrialized trading partners (except Canada), average hours in the United States are rising. Overtime hours are rising as well.' Lonnie Golden, 'Family friend or foe? Working time, flexibility, and the Fair Labor Standards Act,' Economic Policy Institute, Washington, DC, 1997.

45 Steve Biddulph, an Australian family therapist, believes that sons of men who spend more than fifty-five hours a week in the office are 'emotionally handicapped.' 'Notebook,' *Time* (June 30, 1997).

46 Cited in Elaine Carey, 'Women find there's no place like ... work,' *Toronto Star* (August 12, 1997).

47 An analysis of U.S. data shows that between 1973 and 1988, 'the combined average husband-wife hourly wage increased by only 1.8 percent – the equivalent of a real hourly wage increase of less than 30 cents over the entire period, or 2 cents each year! ... American mythology holds that long hours will pay off in a steadily increasing standard of living; in other words sacrificing time with family can pay for a dishwasher or microwave and, down the road, a more expensive college for one's children. Yet from a purely material perspective, all the extra hours from the 'average' working family have yielded only a very modest improvement in the amount of goods and services they can buy ... Most Americans are not working harder so they can afford a fancier minivan; they're just trying to make payment on their old car or cover the rent.' Barry Bluestone and Stephen Rose, 'Overworked and underemployed,' *The American Prospect* (March/April 1997). These data cover the relative boom years before the economic downturn of the 1990s; since then the situation has gotten worse.

48 Leslie Scrivener, 'In changing world, men flock to Jesus,' *Toronto Star* (September 24, 1995). See also Joe Conason, Alfred Ross, and Lee Cokorinos, 'The Promise Keepers are coming: The third wave of the religious right,' *The Nation* (October 7, 1996).

49 David Blankenhorn, *Fatherless America: Confronting Our Most Urgent Social Problem* (New York 1995), 1–2.

50 See Martin, *With God on Our Side*, 349–53.

51 Joan Breckenridge and Gay Abbate, 'Movement issues "wakeup call" to Canadian men,' *Globe and Mail* (September 25, 1995).

52 See Thomas Y. Canby and Steve McCurry, 'After the Storm,' *National Geographic* (August 1991), 2–35.

53 John Keegan, *A History of Warfare* (Toronto 1993), 59–60.

54 See Linda Bird Francke, *The Gender Wars in the Military* (New York 1997); 'In the company of wolves,' *Time* (June 2, 1997); Randy Shilts, *Conduct Unbecoming: Gays and Lesbians in the U.S. Military* (New York 1993), 28; and Kathy Dobie, 'A few nice men,' *Vogue* (February 1993).

55 M.A. Messner and D.F. Sabo, 'Changing men through changing sports: An eleven point strategy,' in M.A. Messner and D.F. Sabo, eds, *Sex, Violence, and Power in Sports: Rethinking Masculinity* (Freedom, CA, 1994).

56 Michael Messner, ' "Changing men" and feminist politics in the United States,' *Theory and Society* 22 (1993), 723. Messner argues that new manifestations of men's changed consciousness – the greater (though still unequal) involvement of middle-class men in household and childrearing tasks known as the 'New Fathering'; the 'mythopoetic movement' exemplified by Robert Bly's *Iron John*; and the recent spate of powerful men such as General Schwarzkopf and Michael Jordan shedding tears in public – can be interpreted as a sign that men would like to stop

Makin, Kirk. 'The peanuts and beer on Canada's spectator sport.' *Globe and Mail*, May 21, 1994.

Malszecki, Greg. 'Fight like a man: Metaphors of war in sport and the political linguistics of virility.' Unpublished Research Paper, Social and Political Thought Program, York University, Toronto, 1994.

Malthus, Thomas. *An Essay on the Principle of Population, and a Summary View of the Principle of Population*. London: Penguin, 1970.

Managan, James A. *Athleticism in the Victorian and Edwardian Public Schools: The Emergence and Consolidation of an Educational Ideology*. Cambridge: Cambridge University Press, 1981.

– 'Social Darwinism, sport and English upper class education.' *Stadion* 7(1), (1981), 93–116.

Mandel, Ernest. *Delightful Murder: A Social History of the Crime Story*. London: Pluto Press, 1984.

Mandell, Richard. *The Nazi Olympics*. New York: Macmillan, 1971.

Mandese, Joe. 'Marketers' plans for '92 games are less than Olympic.' *Advertising Age*, August 12, 1991.

Mannis, Robert Frank. 'Husbandry.' *Utne Reader*, May/June 1991, 70–1.

Mantle, Mickey. 'My life as an alcoholic.' *Sports Illustrated*, April 18, 1994, 66–77.

Marcus, Steven. *The Other Victorians: A Study of Sexuality and Pornography in Mid-Nineteenth-Century England*. New York: W.W. Norton, 1985.

Marcuse, Herbert. *Eros and Civilization: A Philosophical Inquiry into Freud*. New York: Alfred A. Knopf, 1962.

– *One Dimensional Man: Studies in the Ideology of Advanced Industrial Society*. Boston: Beacon, 1964.

Martin, William. *With God on Our Side: The Rise of the Religious Right in America*. New York: Broadway Books, 1997.

Marx, Karl. *German Ideology*. Moscow: International Publishers, 1968.

McCallum, Jack. 'The record company.' *Sports Illustrated*, January 8, 1990.

McClintock, Anne. *Imperial Leather: Race, Gender, and Sexuality in the Colonial Contest*. New York: Routledge, 1995.

McDonald, Mark. 'Pushing the envelope.' *Civilization*, May/June 1996, 40–7.

McGrath, Charles. 'Rocking the pond.' *The New Yorker*, January 24, 1994.

McKay, Jim. 'The "moral panic" of drugs in sport.' Paper presented to the Australian Sociology Association Annual Conference, Brisbane, December, 1990.

– *No Pain, No Gain? Sport and Australian Culture*. New York: Prentice-Hall, 1991.

– 'Sport and the social construction of gender.' In Gillian Lupton, Patricia M. Short, and Rosemary Whip, eds, *Society and Gender: An Introduction to Sociology*. Sydney: Macmillan, 1992.

- '"Just do it": Corporate sports slogans and the political economy of "enlightened racism."' Paper presented at the Fifth Congress of the International Association for Semiotic Studies, University of California, Berkeley, June 1994.
- 'Masculine hegemony, the state, and the incorporation of gender equity discourse: The case of Australian sport.' *Australian Journal of Political Science* 29 (1994), 82–95.

McNeal, James U. 'From savers to spenders: How children became a consumer market.' *Media and Values*, Fall/Winter 1990, 4–6.

McPherson, B.D. 'The segregation by playing position hypothesis in sport: An alternative hypothesis.' *Social Science Quarterly* 55 (March 1975), 960–6.

Mead, Margaret. *Coming of Age in Samoa*. New York: William Morrow, 1961.
- *Male and Female: A Study of the Sexes in a Changing World*. New York: Dell Publishing, 1968.

Meggyesy, David. *Out of Their League*. New York: Paperback Library, 1971.
- 'Platform: Football and war.' *Los Angeles Times*, February 8, 1991.

Mellen, Joan. *Women and Their Sexuality in the New Film*. New York: Dell, 1973.
- *Big Bad Wolves: Masculinity in the American Film*. New York: Pantheon, 1977.

Merchant, Carolyn. *The Death of Nature: Women, Ecology, and the Scientific Revolution*. San Francisco: Harper and Row, 1982.

Messerschmidt, James W. *Capitalism, Patriarchy, and Crime: Toward a Socialist-Feminist Criminology*. Totowa, NJ: Rowman and Littlefield, 1986.
- 'Feminism, criminology and the rise of the female sex "delinquent," 1880–1930.' *Contemporary Crises* 11 (1987), 243–63.

Messner, Michael. 'The changing meaning of male identity in the lifecourse of the athlete.' In Michael Messner, ed., *Sport, Men, and Masculinity. Arena Review* 9(2), special issue (November 1985), 31–60.
- 'Jocks in the men's movement.' *Changing Men*, Spring 1985, 34–5.
- 'The life of a man's seasons: Male identity in the life course of the jock. In Michael S. Kimmel, ed. *Changing Men: New Directions in Research on Men and Masculinity*. Beverly Hills, CA: Sage Publications, 1987.
- 'Sports and male domination: The female athlete as contested ideological terrain.' *Sociology of Sport Journal* 5 (1988), 197–211.
- 'Masculinities and athletic careers.' *Gender and Society* 3(1) (March 1989), 71–88.
- 'Boyhood, organized sports, and the construction of masculinities.' *Journal of Contemporary Enthnography* 18(4) (January 1990), 416–44.
- 'Men studying masculinity: Some epistemological issues in sport sociology.' *Sociology of Sport Journal* 7 (1990), 136–53.
- '"Changing men" and feminist politics in the United States.' *Theory and Society* 22 (1993), 723–37.

- 'When bodies are weapons.' In Michael A. Messner and Donald F. Sabo, eds, *Sex, Violence, and Power in Sports: Rethinking Masculinity*. Freedom, CA: Crossing Press, 1994.
- 'Women in the men's locker room?' In Michael A. Messner and Donald F. Sabo, eds, *Sex, Violence, and Power in Sports: Rethinking Masculinity*. Freedom, CA: The Crossing Press, 1994.
- *Power at Play: Sports and the Problem of Masculinity*. Boston: Beacon, 1995.
- Messner, Michael A., and D.F. Sabo. 'Changing men through changing sports: An eleven point strategy.' In Michael A. Messner and Donald F. Sabo, eds. *Sex, Violence, and Power in Sports: Rethinking Masculinity*. Freedom, CA: Crossing Press, 1994.
- eds. *Sex, Violence, and Power in Sports: Rethinking Masculinity*. Freedom, CA: Crossing Press, 1994.
- *Sport, Men, and the Gender Order: Critical Feminist Perspectives*. Champaign, IL: Human Kinetics Publishers, 1990.
- Messner, Michael A., and William R. Solomon. 'Outside the frame: Newspaper coverage of the Sugar Ray Leonard wife abuse story.' *Sociology of Sport Journal* 10 (1993), 119–34.
- Mickleburgh, Rod. 'Young gymnasts suffering in gold quest, doctors told.' *Globe and Mail*, August 18, 1992.
- Milhill, Chris. 'Poverty is the world's greatest killer.' *Guardian Weekly*, May 7, 1995.
- Miller, Laura. 'The humiliator.' *San Francisco Examiner*, August 1994.
- Miller, Mark Crispin. 'Free the media.' *The Nation*, June 3, 1996.
- 'The crushing power of big publishing.' *The Nation*, March 17, 1997.
- Miller, Mark Crispin, and Janine Jacquet Biden. 'The national entertainment state.' *The Nation*, June 3, 1996, 23–6.
- Miller, Alice. *For Your Own Good: Hidden Cruelty in Childrearing and the Roots of Violence*. Trans. Hildegarde and Hunter Hannum. New York: Farrar, Straus and Giroux, 1983.
- *Thou Shalt Not Be Aware: Society's Betrayal of the Child*. Trans. Hilda and Hunter Hannam. New York: Farrar, Straus and Giroux, 1984.
- *Banished Knowledge: Facing Childhood Injuries*. Trans. Leila Vennewitz. New York: Doubleday, 1990.
- *Breaking Down the Wall of Silence: The Liberating Experience of Facing Painful Truth*. Trans. Simon Worrall. New York: Dutton, 1991.
- Mitchell, Alanna. 'Toward a saner, simpler workstyle.' *Globe and Mail*, March 5, 1994.
- 'Unpaid housework valued to $319-billion, Statscan say.' *Globe and Mail*, April 7, 1994.

- 'Are women becoming as violent as men?' *Globe and Mail*, July 15, 1995.
- 'Women take laborious road to work for pay.' *Globe and Mail*, January 2, 1997.
- 'Hockey coach pleads guilty to sexual assault charges.' *Globe and Mail*, January 3, 1997.
- 'Rich, poor wage gap widening.' *Globe and Mail*, May 13, 1997.
Mitchell, Juliet. *Psychoanalysis and Feminism: Freud, Reich, Laing, and Women*. New York: Vintage Books, 1974.
Molnar, Alex. *Giving Kids the Business*. Boulder, CO: Westview Press, 1996.
Money, John. *Venuses Penuses: Sexosophy and Exigency Theory*. Buffalo: Prometheus Books, 1986.
- *Gay, Straight, and In-Between: The Sexology of Erotic Orientation*. New York, Oxford University Press, 1988.
- 'Reinterpreting the unspeakable: Sexuality in human behaviour.' *Continuum*, May 1994.
Montville, Leigh. 'Super Bowl XXV: Super ... and surreal.' *Sports Illustrated*, February 4, 1991.
- 'Olga Korbut.' *Sports Illustrated*, September 19, 1994.
- 'Listen up!' *Sports Illustrated*, November 4, 1996.
Moore, Kenny, 'Missing the mark.' *Sports Illustrated*, January 20, 1992.
- 'A scream and a prayer.' *Sports Illustrated*, August 3, 1992.
- 'The eternal example.' *Sports Illustrated*, December 21, 1992.
Moore, Robert, and Douglas Gillette. *King Warrior Magician Lover: Rediscovering the Archetypes of the Mature Masculine*. San Francisco: HarperCollins, 1991.
Moraga, Cherie, and Gloria Anzaldua. *This Bridge Called My Back: Writings by Radical Women of Colour*. Watertown, MA: Persephone Press, 1981.
Morse, Margaret. 'Sport on television: Replay and display.' In E. Ann Kaplan, ed., *Regarding Television*, Los Angeles: American Film Institute, 1983.
Mrozek, Donald J. *Sport and American Mentality, 1880–1910*, Knoxville: University of Tennessee Press, 1985.
Mukherjee, Sougata. ' "Sports welfare" growing with more subsidies to U.S. stadiums.' *Houston Business Journal*, September 16, 1996.
Mulvey, Laura. 'Visual pleasure and narrative cinema.' *Screen* 16(3) (Autumn 1975), 412–28.
Nack, William. 'A gruesome account.' *Sports Illustrated*, February 10, 1992.
Nack, William, and Lester Munson. 'Sport's dirty secret.' *Sports Illustrated*, July 31, 1995.
Nash, J. Madeleine. 'Fertile minds.' *Time*, June 9, 1997.
National Council of Welfare. *Poverty Profile 1992*. Ottawa, Spring 1994.
Navarro, Vincente. 'The Olympics' untold stories.' *In These Times*, September 2–15, 1992.

Neale, Steve. 'Masculinity as spectacle: Reflections on men and mainstream cinema.' *Screen* 25(4–5) (July–October 1984), 2–16.

Nelson, Joyce. *The Perfect Machine: TV in the Nuclear Age.* Toronto: Between the Lines, 1987.

Nelson, Mariah Burton. 'Jock violence hits home.' *Globe and Mail/New York Times*, June 23, 1994.

Nichols, Bill. *Movies and Methods.* Berkeley: University of California Press, 1976.

– *Ideology and the Image.* Bloomington: Indiana University Press, 1981.

Nicholls, Peter, and John Clute. *Grolier Science Fiction: The Multimedia Encyclopedia of Science Fiction.* Danbury CT: Grolier, 1995.

Nicholson, Jennifer. 'The advertiser's man.' *Adbusters*, Summer/Fall 1992, 20–6.

Nickson, Liz. 'She's not heavy, she's my sister.' *Globe and Mail*, April 13, 1996.

Nixon, Lucia. 'Rituals and power: The anthropology of homecoming at Queen's.' *Queen's Quarterly* 94(2) (Summer 1987), 312–31.

Novak, Michael. *The Joy of Sports: End zones, Bases, Baskets, Balls, and the Consecration of the American Spirit.* New York: Basic Books, 1976.

Novogrodsky, Myra, Michael Kaufman, Dick Holland, and Margaret Wells. 'Retreat for the future: An anti-sexist workshop for high schoolers.' *Our Schools/Our Selves* 3(4) (April 1992), 67–88.

O'Brien, Mary. *The Politics of Reproduction.* Boston: Routledge & Kegan Paul, 1981.

O'Brien, Richard, and Hank Hersch, eds. 'Scorecard: The Class of '47.' *Sports Illustrated*, March 10, 1997, 13.

'On the ropes.' *Inside Track*, CBC Radio, January 23, 1994.

Orbach, Susie. *Fat Is a Feminist Issue: The Anti-Diet Guide to Permanent Weight Loss.* New York: Berkeley Books, 1979.

Osterland, Andrew. 'Field of nightmares.' *Financial World*, February 14, 1995.

Overall, Christine, ed. *The Future of Human Reproduction.* Toronto: Women's Press, 1989.

Packard, Vance. *The Hidden Persuaders.* New York: Random House, 1957.

Paglia, Camille. *Sexual Personae: Art and Decadence from Nefertiti to Emily Dickinson.* New York: Random House, 1991.

Palomo, Juan R. 'Affirmative action takes athletic twist.' *USA Today*, April 10, 1997.

Papp, Leslie. 'Child abuse issue in gym.' *Toronto Star*, July 27, 1996.

Pappas, Gregory. (Editorial) 'Elucidating the relationship between race, socioeconomic status, and health.' *American Journal of Public Health* 84(6) (1994), 892–3.

Pascal, A.H., and L.A. Rapping. 'The economics of racial discrimination in organized baseball.' In A.H. Pascal, ed., *Racial Discrimination in Economic Life.* Lexington, MA: Lexington Books, 1972.

Pate, Russell R., et al. 'Physical activity and public health – A recommendation from the Centers for Disease Control and Prevention and the American College of Sports Medicine.' *Journal of the American Medical Association* 273 (1995), 402–7.

Pelletier, Kenneth. *Mind as Healer, Mind as Slayer: A Holistic Approach to Preventing Stress Disorders.* New York: Dell, 1975.

Pendleton, Don. *The Executioner.* New York: Avon, 1988 (Executioner titles available from www.Amazon.com).

Person, Ethel Spector. 'Sexuality as the mainstay of identity: Psychoanalytic perspective.' In Catharine R. Stimpson and Ethel Spector Person, eds, *Women: Sex and Sexuality.* Chicago: University of Chicago Press, 1980.

Person, Ethel Spector, and Lionel Ovesey. 'Psychoanalytic theories of gender identity.' *Journal of the American Academy of Psychoanalysis* 11(2) (1983), 203–26.

Phillips, J.C. 'Race and career opportunities in major league baseball: 1960–1980.' *Journal of Sport and Social Issues* 7(2) (1983), 1–17.

Pilz, Gunter A. 'Attitudes toward different forms of aggressive and violent behavior in competitive sports: Two empirical studies.' *Journal of Sport Behavior* 2(1) (February 1979), 3–26.

Place, Janey. 'Women in film noir.' In E. Ann Kaplan, ed., *Women in Film Noir.* London: British Film Institute, 1978.

Pleck, Elizabeth H., and Joseph H. Pleck. *The American Man.* Englewood Cliffs, NJ: Prentice-Hall, 1980.

Plimpton, George, moderator, with Howard Cosell, Robert Lipsyte, Harry Edwards, Tom Sanders, Digger Phelps, Billie Jean King, and David J. Stern. 'Sports: How dirty a game?' Forum based on a discussion at the New School for Social Research, New York City. *Harper's,* September 1985.

Pomeroy, Sarah B. *Goddesses, Whores, Wives, and Slaves: Women in Classical Antiquity.* New York: Schocken Books, 1976.

Pope, Harrison G., and David L. Katz. 'Affective and psychotic symptoms associated with anabolic steroid use.' *American Journal of Psychiatry* 145(4) (April 1988), 487–90.

Powell, Linda C. 'Review: Black macho and the myth of the superwoman.' *Conditions: Five. The Black Women's Issue* (Special issue), 1979, 165–172.

Press, Aric. 'Old too soon, wise too late.' *Newsweek,* August 10, 1992.

Price, Robert. 'Some performance enhancing drugs in use by athletes prior to and in 1994.' *MuscleMag International,* June 1994.

'The prison boom.' *The Nation,* February 20, 1995.

Pronger, Brian. *The Arena Of Masculinity: Sports, Homosexuality, and the Meaning of Sex.* Toronto: Summerhill Press, 1990.

– 'The unspoken sexuality of sport.' *Globe and Mail,* July 30, 1990.

– 'Fear and trembling: Eros, patriarchy, and the mythology of male homophobia in athletics.' Paper presented to the joint meeting of the North American Societies for the Sociology of Sport and the Philosophic Study of Sport, Washington, DC, November 1989.

Proudfoot, Jim. '4-foot-8 Texas moppet makes ice history.' *Toronto Star*, March 23, 1997.

Pujadas, Xavier, and Carles Santacana. 'The popular Olympic games, Barcelona 1936: Olympians and Antifascists.' *International Review for the Sociology of Sport* 27(2) (1992), 139–49.

Purdy, Dean A., D. Stanley Eitzen, and Rick Hufnagel. 'Are athletes also students? The educational attainment of college athletes.' *Social Problems* 29(4) (April 1982).

Quinty, Lee. 'Spectacular men: Power, masculinity, and self-surveillance in the age of the image.' Paper presented to the Popular Culture Association National Meeting, Montreal, March 1987.

Rabinovitch, Sandra. 'The new warriors.' *Ideas*, CBC Radio, November 7, 14, 1986.

Rader, Benjamin G. 'The quest for subcommunities and the rise of American sport.' *American Quarterly* 29(4) (1977), 355–69.

– 'Modern sports: In search of interpretations (review essay).' *Journal of Social History* 13(2) (Winter 1979), 307–21.

Ramsamy, Sam. *Apartheid: The Real Hurdle*. London: International Defence and Aid Fund for Southern Africa, 1982.

Reich, Wilhelm. *The Sexual Revolution*. New York: Farrar, Straus, 1962.

– *Early Writings*. Vol. 1. New York: Farrar, Straus and Giroux, 1975.

Reilly, Rick. 'Somebody, please, postpone the fight: One man's opinion.' *Sports Illustrated*, September 23, 1991.

– 'Strokes of genius.' *Sports Illustrated*, April 21, 1997, 31–49.

Reiter, Rayna R., ed. *Toward an Anthropology of Women*. New York: Monthly Review Press, 1976.

Remnick, David. 'Kid Dynamite blows up.' *The New Yorker*, July 14, 1997.

Reynaud, Emmanuel. *Holy Virility: The Social Construction of Masculinity*. London: Pluto Press, 1983.

Richardson, Bob. 'Hockey violence: Street gangs on skates.' *Toronto Star*, January 26, 1990.

Richman, Alan. 'The death of sportswriting.' *This World*, October 20, 1991.

Riddell, Ken. 'Games provide wealth of sponsorship opportunities.' *Marketing*, July 1991.

Riesman, David, and Reuel Denney. 'Football in America: A study in cultural diffusion.' In Eric Dunning, ed., *The Sociology of Sport: A Selection of Readings*. London: Cass, 1971.

Riess, Steven. *City Games: The Evolution of American Urban Society and the Rise of Sports.* Urbana: University of Illinois Press, 1989.

Rifkin, Jeremy. *Time Wars: The Primary Conflict in Human History.* New York: Simon & Schuster, 1987.

– *Biosphere Politics: A Cultural Odyssey from the middle ages to the New Age.* San Francisco: Harper, 1992.

– *The End of Work: The Decline of the Global Labor Force and the Dawn of the Post-Market Era.* New York: Putnam, 1995.

Riordan, Jim. *Sport in Soviet Society.* Cambridge: Cambridge University Press, 1971.

– *Sport under Communism.* Montreal/Kingston: McGill-Queen's University Press, 1981.

Robertson, Sheila. 'The life and times of CAAWS.' *Canadian Woman Studies* 15(4) (1995), 16–21.

Robinson, Laura. 'Beating the Pink Ribbon Syndrome.' *Globe and Mail*, August 23, 1990.

Rojeck, Chris. *Capitalism and Leisure Theory.* London: Tavistock, 1985.

Rosenberg, Emily S. '"Foreign affairs" after World War II: Connecting sexual and international politics.' *Diplomatic History* 18(1) (Winter 1994), 59–70.

Rosenblatt, A. 'Negroes in baseball: The failure of success.' *Transaction* 4 (September 1967), 51–3.

Rothenberg, Randall. 'PGA flap shakes business backers.' *Globe and Mail*, August 11, 1990.

Rotundo, E. Anthony. 'Body and soul: Changing ideals of American middle-class manhood, 1770–1920.' *Journal of Social History* 16 (1983), 23–38.

– 'Patriarchs and participants: A historical perspective on fatherhood in the United States.' In M. Kaufman, ed., *Beyond Patriarchy: Essays by Men on Pleasure, Power, and Change.* Toronto: Oxford University Press, 1987.

– *American Manhood: Transformations in Masculinity from the Revolution to the Modern Era.* New York: Basic Books, 1994.

Rowbotham, Sheila, and Jeffrey Weeks. *Socialism and the New Life: The Personal and Sexual Politics of Edward Carpenter and Havelock Ellis.* London: Pluto Press, 1977.

Rubin, Gayle. 'The traffic in women: Notes on the "political economy" of sex.' In Rayna R. Reiter, ed., *Toward an Anthropology of Women.* New York: Monthly Review Press, 1976.

– 'Thinking sex: Notes for a radical theory of the politics of sexuality.' In Carole S. Vance, ed., *Pleasure and Danger: Exploring Female Sexuality.* Boston: Routledge & Kegan Paul, 1984.

Rubin, Lillian Breslow. *Worlds of Pain: Life in the Working Class Family.* New York: Basic Books, 1976.

Ruitenbeek, Hendrik M., ed. *Sexuality and Identity*. New York: Dell, 1970.

Russett, Cynthia Eagle. *Sexual Science: The Victorian Construction of Womanhood*. Cambridge, MA: Harvard University Press, 1991.

Rushin, Steve. 'How we got here.' *Sports Illustrated*, August 16, 1994.

– 'Jock schools USA.' *Sports Illustrated*, April 28, 1997.

Sabo, Donald F. 'Doing time doing masculinity: Sports and prison.' In Michael A. Messner and Donald F. Sabo, eds, *Sex, Violence, and Power in Sports*. Freedom, CA: Crossing Press, 1994.

– 'Pigskin, patriarchy and pain.' In Michael A. Messner and Donald F. Sabo, eds, *Sex, Violence, and Power in Sports*. Freedom, CA: Crossing Press, 1994.

– 'Sport, patriarchy, and male identity: New questions about men and sport.' *Arena Review* 9(2) (1985), 1–30.

Sack, Allen L. 'When Yale spirit vanquished Harvard indifference.' *Harvard Magazine*, November 1975, 26–9, 50–1.

Sack, Allen, and David Westby. 'The commercialization and functional rationalization of college football: Its origin.' *Journal of Higher Education* 47(6) (November–December 1976), 625–47.

Sanday, Peggy Reeves. *Female Power and Male Dominance: On the Origins of Sexual Inequality*. Cambridge: Cambridge University Press, 1982.

Sanders, Scott Russell. 'The men we carry in our minds.' *Utne Reader*, May/June 1991, 76–8.

Sapolsky, Robert, 'The graying of the troops.' *Discover*, March 1996, 46–52.

Saunders, Doug. 'And now, some words from their sponsors.' *Globe and Mail*, May 10, 1997.

Scher, Jon. 'Death of a goon.' *Sports Illustrated*, August 24, 1992.

Schiller, Herbert I. *Culture Inc.: The Corporate Takeover of Public Expression*. New York: Oxford University Press, 1991.

Schmidt, Véra, and Annie Reich. *Pulsions sexuelles et éducation du corps*. Paris: Union Générale d'Éditions, 1979.

Schneider, John, and D. Stanley Eitzen. 'Racial discrimination in American sport: Continuity or change.' *Journal of Sport Behavior* 2(3) (1979), 136–42.

– 'Racial segregation by professional football positions, 1960–1985.' *Sociology and Social Research* 70 (July 1986), 259–62.

Scott, Ann Crittenden. 'Closing the muscle gap.' *Ms*, September 1974.

Scrivener, Leslie. 'In changing world, men flock to Jesus.' *Toronto Star*, September 24, 1995.

Scully, Gerald. *The Business of Major League Baseball*. Chicago: University of Chicago Press, 1989.

Seccombe, Wally. *A Millennium of Family Change: Feudalism to Capitalism in Northwestern Europe*. London: Verso, 1992.

– *Weathering the Storm: Working Class Families from the Industrial Revolution to the Fertility Decline*. London: Verso, 1993.

Seglins, David. ' "Just part of the game": Violence, hockey and masculinity in central Canada, 1890–1910.' Unpublished master's thesis, History Department, Queen's University, Kingston, ON, 1995.

Segrave, Jeffrey O. 'The perfect 10: "Sportspeak" in the language of sexual relations.' *Sociology of Sport Journal* 11(2) (June 1994), 95–113.

Sewart, John J. 'The commodification of sport.' *International Review for the Sociology of Sport* 22(3) (1987), 171–91.

– 'The rationalization of modern sport: The case of professional football.' *Arena* 5(2) (1981), 45–53.

Seidman, Steven. *Romantic Longings: Love in America, 1830–1980*. New York and London: Routledge, 1993.

Shanor, Karen. *The Shanor Study: The Sexual Sensitivity of the American Male*. New York: Ballantine, 1979.

Sheard, K.G., and E.G. Dunning. 'The Rugby football club as a type of "male preserve": Some sociological notes.' *International Review of Sports Sociology* 8(3/4) (1973), 5–24.

Shephard, Roy J., and Claude Bouchard. 'Population evaluations of health related fitness from perceptions of physical activity and fitness.' *Canadian Journal of Applied Physiology* 19(2) (1994), 151–73.

Shilts, Randy. *Conduct Unbecoming: Gays and Lesbians in the US Military*. New York: St Martin's Press, 1993.

Signorile, Michelangelo. 'The incredible bulk.' *Out*, May 1997.

Simri, Uriel. 'The development of female participation in the modern olympic games.' *Stadion* 6 (1980), 187–216.

Simson, Vyv, and Andrew Jennings. *The Lords of the Rings: Power, Money and Drugs in the Modern Olympics*. Toronto: Stoddart, 1992.

Sipes, Richard G., 'War, sports and aggression: An empirical test of two rival theories.' *American Anthropologist* 75 (1973), 64–86.

Skene, Wayne. *Fade to Black: A Requiem for the CBC*. Vancouver/Toronto: Douglas and McIntyre, 1993.

Skrzypzak, J.-F. 'Le sport est-il politique?' *Anthropophagie du sport*. Special issue of *Quel corps?* no. 41 (April 1991), 22–36.

Smith, Barbara, ed. *Home Girls: A Black Feminist Anthology*. New York: Kitchen Table, 1983.

Smith, Gary. 'Forty for the ages.' *Sports Illustrated*, 40th Anniversary Issue, September 19, 1994.

Smith, Geoffrey S. 'National security and personal isolation: Sex, gender, and disease in the cold-war United States.' *The International History Review* 14(2) (May 1992), 307–37.

– 'Security, gender, and the historical process.' *Diplomatic History* 18(1) (Winter 1994), 79–90.

Smith, Michael D. 'Hockey violence: A test of the violent subculture hypothesis.' *Social Problems* 27(2) (December 1979), 235–47.

Smith, Shelley. 'Death on the court.' *Sports Illustrated*, March 12, 1990.

Smolowe, Jill. 'When violence hits home.' *Time*, July 4, 1994.

Smuts, Barbara. 'Apes of wrath.' *Discover*, August 1995.

Snitow, Ann, Christine Stansell, and Sharon Thompson, eds. *Powers of Desire: The Politics of Sexuality.* New York: Monthly Review Press, 1983.

Sobachak, Vivian. 'New age mutant ninja hackers: Reading mondo 2000.' In Mark Dery, ed., *Flame Wars: The Discourse of Cyberculture. South Atlantic Quarterly*, Special Issue, 92(4) (Fall 1993), 569–84.

Sokol, Al. 'The sports business.' *The Economist*, July 25, 1992.

– 'After the gold rush.' *Toronto Star*, October 1, 1994.

– 'The body beautiful.' *Toronto Star*, May 11, 1996.

Solotaroff, Paul. 'The power and the gory.' In Thomas McGuane, ed., *The Best American Sports Writing 1992.* Boston: Houghton Mifflin, 1992.

Soloway, Colin, 'More than a football game.' *The Nation*, January 22, 1990.

Sparhawk, Ruth M., Mary E. Leslie, Phyllis Y. Turbow, and Zina R. Rose. *American Women in Sport, 1887–1897: A 100-Year Chronology.* Metuchen, NJ, and London: Scarecrow Press, 1989.

Sperber, Murray. 'Flagrant foul.' *Lingua Franca*, November/December 1993, 1, 26–31.

'Sports stadiums bring no economic boom.' *USA Today Newsview*, special newsletter edition, December 1996.

Springer, Claudia. 'Sex, memories, and angry women.' In Mark Dery, eds., *Flame Wars: The Discourse of Cyberculture. South Atlantic Quarterly* 92(4), 713–33.

Starkman, Randy. 'Gut reaction.' *Toronto Star*, November 10, 1996.

– 'Tiger Woods: A man on a mission.' *The Toronto Star's Golf '97 Preview*, April 13, 1997.

'Starving to win.' *UMDNJ News*, University of Medicine and Dentistry of New Jersey Newsletter, Newark NJ, Spring 1996.

Starzynski, Bob. 'Michael Jordan scores for WorldCom, EPB.' *Washington Business Journal*, May 19, 1997.

Statistics Canada. *Sport Participation in Canada.* Prepared on behalf of Sport Canada. Ottawa, February 1994.

– *Women in the Labour Force.* Ottawa, 1994.

– *National Population Health Survey Overview, 1994–95.* Ottawa, 1995.

– Women in the Labour Force. Ottawa, 1995.

– 'Labour force update: Hours of work, first quarter 1997.' Ottawa, July 14, 1997.

– *National Population Health Survey Overview, 1996–97.* Ottawa, 1997.

Steele, Valerie. *Fashion and Eroticism: Ideals of Feminine Beauty from the Victorial Era to the Jazz Age*. New York: Oxford University Press, 1985.

Stimpson, Catharine R., and Ethel Spector Person. *Women: Sex and Sexuality*. Chicago: University of Chicago Press, 1980.

Al Strachan. 'Gretzky no longer fighting against fighting.' *Globe and Mail*, February 23, 1994.

Strand, David. *The David Strand Workout*. Toronto: Morningstar Productions, 1997.

Strasser, J.B., and Luarie Becklund. *Swoosh: The Unauthorized Story of Nike and the Men Who Played There*. New York: HarperCollins, 1993.

Sullivan, Andrew. 'Flogging underwear: The new raunchiness of American advertising.' *The New Republic*, January 18, 1988.

Swift, E.M. 'Why Johnny can't play.' *Sports Illustrated*, September 23, 1991.

– 'Dangerous games.' *Sports Illustrated*, November 18, 1991.

– 'On a roll.' *Sports Illustrated*, March 11, 1996.

– 'Women of mettle.' *Sports Illustrated*, 1992.

Taafe, William. 'TV to sports: The bucks stop here.' *Sports Illustrated*, February 24, 1986.

Talese, Gay. *Thy Neighbor's Wife*. New York: Dell, 1982.

'Talk of the streets: Osaka: Victims of fashion.' *Time*, October 7, 1996.

Tandy, Ruth E., and Joyce Laflin. 'Aggression and sport: Two theories.' *Journal of Health, Physical Education and Recreation (JOHPER)* (June 1973,) 19–20.

Tannen, Deborah. *You Just Don't Understand: Women and Men in Conversation*. New York: William Morrow, 1990.

Taylor, Ian, *Crime at the End of the Welfare State*. London: Macmillan, 1980.

– 'Class, violence and sport: The case of soccer hooliganism in Britain.' In Hart Cantelon and R. Gruneau, eds, *Sport, Culture, and the Modern State*. Toronto: University of Toronto Press, 1982.

– 'Putting the boot into a working class sport: British soccer after Bradford and Brussels.' Paper delivered to the Annual Conference of the North American Society for the Sociology of Sport, Boston, November 1985.

Taylor, Phil. 'Bad actors.' *Sports Illustrated*, January 30, 1995.

Telander, Rick. 'Something must be done.' *Sports Illustrated*, October 2, 1989.

– *The Hundred Yard Lie: The Corruption of College Football and What We Can Do to Stop It*. New York: Fireside, 1990.

– 'Senseless.' *Sports Illustrated*, May 14, 1990.

– 'In the aftermath of steroids.' *Sports Illustrated*, January 27, 1992.

Tenner, Edward. *Why Things Bite Back: Technology and the Revenge of Unintended Consequences*. New York: Vintage Books, 1997.

Theberge, Nancy. 'A feminist analysis of responses to sport violence: Media coverage of the 1987 World Junior Hockey Championship.' *Sociology of Sport Journal* 6 (1989), 247–56.

Theweleit, Klaus. *Male Fantasies*, vol.1: *Women Floods Bodies History*. Minneapolis: University of Minnesota Press, 1987.

Thomas, Louis-Vincent. *Mort et pouvoir*. Paris: Petite Bibliothèque Payot, 1978.

– *Rites de mort*. Paris: Librairie Arthème Fayard, 1985.

Thompson, Clara M. *On Women*. New York: New American Library, 1964.

Todd, Terry. 'The steroid predicament.' *Sports Illustrated*, August 1, 1983.

Tomlinson, Alan. 'Good times, bad times, and the politics of leisure: Working class culture in the 1930s in a small northern English working class community.' In Hart Cantelon, with Robert Hollands, Alan Metcalfe, and Alan Tomlinson, eds, *Leisure, Sport, and Working Class Cultures*. Toronto: Garamond Press, 1988.

Tomlinson, Alan, ed. *Off the Ball: The 1986 Soccer World Cup*. London: Pluto Press, 1986.

Tomlinson, Alan, and Gary Whannel, eds. *Five Ring Circus: Money, Power, and Politics at the Olympic Games*. London: Pluto Press, 1984.

'Tomorrow's second sex.' *The Economist*, September 28, 1996.

Turner, Dan. 'Super Bowl advertisers spending huge sums to reach fewer viewers.' *Los Angeles Business Journal*, January 20, 1997.

Underwood, John. 'Brutality: The crisis in football.' *Sports Illustrated*, August 14, 1978.

– Special report: 'The writing is on the wall.' *Sports Illustrated*, May 19, 1980.

United Nations Conference on Trade and Development. *Report of the United Nations Conference on Trade and Development*. Geneva, September 11, 1997.

U.S. Surgeon General. *Progress Report for: Physical Activity and Fitness*. Washington, DC: U.S. Department of Health and Human Services, April 1995.

– *Physical Activity and Health: A Report of the Surgeon General*. Washington, DC: U.S. Department of Health and Human Services, July 1996.

Vance, Carole S., ed. *Pleasure and Danger: Exploring Female Sexuality*. Boston: Routledge and Kegan Paul, 1984.

Vanier Institute for the Family. *Canadian Families in Transition: The Implications and Challenges of Change*. Toronto, 1992.

Verducci, Tom. 'Anybody home?' *Sports Illustrated*, May 8, 1995.

Vertinsky, Patricia. 'Feminist Charlotte Perkins Gilman's pursuit of health and physical fitness as a strategy for emancipation.' *Journal of Sport History* 16(1) (Spring 1989), 5–26.

Vigarello, Georges. Interview, 'Le sport est avant tout un rituel de dévotion.' *Anthropophagie du sport*. Special issue of *Quel corps?* no. 41 (April 1990), 51–3.

Vincent, Isabel. 'Every four years "Copa" fever paralyzes a nation.' *Globe and Mail*, May 30, 1994.

Vittala, Kalyani. 'Study links chemical changes, anorexia.' *Globe and Mail*, August 25, 1994.

Walkowitz, Judith R. *Prostitution and Victorian Society: Women, Class, and the State*. Cambridge: Cambridge University Press, 1983.

Wallace, Michèle. *Black Macho and the Myth of the Superwoman*. New York: Dial Press, 1979.

Wallace, Michèle, coordinator, and Gina Dent, ed. *Black Popular Culture*. Seattle: Bay Press, 1992.

Walters, John. 'School spirit.' Scorecard. *Sports Illustrated*, September 30, 1991.

Ward, Olivia. 'Old myths, new realities.' *Toronto Star*, October 29, 1995.

Warshaw, Robin. *I Never Called It Rape: The Ms. Report on Recognizing, Fighting, and Surviving Date and Acquaintance Rape*. New York: Harper and Row, 1988.

Watson, Peggy. 'The rise of masculinism in Eastern Europe.' *New Left Review* 198 (March/April 1993), 71–82.

Watson, Sophie, ed. *Playing the State: Australian Feminist Interventions*. London: Verso, 1990.

Waugh, Thomas. *Hard to Imagine: Gay Male Eroticism in Photography and Film from Their Beginnings to Stonewall*. New York: Columbia University Press, 1996.

Weber, Max. *The Sociology of Religion*. Boston: Beacon Press, 1972.

Weeks, Jeffrey. *Coming Out: Homosexual Politics in Britain from the Nineteenth Century to the Present*. New York: Quartet Books, 1977.

– *Sex, Politics, and Society: The Regulation of Sexuality since 1800*. London: Longman, 1981.

– *Sexuality and Its Discontents: Meanings, Myths, and Modern Sexualities*. London: Routledge & Kegan Paul, 1985.

– *Between the Acts: Lives of Homosexual Men, 1885–1967*. London: Routledge, 1991.

Welch, Paula, and D. Margaret Costa, 'A century of Olympic competition.' In D. Margaret Costa and Sharon R. Guthrie, *Women and Sport: Interdisciplinary Perspectives*. Champaign, IL: Human Kinetics, 1994, 353–71.

Wenn, Stephen R. 'A tale of two diplomats: George S. Messersmith and Charles H. Sherrill on proposed American participation in the 1936 Olympics.' *Journal of Sport History* 16(1) (Spring 1989), 27–43.

Wenner, Lawrence A. 'In search of the sports bar: Masculinity, alcohol, sports, and the mediation of public space.' In Gary Gumpert and Susan J. Drucker, eds, *Voices in the Street: Explorations in Gender, Media, and Public Space*. Creskill, NJ: Hampton Press, 1996.

Wernick, Andrew. 'From voyeur to narcissist: Imaging men in contemporary advertising.' In Michael Kaufman, ed., *Beyond Patriarchy: Essays by Men on Pleasure, Power, and Change*. Toronto: Oxford University Press, 1987.

West, Cornell. 'Nihilism in black America.' In Gina Dent, ed., *Black Popular Culture: A Project by Michèle Wallace*. Seattle: Bay Press, 1992.

White, Jack E. 'Stepping up to the plate.' *Time*, March 31, 1977.

White, Kevin. *The First Sexual Revolution: The Emergence of Male Heterosexualtiy in Modern America*. New York: New York University Press, 1993.

White, Philip G., and James Gillett. 'Reading the muscular body: A critical decoding of advertisements in *Flex* magazine.' *Sociology of Sport Journal* 11(1) (March 1994), 18–39.

White Ribbon Campaign Education Action Kit. Toronto: White Ribbon Campaign, 1996.

Whitson, David. 'The embodyment of gender: Discipline, domination and empowerment. In Susan Birrel and Cheryl L. Cole, eds., *Women, Sport, and Culture.* Champaign, IL: Human Kinetics, 1994.

Whitson, David, and Donald MacIntosh. 'Gender and power: Explanation of gender inequalities in Canadian national sport organisations.' *International Review for the Sociology of Sport* 24(2) (1989), 137–50.

– 'Becoming a world-class city: Hallmark events and sports franchises in the growth strategies of western Canadian cities.' *Sociology of Sport Journal* 10(3) (1993), 21–40.

Wilcox, Merrie-Ellen. 'The power to move.' *The Idler*, May–June 1989.

Williams, Raymond. *Problems in Materialism and Culture.* London: Verso, 1980.

– *Writing in Society.* London: Verso, 1983.

– *Towards 2000.* Harmondsworth, England: Penguin Books, 1985.

Williams, Walter L. 'Ritualized homosexuality in Melanesia.' *Changing Men.* 15 (Fall 1985), 37.

Williamson, Judith. *Decoding Advertisements: Ideology and Meaning in Advertising.* London and New York: Marion Boyars, 1985.

– 'Woman is an island: Femininity and colonization.' In T. Modleski, *Studies in Entertainment.* Bloomington, IN: Indiana University Press, 1986.

Willis, Paul. *Learning to Labor: How Working Class Kids Get Working Class Jobs.* New York: Columbia University Press, 1981.

Wilson, E.O. *Sociobiology.* Cambridge MA: Harvard University Press, 1980.

Wilson, Trish. 'What price glory? Effects of gymnastics on physical and emotional health.' *Sojourner: The Women's Forum* 22(9) (April 30, 1997).

Witt, Howard. 'Churches and comics.' *Montreal Gazette* (Chicago Tribune Service), October 2, 1995.

Wolfe, Morris. *Jolts: The TV Wasteland and the Canadian Oasis.* Toronto: Lorimer, 1985.

Wolff, Alexander. 'The slow track.' *Sports Illustrated*, September 28, 1992.

– 'The first fan.' *Sports Illustrated,* March 21, 1994.

– 'Out of control.' *Sports Illustrated*, May 15, 1995.

Wood, Robin. *Hollywood from Vietnam to Reagan.* New York: Columbia University Press, 1986.

– 'Raging bull: The homosexual subtext in film.' In Michael Kaufman, ed., *Beyond Patriarchy: Essays by Men on Pleasure, Power, and Change.* Toronto: Oxford University Press, 1987.

Wood, Robin, with Andrew Britton and Richard Lippe. *American Nightmare: Essays on the Horror Film*. Toronto: Festival of Festivals, 1979.

Woodman, Marion. *Addiction to Perfection: The Still Unravished Bride*. Toronto: Inner City Books, 1982.

Woodward, Diana, Eileen Green, and Sandra Hebron. 'The sociology of women's leisure and physical recreation: Constraints and opportunities.' *International Review for the Sociology of Sport* 24(2) (1989), 121–33.

Wolcott, James. 'A man's life.' *Vanity Fair*, June 1997.

'The world cup.' *Inside Track*, CBC Radio, May 30, 1993.

Wright, Robert. *The Moral Animal: Why We Are the Way We Are. The New Science of Evolutionary Psychology*. New York: Pantheon Books, 1994.

Wright, Ronald. *Stolen Continents: The 'New World' through Indian Eyes*. Toronto: Penguin, 1993.

Wulf, Steve. 'Hands of stone, hearts of gold.' *Time*, April 10, 1995.

– 'An unwhole new ball game.' *Time*, April 17, 1995.

– ed. 'Scorecard: Old Glory and new wounds.' *Sports Illustrated*, February 25, 1991.

Yalouris, Nikos. 'Women in ancient Greece: Their contribution to letters, science, politics and sport.' Paper presented to the International Olympic Academy, 30th International Session, Olympia, Greece, June 20–July 5, 1990.

Yannakis, Thomas. 'The Olympic games: Their history and philosophy.' Paper presented to the International Olympic Academy, 30th International Session, Olympia, Greece, June 20–July 5, 1990.

York, Marty. 'New stadium for Expos – or else.' *Globe and Mail*, June 18, 1997.

Young, Chris. 'Thomas takes place as true pioneer.' *Toronto Star*, April 22, 1997.

Ziegler, John B. 'Introduction.' In Bob Goldman, with Patricia Bush and Ronald Klatz, *Death in the Locker Room: Steroids, Cocaine, and Sports*. Tucson, AZ: Body Press, 1984.

Zimbalist, Andrew. *Baseball and Business*. New York: Basic Books, 1992.

Index

Acton, Lord William, 80, 290n10
Adidas, 230
advertising: development of, 109, 143–4; for the female market, 266; and homoeroticism, 218–19; for the masculinity market, 105, 109–20, 130, 144–9, 261; mass media, and sport, 136; and Olympic sport, 232; racism, and sport, 210–11; sexuality, and sport, 110
African-Americans: commodification, and nihilism, 205–7; and cult of the black super–athlete, 89–90, 163–5, 201–13; exploitation of in feeder systems, 141; and hypermasculinity, 163–5; and political leadership, 203–6, 209; and styles of masculinity, 203–4. *See also* black nationalism; racism; superstar athletes
aggression, 23; theories of, 40–2, 186–7; and football, 72–3; war, and sport, 186–9
Ali, Muhammad, 204, 206
amateur sport, 49, 224–5
Amazons, 283n59
Arnold, Thomas, 70
Ashe, Arthur, 211

athlete-hero. *See* champions
athletes, identification with, 24, 142, 204–6, 208–9, 211–12. *See also* champions
athletes, professional: alienation of, 136–8; dislocation and exploitation of, 141–2; and steroid use, 222–5. *See also* superstar athletes
athletic beefcake, 95, 151
athletic femininity, 156–61, 267
athleticization: of girls and women, 153; masculinism, and imperialism, 57; in nineteenth century, 47–50, 58; of politics and the military, 68, 185–7
athletoporn, 151, 304n51

Bagnato, Vince, 166
Baker, William J., 14, 108
Bamberger, Michael, 243
Barkley, Charles, 145, 170, 206–7, 210
Barer, Morris, 249
baseball: development of, 48–9, 107–8, 285n9; 1994 players' strike, 140; as spectacle, 135–6
basketball, as spectacle, 135
Bausch & Lomb, 230, 232
Beard, George M., 91

hooliganism, 200; and sport, 88,
98–102, 213–17, 261, 295n88; and
Vietnam representation, 177–8
homophobia, 214, 295n80; and black
nationalism, 203; definition of,
293n41; and fear of the feminine, 100,
312n47; and sport, 102, 261
homosexuality, 295n78; definition of,
293n41; and sport, 98–102, 213–17;
third-sex theory of, 293n75
homosociality, 274; definition of, 293n41
hooks, bell, 206
Horowitz, Gad, 23
Houston, William, 139
hyperfemininity, in women's sports,
156–61
hypermasculinity: and aggressive
physicality, 23, 68, 90–3; and
athleticized male body, 149–50, 161;
and Cold War, 124; and commercialization of sport, 145–9, 263; definition
of, 10; erotics and aggression, 100–2,
186; and fear of the feminine, 99–100,
171–3, 312n47; and gay culture, 217–
19; and gender identity, 128, 190; and
gender order, 122; and high-performance sport, 239–40, 245; and
homoeroticism, 215–18; iconography
of, 150–1; as master-narrative, 33,
192–4, 279n17; and neoliberal/
neoconservative policy, 256–8; and
Olympic sport, 226–7, 243–4; political
ideology, and sport, 183–5, 188–90;
and racism, 202, 211–13; and sexual
display, 35–8, 94–6, 151, 177–8; and
soccer hooliganism, 196–201; and
sport culture, 193–4, 252–3, 258,
309n6; and steroid use, 222–3; and
Vietnam representation, 174–9, 184;
violence and sport, 142, 163–5, 176,

181, 187; war and sport, 179–81, 271;
and warrior culture, 313n59
Hyslop, Paula, 154, 156

IBM, 230
iconography: homoerotic, 218–19; of
athleticized female body, 152, 155–61,
304n51; of athleticized male body,
35–6, 94–5, 149–52, 177–8, 218
ideology of gender, 29
ideology of sport, 7–8, 20–7, 281n37,
282n45, 289–90n4; and gender culture,
30–2. *See also* sport as religion
imperialism: erotics of, 83–4, 88; and football, 72–3; and masculine dominance,
52; masculinism and sport, 57, 96
industrialization: and family structure, 52;
and rise of corporate capitalism, 108;
and sport, 46–9, 69–70, 111–12
injuries, sports-related, 167–8, 196n10,
310n21
International Olympic Committee,
229–32, 234; founding of, 47

Jabbar, Kareem Abdul, 204
Jackson, Jesse, 203
Jeffords, Susan, 150, 174–5, 177–8,
183–4
Jeffries, James J., 89
Jennings, Andrew, 230
Jhally, Sut, 105, 110
jock schools, 228
Johnson, Ben, 221–2, 234
Johnson, Jack, 89
Johnson, Lyndon B., 183
Johnson, William Oscar, 230
Jordan, Michael: as athlete-hero, 206,
212, 253; and endorsements, 145–6,
232; and sport–media complex,
116–18; as violent warrior, 168